Land of Hope

LAND OF HOPE

Chicago,

Black Southerners,

and the

Great Migration

James R. Grossman

The University of Chicago Press
Chicago and London

The University of Chicago Press, Chicago 60637
The University of Chicago Press, Ltd., London
© 1989 by The University of Chicago
All rights reserved. Published 1989
Paperback edition 1991
Printed in the United States of America

09 08 07 06 05   7 8 9 10

Library of Congress Cataloging-in-Publication Data

Grossman, James R.
    Land of hope : Chicago, Black southerners, and the Great Migration
/ James R. Grossman.
        p.   cm.
    Revision of the author's thesis.
    Bibliography: p.
    Includes index.
    ISBN 0-226-30995-9 (paper)
    1. Afro-Americans—Illinois—Chicago—History—20th century.
2. Afro-Americans—Southern States—Migrations—History—20th
century. 3. Chicago (Ill.)—History—1875–   4. Migrations, Internal—
United States—History—20th century. I. Title.
F548.9.N4G76   1989
977.3′1100496073—dc19   88-39125
                                                                CIP

To Howard Grossman and Adele Grossman

Contents

List of Illustrations   *ix*

Acknowledgments   *xi*

Introduction   *1*

Part 1

1. "All I Ask Is Give Me a Chance"   13

2. "The Negro's Natural Home"   38

3. "Tell Me about the Place"   66

4. "Bound for the Promised Land"   98

Part 2

5. "Home People" and "Old Settlers"   123

6. "Don't Have to Look up to the White Man"   161

7. "Eny Kind of Worke"   181

8. "The White Man's Union"   208

9. "What Work Can I Get If I Go through School?"   246

Conclusion   259

Appendix A   269

Appendix B   270

List of Abbreviations   273

Notes   277
Selected Bibliography   355
Index   371

Illustrations

Maps

Southern circulation of the Chicago *Defender*   76
The Illinois Central Railroad system in the South   100
Distribution of black population in Chicago, 1910   124
Distribution of black population in Chicago, 1920   125
The South Side Black Belt   126
State of birth of black Chicagoans, 1910–20   148

Figures

"Main Cause of Migration—the Labor Agent"   45
"The Exodus"   83
"The Awakening"   84
A family arriving in Chicago from the rural South   114
Illinois Central Railroad Station, Chicago   115
Migrants exiting train station in Chicago   118
The Plantation Cafe   119
Plantation home   136
Homes occupied by black families, South Chicago   137
Family in one-room apartment in Chicago   138
Card distributed by the Chicago Urban League   147
Leaflet distributed by the Chicago Urban League   151
Men waiting outside Chicago Urban League employment office   188
Job-seekers being interviewed at Chicago Urban League   189
Swifts' Premiums baseball team   201
A black school in the rural South   248
Moseley School in Chicago   249

Acknowledgments

I began studying the Great Migration ten years ago unaware that the project would draw me into a network of scholars from whom I would learn the meaning of collegiality and community. These individuals, along with a number of institutions, made it possible for me to undertake and complete this book.

I am grateful to innumerable archivists and librarians for their invaluable assistance. Two archivists in particular—Archie Motley at the Chicago Historical Society and Joseph Howerton at the National Archives—led me to material that I otherwise never would have found. I am particularly indebted as well to Frank Conaway, the history bibliographer at Regenstein Library at the University of Chicago. In general, I wish to thank the staffs of the Chicago Historical Society, Library of Congress, DuSable Museum, Moorland-Spingarn Research Center, National Archives, Newberry Library, Rockefeller Archives, Schomburg Collection of the New York Public Library, Washington National Records Center, and Carter G. Woodson Regional Library. Equally helpful were the staffs of the libraries at the University of California, Berkeley; University of California, San Diego; University of Chicago; University of Cincinnati; Earlham College; Fisk University; and University of Illinois at Chicago.

The other form of institutional assistance that made this project possible was financial. The University of California, Berkeley, provided Chester McCorkle and Max Farrand fellowships, along with a Heller Fund grant. A Charles Phelps Taft Postdoctoral Fellowship at the University of Cincinnati permitted me to begin the process of revision, an opportunity enhanced by the hospitality and intellectual engagement offered by Roger Daniels and Zane Miller. A National Endowment for the Humanities Fellowship for Independent Study and Research permitted me to spend a year writing. The Division of

the Social Sciences at the University of Chicago has provided gener-
ous research support.

In this study's earliest stages, as first a seminar paper and subsequently a dissertation, fellow graduate students at the University
of California, Berkeley, discussed research and conceptualization,
read preliminary essays, and provided encouragement and warmth.
Mark Dimunation, Lynn Dumenil, Deena González, Barbara Loomis,
Katherine Mooney, Catherine Schupbach, and Robert Weyeneth will
find much in this book that is familiar. Susan Glenn, James Gregory,
Jeffrey Hanes, and James Oakes tolerated years of conversation about
the Great Migration and read the entire manuscript along with successive versions of various pieces. Their thorough and insightful cri-
tiques challenged me to probe deeper; their suggestions made it
easier to meet that challenge.

When I left Berkeley to undertake the research for this project, I
found a larger community of scholars impressive in its commitment
to shared research and mutual assistance. William M. Tuttle, Jr., encouraged me to pursue the topic and graciously opened both his
home and his boxes of research material on black Chicago. Arvarh
Strickland granted access to his interviews of Chicago Urban League
officials. John Hope Franklin welcomed me to Chicago and provided
context, reason, and a stimulating dialogue during early stages of research. John Vernon guided me through the labyrinths of Suitland
and shared his research on Robert R. Moton. As the dissertation
evolved into a book, Peter Gottlieb and Spencer Crew generously
shared their sources and considerable expertise. Colleagues at the
University of California, San Diego, and the University of Chicago
have stimulated my thinking about conceptualization and presentation; I am particularly grateful to John Coatsworth, Michael Conzen,
Dolores Janiewski, Peter Novick, and Roy Ritchie.

A number of students at the University of Chicago have contributed to this book by listening, discussing, and questioning. A few,
however, deserve specific recognition. Andrea Atkin provided word-
processing assistance and rescued me from innumerable stylistic
gaffes. Myra Young Armstead skillfully conducted interviews. Robin
Einhorn painstakingly plotted *Defender* circulation and organized statistical material. Alexis Papadopoulos helped to conceptualize the
maps and supervised their preparation. To Tim Hall and Frank Biletz
fell the often tedious task of checking citations, and I am grateful
for their persistence and their attention to detail. Alex Mann and
Maureen Harp proofread with equal diligence and care. Maureen also
assisted with the index; without her perseverance and generosity,
this book might still be lingering in page proofs.

So many people have read various parts of various versions of the manuscript that I sometimes question whether there is anyone left to buy the book. William Cohen and Harold Woodman offered advice on Part 1, and saved me from some egregious errors. David Katzman, Nell Painter, and Joe Trotter offered especially useful suggestions in response to papers that laid out the main themes of the study. Ira Berlin, Roger Daniels, Paula Fass, David Katzman, August Meier, Zane Miller, Albert Raboteau, Howard Rabinowitz, Joe Trotter, and William Tuttle read the entire manuscript. Their suggestions shaped much of the revision process. At a critical moment Mark Kishlansky provided a particularly thorough critique; I especially appreciate his desperate search for an aspect of the argument with which he could agree.

Leon Litwack and Kathleen Conzen encountered this project at different stages, and each has been essential to its progress. As friend and teacher, Leon listened, argued, encouraged, prodded, praised, and criticized. If I have finally learned how to listen to sources, how to respect and understand those about whom I write, it is because of Leon's influence. As friend and colleague, Kathy Conzen has read draft after draft after draft; no doubt by now she has memorized complete passages. Her criticisms have invariably been accompanied by helpful suggestions. Her perseverence eventually proved a match for my stubbornness, and I am certain that the book is better for it.

Finally, I wish to thank Ann Billingsley for her patience, forbearance, and willingness to endlessly discuss, criticize, and suggest. From the day she explained to me the intricacies of the CTA map, Ann has been a part of this project, first as a librarian at the Chicago Historical Society and subsequently as critic and editor. She has lived with this book. So have Ruth and Alice Grossman, although not as long and not as painfully.

The book is dedicated to the two individuals who have waited the longest. I can only hope that it has done justice to what I have learned from them.

Introduction

En route from his Augusta, Georgia, home to Chicago in 1899, Richard Robert Wright encountered his first of many surprises. The future clergyman and editor later vividly remembered "the morning I crossed the Ohio River and went into the 'white people's coach.'" Having always assumed "that white people's things were better," he had not expected to see "a car littered with papers, discarded lunch boxes, etc., and men and women who gave out none too pleasant odors, sprawled out on their seats." At the first empty seat, Wright took a significant step away from the southern way of life he had known during his first twenty-one years: he sat down.[1]

Patterns of behavior, however, were not shed easily. When a white man took the seat beside him, the young Georgian grew uncomfortable and wary. "Here I was sitting beside a white man, and he said nothing. He did not try to make me get up or in any way embarrass me; where I came from the white man would have said 'Boy, get up from here, and let me sit down,' and I would have had to get up. Finally I gained courage and spoke. 'How far is Chicago?'"

Upon arrival, Wright immediately experienced a new series of shocks to his southern sensibilities. Despite what he had heard about the North, he was not prepared for what seemed like a virtual absence of familiar prescribed racial roles. Gazing at a work crew along the railroad tracks outside Chicago, he took note of their color:

I had seen hundreds and hundreds of gangs of black men working on railroads, but I had never seen such a gang of white men. I had seen white bosses but not white laborers. My eyes and mouth were wide open as I stared at this unusual spectacle, white laborers were acting like Negro-Americans, except that Negro-Americans sometimes sang as they worked. . . . It had never occurred to me that white men actually used the pick and shovel with no Negro Americans around to help them. The whole situation seemed unnatural; I felt that there must be a mistake.

Gradually, Wright tested the new freedom. For the first time in his life, he voluntarily spoke to a policeman. He was pleasantly surprised to receive "a civil answer." However, Wright soon learned that Chicago had its own racial etiquette, its own unwritten laws and patterns of discrimination. Regardless of how honest and hardworking a black Chicagoan might be, he noted in 1901, only the most menial and low-paying jobs were available. But the first days in the city stuck in his memory, because "the seeming equality I found in Chicago gave me quite a lift."

On a rainy Saturday night in 1925, another young Richard Wright climbed aboard a northbound train in Jackson, Mississippi. His immediate destination was Memphis, but he intended to remain there only a short time. He planned to leave as soon as he could accumulate enough money to move on to Chicago, which he envisioned as a land of opportunity. "It's my life," he told himself; "I'll see now what I can make of it." Finally leaving Memphis two years later, he once again reflected on the meaning of northward migration to his identity and his future: "If I could meet enough of a different life," mused the future novelist, "then, perhaps, gradually and slowly I might learn who I was, what I might be."[2]

Like his predecessor, this Richard Wright also brought with him the "scars, visible and invisible," of his southern boyhood. He, too, was both fascinated and intimidated. "I was seized by doubt," he recalled of the moment he walked out of the railroad station in Chicago. "Should I have come here? But going back was impossible. I had fled a known terror, and perhaps I could cope with this unknown terror that lay ahead." For along with the "unknown terror" of the big city came the liberating realization that a white man sitting beside him on the streetcar seemed unconscious of his blackness. "Black people and white people moved about," he noticed, "each seemingly intent upon his private mission. There was no racial fear. Indeed, each person acted as though no one existed but himself."[3] The new rules would require adjustment, but they also promised hope. Although he, too, grew disillusioned rather quickly, Richard Wright did not regret coming to Chicago in 1927. For in the South, an ambitious black American could find even less nourishment for hopes and dreams than in the North.

That the two Wrights so similarly recalled their migratory experience might seem surprising. The son of a prominent Georgia educator, Richard Robert Wright was headed for the University of Chicago in 1899. His middle-class background and college education sharply distinguished him from the son of a Mississippi sharecropper who twenty-eight years later arrived in Chicago with no prospects and a vague dream of becoming a writer. Yet they shared two characteristics that overshadowed these differences: they were black southerners, and they recognized that their future lay in the North.

Although their journeys chronologically offer only a rough frame, the recollections of these two men provide insight into a crucial moment in Afro-American history—the first mass movement of black southerners to northern cities, during and immediately after World War I. Few participants in this "Great Migration" left such vivid recollections of their experience. Most were barely literate and never attained the prominence of either the African Methodist Episcopal Church bishop or the author of *Black Boy* and *Native Son*. Yet black southerners who ventured North to "better their condition" brought with them experiences, memories, and expectations similar to those of the two Richard Wrights. Many had more modest goals—a job in a Chicago packinghouse or steel mill—but they likewise had decided that, as one Greenville, Mississippi, man explained, "I want to get my famely out of this cursed south land down here a negro man is not good as a white man's dog." Like R. J. Bennett of Austell, Georgia, who was "truly tired of Living in a country where the Poor negro has no Privalige," most migrants viewed the North as a land of opportunity.[4] During World War I, northern cities were just that, especially compared with the South and within the context of the migrants' short-term expectations and early experiences. Despite race riots and a severe depression during the winter of 1920–21, most black migrants retained their faith in the promise of the northern city; few returned South, except for an occasional visit.

The Great Migration turned the attention of thousands of black southerners toward a northern industrial world previously marginal to their consciousness. With northern employers unwilling to hire blacks as long as white immigrants from Europe remained available, northward migration had played little role in southern black life until World War I shut off immigration. Catalyzed in early 1916 by recruiters from northern railroads suffering from the wartime labor shortage, the Great Migration soon generated its own momentum. "Northern fever" permeated the black South, as letters, rumors, gossip, and black newspapers carried word of higher wages and better treatment in the North. Approximately one-half million black southerners chose to "say fair wel to this old world" and start life anew in northern cities during 1916–19, and nearly one million more followed in the 1920s. From cities, towns, and farms, they poured into any northern city where jobs could be found. New York's black population grew from 91,709 in 1910 to 152,467 in 1920; Chicago's, from 44,103 to 109,458; Detroit's small black community of 5,741 in 1910 mushroomed to 40,838 in a decade. Harlem became the mecca of black culture; as home to such luminaries as W. E. B. Du Bois, James Weldon Johnson, and Marcus Garvey, it was also the center of political activity and ferment. But in much of the Deep South, it was Chicago that captured the attention and imagination of restless black Americans.[5]

Among the many cities offering new employment opportunities, Chicago represented a logical destination for black men and women preparing to leave homes in southern communities. "The packing houses in Chicago for a while seemed to be everything," observed one man from Hattiesburg, Mississippi. "You could not rest in your bed at night for *Chicago*." The meat-packing firms were known even in the rural South, where their storage facilities dotted the countryside. Many black southerners had heard of the "fairyland wonders" of Chicago's spectacular 1893 Columbian Exposition. Others knew of Chicago as the home of the Overton Hygienic Manufacturing Company, maker of High Brown Face Powder. Baseball fans might have seen or heard of Chicago's black American Giants, who barnstormed through the South every summer in a private railroad car. The Chicago *Defender*, the most widely read newspaper in the black South, afforded thousands of prospective migrants glimpses of an exciting city with a vibrant and assertive black community. Finally, the city was easily accessible via the Illinois Central Railroad, whose tracks stretched southward from Chicago into rural Tennessee, Mississippi, and Louisiana, with easy access from adjoining states as well.[6] Regardless of where someone "stopped on the way," recalled one migrant from Mississippi, "the mecca was Chicago." From 1916 to 1919, between fifty and seventy thousand black southerners relocated in Chicago, and thousands more passed through the city before moving on to other locations in the North.[7]

This book explores the meaning of the Great Migration from the perspective of its participants, with a particular focus on their adjustment to a northern industrial city and on their perceptions of their place in that city. Whether because of a paucity of sources generated by migrants, a preoccupation with institutional issues, or an inclination to view black southerners as objects of broader social and economic forces, few historians have probed deeply into those perceptions. Instead, the Great Migration has received attention primarily as an aspect of the changing wartime labor market or as an essential element in the development of northern urban ghettos and racial problems. The most significant and most informative descriptions of the movement until recently have been chapters in studies of either black urban communities or race riots. The community studies focus primarily on spatial and institutional development, along with the patterns of race relations that defined the ghetto; riot scholarship traces the patterns and meaning of racial conflicts that punctuated the process of Afro-American urbanization and ghetto formation. Only recently has the community-study genre moved closer to an understanding of the migrants' experience by focusing on their importance as the first Afro-American industrial working class. Still, the focus remains fixed on the community rather than on migration and adaptation as social processes.[8]

But neither the economic changes that made the movement possible nor the institutional developments that it either shaped or accelerated provide sufficient insight into the migrants, their values, or their experiences. As the first generation of black Americans to secure a foothold in the northern industrial economy, the migrants represent a crucial transition in the history of Afro-Americans, American cities, and the American working class. That transition was shaped by a complex interaction between structural forces in the South, the migration experience, structural forces in the North, racial attitudes, and the migrants' perceptions of each of these. Migrants made important decisions based on those perceptions, and only an analysis of the total context of migration—North and South—affords an understanding of either those decisions or the policy implications of responses to the movement. It is this total context that is missing from scholarship on the Great Migration. The best book-length examination of the movement, a recent study of black migration to Pittsburgh, incompletely explicates the migrants' interpretation of their place in the urban-industrial North. Its insightful analyses of migration dynamics, work culture, and industrial context are not matched by equal attention to the migrants' racially centered view of their world.[9] Sensibilities shaped by their experiences as black people in a racially structured southern society contributed to most decisions that migrants made at all stages in the process of migration and settlement. Those decisions, along with the northern and southern responses to the Great Migration, helped to shape the experience not only of the migrants, but of those who followed them North or remained in the South.

The key to a full understanding of the Great Migration and its meaning is to place the movement within the context of southern history, class formation in the North, ghettoization, and racial ideology. No study has yet managed such a synthesis, which would require a sharper and broader focus on the migrants themselves and on the migration process as they experienced it: from South to North.

This investigation, therefore, begins in the South, in particular the broad region from which Chicago drew its migrants—Mississippi, Louisiana, Alabama, Texas, Arkansas, and parts of Georgia and Tennessee. The process of migration can then be reconstructed, from its roots in earlier geographical mobility, through the transmission of information about new opportunities, to the decision-making process, and finally to the departure for the North. This "dynamic of migration" not only affected how migrants reacted to what they found, it also informs our understanding of those reactions. The particular ways in which migrants learned about the North, and then moved and resettled, drew upon and strengthened aspects of southern black culture, especially the role of kin and community. Decisions that migrants made, first about migration and later about northern institutions, reflected their ideas about themselves as black people, Americans, and workers.

The determination to leave the South and head north, viewed as a conscious and meaningful act rather than as a historical imperative, provides a foundation for an understanding of the movement and its implications. This was not necessarily an easy decision, given the risks of a long-distance move. To many black southerners, northward migration meant abandoning the dreams of independence through land ownership that had been central to southern black culture since emancipation. Communal and familial ties would have to be stretched or transplanted, if not severed entirely. Many migrants had to surmount legal and extralegal obstacles devised by southern whites dependent on black labor. In the end, those who left tended to be motivated by a combination of factors, which they often summarized as "bettering my condition," a phrase that embodied a broad comparison of conditions and possibilities in the South with images of the North.

By unraveling and then reweaving central elements of the Great Migration, Part One of this book establishes both a narrative and analytical foundation for understanding what black southerners did and thought after they arrived in the North. The ways in which migrants approached urban schools, politics, workplaces, unions, and other institutions grew out of their experiences as black southerners and participants in the Great Migration itself. Adjustments clearly took place within certain constraints, most of which have been comprehensively analyzed by scholars interested in the emergence and development of northern urban ghettos. At the same time, however, the migrants helped to shape that adjustment and the institutions it involved, and we can understand their decisions and actions in the North only by understanding how and why they came and what cultural baggage they brought with them.

The second half of the book will focus on the experiences of migrants in Chicago, which offers a variety of attractions as the locus of a case study. The broad reach of the *Defender* meant that even to many who migrated elsewhere, Chicago symbolized the promise of the North. More particularly, the city already had a black community sufficiently established to permit the emergence of a complex relationship between "Old Settlers" and newcomers. At the workplace the nature of the migrants' non-domestic employment in Chicago— largely in steel mills and packinghouses—required a sharp transition from nonindustrial to industrial work patterns. Unionization campaigns, especially in the meat-packing industry, forced the newcomers to define their relationship to an industrial economy whose accessibility had been central to migration itself. Part Two examines the environment black southerners found in Chicago and explores the ways in which the migrants' backgrounds and experiences shaped their perceptions of and responses to that environment.

Although the Great Migration drew only a small minority of black southerners, it represented what Alain Locke labeled in 1925 "a new vision of opportunity." In the same tradition, Amiri Baraka has called the movement "a reinterpretation by the Negro of his role in this country."[10] That reinterpretation lies at the center of this study, alongside the cultural and ideological continuities that help to explain the reactions of newcomers to what they found in northern cities. New structures of racial and class relations demanded new choices, best understood within the context of what the migrants had learned in the past, what they perceived at the time, and what they hoped for and expected in the future. An examination of the decisions that migrants made when confronted with issues that spoke to their sense of identity and to the realization of their hopes provides insight into their perceptions of American society and their changing role in that society.

At the heart of that changing role were the twin processes of ghetto and class formation. What was most continuous was the migrants' interpretation of both the Great Migration and American industrial society within the context of race as a social category. Migrants came from a region in which the ideology of race defined central aspects of social relations and in which individual relationships were regulated by racial protocols. If it is becoming increasingly apparent to historians that structures of class and gender relations were at least as important as race in shaping social relations in the early twentieth-century South, the influence of class and gender was at the time probably more real than apparent. Comparisons that stimulated black southerners to migrate drew largely on perceptions of the opportunities available to them as black people. The migration process itself drew upon and extended networks in which black institutions played a central role. Thus, when they went North migrants brought with them a consciousness of racial categories, and what they found easily reinforced that world view. Newcomers lived not near their workplaces as most white workers did, but in neighborhoods whose obvious defining characteristic was race. Although entrance into the industrial economy represents a crucial stage in the development of the Afro-American working class, the contours of that class were shaped by racial preconceptions of employers, black workers, and white workers. Given those preconceptions and the segregation of black communities away from the workplace, it is not surprising that black institutions and leaders offered an appealing alternative organizing matrix for black workers. When options existed, most migrants apparently chose the comfort and familiarity of black institutions; their view was less integrationist than pluralist.

Many migrants viewed migration as an opportunity to share—as black people—the perquisites of American citizenship. These included not only participation in what seemed to be an open industrial economy from which they had previously been excluded, but also good schools, the right to vote, the right to be left alone or to share public accommodations with other Americans, and in general the right to live a life free from the fears and daily indignities that characterized southern race relations. What they would eventually learn was that access defined as mere entry was not enough. Jobs did not mean promotions or economic power; votes and patronage implied neither political power nor even legitimacy as civic actors; seats in classrooms did not set their children on the road toward better jobs or places of respect in the city. Their initial optimism might seem naive in this retrospective light, and in many ways it was. But they had come from a society legally, socially, and seemingly economically defined by racial categories, and it was not at all illogical for them to assume that, freed from racial proscriptions, they could share American freedom and prosperity.

Seventy years after the Great Migration it is clear that many of the migrants' hopes foundered on the shoals of northern racism, the business cycle, and class relations. If the history of the South since emancipation embodies what one historian has called "the terrible paradox of black men and women seeking admission into a society that refuses to recognize their essential humanity," then the Great Migration perhaps represents a prologue to a further stage of disillusion. State Street once symbolized Chicago's opportunities and excitement to thousands of black southerners preparing to journey North; it is now lined with dismal high-rise public housing projects sheltering thousands of black urbanites who have little hope of escaping poverty or the physical environment in which it thrives. But the movement cannot be dismissed as a failure or as merely part of the evolution of the inner city.[11] Viewed forward, rather than backward, the Great Migration and the men and women who shaped it can teach us much about not only the Afro-American diaspora, but the meaning and boundaries of American citizenship and opportunity as well.

Part 1

1

"All I Ask Is Give Me a Chance"

James Reese, a black Floridian "looking for a free state to live in," set out for Chicago in 1917. Fifty-two years had passed since the enactment of the Thirteenth Amendment, yet he and others who left written testimonies to their reasons for participating in the Great Migration drew upon a familiar vocabulary. A half-century earlier the Reverend James Lynch, touring the South after the Civil War, had declared that blacks considered themselves "part and parcel of the American Republic" and expected to be treated as such. For most freedmen and their children the security of this citizenship appeared to lie in independence through land ownership. By 1916, however, a new generation of black southerners had begun to turn to industry, to the city, and to the North for access to the perquisites of American citizenship.[1]

Before they could make this decision, black southerners had to have an alternative that had been unavailable to blacks before World War I—industrial employment. World War I and the economic boom that accompanied it created the conditions that made possible the entrance of black migrants into northern industries. Until then, immigrants had been arriving from Europe at an annual rate that surpassed the North's total black population, thereby providing employers with a pool of labor that they considered preferable to black Americans. The outbreak of war in 1914, however, abruptly halted the flow of European immigrants. Initially, the cessation of immigration had little impact on labor markets, as a slight economic downturn had already reduced demand for industrial workers. By 1916, increasing orders both from abroad and from a domestic market stimulated by military preparedness raised prospects for spectacular profits in most major industries. Confronted with the loss of their traditional source of additional labor, northern employers looked to previously unacceptable alternatives: they opened the factory gates to white women and black southerners, although only as a temporary measure. The mobilization of the armed forces in 1917 exacerbated the labor shortage, and created still more opportunities for newcomers to the industrial labor force.[2]

The simplest explanation of the causes of the Great Migration, at what one might call the macro-historical level, is that it happened because of the impact of the war on the labor market. With northern jobs available at wages considerably higher than what a black southerner could earn at home, migration represented a rational response to a change in the labor market. At the same time, a series of economic setbacks drove blacks from the rural South. Boll weevils, storms, floods, tightening of credit: all made farming more tenuous in the South. Changes in northern and southern labor markets thus occurred simultaneously, and the major question for labor economists has been whether the push was stronger than the pull. More sociologically oriented observers have added to the equation the push of racial discrimination in the South and the pull of less oppressive race relations in the North, along with the attractions of the urban environment. But this line of inquiry has its limits. As Carter G. Woodson argued in 1918, it is not clear that given an alternative, blacks would not have long ago fled the South and its oppression. Conversely, he explained, had they been treated "as men," blacks might have stayed in the South despite the new jobs in the North. Analysis of the changes occasioned by the onset of World War I can tell us why the Great Migration happened when it did, but cannot fully explain why people decided to leave. Causes are not the same as motivations.[3]

A white Alabamian who wrote in the Montgomery *Advertiser* that "it's plain as the noonday sun the Negro is leaving this country for higher wages" might have simplistically overstated his case, but he was aware of the most obvious attraction of the North. A Hawkinsville, Georgia, black laborer, unable to afford a railroad ticket, concurred, explaining, "the reason why I want to come north is why that the people dont pay enough for the labor that a man can do down here." From Carrier, Mississippi, a prospective migrant wrote that he was "willing to work anywhere" to earn decent wages. "Wages is so low and grocery bills is so high," he complained, "untill all I can do is to live." "There is no work here that pays a man to stay here," agreed a South Carolinian.[4]

These men believed they could do better in the North. Readers of the popular Chicago *Defender* learned that anyone could find a job "if you really want it." Chicago daily wages in 1916 started in the

$2.00–$2.50 range for men; most workers earned at least $2.50. The minimum in the packinghouses, soon to be increased by 50 percent, was 27 cents per hour in March 1918. Women reportedly earned $2.00 per day as domestics—as much as many earned in a week in the South. In the factories women's wages were even higher, and southerners could not help but be impressed. Even unskilled laborers supposedly could earn an astronomical $5.00 per day. By 1919, the average hourly manufacturing wage in Chicago was 48 cents, a rate unheard of in the South. Although many were aware of Chicago's high cost of living, they expected these "big prices for work" to be more than adequate.[5] "Willing to do most ennery kind of Work," prospective migrants did not expect "to live on flowry Beds of ease." But they were confident they could earn high wages, even if that required learning new skills.[6]

Most contemporary examinations of the migration emphasized the primacy of wage differentials, along with the economic setbacks caused by the boll weevil, natural disasters, and low cotton prices in 1914 and 1915. James H. Dillard, Emmett J. Scott, and George E. Haynes, whose studies dominated discussion of the migration for many years, regarded economic considerations as "primary," "fundamental," and "paramount." Charles S. Johnson, who was responsible for much of Scott's monograph and analyzed the exodus for the Urban League and the influential Chicago Commission on Race Relations, stressed "the desire to improve their economic status." Twenty years later, sociologists St. Clair Drake and Horace Cayton, in their classic *Black Metropolis*, drew on these studies and others to conclude that the migration's "basic impetus has remained economic."[7]

Wartime considerations probably led Dillard, Scott, and Haynes— all federal officials—to stress the needs of the labor market, which the Department of Labor was attempting to control in the interest of war production. By emphasizing economic motivations, they reflected the Wilson administration's hope that the migration, with its unsettling effects on both northern cities and the southern labor market, would abate after the war boom.[8] Scott, Woodrow Wilson's wartime ambassador to black Americans and former secretary to Booker T. Washington, encouraged blacks to remain in the South. The Wilson administration, furthermore, never considered attacking white racism in the South. It could hardly ascribe migration to such factors as Jim Crow, which it had introduced into the federal government, and lynching, which it had denied was either representative or common in the South.

Johnson, the most knowledgeable student of the movement, had the most unusual yet strategic reason to highlight economic motivations. Writing as a National Urban League official, the young black sociologist did not want northern employers to think of the migrants as impulsive or irrational. Migration to "improve their economic status," represented "a symptom of wholesome and substantial life purpose; the other [flight from southern persecution], the symptom of a fugitive incourageous opportunism." Although later students of the exodus might have been more disinterested than Johnson or the compilers of federally sponsored studies, most have justifiably leaned on these analyses as authoritative and relatively free of the polemical tone of most other contemporary commentaries. Recent quantitative studies have also reiterated the conventional wisdom that persecution had long plagued black southerners and therefore could not have "caused" the migration.[9]

Racial oppression cannot, however, be dismissed quite so easily, even if the impossibility of quantifying either its incidence or impact renders it difficult to measure as an "input" into an equation of causation. Although the Chicago *Defender* might have been concentrating more on attacking the South than on careful analysis when it announced that "the maltreatment . . . of the Race is the sole cause of the exodus," a more restrained and cautious W. E. B. Du Bois found much truth in the "race paper's" exaggeration. A group of migrants leaving Louisiana for Chicago told Du Bois what they would have been reluctant to tell a white investigator: they were "willing to run any risk to get where they might breathe freer."[10] As editor of the NAACP's official journal, Du Bois was not a disinterested observer, but his observation highlights a crucial issue: the breadth of the meaning of "freedom" and other terms used by the migrants themselves.

The physical abuse that sent many migrants North assumed a variety of forms, from mistreatment by law enforcement officials to rape and lynching. The fear of such violence could induce flight as easily as the acts themselves. Blacks from Florida told investigators that they had gone North because of "the horrible lynchings in Tennessee." In Meridian, Mississippi, "migration fever" broke out after news reached town of the lynching of a woman in Louisiana. "Everyone began to circulate that story. Men feared for their wives and women feared for their lives," remembered a man who later relocated in Chicago. Chicago Urban League workers found that after a lynching, "colored people from that community will arrive in Chicago inside of two weeks."[11]

In some cases, what James Weldon Johnson called "the tremendous shore of southern barbarism" literally forced blacks to migrate. Practicing a half-century-old practice known as "whitecap-ping," whites in scattered nonplantation districts physically drove blacks from their land. In 1917, twenty-five hundred blacks were reportedly forced out of two Georgia counties. At the same time, an observer described agricultural Carroll County, Mississippi, as a "white cap county in a mild form," noting that it was now possible to "ride for miles and not see a black face." Blacks had been "driven from the county and their property confiscated."[12] This activity con-tinued into the 1920s, with the revived Ku Klux Klan often lending organizational effectiveness. In 1920, Klansmen posted notices in the environs of one Georgia town, notifying blacks they would no longer be permitted to "live from the river north of the town to the Blue Ridge Mountains." Few blacks were forced out of homes in areas heavily populated by blacks, but as one southern white reformer noted, such acts of terrorism were "widely discussed among the ne-groes and have been a big factor in their unrest."[13]

Along with sporadic violence, continuous discrimination stimu-lated the exodus. One black church elder in Macon, Georgia, pointed to "unjust treatments enacted daily on the streets, street cars and trains . . . driving the Negro from the South." It was this kind of day-to-day indignity that led Jefferson Clemons, "tired of bein' dog and beast," to leave his DeRidder, Louisiana, home. In a South permeated with an "atmosphere of injustice and oppression," the *AME Church Review* observed, migration had become the only solution for those who sought to "stand erect as men."[14]

Most analysts of the migration grouped these "causes" of the exo-dus under the general category of "social" or "sentimental" factors. Also included among these were disfranchisement, inferior educa-tional facilities (sometimes included under economic factors), unfair treatment in the courts, peonage, and "poor treatment" in general. Usually this group fell into the "secondary" category of explanations for the exodus. Some commentators assigned to them an order of relative significance; others simply recited a list, best summarized as "conditions were bad." The black Houston *Observer* offered a poi-gnant recitation of dissatisfactions:

> Take some of the sections from which the Negro is departing
> and he can hardly be blamed when the facts are known. He is
> kicked around, cuffed, lynched, burned, homes destroyed,
> daughters insulted and oftimes raped, has no vote nor voice, is
> underpaid, and in some instances when he asks for pay receives a
> 2 × 4 over his head. These are facts. If he owes a bill he must pay
> it or his body and family will suffer the consequences. But if cer-
> tain people in the community owe him, he must wait until they

get ready to pay him or "sell out." In some settlements, if his crop is better than the other fellow's, his early exit is demanded or forced. When such conditions are placed and forced upon a people and no protest is offered, you cannot blame a race of people for migrating.[15]

The *Observer* succeeded better than most in avoiding laundry lists of "causes," and bifurcating "economic" and "social" factors. But like many others, it examined in isolation those forces driving blacks from the South.

Analysts who examined the appeal of the North—the "pull" forces—also compiled innumerable lists, citing high wages, equality, bright lights, "privileges," good schools, and other attractions describing the obverse of what the migrants were fleeing in the South. Indeed, as Richard Wright would later learn, southern black images of Chicago, and the North in general, "had no relation whatever to what actually existed." He and other children in Jackson, Mississippi, had heard that "a white man hit a colored man up north and that colored man hit that white man, knocked him cold, and nobody did a damn thing." Adults shared impressions of the North as a paradise of racial equality. Wellborn Jenkins of Georgia thought that "when white and black go into the courts of the north they all look alike to those judges up there."[16] Misinformed or not, southern blacks were certain they could find racial justice and opportunities for improvement in Chicago.

Regardless of how much priority is placed on which factor, lists of "push" and "pull" forces suggest mainly the range of injustices and privations driving blacks from the South. No list can implicitly weave together its various components to compose an image of the fabric of social and economic relationships which drove black southerners to look elsewhere for a better life. Nor can lists communicate the fears, disgust, hopes, and goals that combined to propel blacks from the South and draw them northward.[17]

An explanation of motivation, of the decision to move North, lies in the continuity of southern black life, as much as in the changes caused by the wartime economy. A Mississippian tried to explain the problem:

Just a few months ago they hung Widow Baggage's husband from Hirshbery bridge because he talked back to a white man. He was a prosperous Farmer owning about 80 acres. They killed another man because he dared to sell his cotton 'off the place.' These things have got us sore. Before the North opened up with work all we could do was to move from one plantation to another in hope of finding something better.[18]

All the exploitation—legal, social, economic—was bound together within his use of the impersonal "they." This reference to a web of social relations has broad implications for both the causes and meaning of the Great Migration, especially when considered within the context of the tradition of black migration and persistence in the South.

The Great Migration both constituted a stage in the long-term process of Afro-American urbanization and accelerated a northward trend that had begun in the 1890s. Urbanization had started before the guns of the Civil War had quieted and has continued into the 1980s. In absolute terms, the approximately three million blacks who left the South between 1940 and 1960 formed an exodus twice as large as that of 1910–30.[19] The Great Migration, however, represents an important shift in direction, with the center of black population moving northward during World War I, rather than toward the south and west as it had in previous decades. It also marks an important transformation in outlook among a growing minority of black southerners. Since emancipation, both migration and persistence had usually involved strategies directed towards a degree of autonomy based on land ownership. The Great Migration, by contrast, drew upon black southerners who looked to urban life and the industrial economy for the social and economic foundation of full citizenship and its perquisites. It was, as observers noted then and since, a "second emancipation," and accordingly it must be considered within a historical context anchored by the first emancipation and as a similarly transforming event.[20]

As a symbolic theme and social process, migration has epitomized the place of Afro-Americans in American society. Slaves suffered both restrictions on their freedom of movement and coerced migration within the South, and many blacks came to regard the ability to move as, in writer Howard Thurman's words, "the most psychologically dramatic of all manifestations of freedom."[21] Upon emancipation exslaves seized upon spatial mobility as one of the most meaningful components of their newly won status. Subsequently they and their children moved, within the rural South, to southern cities, and finally to northern cities, in a frustrating quest for equality and opportunity. Conversely, southern planters viewed black migration as a threat to economic and social stability. Until the mechanization of cotton culture in the mid-twentieth century, black geographic mobility—like black social and economic mobility—threatened the racial assumptions and labor relations upon which southern economy and society rested. Debt peonage and the crop lien system seldom inhibited local movement but, when combined with contract enforcement laws, did make it difficult for blacks to move longer distances. Various forms of labor enticement legislation inhibited the activities of labor agents, whose role whites invariably overemphasized but who did provide information about faraway opportunities. The narrow range of employment opportunities open to black workers, both inside and outside the South, was perhaps the greatest impediment to black migration until World War I.

Until the Civil War, few black southerners could move about freely. Although perhaps as many as twenty-five thousand slaves escaped during the American Revolution, and more than three thousand eventually made their way to Nova Scotia at the end of the war, the first major migration of black southerners was no more voluntary than the one that had brought them to America in the first place. The opening of the trans-Appalachian West to settlement by slaveholders brought new opportunities to whites. For approximately a hundred thousand blacks between 1790 and 1810 it meant the destruction of family and community ties that had developed in what had been a relatively stable slave society in the Chesapeake. The enormous expansion of cotton cultivation in the early nineteenth century, coupled with the closing of the foreign slave trade in 1808, soon transformed a forced migration dominated by planters carrying their own slaves westward to one increasingly characterized by the professional slave trader. Although the Chesapeake remained the major source for the interstate slave trade, after 1830 North and South Carolina, Kentucky, Tennessee, Missouri, and eventually Georgia also became "exporters" of slaves. The plantations of Alabama, Mississippi, Louisiana, Florida, Arkansas, and Texas were worked largely by these early black "migrants" and their children. Although it is difficult to determine the volume of the domestic slave trade, it appears that more than one million black southerners were forcibly relocated between 1790 and 1860.[22]

Barriers against voluntary movement complemented forced migrations in the antebellum South. The hundreds of slaves who escaped each year constituted only a fraction of the southern black population. By the 1830s even free black southerners were hemmed in, their movement across state lines either restricted or prohibited. Furthermore, the security of family and community ties discouraged them from moving, given the limited opportunities available to free blacks in both northern and southern cities. A few black southerners did find their way North, however, and as early as the 1840s, Chicago had a small community of escaped bondsmen.[23]

During the Civil War, white fears and black hopes generated opposing migration streams. Many slaveowners responded to the approach of Union troops by taking their slaves west, either to the upcountry in the eastern states or from the Deep South to Texas and Arkansas. The last of the great forced migrations followed the fall of New Orleans, as more than 150,000 slaves were transported from Louisiana and Mississippi into Texas. At the same time, thousands of slaves fled toward the advancing Union army and the freedom that they expected the war to bring. The Emancipation Proclamation did not set this movement in motion. Indeed, the executive order cannot be separated from the actions of deserting slaves, who forced Union generals and subsequently President Lincoln to confront the issue of what were at first considered contraband of war. If Union army camps did not constitute a Promised Land they at least provided a destination that made this unorganized mass migration possible.[24]

Former slaves continued to move after the war, with many freed men and women associating their former homes with their former status. Most ex-slaves traveled only short distances, often merely to the next plantation or a nearby settlement. Migration, even if only local, permitted ex-slaves to prove to themselves and their former masters that they now controlled their own labor and their own family life; the act of moving constituted a test of the meaning of emancipation. Some ex-slaves moved in search of family separated by antebellum forced migration; others headed back to plantations from which they had been removed during the war. Much of the movement grew out of a search for favorable social, political, and economic conditions. Former slaves recognized that planters needed their labor and used their new freedom to move as a means of extracting the best possible arrangements from the whites who remained in control of the land. One Georgia freedman, explaining that he did not want to sign a contract because it would strip him of this option, and in a more abstract sense limit his freedom, insisted that he did not have to worry about the planter refusing to pay, because "den I can go somewhere else." Freedpeople who removed to the upcountry or either acquired or squatted on poor land wanted, according to one northern observer, to be "entirely independent of white men." Related to the reluctance of many ex-slaves to produce more than a subsistence, this drive for autonomy might have reflected hostility towards the market as much as an attempt to avoid contact with whites. But it is difficult to separate whites and the market as objects of concern, because involvement with the market implied dealing with whites; and ex-slaves had good reason to be suspicious of any such dealings.[25]

Perhaps most essential to the impulse to move was the search for "independence," which was closely associated with land ownership.

With high hopes and unrealistic expectations of acquiring land, some freedpeople journeyed to developing regions within the South, sometimes following labor agents representing planters confronting a labor shortage. Although it more often tried to dissuade freedpeople from changing employers, the Freedmen's Bureau occasionally tried to send workers to areas with labor shortages, thereby stimulating some long-distance relocation. More frequently, labor agents provided the information and transportation necessary for interstate migration. But land ownership remained elusive for most families, as emancipation teased ex-slaves with the right to own land without providing the wherewithal to obtain it.[26]

Not all former slaves concluded that the countryside offered the best chances to enjoy the perquisites of freedom. Indeed, in many respects cities were "freer," given widespread rural violence and the threat of retribution from former slaveholders. Aware of their vulnerability on scattered plantations and farms, some freedmen looked to cities for security, in the form of federal troops, Freedmen's Bureau officials, and sheer numbers of blacks. Cities also offered ready accessibility to black churches and benevolent societies, schools and relief services established by the Bureau, and possibilities for political participation. It is impossible to measure this move to the cities, given problems with the 1870 census and the fallacies inherent in using a decennial count to chart a period characterized by considerable instability, if not chaos. But if most freedpeople looked first to the land for the fulfillment of the promise of emancipation, it is clear that many others flocked to nearby cities and towns during and after the war.[27]

Dismayed by the social and political implications of an urban black population, city officials resorted to both legal and extralegal devices to push former slaves back to the land, where planters wanted to keep them as a dependent labor force. Presaging the response of the white South to future black migration, especially the Great Migration North during World War I, whites combined repressive measures with the argument that black urbanization owed more to external agitation (in this case Radical Republicans) than to black initiative or problems in rural areas. But "outside influences" more often tended to discourage urbanization. Freedmen's Bureau and army officials, along with many black leaders influenced by the nineteenth-century agrarian ideal, advised ex-slaves to eschew urban life. Although most Bureau officials and other northern Republicans involved in Reconstruction did not share the planters' goal of reviving the plantation on the backs of a dependent labor force, they did want to resume production quickly and envisioned a black yeomanry that first had to be "disciplined" into the norms of a free labor system. Despite their

divergent visions of southern agricultural structure, planters and federal officials could agree on the outlines of a policy designed to limit
black workers' choices and return them to the farms. Vagrancy laws,
passed by unreconstructed governments with the cooperation of the
Bureau, provided a temporary mechanism. As early as the latter part
of 1865, hungry refugees, forced to abandon an urban framework for
freedom, began to return to the plantations. [28]

Northern cities even more successfully resisted the influx that
many northerners feared would follow emancipation. Before the Civil
War, many northern states restricted "Negro immigration," and Illinois prohibited it entirely in its 1848 constitution. Generally unenforced and ineffective, the laws did reflect attitudes that were
unlikely to change quickly. Northern whites, however, had little to
fear. Few freedpeople even considered northward migration, and
many of those who did recognized that it was impractical, given the
costs of transportation and the paucity of opportunities for employment. In its attempt to match the supply of black workers with the
demand, the Freedmen's Bureau did send some ex-slaves North, but
insufficient—if not nonexistent—demand severely limited such activity. The approximately nine thousand freedpeople sent North from
Washington, D.C., constituted an exception. With the District strain-
ing under the burden of relief for thousands of refugees, many of
whom refused to return to the South, Bureau officials in this case
ignored their normal opposition to relocation outside the South. Bureau policy aside, however, most ex-slaves had little information
about the North, few resources to get there, and greater interest in
the possibility of landed independence in the more familiar South. [29]

As the promise of Reconstruction dissolved in state after state during the 1870s, many black southerners began to consider leaving the
South, although generally still within the context of a commitment to
farming. With the southern economy dependent on a landless black
labor force, and with blacks placing the highest value on the independence associated with the ownership of productive land, something
had to give, and usually it was black aspirations. One logical alternative was to seek land elsewhere. A variety of emigration projects attracted considerable interest between the 1870s and 1910s.

Like thousands of other Americans in the nineteenth century,
black southerners looked west during the 1870s. Nearly ten thousand
blacks from Kentucky and Tennessee made their way to Kansas
during that decade, many under the leadership of Benjamin "Pap"
Singleton, who emphasized the potential value of homesteading and
the formation of black colonies. But it was the "Kansas Fever Exodus"
of 1879–80 that attracted national attention, although it actually in-

volved fewer settlers than the movement into the state earlier in the decade. In the aftermath of the often bloody repression that accompanied the collapse of Reconstruction, more than six thousand black Texans, Mississippians, and Louisianians went to Kansas in search of political freedom and land. Perhaps an equal number followed over the next few years, but most important, Kansas Fever infected thousands of other black southerners who could not muster the financial resources to participate in the movement or who ran out of money in St. Louis. Seeking to organize black southerners for political activity in the mid-1870s, Henry Adams found that many preferred simply to leave. He later estimated—perhaps with some exaggeration—that ninety-eight thousand of his people were ready to leave the Deep South. Thousands of others actively debated the proposition. The opportunity to own land formed the wellspring of the "Kansas Fever Idea" and in that respect the Exodus resembled most other nineteenth-century black migration. Yet other features anticipated later movement to northern cities. Although the Exodus seemed unorganized and haphazard, many "Exodusters" wrote for information before leaving home, traveled in organized groups, and considered their move part of a broad popular impulse. Moreover, they contrasted the promise of full citizenship in Kansas—based on the possibility of land ownership in this case—with the future shaped by southern white "Redemption" achieved through fraud, violence, and intimidation. Both the debate that the Exodus engendered among black leaders and the hostility it provoked from white southerners would characterize the later Great Migration."[30]

If the Kansas Exodus left in its wake more frustration than hope, it hardly spelled the end of westward ventures based on the lure of open land and the promise of "independence." More than seven thousand blacks participated in the 1889 Oklahoma land rush, and over the next two decades, approximately one hundred thousand more followed. The formation of "Oklahoma Clubs" suggests once again at least a modicum of organizational activity. In an expansion of what had been only a minor theme in the Kansas Exodus, towns established, developed, and inhabited exclusively by blacks constituted an important part of the drive for land and for both political and economic self-determination. Promoters of such towns linked the ownership of property—particularly productive land—to the attainment and protection of full citizenship. Segregated communities, according to the most complete study of these towns, represented not rejection of American identity, but "the promise of eventual entrance into the mainstream of American life complete with economic prosperity and full social and political rights for all." The approximately twenty-five black towns established between 1891 and 1910 promised, in this sense, one solution to the eternal dilemma that W. E. B. Du Bois referred to as the "twoness" of being both black and American.[31]

But if Oklahoma's black towns offered economic and political autonomy unavailable anywhere else in the United States, these struggling communities also brought disappointment, disillusion, and hardship. Economic difficulties plagued the towns from the beginning, and the transition to statehood in 1907 led to disfranchisement accompanied by racial violence. Even as black southerners were still streaming into Oklahoma during the early twentieth century, despair had driven many earlier settlers to look outside the United States for refuge from what seemed to be a ubiquitous racial order.

Although prospective emigrants considered other destinations, Africa remained the focus of the most enduring, and perhaps quixotic, migration project involving black Americans. Before the Civil War, the American Colonization Society, comprising mainly philanthropic—if usually Negrophobic—whites, had transported twelve thousand black colonists to Liberia. Most black leaders opposed the Society's efforts, considering colonization akin to deportation. A minority, increasingly visible by the 1850s, accepted emigration as a legitimate alternative to the limited freedom available in the United States, but rejected Liberia as "a mere dependency of southern slaveholders." Liberia would remain, however, the major focus of Afro-American emigrationism. During the half-century after the Civil War, each successive low point in American race relations—first the end of Reconstruction and later the passage of Jim Crow laws and the upsurge of lynchings during the 1890s—stimulated renewed interest in Liberia among black Americans. Not only was land available, but neither economic nor political structures required interaction with whites. Only one thousand black southerners actually sailed to Liberia during the twenty years after 1890, but thousands otherwise participated in a movement generally associated with Henry McNeal Turner. Many bought shares in joint stock companies which promised passage across the Atlantic. Others joined emigration clubs, listened receptively to speeches, or enthusiastically read newspapers advocating emigration. But with the bulk of its appeal in the poorest areas of the rural Deep South, emigration to Africa remained financially impossible.[32]

If most black southerners either could not or did not wish to leave the South, they did not remain passively in one place awaiting salvation. Like white Americans, they were remarkably mobile during the half-century after the Civil War. Kansas and Liberia captured the imaginations of thousands of black southerners hungry for land and autonomy, but less exotic destinations within the South provided more practical outlets for dissatisfaction, restlessness, and even hope. Although most movement continued to be local and individualized, as it had been during Reconstruction, many black southerners undertook longer journeys, often within the framework of a group enterprise. Continuing the quest for land ownership, most of those who migrated longer distances headed for rural destinations, generally towards the south and west.

Since Reconstruction, blacks working worn-out land in the Carolinas and Georgia had been responsive to rumors of supposedly higher wages and better tenure arrangements in the Mississippi Delta and other areas in the Gulf states. In many cases, labor agents representing agricultural interests in these regions played a significant role in both transmitting information and organizing departures. Much of the information about fertile land and crops "high as a man on horseback" traveled by way of black workers moving about looking "for betterment." These migrations remain obscure, but a study of the movement of between three thousand and five thousand blacks from eight counties in Georgia to Mississippi at the end of 1899 suggests that labor agents enjoyed considerable credibility in the black South. This exodus was also, however, "an indigenous movement among working-class blacks to achieve a better life," and encouragement from agents was less necessary than the transportation they provided. In at least one county, local people took the initiative and held meetings to discuss and plan migration. Similarly, in South Carolina, "emigration societies" formed, with membership dues used to finance the expeditions of scouts, who would travel to Florida, Mississippi, Arkansas, or Texas and report back as to whether actual conditions had been honestly represented. Frequently these scouts sent back reports only slightly less inaccurate than the fraudulent promises of the agents, and hopeful emigrants would pack up and leave, only to find themselves once again sharecropping on halves, under equally oppressive racial codes. [33]

This constant movement, especially to more fertile land to the south and west, disturbed whites who not only feared diminution of their labor supply but also recognized—if only implicitly—the relationship between immobility and dependence. After the Civil War landowners in the areas of greatest black population had remained committed to the plantation system. Stability—both of the plantation system itself and of the labor force required to maintain it profitably—remained a high priority to a landed class cognizant of its need to control its black labor force. Complaining that the labor market

remained chaotic because of the "migratory habits" of blacks, southern whites fashioned legal and economic institutions designed partly
to stabilize that market. Even movement within the South encountered such opposition from whites that some prospective migrants
had to overcome barriers erected to protect landlords and agricultural
employers from threats to "their" labor force.[34]

A combination of vagrancy laws, legislation circumscribing the activity of "emigrant agents," and criminal (rather than civil) enforcement of sharecropping contracts formed a legal system that enhanced
planter control over black labor. Complementing this structure was a
cycle of indebtedness that could limit the options of black farmers for
long periods of time. Landlords had to ensure that once a black renter
or wage laborer planted a crop, he would stay on hand to cultivate
and harvest it. Both the contract and the debt incurred in order to
secure everyday necessities provided a legal basis for labor stability
in any given year. As one Mississippi planter explained with reference to a tenant in debt, "If he goes away, I just go and get him."
Thus, the easiest time to move was between settlement time around
Christmas and the beginning of new advances, which even after a
good year could be as early as February. In some cases, tenants and
laborers never paid off the debt—at least not according to the landlord or merchant who kept the accounts. As one Mississippi sharecropper observed, "I have knowed lots of people in Mississippi who
cain't leave, because if you make a crop and don't clear nothin' and
you still wound up owin' on your sharecrop and on your furnish' and
you try to move, well the police be after you then all right." Many
planters even limited the amount of land that tenants could rent, to
ensure not only intensive cultivation but also continued dependence
and therefore "labor available for hire." The freedmen who had
fought for control over their time and their crop had understood the
issue quite clearly. But laws, markets, and social relations secured to
planters and merchants sufficient control to stimulate blacks to move
while making it difficult to do so.[35]

On the whole, however, it is likely that most black southerners
who wanted to move could manage to evade legal impediments if
necessary. In the Southeast, as land became less productive white
resistance to black migration declined along with the demand for
labor. In most of the South, much of the legislation was directed
against labor agents, who while influential were not as essential
to long-distance moves as whites assumed and were irrelevant to
local movement. Tenants circumvented ties of indebtedness through
surreptitious departure or more often by simply transferring the
debt to a new landlord. Where a merchant rather than a landlord held

the note, a debtor could try a new piece of land with even less difficulty. The system did keep most movement local, as the need for credit inhibited most rural black southerners from moving to new communities where they would lack "standing" with landlords and merchants. The visibility of interstate migration and schemes for emigration, along with intense opposition to any threat to the stability of the agricultural labor force, tends to obscure the prevailing practice of short-distance moves.[36]

Whether changing landlords, trying out a new piece of land, buying a small farm with a surplus obtained after a few particularly good years, lapsing back into tenancy after a bad year, or venturing to town or city seeking wage work, black southerners seldom stayed in one place for very long. Movement became as central to southern black life as it has been to the American experience in general, emerging as a major theme in black music, with the railroad recurring as a symbol of the freedom to move and start life anew. White efforts at social control, motivated in part by the refusal of blacks to remain satisfied with their "place," only fueled black dissatisfaction and stimulated the migratory impulse.[37]

To a considerable extent, this instability was class-based, correlated more closely with one's place in the southern economy than with race. Mobility rates among black farmers exceeded those of their white counterparts because blacks constituted a disproportionately large segment of the most mobile group of farm operators—share tenants. Within any given tenure category, black farmers tended to be more stable than whites. Even share tenants were probably less mobile than statistics suggest, because the census recorded as "moves" any shifts from tract to tract on a given plantation. Black southerners moved not because they had a "penchant for migration," but because the economic, political, and social equality presumed to be a perquisite of American citizenship remained beyond their grasp. A different region, a different plot of land, a different landlord—all seemed worth a try.[38]

During the decade preceding World War I, a series of setbacks to the cotton economy of the Deep South contributed to the migratory impulse, while narrowing the alternatives. The opening decade of the twentieth century marked the end of the westward expansion of southern cotton cultivation. Meanwhile, the boll weevil began to widen its swath across the cotton fields. A significant proportion of black migration between 1900 and 1910 coincided with the coming of the weevil, which had entered the United States from Mexico in 1892, and reached Louisiana in 1903 and Mississippi four years later. Moving eastward as blacks moved westward, the insect forced black farmers either to keep moving or accept its depredations, given the ineffectiveness of most methods of combating its attacks on ripening cotton bolls. In the area around Shreveport, Louisiana, it struck hardest between 1906 and 1910, with yields returning to normal by 1914. Mississippi, on the other hand, suffered greatest devastation after 1913, and Alabama after 1916. Intrastate variation in the impact of the weevil further contributed to the tendency of its attacks to stimulate migration, as black farmers tried to stay one step ahead of the threat.[39]

> De white man he got ha'f de crap
> Boll-Weevil took de res'.
> Ain't got no home,
> Ain't got no home.[40]

As if the weevils themselves were not sufficient to ruin black farmers, many tenants found themselves forced to absorb their landlords' losses as well as their own. One United States Department of Agriculture analyst noted that "the advances furnished to the negroes can be held down to very low limits in case of necessity," which suggests that when "necessity" struck in the form of the boll weevil, the already depressed standard of living among black tenants dropped even further. Indeed, the impact of the weevil must be evaluated within the context of specific forms of productive relations in southern agriculture. Neither black farm owners nor white farmers moved as readily as black tenants from infested areas, largely because the latter had the least latitude to react by changing the crop mix and were most subject to the impact of the boll weevil on the availability of credit.[41]

The credit system that economic historians have demonstrated was essential to the structure of southern agriculture compounded the impact of the weevil on black tenants and wage laborers. For years, unharvested cotton had been readily accepted as collateral for agricultural loans. Indeed, by accepting only cotton, merchants and bankers had forced even farm owners into the same one-crop dependency as tenants. To the lender, these loans were safe so long as a good crop could be expected. Even when prices dropped, the loan was secure, as the merchant and banker held first liens on the crop. But by 1916–17, the weevil had spread uncertainty throughout the South. Banks failed and loans became difficult to secure. Many farm owners found themselves forced to sell their land at depressed prices and either turn to renting or head for the city. Again, tenants fared even worse, as the credit crunch further limited advances of food and other supplies, while driving up the already exorbitant interest they paid for those advances.[42]

Belatedly, some planters recognized the folly of their obsession with cotton and began, as one historian has explained, "to look up from their almanacs and listen to agricultural experts." For many, this meant diversification, even if only temporarily. Had such diversification occurred earlier, more black farmers would have survived the boll weevil. But now the decision operated to drive many of them from the land, because such crops as corn and soybeans—whether raised as food or fodder—required less labor and were less conducive to a sharecropping system. Newly diversifying sections around Jackson, Mississippi, noted sociologist Charles Johnson in 1917, had recently decreased their labor force from 30 to 60 percent. On the whole, however, diversification touched only a small percentage of the cotton South, as most farmers and agricultural experts put their energy into protecting the cotton crop.[43]

A Mississippi woman who told Johnson of a "general belief [among blacks] that God had cursed the land," described a reaction to more than just the boll weevil. The Mississippi River flooded in 1912 and 1913, and a drought was followed by driving rainstorms in late 1915. The tightened credit market exacerbated economic distress, as both black farmers and whites employing blacks had difficulty obtaining capital to help recover from the disasters.[44]

Combined with the continuing problem of soil exhaustion in older cotton-growing regions, the chronic instability of the cotton economy, and the endless dissatisfaction inherent in the credit system, the boll weevil and bad weather contributed to a situation characterized by Charles Johnson as "profound restlessness." By 1910, most southern black farmers had moved at least once in the previous four years, and a third had lived in their current residence only a year or less. Johnson found in 1917 that "fundamental unrest" had been rife in Mississippi and Arkansas for at least a decade. But there had been nowhere to go. Constant movement between Mississippi and Arkansas, and from the hills to the Delta and back again, fell within the tradition of the search for land, but the potential clearly existed for other outlets. "Negroes were churning about in the South, seeking a vent," Johnson later recalled, with the benefit of hindsight. An analyst for the federal Bureau of Agricultural Economics picked up the hints in 1913, when he commented on the increased tendency of black tenants to skip debts, perhaps a symptom not only of increasing desperation on the part of some, but of an increasing refusal on the part of young blacks to play by the accepted rules of southern agriculture.[45]

Movement was hardly new to young black southerners. The cycle of cotton cultivation, leaving little work to do for weeks at a time between spurts of intense activity, stimulated a search for nonagricultural employment, especially among young blacks. As teenagers, many were "hired out" by parents or found wage work in various nonfarm occupations. Turpentine camps, sawmills, cottonseed-oil mills, and other industries closely related to the agricultural economy provided young black men with opportunities to acquire cash wages and glimpse a wider world. Young women ventured into cities and towns to earn extra cash washing, cooking, or cleaning. Although most black southerners continued to seek some form of landed independence or simply did not consider leaving the countryside, increasing numbers began to move off the farms in the last decade of the nineteenth century. Many of these men and women moved back and forth between town (or less frequently, city) and farm, leaving the countryside after picking in the late fall and returning to plant in March. They could take advantage also of the slack times during the growing season, which provided additional openings in the traditional way of life and permitted a gradual acculturation to geographical and economic mobility. Like the thousands of Europeans who lived in nonurban settings, similarly unstable in the late nineteenth century but also too rigid to permit younger individuals to seek new places without venturing into a wider world, a generation of black southerners took first steps into a labor market that stretched far beyond familiar boundaries.[46]

Some left the countryside permanently, as part of a general pattern of gradual urbanization in the South. Despite considerable economic expansion in the early twentieth-century South, however, blacks continued to find few opportunities outside agriculture. Women could find service positions in cities and towns, but expanding textile, furniture, oil and gas, paper and pulp, and chemical industries remained virtually closed to black workers. Electricity, streetcars, and other new and skilled areas of urban employment remained equally white. Whether agricultural interests successfully prevented industrial development that they could not control and that would compete for black labor, or whether exclusion emerged from some other dynamic, the fact was inescapable to black southerners: with scattered exceptions (especially in the Birmingham region) the southern urban-industrial economy promised few opportunities for black people.[47]

By 1890, 13.5 percent of black southerners lived in cities; two decades later, the proportion had risen to 19.7 percent. This rate of urbanization, although lower than that of southern whites and partly a result of extended city boundaries, was not insignificant. Nonfarm rural employment and even modest urbanization contributed to a gradual weaning from the land and represented an increasing dissatisfaction among younger blacks with the "place" that their parents had accepted in the economy. Given the casual nature of most employment open to them, black urbanites, especially men, had few opportunities to settle down. For some, movement to a southern city represented an initial step toward a more dramatic move outside the region. Before 1916, few black southerners went directly from the rural South to northern cities. Migration to a nearby town or city often led to subsequent relocation to such places as New York, Philadelphia, Boston, or Chicago.[48]

Black migration out of the South increased dramatically in the 1890s, from only 156,000 in the previous twenty years to 185,000 in a single decade. Frequently referred to as "the migration of the talented tenth," the 1890s movement has been attributed to the deterioration of race relations in the South and the difficulties experienced by aggressive black leaders.[49] Indeed, many of those who went North during this and the following decade were better educated and more affluent than most black southerners, as are most self-selecting migrating populations. The most visible northbound migrants, like Ida B. Wells, who was run out of Memphis because of her outspoken opposition to lynching, were militant leaders who could not remain safely in the South if they continued to reject the accommodating stance summarized in Booker T. Washington's Atlanta Compromise. Race riots, such as those in Wilmington, North Carolina, in 1898 and in Atlanta in 1906, were but the most extreme manifestations of white attempts to root out black participation in community affairs. Both riots accompanied disfranchisement campaigns, and each was followed by heavy black migration to the North. The first to go were often the most successful, best educated, and most outspoken blacks, who had borne the brunt of white violence. After the Atlanta riot, for example, local whites confronted Jesse Max Barber, editor of the *Voice of the Negro*, with three options: leaving town, recanting his comments about the causes of the riot, or serving on the chain gang. He headed for Chicago. W. E. B. Du Bois explained in 1902 that "a certain sort of soul, a certain kind of spirit finds the narrow repression, the provincialism of the South almost unbearable." He left eight years later.[50]

The notion of a "migration of the talented tenth," however, is misleading, especially as northward migration began to accelerate after 1890. Like most long-distance migrants, the black southerners who went North during the late nineteenth and early twentieth centuries differed in the aggregate from those who stayed behind. The most detailed case study, focusing on the period 1865–1900, indicates that those who went to Boston, for example, were disproportionately urban, mulatto, literate, and from the Upper South. And overall, the Upper South provided the bulk of northbound black migrants until

World War I. The prominent figures whose individual experiences suggest the "talented tenth" label differed sharply from most of the men and women who went North. The sheer volume of migration indicates that even if a "talented tenth" was overrepresented, the movement had to have drawn heavily upon the impoverished farmers and laborers who constituted the overwhelming proportion of black southerners. There is no evidence that the small southern black middle class was decimated—or even significantly affected—by migration during this period. Although perhaps better prepared for urban life than most black southerners, most newcomers to northern cities during these years brought few resources with them. [51]

Most black southerners who went North before World War I headed for a handful of major cities; by 1910, New York, Philadelphia, and Chicago housed nearly one-fourth of the northern black population. Yet neither these cities nor others in the North seemed to offer an alternative for most black southerners during the half-century after the Civil War. Few industrial employers considered hiring blacks except as strikebreakers or porters, and the service economy could not absorb a substantial influx. Most black southerners who moved to northern cities before 1916 did find jobs, but mainly as menials, and it is not clear how much black unemployment might have resulted from more extensive migration northward at this point. With some justification, most black leaders—North and South—advised black southerners to heed Booker T. Washington's admonition to "cast down their buckets where they are." Editor Robert Abbott of the Chicago *Defender*, himself a migrant from Georgia, advised black southerners to be more militant than Washington did, but agreed that "the only wise thing to do is to stick to the farm." [52]

What emerges from this pattern of restlessness, persistence, and migration are three interrelated themes: a continuing commitment to landed independence, despite its increasingly evident impossibility; a localistic perspective; and growing tension. Those who moved—or wanted to move—long distances tended to remain oriented towards the land. But by the early twentieth century, both inside and outside the context of southern agricultural life, blacks were widening their perspectives and beginning to extend kin and community networks to an urban-industrial world that would eventually create important links to northern cities. To many black southerners, movement continued to be the most effective means of asserting the freedom and independence that they had hoped to attain through land ownership. They moved when the ubiquitous exploitation reached intolerable levels, and they moved when something better beckoned. "Whenever we get an opportunity and inducement and [are] in position to take care of ourself, we moves," commented one Mississippian in 1917.[53]

Neither stability nor geographic mobility, however, enabled very many blacks to fulfill the promise of emancipation. In some places whites refused to sell land to blacks. Even cash tenancy loosened the close supervision a landlord exercised over a sharecropper, and most southern landowners assumed that black farmers could not work land efficiently without such supervision. After fifty years of "hoping against hope," the *AME Church Review* observed in 1917, black southerners had learned that "neither character, the accumulation of property, the fostering of the Church, the schools and a better and higher standard of the home" had brought either respect or the chance for substantial mobility. "Confidence in the sense of justice, humanity and fair play of the white South is gone."[54] Even those who had followed all the rules and had lived (at least outwardly) according to the values preached to them ever since white missionaries had followed the Union armies South, had nothing to show for it. They had been told to be thrifty, but as journalist Henry Reed reported from Pittsburgh, Texas, "if they try to save any money the whites will lay them off for two or three days out of each week." A farmer in Alpharetta, Georgia, knew that he "better not accumulate much, no matter how hard and honest you work for it, as they—well you can't enjoy it." One Tennessee black newspaper reported in 1909 that a black farmer's "signs of prosperity" could attract "nightriders" who would drive him from his land. Working hard as an employee was equally unlikely to bring advancement; most black southerners were well aware of the "Dixie limit" beyond which no black could advance. Black sharecropper and occasional lumber hauler Ned Cobb later recalled how whites reacted to his ambitious ways: "Whenever the colored man prospered too fast in this country under the old rulins, they worked every figure to cut you down, cut your britches off you." His brother Peter had given up, deciding to work as little as possible and accumulate nothing. "It might have been to his way of thinkin' that it weren't no use in climbin too fast; weren't no use in climbin slow, neither, if they was goin to take everything you worked for when you got too high." Little had changed since Reconstruction, when, as W. E. B. Du Bois later argued, the white South had feared black success above all else.[55]

But if southern blacks realized that the American success ethic had offered them nothing but false promises in the South, they did not dismiss the ethic itself as invalid. Few white tenants lived in the South's "Black Belt." Black tenants who did live near whites might well have shared the oversimplified conclusions of the 1910 census—that young whites, starting as tenant farmers, moved into the ranks of ownership "at a much more rapid rate" than blacks. Tenancy rates for farmers of both races in the South were steadily increasing, but the higher average age of black tenants suggests a continuing difference in the likelihood of ownership. The number of white farmers who were able to move up the "agricultural ladder" did make it appear that while whites could "leave the tenant class entirely," most blacks could merely move "from one class of tenancy to another."[56] Even progress from sharecropper to share tenant to cash tenant represented a tenuous accomplishment which could be erased in a single bad year. The problem, then, seemed to be essentially racial. Success in America through hard work was possible, but not for blacks in the South. Whites, a migrant from Mississippi later explained, would not permit any black to occupy a place higher than that which they considered appropriate for that individual.

Voices from the North reinforced black southerners' belief in the possibility of success, while convincing them that they could open the door of opportunity by moving North. The "masses of the Negro people," observed the head of the United States Department of Labor's Division of Negro Economics in 1919, "received the impression that all kinds and types of work might at some time be open to them."[57] The *Defender* had long preached the virtues of patience and hard work, reminding its readers that blacks did face obstacles, "perhaps a few more than their white brother, but none they could not surmount." In 1916, it began emphasizing that such homilies pertained only to the North, "where every kind of labor is being thrown open." As proof, it could offer biographies of such southerners who had "made it" in Chicago as prominent lawyer and politician Louis B. Anderson and editor Robert Abbott himself. These men had traveled the road to success in Chicago earlier, when fewer occupations had been open to blacks. For the mass of the race, the newspaper announced, "our chance is now."[58] Migrants' letters, written on the eve of their departures, suggest that they shared both the values and the optimism expressed in the *Defender*.

Most of the migrants who left oral or written testaments to the migratory impulse conflated economic and social stimuli into the goal of "bettering their position." Variants of this theme abound: "Better his Standing"; "better my conditions in the business world"; "aspire to better my condition in life"; "elevate myself"; "better my condishion in as much as beaing asshured some protection as a good citizen"; "chance for advancement."[59] They moved North in search of many of the same things black Americans had once hoped would accompany emancipation: good schools, equal rights before the law, and equal access to public facilities. Those black men and women who decided to leave the South saw all of these, as well as the numerous other "privileges" they expected in Chicago, as the foundation of freedom and citizenship. A New Orleans woman was typically attracted to "the great chance that a colored parson has in Chicago of making a living with all the priveleg that the whites have and it mak me the most ankious to go."[60]

The recent opening of industrial employment to blacks, a direct result of the war, made it possible to translate these goals into a decision to leave the South and the agricultural economy that had once promised their fulfillment. Unlike their parents and many of those who remained behind, northbound migrants looked to industrial occupations, rather than to landed independence, as the means of attaining these goals. After two generations of economic, educational, social, and political stultification in the South, it appeared that northern factories and cities offered a final chance to obtain what other Americans supposedly had—the opportunity to better their condition by hard work. "All I ask is give me a chance," wrote one Louisiana man, "and I will make good."[61]

Those who were less sanguine about improving their own position voiced aspirations for their children. For the first time since the heyday of the Freedmen's Bureau schools, black southerners could entertain expectations that their children might receive an education that would enable them to compete with whites. In the South, black schoolchildren walked miles to "wretched little hovels," to be taught by people whose schooling barely exceeded that of their pupils. Through the *Defender*, black southerners knew of Chicago's Wendell Phillips High School, whose integrated education promised hope to their children. One man, who already earned a comfortable living, was not moving "just to get a jobe . . . [but] . . . want some places to send my children to school." Another, also careful to state he already had a job, was leaving for Chicago "where I can educate my children." From Anniston, Alabama, a man desperate to "do any kind of work," pleaded for aid so he could "get where i can put my children in schol."[62] These prospective migrants assumed that access was the crucial issue and that it was race and region that limited access. Only later would their children learn the limited efficacy of access in the absence of community power and economic resources.

To black writer Alain Locke, commenting upon this "new vision of opportunity," the migration represented "a spirit to seize . . . a chance for the improvement of conditions."[63] The vision was new, because blacks had never before anticipated economic security or social mobility through mass entrance into American industry. But of equal import was Locke's choice of the verb "seize." The migrants acted to better their condition by seizing control over their own destiny. The southern system had rested on their dependence on whites and on its ability to restrict their options. To those like the Kentuckian who migrated to Chicago because he "was tired of being a flunky," migration constituted a rejection of that dependence. "Negroes are not so greatly disturbed about wages," a black leader in Florida commented. "They are tired of being treated as children; they want to be men."[64] "Pushes" and "pulls" might be abstractly separable, but they operated together in the minds of black southerners comparing one place to another. To the ambitious men and women venturing North seeking independence and mobility, the Great Migration represented a new strategy in the struggle for the full rights of American citizenship, including the right to equality of opportunity.

2

"The Negro's Natural Home"

The Great Migration sparked a firestorm of controversy, igniting reactions that intensified prospective migrants' dissatisfaction with both the South and its black leadership. At the same time, the form and content of the debate illuminate the distance between impulses central to the movement and the world views of black and white elites in the South. Whites discussed the impact of the exodus on production, economic structure, and social order. Optimists predicted an end to the "Negro Problem" or hailed the likelihood of agricultural revitalization based on white labor and diversification. Opponents of black migration, who dominated influential white opinion, reacted most visibly to the threat to the South's labor force. This opposition took various forms, from reform agendas addressing specific black complaints to varying degrees of coercion. Regional black leaders, skeptical about the wisdom of abandoning agriculture and vulnerable to white pressure, also grew concerned about how the exodus might affect their businesses, institutions, and status. The agricultural orientation and accommodationist rhetoric of the Washingtonian establishment accentuated its growing distance from black southerners interested in northward migration.

A migrant's decision to act, Richard Wright recognized just before leaving Memphis, could be taken as a challenge, an aggressive statement of dissatisfaction. Such autonomy and ambition constituted a direct threat to the fiber of social and economic relations in the South. Public values rested upon the assumption that blacks were by nature docile, dependent, and unambitious, even if the system itself depended on repressive devices to ensure that docility. If enlightened southerners like Edgar Gardner Murphy believed that the Negro "will accept in the white man's country the place assigned him by the white man," the Great Migration represented a refusal by one-half million black southerners to cooperate.[1] Dissatisfaction and aggression were characteristics that most white southerners preferred not to associate with "their Negroes."

Although the world view threatened by such assertive black behavior might be traced back to the paternalistic ideology avowed by antebellum slaveowners, this particular image of blacks emerged most clearly at the end of Reconstruction. During the 1880s most southern whites began to abandon their obsession with black treachery during the Civil War, and convinced themselves that the freed men had been "hoodwinked by the Radicals" during Reconstruction. Blacks, as Henry Grady explained reassuringly in 1876, were "peaceable and harmless," except when inflamed by troublemakers. Nearly half a century later an article appearing in two southern journals voiced the same sentiment, reminding readers that "the Negro race is a child race," except when aroused by a "disreputable, dishonest, scoundrelly element." Many southern employers and landlords seemed to agree, assuming that somebody ("German agents" in a few cases) had to be stirring up local blacks and causing them to leave the South. Even attempts to halt migration were sometimes undermined by the inability of many prominent white southerners to recognize blacks as active and rational participants in the historical process. To face a black person—even a high-level official of the United States Department of Labor—on a level of equality was impossible given their analysis of "Negro character."[2]

Few whites, however, perceived—or at least articulated—the challenge the migration posed to their own values. Most found another threat more obvious and more immediately ominous: the loss of their labor supply. If dependency existed anywhere in the South, it was in the economic relations between white employers and black laborers. Blacks, until they learned of the new opportunities in northern cities, depended on white landowners and businessmen for their survival; whites depended on blacks to work their crops, cook their meals, and perform countless other tasks usually referred to as "nigger work." The plantation, whether worked by slaves, contract labor, indentured labor, sharecroppers, cash renters bonded by debt, or forced labor in the form of peonage, depended on the landowner's ability to keep his work force on his land. And whether the antebellum planters as individuals or families had "persisted" into the late nineteenth century, or whether a new planter class had emerged, the commitment to the plantation remained. The southern economy, Booker T. Washington recognized in 1914, was "based on the Negro and the mule."[3]

Cognizant of this dependence, many whites logically feared that mass migration could strip the South of its labor force. If the Negroes go, warned the Montgomery *Advertiser*, "Where shall we get labor to take their places?"[4] The South had faced this prospect once before, immediately after the Civil War, when amid frenzied fears that the freed men would refuse to work, some white southerners advocated encouraging immigrants to settle in the South. Although such efforts continued until the first decade of the twentieth century, few immigrants could be enticed to work under conditions approximating those which were accepted by blacks because they had little choice. And by the turn of the century, whites had begun to recognize that only immigrants from southern and eastern Europe were available, a development rendering the whole enterprise less attractive. By 1916, most whites agreed with the Columbia, South Carolina, *State*'s conclusion that "black labor is the best labor the South can get, no other would work long under the same conditions."[5] Only in Texas, where planters had begun recruiting Mexican laborers to work in cotton fields at least as early as the first decade of the twentieth century, did anybody find a workable solution to the problem that vexed the South during the Great Migration. When planters in the Mississippi Delta brought in "hundreds" of Mexicans to pick cotton, disease took a heavy toll and ended the experiment. The Montgomery *Advertiser*'s recognition that "the farmers of the Black Belt of Alabama cannot get on without Negro labor" applied to much of the South.[6]

Some areas of the South did suffer labor shortages caused by the Great Migration. In Louisiana, a federal official found "hundreds of acres of untouched land formerly cultivated . . . scores of mules in pasture because there was no help to hitch them to the plow." Sugar and rice fields were reported by a Tuskegee agent to "have grown up in grass." Near Dallas, a *Defender* correspondent found "grass . . . grown up around the cotton."[7] In Kentucky and Mississippi, such minor crops as strawberries and hay suffered from a "scarcity of labor." In Lithonia, Georgia, the exodus forced the granite quarry to shut down. In a few cases, entire communities feared "depopulation." With black tenants renting over one-fifth of its farmland in 1910 and black wage laborers working thousands of acres more, Georgia could ill afford massive emigration; by 1923, its bankers were describing the exodus as comparable only to Sherman's march to the sea in its damage to agriculture in the state.[8]

Fears of imminent bankruptcy, however, remained overstated, if not unwarranted. At the opposite extreme, the Macon *Telegraph*, a few months before it sounded the "bankruptcy" alarm in 1916, had advocated sending some of the South's surplus black labor to conquer Mexico. There were indeed fewer laborers available by 1918, although with the supply at 75 percent of "normal" that year the South was slightly better off than agricultural employers in the rest of the country. Reliable observers reported sufficient numbers of workers still available. From Georgia, a correspondent informed Secretary of Labor Wilson that "in various sections of the South there is a surplus of laborers."[9] The problem entailed less a drastic shortage than, as one white southerner perceptively suggested, "a decline from an oversupply." Lieutenant Robert Owen, investigating the situation for the Department of War, offered an incisive explanation for the South's complaints. While the shortage was "undoubtedly acute at certain centers such as Louisiana, it is not clear how severe it is all over the south. Allowance must be made for the fact that part of the clamor may be due to employers who object to paying high living wages called for by the removal of an idle surplus population." Southern landowners and employers were accustomed to this surplus, even if it was hardly "idle"; it assured sufficient hands at picking time, and in general facilitated the exploitation of black workers which lay at the foundation of the southern economy. White southerners did not want to lose their grip on what one Georgia cotton merchant referred to as "a very amiable peasantry."[10] Migration simultaneously threatened the ready availability of that peasantry and planted doubts as to its continued amiability.

Some white southerners, especially those less dependent on black labor, ignored the migration's threat to southern ideological assumptions and rejected the premise that the region's economy could not afford to lose a large share of its black labor force. In Nashville, Tennessee, and Birmingham, Alabama, white newspapers resurrected the old plea for white immigration. The black exodus, the editors hoped, would "clear the way" for such immigration. The president of Atlanta's Oglethorpe University located replacements closer to home, expecting that a new demand for labor would create opportunities for poor whites. Aware that he expressed a minority perspective, he urged agriculturalists to replace the migrants with well-paid white labor. The weakness of southern farming, he argued, was a result of the inefficiency of its black workers. The USDA statistician in Montgomery, Alabama, agreed, attributing the migration itself to the inability of black farmers to cope with the boll weevil. The exodus, therefore, would increase labor efficiency on the farms by eliminating the worst farmers.[11]

Other optimists saw even more substantial gains resulting from the mechanization and diversification which they predicted would follow in the wake of the exodus. The Vicksburg, Mississippi, *Herald* expected that once rid of "thousands of Negroes," farms all over southern Mississippi would finally diversify and become more productive. P. O. Davis of Alabama Polytechnic Institute agreed that "no serious cotton shortage but a better farming system should be one result of the exodus of Negroes." Blacks were "unintelligent farmers" incapable of growing anything but cotton. Their departure, especially since it would also raise the proportion of owners to tenants, would elevate the southern farm operator, who would be more likely to diversify into more capital-intensive crops.[12] After years of preaching diversification and mechanization, southern agricultural reformers hoped the migration would both enable and force landowners to adopt more efficient techniques. But they had incorrectly identified the impediment to innovation. Black farmers raised mostly cotton because they were forced to by landowners and local merchants who demanded a cash crop. Given the credit structure and sharecropping system, none of the actors had much incentive to diversify or improve agricultural land. If anything promised to change the southern crop mix, it was the devastation and frustration wrought by the boll weevil; even that shift was only transitory at best. Dramatic and enduring transformation would await new forces set in motion by the Great Depression and the New Deal in the 1930s.[13]

Whites who approached black out-migration optimistically celebrated more than the South's imminent relief from dependence on supposedly inferior black farmers. Many envisioned the lifting of an even greater burden from the shoulders of the white South—that of "educating and civilizing" its black dependents. Less paternalistically oriented whites equally applauded the departure of "worthless" blacks, although none matched the cynicism embodied in a former Arkansas governor's proposal to pardon black convicts on the condition they migrate to Massachusetts. Judge Gilbert Stephenson of Winston-Salem, North Carolina, however, did revel in the knowledge that "many of these young bucks already have criminal records and, going North, add to their bad reputations."[14] Others, although less crude, also looked forward to the North's imminent sharing of the South's racial albatross. "A more equitable distribution of the sons of Ham," hoped the Vicksburg *Herald*, "will teach the Caucasians of the northern states that wherever there is a negro infusion, there will be a race problem."[15] Some white southerners even contemplated the possibility that eventually all blacks would leave the South, solving the "race problem" once and for all. Although black and white leaders ascribed this sentiment to poor whites, who often drove blacks from their homes, it did attract others as well, especially in nonplantation districts and in some cities, where black men represented more of a threat than an economic resource. Speaking for "a growing number" of optimistic whites, the New Orleans *Times-*

Picayune looked beyond the temporary labor problem and cheerfully concluded that "as the North grows blacker the South grows whiter."[16]

Most influential white southerners realized that the South could not afford to be "a white man's country," if that term implied racial homogeneity rather than a power relationship. Cognizant of the crucial role black labor occupied in the southern economy, they neither encouraged migration nor welcomed its implications. Even these individuals, however, initially remained unperturbed, certain that after a short sojourn the migrants would return home.

These expectations did not seem unreasonable to many whites. In Mississippi, Charles Johnson found many who attributed the whole movement to "the Negro's love of travel." Others assumed that jobs in the North would eventually become scarce, or that northern employers would grow dissatisfied with lazy black workers.[17] Nor would the migrants themselves be satisfied. "Happy and healthy . . . when engaged in agricultural occupations," blacks would not be able to adjust to urban tenements, argued an official at the Associated Charities of Atlanta. In October 1916, the Montgomery *Advertiser* reassured its readers that Chicago's chilling winds would send the migrants scampering home "within three months." Nor would they be able to adjust to new racial arrangements, suggested Kingsley Moses, a journalist. He recited a "well-known story to the effect that a certain Southern negro, ancient, cold, and penniless," fruitlessly begs fifty northerners for food and shelter. When he finally reaches the "modest cottage" of an old Virginia "Cunnel," the gentleman curses his effrontery. "Yuh, yuh black, good for nothin' worthless houn'; get on 'round to the back do' an' yuh'll find a place to eat an' sleep." "Thank Gawd," responds the grateful beggar, "I's home again." Perhaps white southerners did find "more truth than fiction" in the tale; many no doubt tried to convince themselves of its authentic flavor, confirming in their minds blacks' dependence on southern paternalism and charity. Either way, it reassured them that "their Negroes" would return.[18]

Few did come back, and some southerners recognized that even those returnees might not reassume former roles. A leading Georgia businessman, after visiting Chicago in 1919, informed his state's commissioner of commerce and labor that "it would be unwise to encourage the return of the Negroes in Chicago," because they had acquired new attitudes toward the South. Although it took some longer than others, white southerners eventually began to believe black leaders who told them that the exodus was "not a temporary migration, but a movement likely to continue for an indefinite period."[19] Few faced this future with the equanimity displayed by the New Orleans *Times-Picayune*, which although "sorry to see so many able bodied Negroes leaving this community," preferred migration to "loafing around doing nothing. . . . We fancy they will be needed hereafter, and that their places will be hard to fill. But if they cannot find work here at living wages, it is better that they should go where it is offered them. . . . It would be very selfish not to want any man, black or white to go and do the very best he can for himself and his family." Most journals preferred contradictory responses, one day chronicling the migrants' return, the next bewailing their loss and advocating measures to keep workers in the South.[20]

Either immediately or eventually, civil authorities and whites dependent on black labor sought to halt the exodus, through coercion, persuasion, or some combination of the two. Repressive responses generally took the form of impediments either to the transmission of information about opportunities in the North or to departure itself. Like their antebellum forbears, who had halted the dissemination of abolitionist literature and had forbidden slaves to play drums or trumpets because they might be used to pass signals, white southerners during the Great Migration thought they could control communication sufficiently to prevent the spread of knowledge that threatened the labor system. The Chicago *Defender*, a strident critic of the South and most enthusiastic advocate of northward migration, posed an obvious target. In Meridian, Mississippi, the chief of police ordered the newspaper confiscated from dealers. Scores of other communities took similar measures, forcing the militant "race paper" underground, able to reach its subscribers only through the mail. With the authorities watching ministers, teachers, and other local notables apt to read and distribute the newspaper, resourceful *Defender* agents even resorted to folding copies into bundles of merchandise. Nor was the *Defender* the only target. In Franklin, Mississippi, a black minister was sentenced to five months on the county farm and a four hundred dollar fine for selling the NAACP's *Crisis*.[21]

Most official efforts to maintain the relative isolation of the southern labor market were directed at a more traditional menace—the labor agent, who not only transmitted information about new opportunities but even assisted migrants. As they had in the past, especially during the Kansas Exodus of 1879, southern white elites ascribed black migration from the region to the influence of outsiders. Thus, many white southerners assured themselves that labor agents constituted not only the migrants' main source of information but the very cause of the migration itself. "The Negroes who have gone North haven't gone because of any bad treatment accorded them

Main Cause of Migration—the Labor Agent

—JCSMITH.

Labor agents became convenient scapegoats to white southerners unwilling to confront the reasons underlying the Great Migration (courtesy of the Smithsonian Institution).

here," insisted the Nashville *Banner* in November 1916. "They have gone because agents in search of labor needed in the great industries of the North came South in search of labor and offered them higher wages than they were making here." A month earlier the influential New Orleans *Times-Picayune* had accused labor agents of "enticing away" southern labor.[22] Houston's Chamber of Commerce and a Shreveport, Louisiana, congressman considered agents so essential to the migration that they called on the federal government to interdict them in the interest of war production. Similarly, the Tennessee Coal and Iron Company tried to convince a federal investigator that there was a plot by "agents or sub-agents of some northern conspiracy" to scare blacks into fleeing from the South.[23]

Convinced that the migration depended upon outside agitation by sophisticated recruiters, white southerners thought they could hold their labor supply by expelling the agents. Anti-enticement laws dating back to 1865 were dusted off, reenacted, or tightened, and by 1917, states, counties, and municipalities had established expensive licensing procedures for outside solicitation of labor. To operate in Birmingham, Alabama, a recruiter needed a $500 Alabama license along with city and county permits costing $250 and $500. Scores of towns, cities, and counties required agents to purchase such permits; Jacksonville, Florida, charged emigration agents a prohibitive $1,000 to operate. Some places enjoined any outsider from recruiting workers. In Mississippi, imprisonment and a $500 fine awaited any agent guilty of "inducing" labor from the state.[24] The city fathers of Montgomery, Alabama, demonstrating an acute awareness of the murky definition of "labor agent" and the breadth of the migration information network, adopted an ordinance prescribing a $100 fine and six months in the workhouse for

> Any person, firm or corporation who publishes or prints or writes or delivers or distributes or posts, or causes to be published, printed or written or delivered or distributed or posted, any advertisement, letter, newspaper, pamphlet, handbill, or other writing, for the purpose of enticing, persuading, or influencing any laborer or any other person to leave the city for the purpose of being employed at any other place as a laborer.[25]

The Montgomery *Advertiser*, certain that the agents were "instrumental," expected this ordinance to check the exodus. But neither this "ironclad ordinance," sentences to labor on the public roads, nor expulsion of agents by local vigilantes could stamp out the migratory impulse.[26]

Even after it became apparent that this campaign against northern recruiters had failed to slow the exodus, white southerners persisted in blaming the movement on labor agents, soon accusing them of "working through the mails." As migration continued through the 1920s, many southern whites could not abandon their belief that labor agents were solely responsible for the departures. Such notions were so widespread that in 1923 Georgia banker James S. Peters felt compelled to tell his colleagues that "it is useless to talk about labor agents or undertake to legislate against their activities." [27] Few whites shared Peters' view that labor agents had become insignificant. Unable to recognize "their Negroes'" ability to make independent, rational decisions of such magnitude, and unwilling to confront the exploitative and oppressive nature of southern race relations, many preferred to assign to outside influences—northern whites—the pivotal role in the decision-making process of black southerners.

White southerners were not completely mistaken. Labor agents did operate effectively in the Deep South, although less as "causes" of migration than as facilitators. Most whites misunderstood the dynamics of recruitment. Their assumptions about the passive character of "the Negro" led them to believe that the agents were either whites or naive black hirelings, rather than purposeful and informed members of the local black community itself. By removing or discrediting outside influences, they thought they could sustain the fiction that black Americans were best off in the South. But by 1917 it was too late; northern employers had virtually ceased sending recruiters south. They no longer had to. Stories of labor agents' activities had circulated more widely and more rapidly than the agents themselves. Most of the labor agents still operating were blacks acting on their own initiative, organizing group travel or writing North to offer their own labor and that of others. Those who did come from the North were probably visiting home, carrying small sums from employers willing to finance the journeys of friends or relatives of the recruiter. Both whites and blacks exaggerated the importance of labor agents. For whites, the mistake led to repressive actions which only fueled discontent. For blacks, it brought hope and produced a folklore which heightened the anticipation and excitement of the moment.

Unable to keep information from their black employees and tenants, whites tried various devices to tighten their hold on blacks and keep them away from the train stations. By refusing to gin the whole cotton crop or make settlements until the following year's crop was planted, landlords deprived tenants of even the small capital required for railroad fare. By the time they settled their accounts, tenants would have incurred enough new debts to justify the planter's complete withholding of cash. [28] Blacks fortunate enough to receive prepaid passes from friends or relatives in the North often found themselves no closer to departure. Not wanting "to have colored labor leaving the South to go North," southern railroads refused to honor prepaid tickets bought through northern railroads. Even after the federal government assumed control over the railroads during World War I, this practice continued, until pressure from the NAACP and northern congressmen led to its abrogation in July 1919. When railroads were returned to private control in 1920, they resumed the old policy. Railroads that refused to cooperate in such efforts found themselves subject to southern employers' threats to influence juries sitting on damage suits against the railroad involved.[29]

Some localities applied more direct measures to keep blacks off the trains. In Macon, Georgia, police forcibly evicted several hundred Chicago-bound blacks from the railroad station. Unsure he could continue to intimidate "surly" blacks without more firepower, the chief of police promptly requested forty rifles to augment the pistols and clubs carried by his men. Outside nearby Americus, police boarded a train and arrested fifty would-be migrants. At Summit, Mississippi, local officials simply closed the railroad ticket office and had the trains pass through without stopping. "The southern white are trying very hard to keep us from the north," understated an anxious Louisianian hoping to leave for Chicago as soon as possible.[30]

These efforts were not confined to the local level. Southern employers understood that the migration was a national phenomenon and turned to the federal government to shut it off. Charging federal agencies with encouraging and aiding the migration in the interest of war production, southern employers lobbied senators, congressmen, the Departments of Agriculture, Labor, Commerce, Justice, and War, and the War Labor Policies Board for protection and aid.[31] There was some truth to these complaints, but mainly with regard to labor recruitment for federal munitions plants in the South, hardly a threat to the long-term labor supply in the South.[32] The United States Employment Service (USES) and its parent agency, the Department of Labor, were sharply criticized for disrupting the South's labor market. But the USES, which did assist northward migration to fill labor demand in northern war industries, could hardly have been a major factor, as it "withdrew its facilities from group migration" in the summer of 1916, continuing only to "serve individual citizens regardless of race." And by June, 1918, the USES director for the Southern District (southern Florida, southern Alabama, Mississippi, Louisiana, East Texas) was a Meridian, Mississippi, man who quickly announced his intention "to see that Niggers were stopped from going North."[33] There is no evidence of his effectiveness in this quest, but it is unlikely that his office succored the migration. Inactivity, however, was not sufficient; southern employers wanted federal agencies to take positive steps to keep blacks on their farms and payrolls.

Although both the USES and the Department of Labor's Division of Negro Economics did try to convince unemployed Chicago migrants to return South, the department never considered the use of force or deception in trying to slow or reverse the movement North. Despite complaints from southern congressmen and their constituents, Secretary of Labor William B. Wilson's policy remained firm. He agreed in 1919 that the exodus had begun to impair labor efficiency but refused to reverse a 1917 ruling that interference with "the natural right of workers to move from place to place at their own discretion" fell beyond the authority of his department.[34]

Other cabinet departments usually referred complaints to the Department of Labor or to war-related agencies.[35] The War Labor Policies Board, despite its ambitious plan for a controlled and efficient labor market, does not appear to have acted any more forcefully than the Department of Labor. Much of its program, moreover, was implemented through USES. There is no evidence that the numerous complaints about labor agents luring agricultural labor to munitions factories elicited a substantial response from the board. Colonel Arthur Woods, who headed the War Department's postwar employment activities and cared less about the interests of black servicemen discharged in the North than about the labor needs of the South, also had to work through USES. Despite his dissatisfaction with the USES's position that "compulsion is impossible," he could do nothing to force discharged "darkies" to return to their southern homes.[36] Only the state Councils of Defense offered southern employers the coercive services they requested. In their attempt to allocate labor according to their mandate from Washington, councils in the South frequently resorted to intimidation of black laborers.[37]

Many planters, mill operators, and local officials prevented individual blacks from leaving, but the campaign of harassment and repression did not check the migratory flow. Even where prospective migrants reported that whites had "stopped the exodus," they continued to write North asking for free passes or information about reduced rate excursions. Although sufficiently intimidated to ask the *Defender* not to print such letters, these men and women were not deterred. Coercive measures to forestall migration often reinforced many black southerners' awareness that bettering their condition was not possible in the South.[38]

Many whites, especially those who counted themselves among the "best people" of the South, recognized the inefficacy of the use of force to prevent migration. "We are not slaveholders," the Macon *Telegraph* reminded its readers. "We do not own the Negroes; we cannot compel them to stay here. Therefore we want to keep the Negroes here."[39] To do so presumably required promising changes addressed to the migrants' dissatisfactions: higher wages; checks on mob violence; better schools. Recommended methods of blunting the migratory impulse, however, involved only modification of conditions. Few whites questioned the fundamental social and economic relations that frustrated blacks' aspirations to better their condition.

The assumption that blacks preferred to remain in the South underlay many arguments for improvements that would convince them to stay. "These Negroes who are leaving the South in large numbers and others who are thinking of going do not want to go," the Montgomery *Advertiser* reassured its readers.

> They prefer to remain here. But they want something to eat
> and to wear. They want a brighter future held out to them; they
> want to be reasoned with by their landlords, and want things
> made plain to them in the adjustment of yearly accounts; they
> want to be protected against lynching and personal abuse; they
> want better treatment on the farms, on the common carriers, and
> in public places in general.

Similarly, the Atlanta *Constitution* cited lynching, low wages, and poor schools as driving away people who would "prefer to stay."[40]

Recognizing that they had to convince blacks that their lives would improve in the South, southern white reformers set agendas for change. But first they had to sell reform to other whites. Throughout 1916–17 newspapers stated and restated black dissatisfactions that were provoking migration: lynching, low wages, "making money at the expense of the Negro's lack of intelligence," charging unfair prices, poor housing on farms and in cities, poor schools, unfair treatment by police, lack of legal protection, and even selling liquor too freely to blacks.[41] Without calling for major attitudinal or structural shifts, prominent whites prodded their communities to make adjustments necessary to retain their labor supply.

First and foremost, reformers concentrated on curbing the activities of white mobs. Lynchers and "night-riders" had long acted with impunity, with newspapers and law enforcers tending to look the other way and occasionally chiding the mob afterwards. But if Mississippi's Governor Theodore Bilbo still considered himself in 1919 "utterly powerless" to prevent an announced lynching, and if "respectable citizens" continued to blame terrorism on "shiftless poor whites," some editors began taking stronger positions against racial violence. Georgia's "indifference in suppressing mob law," argued the Atlanta *Constitution*, was costing the state its "best labor." The Macon *Telegraph* similarly condemned night-riding.[42]

In addition to efforts to stem white violence against blacks, reforms designed to keep blacks in the South ranged from decent schools, to aid in creating charitable organizations, to higher wages.[43] Concerned white spokesmen frequently focused on the plantation system, since it was on the farms where blacks were crucial to the South's economy. Blacks were not getting a "square deal," the Albany, Georgia, *Herald* lectured its readers. In Mississippi, a representative of the state Chamber of Commerce told landlords they had to stop cheating their tenants on the price of cotton. "Good darkeys," he lamented, were easy prey for labor agents whenever they were mistreated by landlords, merchants, and courts. Editors, agricultural reformers, and business leaders spelled out the antidote to migration: pay good wages; give tenants land and free time for garden plots; build better, "though inexpensive" plantation cabins; make fair settlements. The Montgomery *Advertiser* even went so far as to condemn the South's agricultural "system," which was "wrong and so had to fail." But the reference was to the one-crop system, to the South's dependence on cotton and its consequent inefficient use of labor.[44]

While it is possible that a shift away from one-crop dependence might have stimulated a change in the South's credit structure and perhaps even in landholding relationships, none of the proponents of diversification voiced such hopes or goals. The reforms intended to convince blacks that they were better off in the South addressed only symptoms of black dissatisfaction. Even Will W. Alexander, always in the vanguard of southern racial reform, not only agreed that "many don't really want to leave," but listed only poor schools, mob violence, threats, poor crops, and "market conditions" as repelling forces. As a remedy he ambitiously suggested better protection of prisoners, changes in labor-contract law to prevent peonage, new schools and hospitals, more public health nurses, and additional efforts in the field of agricultural extension. His was the extreme liberal position; yet while it acknowledged "widespread discouragement among southern Negroes," it excluded any proposals to revise the economic and social relations that could only perpetuate such discouragement.[45] Blacks would remain subordinate, but might not detest their position to the point where they felt obliged to leave. It is possible that Alexander did favor more sweeping measures but chose to keep his program within the limits of political possibility. No white southerner of any prominence advocated changes that addressed the fundamental concern of growing numbers of blacks: condemned to dependency and subordination, they could not significantly better their condition within the South.

In some areas, scattered reforms materialized, if only temporarily. Believing that the migration drew its main impetus from the lure of high wages in the North, many employers chose to compete by offering laborers more money. By summer 1917, sawmills in Hattiesburg and Laurel, Mississippi, had raised wages from the $1.10 daily rate of 1916, to $1.40–1.75. Cotton picking outside Greenville, Mississippi, brought $2.00 per hundred pounds in November 1917, compared with $ .60–.75 a year earlier. By 1918 common labor in southern rural districts had risen in two years from $ .75–1.00 per day to $1.75–2.50. Farm wages in the South, as elsewhere in the nation, more than doubled between 1915 and 1920.[46] As in other regions, they would tumble in 1921 and remain low during the "prosperity decade." But at least during World War I, it appeared that southern farmers, along with town employers, were willing to pay to keep their black workers. As one Georgia black educator carefully reported to the NAACP in 1919, "things are not quite as bad as before the war or before migration began." Except on the farms, women seldom shared this bounty, however, as domestic wages remained stable.[47]

Most of the changes that advanced beyond the advocacy and promise stage related to plantation life. Along with increasing wages, some landowners reduced rents. With black earnings still far below northern wages, rural elites searched for other incentives that would not threaten their control. Banks in Prattville, Alabama, distributed free seed for food crops. Many landlords in Alabama's Black Belt reportedly eased their abuse of tenants. Some sections even began spending more money on black schools. An official of the Russell Sage Foundation, however, identified these educational concessions as oriented almost exclusively toward agricultural training, and he predicted migration would continue anyway.[48] He was right. The changes were designed to make blacks better tenants, rather than to offer alternatives or to ease their economic dependence on whites.

Not all whites who assumed blacks wanted to stay in the South advocated reforms; even the *Advertiser* seemed unsure of its own position. Like others, it argued on occasion that blacks not only did not want to leave, but had no serious grievances outside of crop failures. The same year it enumerated reforms that would stem migration, the newspaper rejected the notion that blacks faced racial barriers in the South. Impersonal economic forces "which he cannot help and which he cannot overcome" were driving the black farmer from Alabama's Black Belt. "He is not being forced out by pressure from the white race," insisted the *Advertiser*'s editors. "The relations between the two races in this section were never better." T. A. Snavely, a federal investigator touring that region, found this confidence in the existence of "perfect harmony" between the races to be widespread among whites. To those who needed proof, a white educator offered Tuskegee Principal Robert R. Moton's relations with whites as an example of black satisfaction with the status quo.[49]

These contradictory positions suggest the confusion which characterized white reaction to the migration. But the contradictions went only so far. In assuming blacks wanted to stay, whites reassured themselves of the soundness of the southern racial system. Those who recognized problems saw abuses, not structural weakness. Injustice occurred, but there was no fundamental unjustice. What inequalities did exist were satisfactory to both races. Like Hugh Ellis, a white man who considered himself an outspoken liberal on racial matters and who thought that "most Negroes prefer the South as a place of abode," most whites were certain that "the average Negro" neither wanted nor expected social equality. The Houston *Post* agreed, and like the New Orleans *States*, was certain that political rights were of no concern.[50] Black poet James Weldon Johnson, expressing some of the black ambivalence toward the South that whites perceived as a preference for that region, recognized the persistence of such assumptions amid the mounting evidence of widespread discontent:

> O Southland, dear Southland
> Then why do you still cling
> To an idle age and a musty page,
> To a dead and useless thing?[51]

Part of the answer to Johnson's question lay in whites' inability to perceive blacks as anything but passive participants in the historical process. Buffeted by floods, insects (among which one observer included the labor agents), and occasional mob violence, blacks supposedly had been helplessly driven out.[52] To many, the "happy negro," unable to cope with agricultural disasters, had been duped by smooth-tongued labor agents whose success owed less to cogency of argument than to black gullibility. Those who acknowledged that injustices had contributed to the process did not understand or perhaps even perceive the existence of blacks' ambitions to full citizenship. Modest comfort, decent schools, and some sense of hope would presumably keep blacks in their "natural home"—the South. By convincing themselves that they were guilty of benign neglect at worst, many whites reassured themselves that limited reforms could prevent the loss of their labor force.

Few reforms, however, advanced beyond the editorial page. Charles Johnson found Jackson, Mississippi, to be typical in its response to the threat to its labor supply: "Whites have counselled themselves that the only way to hold Negroes is to give them better schools, wages, and protection. (newspaper editorials, joint meetings) So far, it is asserted, they have only advocated this. Nothing has yet been done except to increase wages in some occupations."[53] Some employers refused even to raise wages, justifiably fearful that this would only provide workers with the wherewithal to leave. In other communities, Johnson found only "cosmetic" changes. By the mid-1920s, blacks still were registering the same complaints, and white reformers were advocating the same measures to stem the migratory tide.[54]

The failure of southern communities and employers to institute even the limited reforms proposed as antidotes to migration is hardly surprising. Embedded in many of the very statements calling for change lay assumptions that incentives were neither necessary nor of much use. In arguing that "the business of lynching of Negroes is bad," the Memphis *Commercial Appeal* continued that "the worst thing is that often the wrong Negro is lynched." Calling for more honest business practices, it asked merchants to cease exploiting "the Negro's lack of intelligence." Its readers could hardly have been expected to take seriously any suggestions that black dissatisfactions were of any consequence. They were more likely to concur with South Carolina's Governor Thomas McLeod, who labeled any intimation that blacks were leaving because of persecution "sentimental and psychological rot." Not only did blacks not desire equality, but even wage increases were impossible, he insisted, because the South could not afford them.[55] Judge H. B. Abernethy of Birmingham offered a similar response to suggestions that increased funding for black education would slow migration: "From the top of his bonehead to the bottom of his flat foot there isn't a chance to educate the negro. God Almighty made them to be hewers of wood and drawers of water, and I am opposed to educating them."[56] Most white southerners thus could not accept the premises of even the most limited reforms, and little change could occur. Southern optimists who thought a migratory ebb in fall 1917 was due to their reform campaign were handed a harsh reminder by the *Defender*. Prospective migrants, it informed them, were waiting for warm weather, not improved conditions. As Charles Johnson learned in Mississippi, few blacks placed any faith in the sincerity of white promises.[57]

Not all white efforts to persuade blacks to remain in the South required black confidence in white intentions. Exaggerating freely, white opponents of black migration warned that the North's attractions should be weighed against its freezing weather, deadly race riots, and history of employment discrimination. Professing their concern for blacks' health, Mississippi whites advised prospective migrants of the rigors of the northern climate, reciting "exact" figures on death rates of northern blacks from pneumonia. Race riots posed a different kind of threat, and the East St. Louis riot of July 1917 was trumpeted as evidence of widespread white hostility in the North.[58] In the past, such hostility had limited black employment opportunities, the message continued, and after the war, old patterns would reemerge. In the South, blacks' opportunity to work was a "right"; in the North, a "privilege." Whatever the North's passing attractions, white southern newspapers lectured, blacks were better off in the long run in the South. Such arguments were not necessarily disingenuous. Images of black physical attributes, work habits, and attitudes complemented conventional wisdom about the inevitable violence resulting from uncontrolled racial contact, to assure many white southerners that black migration boded disaster for all. But to convince blacks was more difficult, especially when prospective migrants could read in the *Defender* that blacks were not freezing to death and that jobs would remain open.[59]

Two sources of credibility were available to whites seeking to discourage blacks from risking migration—disillusioned returnees and southern black leaders. In Bolivar County, Mississippi, any black returnee who "gave the North a bad name" received widespread publicity from whites. Newspapers eagerly circulated information about migrants who had taken ill in the North and returned South on the brink of death. But it was difficult to locate such models of failure. So in the area around Crystal Springs, Mississippi, as elsewhere, white newspapers fabricated articles reporting migrants coming home after unpleasant experiences in the cold North, with "thousands" of others begging for railroad fare South.[60] Without human evidence, however, few blacks were likely to believe such tales; perhaps their main function was to reassure anxious employers and landlords.

Whites anxious about the labor supply hoped that black leaders could offer more persuasive testimony against the North's image as a Promised Land. In Jackson, Mississippi, whites offered substantial sums of money to influential blacks willing to speak against the movement. Perry Howard, a prominent black lawyer and Republican national committeeman refused such a proposal. Local lumber companies had to settle instead for anointing their own "black leader," I. W. Crawford, who had fewer scruples than Howard and accepted three thousand dollars for encouraging black workers to remain in

Jackson. Forty miles north, in Sunflower County, bankers, merchants, and businessmen made similar, although fruitless, efforts to enlist the aid of black ministers.[61] The New Orleans Chamber of Commerce had greater success, bankrolling a black newspaper that extolled the South as a land of opportunity where blacks could "buy a little piece of property . . . and live in your own ease and comfort." Black "flunkeys" enlisted by "panicked" whites, commented the *Defender*, distributed handbills in Jacksonville, Florida, warning that migrants were being used only as strikebreakers. And where they did not apply monetary incentives, whites instructed black leaders on their patriotic duty. The Negro Councils of Defense in the South were instructed to remind their people "that they render direct patriotic service by remaining at their work on Southern farms." Robert R. Moton, Booker T. Washington's successor at Tuskegee, agreed to make speeches informing black farmers that patriotism and national unity demanded that they remain home and produce as much food as possible. Whenever able to locate a black leader opposed to migration, whites published his views or rushed him to a platform.[62]

As usual, southern whites could find some "dependable negro" or "good negro" whose views coincided with their own. Some, like Giles Jackson of Richmond, Virginia, spoke mainly for their white sponsors. Jackson, whose National Civic Improvement Association was, according to one historian, "a thinly disguised scheme devised by business, planter, and political interests . . . to check the flight of Negroes from the South," probably received more attention from whites than from blacks. The Mississippi Rural Association, which attracted little notice outside the pages of a southern white newspaper, suffered the same fate.[63] Black southerners whose positions as leaders rested more upon their ties to the white community than their ability to influence blacks were not, however, the only blacks to oppose migration.

Like their predecessors during the 1879–80 Kansas Exodus, much of the southern black established leadership reacted coolly to the first stirrings of mass migration from the region. The *Defender* castigated such individuals as "so-called leaders" who used their "wits to get on the good side of the white people," but most black leaders had legitimate reasons for urging people to stay home. Pressure from whites did indeed influence black southerners dependent upon white patronage, tacit support, or even mere tolerance, for the survival of their businesses or schools. But opposition also drew upon both deeply rooted agricultural traditions and the need to protect social and economic institutions from the loss of their clientele and influence. Booker T. Washington fervently believed that "in the last analysis we have got to help ourselves"; but neither he nor his followers envisioned self-help in the form of individual or collective decisions to seek new opportunities in northern industry. His strategy embodied an agricultural vision in a southern milieu that would gradually adapt to a biracial society as blacks proved that they posed no threat to social order, economic development, or racial integrity.[64]

The minority of black southerners who refused to accept their place along the color line and decided to seek full citizenship in the industrial North, however, looked to an entirely different model of both individual and racial integration into American society and economy. Explicitly and implicitly the mostly young men and women leaving home were repudiating relationships and ideas upon which southern black elites had staked their reputations. Mass migration to the North not only threatened to cut into the constituency of the South's Washingtonian leadership, but also questioned its ideological framework.

The most influential leaders who opposed the migration exhibited all of these concerns. From Hampton Institute, Tuskegee, and elsewhere, Washingtonian spokesmen advised black southerners to stay on the farm. Administrators at these institutions knew that whites opposed the movement and did not want to jeopardize the fragile acceptance the schools had won. Southern whites tolerated these institutions because they posed no threat to the existing order; indeed, they helped to strengthen that order by inculcating proper values and accepting a subordinate role for blacks. Whites expected Moton and his colleagues to exercise their influence on behalf of the status quo.

These educators reacted logically to protect their institutional, political, and ideological positions. Tuskegee not only made a "determined effort" to encourage nearby farmers to remain at the plow, but dispatched speakers to carry the message. W. M. Rakestraw, a "Conference Agent" for the Institute, traveled throughout the state and into Tennessee, speaking at rural courthouses "on the importance of staying on the farm and living at home." The school's publication, *The Negro Farmer and Messenger*, first acknowledged the movement in August 1916, reminding its readers, "You are farmers; stick to your job." Thereafter, it seldom mentioned the exodus, pausing only occasionally to offer advice on how to keep teenage children on the farm, warn of the risks of migration, or report on Rakestraw's speeches.[65] With an eye to its white contributors as well as to its black audience, the Tuskegee publication portrayed the movement as a passing folly.

Spokesmen for similar institutions, ranging from Hampton Institute to Central Training School in Charity, Alabama, adopted the same strategy. Sometimes downright obsequious, the principals of these schools praised the "beautiful sunny Southland" as the "natural home" for their race, and warned blacks to be wary of labor agents who would lure them "away to some strange land." Once lured, of course, former agriculturalists might no longer wish to send their children to such schools. A member of the senior class at Hampton Institute had learned his lessons well; noting that "in normal times we have found it easy and desirable to live in the South," he foresaw an "open field for advancement" in that region.[66]

Educators were not the only ones who perceived in the exodus a threat to their status. Black doctors, lawyers, editors, businessmen, and ministers all depended on their own people for a living. The Negro Board of Trade in Jacksonville declared that "running away" would accomplish little, while acknowledging that if migration continued, "Who will support the negro men of business and those in Professions?" In Alabama an African Methodist Episcopal Church conference in 1916 advised its members to "remain on the farms" and seek salvation in the church rather than in the North. In Louisiana, Bishop Elias Cottrell of the Colored Methodist Episcopal Church blamed the movement on white labor agents and advised his listeners at an annual conference to discourage it. Pastors in Meridian, Mississippi, did not have to be advised by bishops; as their income began to diminish, they "talked against" the movement. Like the southern professionals whom the *Defender* accused of "selling their soul for a mess of pottage," such notables did not need any incentive from whites to act to calm the migratory fever. Mass migration threatened to—and did—impede the development of independent black social and economic institutions in the South.[67]

For most of these opponents of migration, the need to protect interests within the black community and relationships with whites coincided with their own experiences and their considered judgments about the future of their race. These individuals were not hypocrites whose arguments against migration were little more than attempts to protect their positions. They had already bettered their condition in the South and attributed their achievements to persistence along with personal characteristics that could be imitated by the next generation. Educated in the Washingtonian tradition, witness to the progress made by black farmers who followed their advice, and aware that as long as blacks remained subject to the whims of whites they remained vulnerable, these men and women believed that the future of black America rested upon the growth of a sturdy, independent yeomanry led by practical men willing to make stategic compromises. After all, in only a half-century of freedom, more than two hundred thousand black southerners (one-fourth of all black farm owners in the South) had reached the ranks of independent farm owners, amassing nearly thirteen million acres of farmland by 1910. And even if the percentage of owners among black farm operators had declined between 1900 and 1910, thirty-one thousand more owners had been added to the ranks during the decade.[68] Mass migration, especially of ambitious young men, would jeopardize these gains, inhibit further progress, and expose southern blacks to the vagaries of a traditionally hostile labor market in the North.

At the heart of this Afro-American variant on yeoman ideology lay the image of the South as the natural home of blacks. Two years before the Great Migration, Booker T. Washington had written that he had "never seen any part of the world where it seemed to me the masses of the Negro people would be better off than right here in these southern states."[69] After his death in November 1915, his disciples retained this loyalty to the South. His secretary, Emmett Scott, later celebrated the region as a land of "exceptional business opportunities," where blacks had "made the most amazing progress." Scott joined such black businessmen as Charles Banks of Mound Bayou, Mississippi, in tying prosperity closely to the businesses black southerners had built on a black clientele, but he recognized that Banks was not unusual in his dependence on black farmers for his commercial success. Farming clearly provided the foundation for black progress, while lying at the heart of blacks' affinity for the South. Robert R. Moton, confident that the region would remain "the scene of the Negro's greatest development," was so committed to his faith in farming as blacks' greatest aptitude that he even suggested that those who did migrate be encouraged to farm lands in the North. Racial as well as individual progress, these men believed, was most accessible in the South. There, blacks had established working relationships with whites, especially in those instances, noted Banks, when "the better elements of both races in the South maintain good relations."[70]

The North, on the other hand, argued Kelly Miller of Howard University, offered little chance for either independence or prosperity. Like others, he warned blacks that while in the South the farmer sold his produce in an impersonal and therefore color-blind market (he ignored such restrictions as those requiring tenants to sell to their landlords at low prices), in the North the black worker competed with whites in the sale of his labor. Unable to fall back on the independence of the family farm, the black northerner could be frozen out of the labor market. To those migrants attracted by the short-term gains the North offered, a southern black business magazine warned that the higher cost of living would absorb any increased wages.

Temptation and vice would sap the migrant's moral fiber while diverting earnings. Migration could do little to help the "average Negro" to better his condition. Instead, predicted Tuskegee's *Negro Farmer*, migrants would end up like those men who had left their farms, "lured to other sections and conditions, in the hope of great personal gain, only to find themselves finally entangled in the great web of disappointment, misery and crime." Sutton Griggs, a Memphis writer, citing statistics that showed an excess of black deaths over births in American cities, foresaw racial as well as individual disaster, culminating in the eventual extinction of the race.[71]

This opposition was hardly unanimous, even among the established leadership. The Birmingham *Weekly Voice*, like some other black newspapers, rejected such dire prognoses, and bade the migrants "Godspeed."[72] The *Southern Christian Recorder* applauded their initiative and hoped that their success in the North would dispel images of blacks as shiftless, indolent, and unreliable. Along with these newspapers, many black ministers favored the movement, according to one minister who traveled through Georgia, Florida, Alabama, "and other southern states" in 1917. Many advised "that it means protection under the law, the right of citizenship, better educational advantages for their children and freedom from the increasing wrongs of the South." Voices from the North proffered the same message, as such national publications as the *Christian Recorder, AME Church Review, Crisis*, and Chicago *Defender* agreed that the movement promised a brighter future for both the migrants and the race as a whole.[73] *Crisis* editor W. E. B. Du Bois directly responded to the pessimists' argument that the North offered little but a different form of racism. "The North is no paradise," he pointed out, "but the South is at best a system of caste and insult and at worst a Hell." In the South however, few were as optimistic as the normally accommodationist *Southwestern Christian Advocate*, which exulted that in the North black laborers were "improving their conditions," while at home the exodus was producing a labor shortage which would increase the bargaining power of those who remained.[74]

If there was any response that typified and unified black leadership, it was the impulse to use the movement and its threat to the southern labor supply as a political lever in the South.[75] As usual, northerners were freer to state the issue clearly and militantly. James Weldon Johnson of the NAACP called the exodus "tantamount to a general strike," and editor Richard R. Wright of the *Christian Recorder* exhorted black southerners to sharpen the weapon. Noting the panic and promises that the migration had elicited in the South, he asked

in 1917, "IF ONE HUNDRED THOUSAND UNORGANIZED NEGROES CAN
DO THIS WHAT COULD ONE MILLION ORGANIZED NEGROES DO?"[76] Few
southern leaders were willing to risk the consequences of such in-
flammatory rhetoric. Their strategy followed similar logic—but they
proceeded in their own characteristic way. Instead of organizing the
masses or threatening to upset traditional power relationships in the
South, they tried to exploit their reputations as moderate "reliable"
blacks by offering whites data on the causative influence of racial discrimination and specific advice on how to discourage migration.[77]

Southern black leaders had good reason to seize upon the Great
Migration as an opportunity to lobby for change in the South. In normal times, public criticism of southern racial protocols or economic
practices could jeopardize the precarious position maintained by the
educational institutions and newspapers from which many black
leaders derived their status. Ministers and business leaders knew
that such criticism also could provoke physical threats, attacks on
their property, or exile. But now, by placing criticism within the
context of support for white efforts to preserve the labor supply
and by offering proposals similar to those of white moderates, traditional black leaders could maintain or even enhance their reputations
among whites. Such men used their positions as recognized spokesmen for their communities by telling whites that only broad reforms
could stem the tide.

Often, these messages were offered within the context of agreement with whites that the South was the "Negro's natural home."
"He loves the Southland," insisted Reverend T. W. Coffee, Presiding
Elder of the Bessemer District, AME Church, and associate editor of
the Birmingham *Reporter*. "All that is near and dear to him is here and
he would like to stay, but being a man of feeling and growing into a
sense of self-respect, how can he stay under the circumstances?" The
Atlanta *Independent* repeatedly invoked the same "natural home"
homilies, adding that "he prefers to be here. He loves its traditions,
its ideals and its people. But he cannot stay here and starve." Standing the "natural home" argument on its head, the *Independent* reminded whites that "the Southland belongs as much to the Negro as
it does to the white man."[78]

Informing whites that blacks "cannot stay" in the South under
present circumstances, moderate voices listed a variety of reforms
that might discourage emigration. Lynching and mob violence were
the safest targets, as the white establishment also condemned such
attacks. Robert R. Moton, whose caution led him to combine his depiction of "genuine restlessness" due "very largely to recent lynch-

ings and burnings of colored people," with support for efforts to
change the "quietly hostile" attitude of blacks, implied that both races
had to change their attitudes. Most other leaders were more assertive,
as was even Moton on other occasions. William Jones, District Superintendent of the Methodist Episcopal Church of Alabama, spelled out
what would keep a prospective migrant at home:

> He must be accorded better treatment, not only better schools,
> but better wages, better accommodations, better protection of life
> and in the pursuit of happiness. He does not want to get into an-
> yone's way, he does not want to crowd anyone out, he does not
> want to infringe on any person's rights. He wants to feel that he is
> wanted and that he has friends. He knows that he has individual
> friends, but he wants to feel that society and the commonwealth
> are friendly toward him. In other words, he wants justice.[79]

Although their lists conformed to the reasons the migrants themselves offered for leaving, these leaders on the whole could not vigorously demand the kinds of changes that would make the South
a place where blacks could substantially better their condition.[80] Better schools would be of little use without job opportunities, and the
term usually referred to the Washingtonian institutions which were
training blacks to be better small farmers and servants. Ironically,
improved educational facilities might well have further stimulated
migration; even the existing institutions could nourish ambitions
incompatible with rural life in the black South. Frustrated Tuskegee
educators complained that too few of their alumni either farmed or
followed a trade learned at the school.[81] Higher wages, protection
from violence, and fair treatment in the courts and in settlement
of contracts would make blacks' present status more bearable and
stave off the starvation that black leaders claimed was driving people
North, but could hardly promise opportunity. None of these leaders
frontally attacked the system of land tenure, although most probably
recognized its exploitative nature. There is little evidence of an understanding that widespread land ownership was incompatible with
an agricultural system that assumed the existence of a dependent proletariat.[82] The Atlanta *Independent* ventured the furthest, telling whites
that they were "responsible for the unrest and uncertainty and migration of the Negro," and attacking the "southern equation" as the
framework that limited the social, political, and economic activities of
black people. But on most other occasions, even the *Independent* eschewed such thoroughgoing analysis in favor of relatively militant but
still meliorative requests.[83]

These men could hardly be blamed for prescribing antidotes that dealt with symptoms rather than with the cause of the South's maladies. By keeping their arguments within the limits of permissable debate in the South, they obtained sympathetic access to white newspapers and magazines, were permitted use of public auditoriums even to attack white "disregard for the law," and were accorded recognition from whites hoping to demonstrate that their own prescriptions were relevant to the discontents of the migrants. The white establishment could afford to lighten the burden of racial oppression, especially if it could be certain of the loyalty of what it considered to be the black leadership in the region. It could not, however, afford structural changes in the economy or threats to the assumption of white supremacy. Thus, cautious bargaining could yield results only slowly, but was essential to any improvements in the South. As John Hope, who in the North defended migration but in the South remained silent, wisely observed, even after the migration "the Negro problem [will remain] still . . . a Southern and rural problem." Black leadership in the South could address this problem most effectively by protecting its relationship with whites, while working the migration for whatever leverage it offered.[84]

Some leaders tried to convey the urgency of their agenda to whites by arguing that they were losing their influence with their people and were unable to discourage the movement without some positive signs that conditions would change. Reverend Coffee told whites that "the ministers are holding him [the prospective migrant] back to great extent," but were losing their grip. Wellborn V. Jenkins, in a letter to the Atlanta *Constitution*, told whites that when he and other black leaders advised against migration, listeners "fly back like children" to the argument that conditions in the North were better. "Nor could Booker T. Washington or even God, Himself, move them away from that," he continued.[85] By arguing that the migration was leaderless, traditional leaders absolved themselves of responsibility while informing whites that it was their move.

Such arguments were more than mere tactics; traditional southern black leaders were indeed powerless to stop the exodus. With characteristic hyperbole, *Defender* columnist W. Allison Sweeney called one purported black opponent of migration "an unsightly wart," and accurately evaluated the chances of a leader's ability to convince people to stay: "As well might he attempt to dig up the Gulf of Mexico in a teaspoon as stop this mighty avalanche marching—can't you hear its tread?—sweeping northward to a NEWER and more significant emancipation." The migrants, concluded Isaac Fisher, editor of the

Fisk University News, "look with great suspicion upon . . . the Negroes who attempt to halt them in their course . . . and are trusting
no one."[86]

By 1916, the Washingtonians, although still looked to by whites for
advice or support, had begun to lose influence among black people
who were forsaking Washington's advice to cast down their buckets
where they were. The buckets had come up empty too often. As Isaac
Fisher recognized in 1917, "great hosts" of blacks had followed the
Washingtonian recipe for success—obedience, humility, restraint—
for twenty years and were not likely now to heed the advice of these
same leaders who had been so mistaken. Nor did the Washingtonians
seem to be learning anything during the migration. In Mississippi,
one of these leaders still argued that "the hope of the Negro . . . lies
in the education and the liberalizing of the [southern] white man." In
Alabama, the principal of the Snow Hill Normal and Industrial Institute reiterated the Washingtonian doctrine of separation and "unself-
ish service," opposed the movement, and offered his services to
whites. These men were out of touch with such prospective migrants
as Isaac West, a railroad laborer in Shreveport, Louisiana, who would
"just as soon Be in hell" as remain in Louisiana.[87]

With recognized leaders predominantly unenthusiastic about the
exodus but unable to dampen the enthusiasm of prospective migrants, the movement seemed leaderless to most observers. A Mississippi preacher quoted by W. E. B. Du Bois claimed that the "leaders
of the race . . . had nothing to do with it," and were "powerless to
prevent" departures. John Hope called the movement "unled, un-
guided," and W. T. B. Williams of Tuskegee agreed that it was a
"movement without organization or leadership. The Negroes just
quietly move away without taking their recognized leaders into their
confidence."[88] Both white and black newspapers agreed the movement was "headless," as did such influential students of the migration as Charles Johnson, Monroe Work, and Emmett Scott. Most
observers were struck by the migrants' seeming disregard for the advice of leaders and their ability to act decisively without the aid of
those leaders. "It would be better," commented the *Southwestern
Christian Advocate,* "if there were a responsible leadership, then many
of the mistakes in the movement would be eliminated."[89]

That the migrants did indeed disregard the advice of established
leaders seems clear. But it is not so certain that the movement lacked
leadership or organization. The activities and importance of two
groups of leaders belie this assumption: leaders in the North, many
of whom were themselves migrants; and men and women in southern towns and cities who organized migration clubs, wrote letters

North offering their services and those of their townsmen, and spoke out within their communities—often hiding such activity from whites—in support of the movement. The Great Migration had its leaders, but they were not the disciples of Booker T. Washington who dominated the southern black press, who occupied whatever positions of political influence whites offered blacks, and who were the recognized spokesmen of black America.

3

"Tell Me about the Place"

Each Saturday the Chicago *Defender* arrived at Robert Horton's barber shop in Hattiesburg, Mississippi, carrying news of life north of the Mason-Dixon line. Habitués of the shop—many of whom had come in from surrounding rural areas for the day—not only purchased the black newspaper from Horton, but often discussed its contents, which in 1916 began to focus increasingly on the growing movement of black southerners to northern cities. Although the *Defender* provided most of his impressions about life in the North, Horton also occasionally received letters from a brother who had moved to Chicago in 1898. During a visit to New Orleans in 1916, Horton encountered in a barber shop a labor agent recruiting for northern industry. Despite dissatisfaction with the limitations he confronted in the South, he declined the agent's offer of free transportation. He continued to think about the increasingly inescapable question of migration and soon afterwards decided to move to Chicago, but he determined not to make the journey alone. The apparently popular barber discussed the proposition with others, and between fall 1916 and January 1917 he recruited nearly forty men and women to join his family in a migration club, which secured a group discount on the Illinois Central Railroad. Soon after his arrival in Chicago, he opened the Hattiesburg Barber Shop, which became a gathering place for migrants from Mississippi.[1]

Having occupied a central position in Hattiesburg's black community as a businessman and Baptist deacon, Horton became the recipient of numerous letters of inquiry about conditions in Chicago. He, in turn, passed along these names and addresses to a boardinghouse keeper who had earlier housed lodgers in Hattiesburg. She had migrated in October 1916, one month after her husband had quit his railroad job and gone to Chicago. She wrote letters offering rooms to people upon arrival, and her home apparently served as an initial stopping place for scores of migrants from southeastern Mississippi.[2]

From Chicago, Horton and other deacons of Hattiesburg's First Baptist Church stayed in touch with their pastor, who had opposed migration. With his congregation slipping away, Reverend Perkins finally agreed in late 1917 to come North to "shepherd them" again. Reverend Harmon, one of his colleagues in Hattiesburg, had needed less urging; he arrived in November 1916. In four months he earned enough to return South for his wife, four children, and "some" of his congregation. By late 1917, three Hattiesburg ministers had reunited with their congregations in Chicago.[3]

Once settled in Chicago, many of these Mississippians sent for family and wrote to relatives and friends. The siphoning process continued almost endlessly, drawing on family and kinship networks that would now extend not only across the South, but between regions as well.[4] Transferring families and communities northward, these migrants ensured continuity in their lives as well as in the Great Migration itself.

The experience of this group from Hattiesburg might not have been entirely typical, but it does suggest some of the salient elements in the dynamic of migration. Contrary to the images drawn by contemporary observers—images which have shaped much of the work of subsequent analysts of the movement—the Great Migration lacked neither organizational forms nor leaders. The movement did indeed grow largely from the initiative of individuals who resisted the warnings and pleas of most of the educators, businessmen, professionals, and editors who constituted the recognized leadership of the black South and who generally discouraged migration northward. But its vitality drew upon an infrastructure, a network held together by social institutions, leaders, and individual initiative. This network stimulated, facilitated, and helped to shape the migration process at all stages, from the dissemination of information through the black South to the settlement of black southerners in northern cities. An examination of the dynamic of migration between the South and one northern city—Chicago—suggests how a grass-roots social movement developed despite the opposition of an entrenched regional leadership.[5]

Before they would leave their southern homes, many migrants wanted specific and reliable information about the North. Black southerners learned about the North from a variety of sources, many of which they sought out on their own initiative. As a case study of one small South Carolina black community has suggested, many people who left for Chicago and other northern cities "consciously formulated their emigration . . . [and] carefully planned" according to information obtained from a network that connected black communities, families, institutions, and individuals. "I like my fellow southerner am looking northward," one migrant wrote in April 1917, "but before leaving the South Id like to know just wher I am goin and what Im to do if posible." Southern blacks had chased chimeras before—to Florida, the Yazoo-Mississippi Delta, Arkansas, and Texas—and had heard about the hard conditions faced by westward migrants to Kansas and Oklahoma. It was clear to many that migration involved risks. One Jackson, Mississippi, woman remembered that a friend, drawn to the Delta by "white agents and white folks niggers" had returned seven years later looking "like a haunt." This time people were more cautious. "I do not wish to come there hoodwinked not knowing where to go or what to do," wrote a New Orleans man to the Chicago Urban League, "so I Solicite your help in this matter." An Anniston, Alabama, migrant put it more succinctly: "I should not like to com in that secson with out no enfremation."[6]

By 1917, an information network had developed through which prospective migrants could learn what jobs were available in the North, how much could be earned, what life was like, what schooling was offered, and virtually anything else they wanted to know before leaving. The emergence of new sources of information during the second decade of the twentieth century has, with some justification, received attention mainly as a "cause" of the Great Migration. But the migrants' participation in this network also suggests one of the ways in which the Great Migration represented a forceful attempt by black southerners to seize control over their future. By forging links with Chicago's black community, prospective migrants facilitated and shaped not only the migration process, but their adaptation to new homes as well.

News of what one prospective migrant referred to as the "great work going on in the north" flowed south through a variety of channels.[7] Labor agents attracted workers' attention with stories of high wages and better living conditions in the North. Men working in railroad yards and trains transmitted information along the tracks. To those who believed only what they saw in print, northern black newspapers—especially the Chicago *Defender*—provided glowing images of the North alongside lurid reports of southern oppression. Letters and visits from previous migrants combined specific information with welcome advice from trusted relatives and friends. Discussion of the North, initiated by news from endless combinations of these sources, came to dominate conversation in homes, churches, barber shops, and poolrooms, along with outdoor gathering places and other focal points of southern black communities.

Although a vague chronology would focus on labor agents at the beginning of the process and on the *Defender* and letters in subsequent stages, it was the interaction of various forms of communication that suggests the concept of a network. By themselves, labor agents would have had little enduring impact, had their pitch not been relayed through the black South along more indigenous lines of communication. Many people listened to the agents skeptically, waiting for confirmation from more trusted sources before embarking. Rumors circulated widely, but also commanded only limited authority. Trainmen were early sources of such stories; they also carried the *Defender*, which developed a growing following in the black South in the 1910s. Had they not reinforced each other, neither the thousands of letters from previous migrants nor the *Defender* would have been as influential as they were. At the same time, kinship networks facilitated visiting, circulated letters and copies of the *Defender*, and brought news of the labor agents. If trainmen, agents, and newspapers spread the message across a broad expanse of territory, the letters and visits provided an essential depth to the information. Contemporary analysts and subsequent historians acknowledged the importance of letters, black newspapers, and other forms of communication, but mainly as causes of the Great Migration rather than as integral aspects of a network and an organizational framework that suggest the self-activating nature of the movement.

The Great Migration's origins are inseparable from specific efforts by employers to recruit black workers from the South. Connecticut tobacco growers, feeling the pinch of a tightening labor market in 1915, secured the cooperation of the National Urban League in recruiting fourteen hundred students from southern black colleges. Massive recruitment of laborers began the following year, when the Erie and Pennsylvania railroads began sending agents and special trains into northeastern Florida urging blacks to come North to work on track crews and yard gangs. The railroads, whose ranks soon grew to include the New York Central, New Haven, Delaware & Hudson, Lackawanna, Philadelphia & Reading, Illinois Central, and Great Northern, needed labor quickly and could transport workers from the Deep South over long distances at low cost. In the face of southern opposition and an inability to retain workers who had been given free transportation, however, the railroads soon drastically reduced "shipments" of black southerners.[8]

In the meantime, other northern industries, also pushing to meet the demands of the wartime economy and unable to secure white immigrant workers, soon began sending recruiters south. When

Charles Johnson toured Mississippi in late 1917, he heard how the previous year an agent "would walk briskly down the street through a group of Negroes, and without turning his head would say in a low tone: 'Anybody want to go to Chicago, see me.' " In Jackson, forty informants told him of labor agents' activities in that city. In small communities he heard about individuals who had gone to New Orleans for free passage to Chicago. Others told him of "free trains that backed up on plantations and carried away hundreds of farm hands with their families." Because northern industrialists seldom financed the transportation of the families of recruited workers, many of these stories were apparently exaggerated. But free transportation did carry some men northward, with agents distributing tickets and perhaps even providing special railroad cars. These "pass riders" operated mainly in large cities, recruiting local workers as well as visitors from outlying areas, who would often carry the message home with them before leaving. During late 1916-early 1917, news spread to many southern towns and cities that "it was possible to get passes without difficulty." Although the agents had all but disappeared by the time of Johnson's arrival in the fall of 1917, their influence lingered. They had touched a nerve among restless black southerners. The "pass rider" became a central part of migration folklore.[9]

A few agents in major southern cities were able to spark discussion and stimulate the spread of information partly because labor recruiters already occupied an important place both in southern economic history and black folklore. Southern planters and other employers had been using labor agents to secure tenants or laborers for newly developing regions since the Civil War. As recently as the first decade of the twentieth century, recruiters from labor-hungry plantations had followed the boll weevil into the Natchez, Mississippi, area and taken "carloads" of black families and their belongings into the bottom lands of the Yazoo Delta. Even during the Great Migration itself, agents from southern munitions industries recruited black workers from plantations and lumber mills.[10] Notwithstanding the measures adopted to prevent such activity, the tradition of the labor agent luring blacks to some new, and supposedly better, employment was firmly established. It was not difficult for many black southerners to believe stories of labor agents' activity on behalf of a new group of employers.

Studies of Pittsburgh, Milwaukee, and other northern cities have demonstrated that industrialists in some cities sent labor agents into the South; but only a handful of Chicago companies seem to have considered such recruitment necessary.[11] In August 1916, Morris & Company arranged with a "white contractor" to bring seventy-five black southerners north to work in its Chicago packinghouses. The following month, Armour & Company transferred two hundred black workers from its Alabama meat-packing facility. A few months later the Chicago *Defender* reported the activity of a packinghouse recruiter in the area of Hattiesburg, Mississippi. In other industries, it is likely that the Illinois Central did some recruiting for a short period, and Commonwealth Edison obtained "small numbers" of black workers in the South to compensate for its labor shortages.[12] But despite reports of agents sending laborers to Chicago from Mobile, Birmingham, Jackson, New Orleans, and Memphis, Chicago employers appear to have done little direct "importing" of black southerners.[13]

Many of the references to and stories of labor agent activity probably referred to black southerners who served the interests of both northern employers and prospective migrants but operated within the context of traditional social networks. Closest to the contemporary definition of a labor agent were those who had already migrated North but then returned home with a few dollars from an employer willing to pay transportation for friends and relatives of a proven worker. Others were black men and women who neither worked for northern employers—directly or by contract—nor received compensation for their recruitment activities. Upon hearing of opportunities in the North, these individuals conveyed the news to friends and relatives and took the initiative in organizing group transportation. Many wrote to Chicago employers, the Chicago Urban League, or the *Defender*, seeking work and offering to bring others along. After asking for "a transportation" for himself, a Chattanooga, Tennessee, man wrote a Chicago foundry that "i can get you good mens here." People casually offered not only their own services, but those of friends, relatives, and townsmen. Although it might seem appropriate to limit the definition of a labor agent to recruiters who provided transportation, many white southerners and black recruits attached the label to anyone who promised Chicago employers that he could "bring along manny more if you want them."[14] These men and women were neither the outside agitators white southerners traditionally had held responsible for black migration nor part of any broad recruiting effort organized by a northern conspiracy. They did, however, disseminate information, encourage migration, and help foster the image of a network of recruiters that could facilitate migration and adjustment to Chicago.

Outside the few major cities of the South, labor agents employed by northern industry tended to be more important as legends than as actual recruiters of labor. "If there are any agents in the south there havent been any of them to Lutcher," wrote one Louisianian seeking the rumored free transportation. To such men, agents became symbols of the new freedom and opportunities beckoning from the North. A Mississippi man who met an agent while visiting New Orleans considered him "an instrument in God's hands" and passed the word to countless friends and relatives back home in Mississippi. Thousands of black southerners heard about the agents through the pages of the *Defender*, which publicized agents' successful attempts to evade southern whites' harassment. Because the *Defender* did not reveal either the names of the agents, the prospective employers, the mode of recruitment, or even the definition of a labor agent, it is difficult to discern the extent to which these stories refer to agents of northern employers or black southerners recruiting friends to travel north with them. But *Defender* readers did find additional evidence that the agents were indeed active—if not in their own community, then elsewhere. From Shreveport, a Louisianian wrote, probably to the *Defender*, "I want to get some infirmation about getting out up there I did learn that they had a man here agent for to send people up there I have never seen him yet and I want you to tell me how to get up there."[15] These shadowy agents added to the excitement of the moment, reinforced other rumors, and sustained the high level of optimism regarding opportunities in the North. Often, visitors were regarded as labor agents, because of both the air of mystery surrounding them and the departures which sometimes followed their visits. Charles Johnson observed in Mississippi in 1917 that

> every strange face came to be recognized as a man from the North looking for laborers and their families. If he denied it, they simply thought that he was concealing his identity from the police, and if he said nothing, his silence was regarded sufficient affirmation. Hundreds of disappointments are to be traced to the rumour that a train would leave on a certain date, (sometimes after the presence of a stranger in town). Hundreds would come to the station prepared to leave and when no agent appeared, would purchase their own tickets.[16]

Swindlers, posing as labor agents, took advantage of this widespread belief in the presence of recruiters. Promising jobs and cheap transportation north, they either absconded with the advance payments or reneged on promises to provide jobs, clothing, or money in Chicago. In Augusta, Georgia, one man paid two dollars to "some so call agent" who had promised to get him to Illinois. Migrants in Chicago reported that agents had promised them clothes, three months' free rent near their work, and "unlimited privilege." Other swindlers were even more lavish. C. Cassani promised work in a Chicago-area steel mill to ten men at wages of eight dollars per day, despite their total lack of experience. By 1917, the *Defender* had received so many letters regarding men collecting money by posing as agents of railroads and northern factories that it warned its readers against such schemes. "There are a number of agents in the south that are collecting money from members of the Race who are planning to leave for the north. No one should pay any one to leave."[17]

Labor agents were hardly the only sources of outlandish rumors. By late 1916, a story began to circulate in Gulfport, Mississippi, that "something is going to happen to Gulfport and you don't want to stay here and get caught." Other rumors were more specific and more farfetched. The war furnished material for tales like the one warning that the Germans were marching through Texas, preparing to conquer the American South. Closer to the truth, one rumor spread "that the new work-or-fight order of the Provost Marshal meant that men would be drafted for labor and put under conditions practically amounting to peonage."[18] Stories relating to jobs in the North tended to be exaggerated: Mississippians heard that Chicago packinghouses needed fifty thousand black workers and that common laborers could earn up to ten dollars per day in the North.[19]

Few migrants were either seduced by labor agents or deceived by imposters or unfounded rumors. Although agents recruited many of the 1915–16 pioneers, the "guiding hand of the labor agent" did not sweep northward the mass of naive, passive ciphers portrayed by many observers. Large numbers of migrants made careful decisions, based on a variety of sources, and knew more about northern conditions than they cared to reveal to whites—be they agents or locals.[20] They did not need labor agents to instill in them a desire to find a better life. W. T. B. Williams of Tuskegee and Charles Johnson agreed that labor agents "did little more than point the way out of the unfortunate situation" in the South. "The agents," a black Mississippian told Johnson, "simply gave definite direction to Negroes who were going north anyhow." Agents did, in many communities, spark the exodus, and in some cases, agents or rumors of agents strongly influenced migrants' choices of destinations. But they usually recruited men (seldom women) ready to go and awaiting the "clew to the job in the North."[21] And the information agents transmitted often moved more quickly along indigenous lines of communication. These lines of communication formed a network anchored by men and women who might be termed the leaders of the Great Migration.

Central to this network were the growing number of black railroad workers. Considerable information moved southward along the same railroads that carried migrants in the opposite direction. Even before the Great Migration, eyewitness accounts of the North reached southern black communities through men working in the rail yards, on the tracks, and in the trains. Charles Liggett, who arrived in Chicago in 1903, was influenced and aided by a friend who worked as a cook for the Rock Island line. Charley Banks, who had quit farming when the boll weevil "eat up all de cotton," worked for the Yazoo and Mississippi Valley Railroad, owned by the Illinois Central. He went to Chicago in 1914 as an Illinois Central employee. A 1916 migrant from southern Mississippi knew that he could not better his $125 monthly salary as a fireman, but "his railroad life gave him a chance to make some comparisons." He "waited his chance" for labor conditions in the North to improve and left Mississippi when racial violence finally drove him past the point of tolerance.[22] By 1910, 103,606 blacks worked for the railroads, and the Illinois Central hired hundreds more as strikebreakers the following year. Black men who labored on section or yard gangs often lived in small southern communities and either visited the North or heard about Chicago from the black trainmen working on any of the numerous lines passing through the nation's rail hub. Shop workers in Vicksburg, Mississippi, for example, often traveled to Chicago on "free passes," and returned telling "interesting stories."[23]

Pullman porters and dining-car waiters commanded particular influence, both within the community of black railroaders and among black southerners in general. These men, many of whom lived in Chicago, spoke proudly of their home town as they traveled through the South. Bluesman Tampa Red, who came to Chicago from Florida, remembered Pullman porters referring to it as "God's country." In Mississippi, porters on the Gulf and Ship Island Railroad regularly informed eager listeners about Chicago.[24] But even more important than their activities as traveling civic boosters was the porters' work as publicists and distributors of the Chicago *Defender*.

Fearless, sensationalist, and militant, the *Defender* advertised the glories of Chicago so effectively that even migrants headed for other northern cities drew their general image of the urban North from its pages. Many also wrote to the newspaper for information and assistance. Founded by Robert Abbott in 1905 on capital of twenty-five cents, the "World's Greatest Weekly" grew into the largest-selling black newspaper in the United States by World War I, with two-thirds of its circulation outside Chicago. Born and raised in Georgia, Abbott had come to Chicago in 1897 after attending Hampton Institute. Although he continued to support Booker T. Washington—especially with regard to educational policy—until the Tuskegeean's death in 1915, Abbott was no accommodationist. He refused to use the term "Negro," because of the derogatory connotation given it by whites. In the *Defender*, blacks were "the Race," and black men, "Race men." All issues were evaluated on the basis of the Race's interests. Abbott opposed "demon rum," but refused to support prohibition until enough racial barriers had been dropped to allow black brewery and saloon workers to find other employment. Abbott's editorial yardstick was consistent and simple: if it fostered discrimination or cost blacks jobs, he opposed it.[25]

To black southerners, the *Defender* represented unapologetic black pride, dignity, and assertiveness. From its inception, it offered itself as a crusader against the white South. Abbott's first issue set the tone, denouncing "WHITE GENTLEMEN FROM GEORGIA" who had condoned a white man's murder of three blacks for committing the crime of refusing to work overtime. More viciously anti-South than any other black newspaper, it loudly denounced racial oppression below the Mason-Dixon line. Front page banner headlines, sometimes drenched in red ink, announced such injustices as,

SOUTHERN WHITE GENTLEMEN
BURN RACE BOY AT STAKE.[26]

In reporting news of white violence against blacks in the South, *Defender* correspondents spared few of the gory details, and the editors reputedly embellished them even further. A lynching in Dyersburg, Tennessee, received the standard coverage:

> Bound to an iron post by the most savage fiends in existence on the face of the globe or even in the depths of hell below, Scott stood one-half hour, while men heated pokers and soothing irons until they were white with heat and were as fiery as the flames that heated them. Scott lay flat on his face beneath the yoke of the iron post. Children on the outskirts of the mob played merrily on and their voices could be heard above the hubbub of the mob.
>
> Then a red streak shot out and the holder began to bore out the prisoner's eyes. Scott moaned. The pokers were worked like an auger, that is, they were twisted round and round.
>
> The smell of burning flesh permeated the atmosphere, a pungent, sickening odor telling those who failed to get good vantage points what their eyes could not see: Smoothing irons were searing the flesh.
>
> Swish. Once, twice, three times a red-hot iron dug gaping places in Lation Scott's back and sides.[27]

Black southerners knew of such events, through either word of mouth or personal knowledge. But the *Defender* demonstrated to

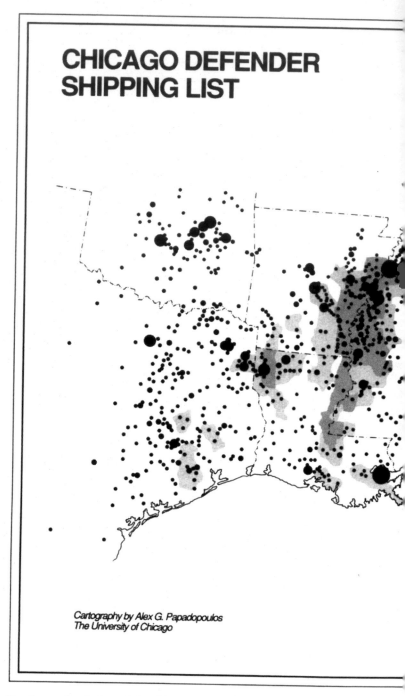

Southern circulation of the Chicago *Defender*.

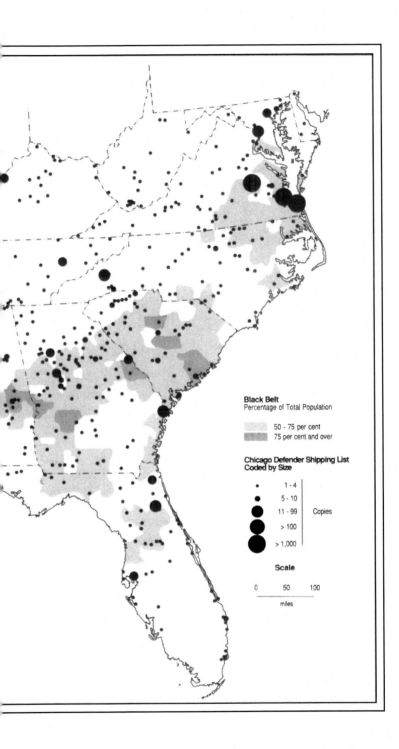

Black Belt
Percentage of Total Population

50 - 75 per cent

75 per cent and over

Chicago Defender Shipping List
Coded by Size

•	1 - 4
•	5 - 10
●	11 - 99
●	> 100
●	> 1,000

Copies

Scale

0   50   100

miles

them that these incidents were systematic and unremitting. Observers and historians who have discounted lynching as a stimulus to
migration, noting the lack of correlation between lynching and migration statistics in southern counties, ignore the *Defender's* influence. A
racial incident anywhere in the South—especially if violent—easily
found its way into the *Defender*, which broadcast it nationwide. The
Defender constantly reminded its readers of their oppression. In the
series "Below the Mason Dixon Line," for example, traveling correspondents would send dispatches from a different place each week,
relating the local horror stories.[28]

Unafraid of pointing an accusing finger, the *Defender* waged a
militant campaign against white southerners, fulfilling its role as
the defender of black America against "the crafty paleface" of the
South. Its editorials sought to make "the 'crackers' squirm under
the lash" of *Defender* attacks. Columnist W. Allison Sweeney, a favorite among black southerners, specialized in what he called "breaking southerners and 'white folks' niggers' on the wheel." Sweeney's
purple prose scattered invective too dangerous to express openly
in the South, identifying white leaders as "looters, grafters, lazy si-
necurists, general 'no-accounts,' persecutors, KILLERS OF NEGRO MEN,
seducers, RAVISHERS OF NEGRO WOMEN." Reading of Theodore Bilbo's
"gubernatorial carcass" in Sweeney's column, black Mississippians
knew they had an outspoken and apparently fearless champion.[29]

The *Defender's* influence in the South did not rest only on its
militant message. Abbott built his wide circulation partly through his
astute cultivation of black railroad men during the newspaper's struggling early years. The *Defender's* railroad column, which ran regularly
as early as 1910, noted who worked on which lines and routes and
related anecdotes about individual workers. Abbott also vigorously
supported the struggles of Pullman porters for higher wages, claiming a major role in a 10 percent increase in early 1916. Occasionally he
reminded them of what they could do for him, as well as for themselves, because the *Defender* represented their interests and but-
tressed their prestige in the community. "A railroad porter of Chicago
feels proud of a paper that does big things, and he shows it to a friend
or an acquaintance in some other clime." The *Defender* successfully
attracted these men as readers, and most important, as publicity
agents and distributors. Managing editor L. C. Harper later noted
that the paper's wide circulation owed partly to its practice of giving
Pullman porters copies to distribute to friends.[30]

Promotion and distribution of the *Defender* drew also upon other
traditional lines of communication in black America. Extensive coverage of black entertainers, for example, prompted stage performers

to enlist as the *Defender*'s traveling salespeople. By 1916, the *Defender* seemed to be everywhere. In many places, readers could buy it in the church or barber shop, two major centers of socializing and discussion. In Savannah, Reverend Daniel Wright regularly sold twenty-five to fifty copies to his congregation. A South Carolina itinerant preacher carried the newspaper to sell as he traveled through the state. In Rome, Georgia, people could buy the *Defender* "at all barbershops." New Orleans readers could purchase it on the jitney buses. By 1919, three news dealers in that city were selling one thousand copies weekly.[31]

By the time of the Great Migration, Abbott's militancy and sensationalism had combined with this vast promotion and distribution network to propel the *Defender* to the forefront of Afro-American journalism. The *Defender*'s circulation, already 33,000 by early 1916, skyrocketed along with the migration. From 50,000 at the end of that year it rose to roughly 90,000 in 1917, 125,000 in 1918, and 130,000 in 1919. Abbott's biographer has suggested that it climbed as high as 180,000 in 1918 and 230,000 in 1919. Estimates during the early 1920s, some slightly exaggerated, ranged from 160,000 to 250,000. The variation in estimates notwithstanding, the *Defender* clearly pioneered a new era in Afro-American journalism, pumping a constant flow of trusted information into southern black communities.[32]

The *Defender* penetrated into some of the most remote corners of the black South. Its 1919 shipping manifest, which included 1,542 towns and cities across the South, listed thousands of names on its sixty-four galley-sized pages. Raging headlines and glowing images of Chicago provoked discussion in Fry's Mill, Arkansas; Bibsland, Louisiana; Tunica, Mississippi; Yoakum, Texas; and countless other tiny communities dotting the South. In Palatka, Florida, one hundred *Defenders* were sold each week. A Hattiesburg, Mississippi, black leader marveled that "Negroes grab the *Defender* like a hungry mule grabs fodder." In nearby Laurel, "people would come for miles running over themselves, to get a Defender."[33] These observations were corroborated weekly, as each issue of the *Defender* contained contributions from far-flung readers.

Neither income nor literacy circumscribed the *Defender*'s audience, which stretched far beyond those people able and willing to spend scarce nickels (or $1.50 per year until 1918; $2 thereafter) for its message. As befitting a newspaper that linked blacks from different regions, the *Defender* was generously shared within communities. "Copies were passed around until worn out," noted one observer. Abbott's biographer claimed that five people read each paper. NAACP official Walter White, conservatively estimating *Defender* southern circulation at 75,000 in 1920, noted that "this means approximately 300,000 readers who see the Chicago *Defender* each week." Countless others listened to someone read a *Defender* aloud at home, in a barber shop, or after church.[34]

To Charles Johnson, traveling through Mississippi and Louisiana in 1917, it seemed as if everybody read the *Defender*. In Gulfport, Mississippi, "a man was regarded as 'intelligent' if he read the *Defender*." Ninety miles north, at Laurel, Johnson heard that "old men who have never known how to read, would buy it simply because it was regarded as precious." In many places the arrival of the *Defender* constituted a major weekly event. A New Orleans woman explained that she "had rather read it then to eat when Saturday comes, it is my heart's delight." With a mass appeal that reached even "the lowly class of Negroes," as one Tuskegeean lamented, the *Defender* transmitted information through the black South on a scale hitherto unknown. Not even Booker T. Washington, despite the cooperation of southern whites, had been able to communicate so easily with so many black southerners.[35]

The *Defender* commanded this loyal following, which dramatically increased during the migration, because black southerners had confidence in it. After reading the Chicago weekly for the first time in 1917, a Texan wrote Abbott that "I never dreamed that there was such a race paper published and I must say that its *some* paper." W. A. McCloud of Wadley, Georgia, considered the editor "a great and grand man and a lover of his rase." Another reader wrote Abbott that "I feal that I know you personaly."[36] Presenting material that southern white papers would not, and southern black papers usually dared not, print, the *Defender* came to be regarded as the final authority on racial matters. Most contemporary southern black newspapers were necessarily cautious of racial boundaries and often were dominated by religious and fraternal news and "stereotyped and utterly innocuous" content. Many of the more assertive journals were controlled by individuals whose political ambitions demanded moderation. Southern black editors seldom presented either harsh criticism of the South or attractive images of the North. Some were so timid as to invite accusations that they received subsidies from planters. A northern white minister perceptively noted in 1918 that in the South, "the Negro pays more attention to northern [black] press than to the southern press because of the suspicion that the local Negro press can be influenced by the white community." Blacks learned even less from white publications. "We pay no attention to what the southern white papers report," remarked one Pullman porter; "I'm waiting to get home and see what my Chicago paper has to say." Southerners took a similar attitude. "I feel that this is the only source from which we can learn of what good Negroes are doing. The white press just will not publish anything good of us," observed one Kentuckian. A Miami, Florida, man believed rumors of the migration only after he had read of it in the *Defender*. The long-standing legends concerning the North assumed heightened authenticity in the *Defender* pages.[37]

Alongside descriptions of lynching, torture, and everyday oppression in the South, the *Defender* counterposed articles picturing Chicago's black community as influential, moderately prosperous, and modern. Southern subscribers read heated denunciations of Jim Crow along with articles calmly describing black Chicago's elected officials or its YMCA basketball teams' games against whites (the *Defender* tended to ignore the politicians' lack of real power and de facto segregation in the YMCA and elsewhere). The exploits of Chicago's black baseball teams, local track stars Binga Dismond and Howard Drew, and especially Chicago's own Jack Johnson, set in sharp relief the *Defender*'s routine depiction of the South as a place of unending toil and constant fear. While southern blacks often faced peremptory retaliation for even the slightest aggressive act, front-page photographs of black Chicago's gun-toting "Famous Eighth" infantry, "THE PRIDE OF ILLINOIS," documented the striking contrast. More pointedly, in April 1917, the *Defender* printed a photograph of a Freetown, Louisiana, one-room shack that passed as a schoolhouse. Alongside appeared the stately pillars of Chicago's modern Robert Lindblom High School. Reminding its readers that Lindblom had no color line, the *Defender* characteristically ignored the fact that few blacks could attend Lindblom, as it was located in a white neighborhood.[38] But the *Defender* could repeatedly point with justifiable pride to Chicago's Wendell Phillips High School, which offered Chicago black youths integrated secondary education. The editors drew these contrasts to boost Chicago as well as *Defender* circulation.

Although it would eventually both symbolize the migration spirit and play a central role in the movement, the *Defender* until mid-1916 advised black southerners to remain where they were. Like Booker T. Washington, Abbott counseled blacks to cast down their buckets in the South and recommended agricultural diversification as the road to prosperity. "The southland is rich and fertile, and it requires brains first and brawn afterward to make farming pay."[39]

Neither Abbott's faith in the possibility of progress in the South, nor his view that "the ultimate salvation of the Afro-American in the South lies in their own strength," implied an accommodationist position.[40] Indeed, his alternative to northward migration readily convinced southern readers that the "World's Greatest Weekly" was truly a "race paper" and that the North must be freer if editors could print such things. It advocated fighting back, "Eye for an Eye, and Tooth for a Tooth." After a Georgia lynching and mob violence in North Carolina, the *Defender* front page counseled,

WHEN THE MOB COMES
AND YOU MUST DIE TAKE
AT LEAST ONE WITH YOU.

This advice continued into 1916. "When you are in Rome, you have to do as the Romans do"; "Call the white fiends to the door and shoot them down."[41]

Most important, the *Defender* told black southerners that the South offered more opportunities for employment. In the North employers could hire immigrants, and trade unions excluded blacks from skilled positions. Abbott's professed belief that "it is best for the ninety and nine of our people to remain in the southland" coincided with the reluctance with which he and other middle-class black Chicagoans greeted poor, "slow-thinking," unemployable migrants to their city.[42]

With the sudden opening of Chicago's unskilled industrial jobs to blacks in the summer of 1916, the *Defender* began to encourage northward migration. Although reference to "steady movement of race families" out of the Deep South had appeared as early as February, the *Defender* had given the initial stirrings of migration little attention. Still cautious in mid-August, the editors now merely noted the exodus, predicted it would continue, and argued that "for the nation as a whole it will be beneficial to have the Colored people more evenly sprinkled through the different states." But by September what had been mere news a month earlier had become a crusade. A front page photograph of black men and women crowding alongside a railroad track, publicized the "exodus of labor from the South. . . . The men, tired of being kicked and cursed, are leaving by the thousands as the above picture shows." From then on, the *Defender* actively, sensationally, and relentlessly promoted migration.[43]

Abbott's shifted position was consistent with his established record of measuring all issues along the yardstick of racial self-interest. The increasing demand for black laborers in the North not only obliterated the old argument that black economic opportunity lay exclusively in the South, but offered blacks as a group the chance to prove their ability to perform industrial labor. "Our problem today," argued Abbott in 1916, "is to widen our economic opportunities, to find more openings and more kinds of openings in the industrial world. Our chance is right now." At the same time, migration to northern cities

THE EXODUS

NORTHWARD BOUND

Laborers waiting for the third section of the labor trains northward bound on the outskirts of Savannah, Ga. The exodus of labor from the South has caused much alarm among the Southern whites, who have failed to treat them decent. The men, tired of being kicked and cursed, are leaving by the thousands as the above picture shows.

Front page photograph, Chicago *Defender*, September 2, 1916 (courtesy of the Chicago *Defender*).

would help to diminish racial prejudice by increasing racial contact. "Only by a commingling with other races will the bars be let down and the black man take his place in the limelight beside his white brother. Contact means everything." [44] The *Defender* did not mention, but Abbott no doubt recognized, that the thousands of employed black workers would bring money into Chicago's black community and that sheer numbers would increase its political clout. Not coincidentally the *Defender*, as the champion of a great racial movement and representative of black Chicago, would gain prestige and increase its circulation.

Once it endorsed the migration, the *Defender* helped to stimulate the movement, with vivid North-South contrasts, advertisements for newly available jobs, exciting images of city life, and reports of "migration fever." Articles on lynchings either lay alongside news of the spreading exodus or ended with reminders that it was foolhardy to

Cartoon from the Chicago *Defender*, August 19, 1916 (courtesy of the Chicago *Defender*).

remain in the South. Arguing that "anywhere in God's country is far better than the southland," the *Defender* abandoned all vestiges of its earlier positions on black progress south of the Ohio River.

> Every black man for the sake of his wife and daughters especially should leave even at a financial sacrifice every spot in the

south where his worth is not appreciated enough to give him the standing of a man and a citizen in the community. We know full well that this would mean a depopulation of that section and if it were possible we would glory in its accomplishment.[45]

Inviting "all to come north," the *Defender* provided concrete evidence that migration now offered the greatest opportunity for both race and individual progress. Not only did it estimate "places for 1,500,000 working men in the cities of the North," but it carried Help-Wanted advertisements directed at black southerners. Unlike earlier employment notices in the newspaper, these called for large numbers of workers and involved factory work. With such messages as "we do not pay transportation, but guarantee you a steady position," they were clearly aimed at southerners.[46]

These advertisements first appeared on September 2, 1916, but then only sporadically until spring 1917, probably because few white employers knew of the *Defender*'s influence. But as employers turned to the more knowledgeable Chicago Urban League for aid and advice in recruitment efforts, the advertisements increased. Throughout 1917–18, the Urban League, Chicago firms and employment agencies, and industries in Wisconsin, Nebraska, Ohio, and Minnesota sought to attract black southerners through classified advertisements in the *Defender*.[47]

Readers of the *Defender* responded enthusiastically to these advertisements. Some wrote directly to employers; others wrote to either the *Defender* or the Chicago Urban League, which gained publicity from news stories as well as advertisements. Many readers assumed that the newspaper, as a spokesman for and representative of the Race, would act as an employment agent. "Being a constant reader of your paper," wrote a Georgia letter carrier willing to give up his civil service job to work as a laborer, "I thought of no one better than you to write for information." A Floridian, willing to "garntee you good and reglar service," not only wanted employment, but "some instruction how i can get there." Like the Marcel, Mississippi, man who knew Abbott to be "a real man of my color," many *Defender* readers thought that the Help-Wanted notices implied that the editor had sufficient influence with employers to secure jobs for his readers. Others, unable to find suitable advertisements, seized the initiative and inserted their own Situations-Wanted pleas for employment in the North.[48]

With the *Defender* as its advertising agent, the Urban League inspired even greater confidence in the Chicago job market. Upon learning in the *Defender* of "the splendid work which you are doing in placing colored men in touch with industrial opportunities," black southerners inundated the League with requests for employment and other assistance. Some offered to "do any kind of work for an honest liveing"; others thought the League "could place mens in iny job or trade they follows." Even more optimistic applicants responded to the advertisements by offering to bring five, ten, twenty, or a hundred friends along with them. The League received "thousands" of letters from hopeful southerners; most mentioned the *Defender*.[49]

Besides impressing readers with the availability of jobs in the North, the *Defender* showed them that Chicago offered attractive leisure activities. One of the earliest black newspapers to include a full entertainment section, the *Defender* dazzled black southerners with its image of "the Stroll"—the strip of State Street from 26th to 39th streets. Here, blacks were supposedly treated politely by white businessmen and could hop from one night spot to the next. Such dance halls as the Pekin and the Palace Garden offered jazz, bright lights, dancing into the wee hours, and even racially mixed crowds. Black Chicago's seven movie theaters (eight by late 1917) broadcast their attractions, which included live orchestras, with large displays in the *Defender*, and southern readers must have found the quantity and variety awesome. Opening the *Defender* on October 7, 1916, for example, a southerner found that—if he lived in Chicago—he could choose from among "The Girl from Frisco," "A Lesson from Life," "The Shielding Shadow," "The Trooper of Company K" ("with an all colored cast"), "Forbidden Fruit," "God's Half Acre," "The Sins of the City," or any of thirty-eight other films. And every theater offered a different show each night. One *Defender* reader in Mississippi expected State Street to be "heaven itself."[50]

In addition, the *Defender* bragged of playgrounds with "all modern equipment" and open access to all beaches along Lake Michigan (a claim accurate in a legal sense only). Baseball fans were repeatedly reminded not only that games between black teams took place nearly every day, in the "shadow of [the] White Sox," but also that Chicago's American Giants were the greatest black team in the country.[51] If black southerners had heard for years of the greater freedom to enjoy oneself in the North, they now had clear evidence that it was all true.

Southern white attempts to inhibit distribution of the *Defender* only assured blacks of its reliability. When many southern communities forced distribution of the *Defender* underground in 1918, blacks responded by going to extraordinary lengths to secure their newspapers. Copies were "folded into bundles of merchandise," or passed around surreptitiously. Even when whites succeeded in preventing distribution, blacks reopened the flow of information by writing directly to Abbott, who apparently passed along many of the letters to social agencies in Chicago.[52]

Observing that the *Defender* "voiced the unexpressed thoughts of many," Charles Johnson noted that the weekly "provided a very good substitute for the knowledge which comes through travel." The newspaper brought hope and direction to thousands who learned more about the northern alternative to southern oppression. "I bought a Chicago Defender," wrote a Memphis man, "and after reading it and seeing the golden opportunity I decided to leave this place at once." To black southerners who "saved [copies of the *Defender*] from the first I have received" or wrote Abbott that "your paper was all we had to go by so we are depending on you for farther advise," the information offered an opportunity to change their lives.[53]

The *Defender* did not limit itself to informing its southern readers of northern attractions and inviting them to Chicago. It also sought to convince them that the migration was a broad-based movement drawing from the entire South. In their copies of the *Defender*, Mississippians and Texans learned that Georgians were leaving in droves; rural people confirmed rumors of the depopulation of towns and cities. The restless but cautious were often stirred by the knowledge that so many others were going.

From its correspondents in scores of southern towns, the *Defender* received reports of migrants leaving the South and printed them under headlines which bragged "300 LEAVE FOR NORTH." Designed to inspire others to leave, these notices often included predictions: "There are so many leaving here that Waycross will be desolate soon." Local gossip correspondents regularly passed along news of mass or individual departures. During the winter of 1917 these items dominated the columns. "The great exodus has struck Talledega county," an Alabama agent reported in early March. A few weeks later it was an "epidemic" in Aberdeen, Mississippi. And any reader who still doubted the magnitude of movement learned from the Summit, Mississippi, column of April 7 that "twenty-four carloads passed through here last week."[54] Into the 1920s, these columns continued to be sprinkled with notices of local residents leaving for the North.

To complement these constant reminders of mass movement, the *Defender* launched a bandwagon by setting a specific date for a "Great Northern Drive"—May 15, 1917. For three months the *Defender* told its readers of an impending group departure on that date. The promotion, widely magnified into rumors of special trains with discount fares, aroused tremendous enthusiasm among *Defender* readers and their friends. Both the influence of the *Defender* and the stimulus of setting a specific date are suggested by the exceptionally large numbers arriving in northern cities during the week following May 15. Although the *Defender* misled readers who thought the "Great Northern Drive" was an organized enterprise, the promotion's impact suggests that many migrants did conceive of their actions as part of a mass movement. For many, like S. Adams of Houston, who wanted to "get in line with the rest," being part of a "movement" was easier than acting in isolation.[55]

Labeled a "black Joshua" by one historian of the Great Migration, Abbott has been credited by his biographer with having "single-handed[ly] . . . set the migration in motion."[56] Because significant migration had occurred before the *Defender* either publicized or supported the exodus, Abbott can hardly be accorded such exalted status, even if the propitious economic conditions created by World War I are taken for granted. He and his newspaper played a central role in the communications network that shaped and facilitated the Great Migration as a social movement. It voiced the discontents of black southerners, urged them to act rather than wait, informed them of opportunities, shaped images of the urban North, encouraged migration, and interpreted the exodus as a racial crusade. But it could not have had the influence it did if community leaders had not served as local correspondents and sales agents, if those who were able to read had not read it aloud, or if it had not been part of an even larger network.

Many local leaders in the black South reached conclusions similar to those expressed by Abbott and other black northerners and agreed that migration represented the best prospect for advancement. Their voices remained muffled, however, because many were afraid to speak loudly. A Newborn, Alabama, minister favored migration and wrote to the *Defender* for help for his departing parishioners. But he would not speak out in public for the movement or against the South. "As leaders," he wrote, "we are powerless for we dare not to resent such [treatment] or to show even the slightest disapproval." A railroad fireman in southern Mississippi who found biblical parallels for the migration told Charles Johnson that the movement lacked a Moses because "it is not safe to be a Moses." After hearing the same message repeatedly during his trip through the South in 1917, Charles Johnson concluded that "leaders who openly encouraged the exodus would be in personal danger." William Pickens, field secretary for the NAACP, reached the same conclusion, and when he gave to the Baltimore *Afro-American* a letter from a Mississippi minister strongly defending migration, he instructed the editors not to publish the writer's name. Aware of the dangers of openly advocating migration, many of these leaders resorted to subterfuge, indulging in the honored tradition of fooling whites by using what Johnson called "a unique method of presentation"—transmitting their message while Uncle Tomming for white consumption.[57] But whether masking their opinions with stereotyped facades or remaining silent in public, many influential black southerners contributed to the movement's reputation for being leaderless.

There were, however, many men and women who were not afraid to lead, to prod their friends and neighbors. Usually unknown outside their communities, these people occupied central positions within the information network that facilitated the spread of migration fever. Ministers, church deacons, *Defender* agents, letter writers, and others acted as grass-roots organizers of the movement by publicizing it and coordinating departures.

The dynamic element in this network was the influence of migrants already in the North, a factor which multiplied as the migration accelerated. Like European immigrants and white southerners who moved north and west, black southerners established migration chains linking North and South by means of kin and community relationships.[58] The first to leave a town often functioned as scouts for the whole community. Relatives and friends anxiously awaited reports of "how things 'broke' " in Chicago. Those unable to write even the simplest note could ask fellow roomers to compose their letters. With the arrival of a note declaring "everything pretty," or "Home ain't nothing like this," others made preparations to depart. These pioneers became, in the words of one Department of Labor analyst, "apostles of exodus to those remaining behind."[59]

Although many letters betrayed loneliness and homesickness for old friends and institutions (often the church), they did so within the context of a recitation of Chicago's attractions. Few letters expressed great disappointment, and in some cases recipients had other reports against which they could balance negative comments. Most correspondents informed friends and relatives that "Everything is just like they say, if not better." The impulse to paint glowing pictures might have sprung as much from a wish to impress the folks back home as from the desire to render an honest report. Exuberant letters were especially enticing, although they could lead to eventual disillusionment by inflating expectations. But even the man who warned his friend that "half you hear is not true," also informed him that "there some thing to see up here all the time." By reading letters from Chicago, black southerners learned about day-to-day life in the North. These messages communicated the excitement of urban life. A Hattiesburg, Mississippi, man read that his "partner" had just been to the ballpark: "I wish you could have been here to have been here to those games. I saw them and beleve me they was worth the money I pay to see them. T.S. and I went to see Sunday game witch was 7 to 2 White Sox and I saw Satday game 2 to 1 White Sox." An equally impressed woman wrote home of "one of the greatest revivals in the history of my life—over 500 people joined the church. We had a Holy Ghost shower." Outdoor leisure, the huge churches, the bright lights of State Street—all acquired immediacy and accessibility to restless black southerners reading letters from the North.[60]

Chicago letters provided concrete images of not only the attractions of the city, but also the freedom and privileges enjoyed in the North. The Ohio River had long symbolized freedom to black Americans; letters from northern cities lent contemporary substance to this tradition. A southerner might tear himself away more easily once he knew that his friend could "just begin to feel like a man" in Chicago where he "got some privilege My children are going to the same school with the whites and I don't have to umble to no one. I have registered—Will vote the next election and there isn't any 'yes sir' and 'no sir'—its all yes and no and Sam and Bill."[61] The advantages of racial equality—unthinkable in the South—were thus presented in unmistakably attainable and personal terms. Integrated schools, respect, the franchise: if his friend could acquire such privileges, so could he.

Mail from Chicago also documented the city's material advantages. One migrant reported inducing several friends to join him by sending "letters which represented wages as being enormous." Many correspondents provided concrete evidence of Chicago's economic opportunities by enclosing cash with their letters home.[62] *Defender* columnists in southern towns referred to migrants "sending the bacon home" from Chicago, and banks in the Deep South reported heavy deposits of drafts drawn on northern banks. Charles Johnson found many Mississippi wives, husbands, children, and parents regularly receiving substantial sums from the North in 1917. Along with encouraging migration, these remittances facilitated it by providing railroad fare or prepaid tickets.[63]

Not content to wait, many prospective migrants injected themselves into the communications network by cultivating contacts in the North. They wrote to churches, the *Defender*, the Urban League, friends, and relatives asking for information and aid. "I want you to write me what ar you doing and what ar you making and where is your son w—— and how do you think it would soot me up there," a Nashville resident wrote to a "dear friend" in Chicago; "Do you think that I could get a job up there if I would come up there where you are." Frequently these letters would cement old ties with news of home and reminders of bonds between writer and recipient. Before begging her old friend Mary to "tell me about the place," a Macon, Georgia, woman supplied an update on church events and community gossip, mentioning twenty-two individuals in her brief letter. It is impossible to discern how assiduously migrants responded to such letters, as some, like the man who reported receiving two per week from friends "anxious to come," could hardly answer them all.[64] But by helping migrants in Chicago to remain a part of their former communities, black southerners perpetuated old ties that now linked North and South.

More than any advertisement, agent, or publication, letters spoke to black southerners in their own language and addressed their major concerns. Like "America letters" to Europe during the half-century before World War I, these messages were circulated, read before large gatherings, and heatedly discussed.[65] A man who promised to tell his friends how he fared needed to write only one letter, which was then shared by all. A woman who received a jubilant letter from her husband in Chicago promptly showed it to her "closest friends"—ten of them. Another letter was rumored to have "enticed away over 200 persons." A letter to Georgia found its way to Mississippi where it was handed to a woman by her "husband's brother's wife." After arriving in Chicago she began to write urging others to follow. In this fashion the chain lengthened with every new migrant. In 1917, Johnson estimated that "fully one-half, or perhaps even more of those who left, did so at the solicitation of friends through correspondence."[66] This proportion probably increased as continuing migration swelled the ranks of letter-writers. Although some letters were probably part of a private correspondence—usually between family members—they also had a broad impact; that impact frequently occurred within the context of familiar patterns of group activity, including the exercise of influence by group leaders.

Less broadly influential but probably even more convincing was the information conveyed by travelers between North and South. Most of those black southerners who could offer firsthand knowledge of conditions in northern cities were likely to be prominent participants in the social affairs of their communities. Excursions to northern cities had permitted a few black southerners to see Chicago before the Great Migration. A handful of middle-class black southerners had sent their children North for schooling; the paucity and poor quality of secondary schools in the South made Chicago's Wendell Phillips High School especially attractive. As the possibilities for boarding children with relatives expanded during the migration, more families seized this opportunity. Other members of the southern black bourgeoisie gained exposure to Chicago while "summering" there. G. W. Mitchell, who lived in Chicago from 1907 through 1916, later recalled that in the period 1908–10, "excursions to the north during the summer months were in flower." Chicago's Half-Century of Negro Progress exhibition during the summer of 1915 included exhibits from most southern states and attracted perhaps as many as twenty-five thousand out-of-town visitors. During the war visiting became easier and more frequent, as railroads stimulated passenger traffic with special excursion fares and many black southerners could now stay with family in Chicago.[67]

Chicago attracted even more visitors to fraternal conventions and religious conferences, usually attended by people chosen to represent their communities or able to afford to finance their own journeys. Fraternal societies and churches, vital social institutions in the black South, played a connective role in the migration, first by drawing visitors North to see Chicago and then by providing migrants with links to institutions. Between 1912 and 1925, thousands of black Americans from communities throughout the country attended conventions in Chicago. The fifteen to twenty thousand delegates to the 1915 National Baptist Convention, representing 2,600,000 black Americans, carried home stories of the Windy City. Ministers of the Colored Methodist Episcopal Church, whose greatest strength lay in the South, did the same three years later. Masons, Knights Templar, and Elks all returned to southern lodges with information after large conventions in Chicago.[68]

Fraternal and religious conclaves not only brought southerners to Chicago; they showed visitors the city at its best, or at least its most exciting. Special State Street carnivals highlighted meetings of the National Negro Business League in 1912 and the Masons in 1916. On the eve of the Masons' gathering, the *Defender* noted that State Street "will be ablaze with electricity, fireworks, music."[69] Showing their southern comrades a good time, black Chicagoans sent them home with images that would be described and exaggerated in lodges and churches all over the South.

Like letter writing, visiting both fueled the momentum of migration and was itself stimulated by the movement. As more jobs became available in Chicago, southern teachers and college students traveled there for summer employment. Respected and widely connected through such activities as women's clubs, farmers' clubs, organizations for boys and girls, and school improvement leagues, these teachers could easily disseminate information upon their return. More broadly, as family networks branched northward, southerners increasingly ventured forth to find out for themselves, returning home with stories to tell in church, at the barber shop, and in other gathering places.[70]

Travelers southward similarly carried information through both informal and institutional connections. When Ethel Peacock graduated from Wendell Phillips High School, she decided to serve her people by teaching in a Florida country school district. Like nurses trained at Chicago's Provident Hospital, who "in turn take charge of colored hospitals throughout the South and educate other colored nurses," she provided black southerners with striking impressions of what blacks could attain in Chicago.[71] In a more transitory fashion, Rube Foster's American Giants baseball team symbolized Chicago's polish and prestige during its frequent barnstorming tours through the South.[72]

The most influential travelers were earlier migrants who returned home to visit, looking prosperous and urbane and bursting with wondrous tales of their exploits. Although most migrants used the mail to report their progress, many could not resist returning "just to tell how well they had done in the North." Others returned to attend weddings or funerals or to visit ailing family members. Local columns in the *Defender*, filled by 1917 with such items as "Mrs. Helen Scales, Chicago is visiting relatives and friends in Corinth, [Mississippi]," suggest the frequency with which these visits occurred and were noticed in the community. That same year, Charles Johnson found that in towns and cities throughout Mississippi, returnees were heavily influencing friends and relatives. A few of them might even have been "labor agents," he noted, perceiving a "strong suggestion of truth" in the suspicion that some who returned North with thirty or forty friends had been given funds by their employers in the North. But in most cases, visiting was primarily family oriented.[73]

Family visits provided concrete information, most likely from migrants who had been successful enough that they could flaunt their accomplishments. John Wesley Rule, a prosperous Mississippian, sold everything he owned after his son returned from Chicago in late 1916 with a considerable sum of money and the claim that in the North he "could stand up like a man and demand his rights." A decade later New Orleans teenager Mahalia Jackson "could hardly believe" her visiting uncle's stories of life in Chicago. Such information usually circulated rapidly around the community. A Meridian, Mississippi, woman, whom everyone had accused of lying in letters reporting two dollars daily earnings in the stockyards, returned home to visit. As news spread that she had been telling the truth, former skeptics began preparing to leave, certain that they were better wage earners than their former neighbor.[74] New clothes and rolls of bills entitled returnees to bragging rights while providing prospective migrants with convincing documentation of Chicago's rewards.

Chicagoans encouraged southern relatives to visit so they could see for themselves why they should leave the South. Southerners asked relatives in Chicago to visit so they could evaluate how those relatives "looked" before uprooting themselves and migrating North. Others who could not bring themselves to leave sent their children North, and by 1919 Chicago school officials were complaining of the number of southern black children living in Chicago with aunts and uncles.[75] Homes were also opened to newly arrived relatives, thereby eliminating one concern of cautious prospective migrants. Kinship, religious, and community ties were sufficiently flexible to permit separation and were strong enough both to draw people northward and to re-form in a new locale. Once reestablished in Chicago, these families, churches, and other social institutions acted as magnets to others still back home.[76]

As the migration grew, a continuous communication process mush-roomed, as some family members kept closely in touch, informed each other of opportunities, and persuaded relatives to join them in Chicago. This process often started with a male venturing North alone. Free trains usually carried only men, and many who paid their own transportation traveled without families because meager funds could finance only one fare.[77] Once employed in Chicago, this scout could begin to send for the family.

Like families, churches could provide North-South links based in a traditional, stable institution. Southern ministers occasionally preached in Chicago churches and then related their impressions to their home congregations. Through such visits, denominational con-nections, and the *Defender*, black southerners learned of Chicago's religious institutions, and many wrote to them asking for advice. In March 1917 Chicago's Bethlehem Baptist Association, headquartered in Olivet Baptist Church, advertised in the *Defender* that it would help newcomers find jobs and housing. Black southerners' faith in the *Defender*'s race consciousness, coupled with the familiarity of the church as a trusted institution, induced "hundreds" to write.[78] Grasping a connection that a letter to the Urban League or *Defender* could not draw upon, some supplicants appealed as fellow Baptists. W. M. Agnew of Aberdeen, Mississippi, addressing his plea to "Brothers," claimed "I am a Baptist member my mother has Ben the mother of the Baptist Church for 30 years."[79] Others who never wrote to Chi-cago churches could rely on them for initial connections by obtaining letters of transfer from their home ministers.

With migration beginning to draw away members from some southern churches, ministers prepared to follow their congregations. At an African Methodist Episcopal conference in Ensley, Alabama, in 1917, one minister reported losing fifty-two of his ninety-six members in the previous six months. "Bishop," he declared, "I just come up here to notify you that I'm getting ready to follow my flock."[80] In November of that year a pastor in Vicksburg, Mississippi, where churches had already lost a third to a half of their members, was try-ing to sell his property and follow his congregants to Chicago. In some cases a clergyman would visit his former deacons who, discontented with their lack of status in Chicago's churches, once again felt comfortable when he conducted a service for them. The deacons would then invite the minister to stay on and start a new church (usually in a storefront) in Chicago. Once the minister decided to follow the first migrants from his church northward, other members joined the trek. Like families, churches demonstrated their resilience by separating, re-forming in Chicago, and then attracting members still in the South.[81] The central actors in this process were likely to have exercised local leadership in the South, whether as deacons or as ministers.

Churches also functioned as centers of conversation and dissemination of information in the South. In this role they were supplemented by such other gathering places as poolrooms, grocery stores, and barber shops. In 1917, Charles Johnson found that the conversation in these social centers was "one of the chief stimuli" to migration. Men assembled regularly in grocery stores and barber shops, Johnson observed, to review all the instances of mistreatment and injustice which fell to their lot in the South. It was here also that letters from the North were read and fresh news on the exodus was first given out.[82]

Robert Horton's barber shop was one such establishment, and like Horton, most of the people who dominated discussion and organizing efforts were prominent in their communities. The reader of a letter from the North or the writer of a letter to the North, offering to a northern employer or employment agency the services of anywhere from a handful to more than one hundred "good hard working men," was probably better educated than many others in the community. Although many of the letters themselves reflect a smattering of education at best, one-third of all southern blacks were still classified in 1910 as illiterate by the United States Census.[83] Local representatives of the *Defender* might have commanded a degree of respect based upon their link to the trusted newspaper. Those who had visited the North possessed the authority of experience, of direct knowledge.

Innumerable other links touched individual black southerners, influencing and facilitating their movement North. Jazz musicians had their own network, as Chicago musicians would bring others North—usually from New Orleans or Memphis—to join their bands. When Chicago became the home of black recording companies in the 1920s, musicians naturally gravitated there. Seasonal workers in lumber and turpentine camps, sawmills, railroad labor camps, and fertilizer plants learned of northern jobs and living conditions from older men who had traveled North or had heard stories. Young men, often at their first nonfarm employment, thus received their initial exposure to other opportunities. Business and professional men followed their clientele, especially in communities suffering the heaviest losses.[84] Some people were drawn North by the overflowing trains passing through their towns or outside their windows. Others were stirred by poems and songs. "Bound for the Promised Land," "Farewell, We're Good and Gone," "Northward Bound," and "The Land of Hope" made the rounds of black communities in the Deep South, drawing on the importance of oral tradition in communication within the group.[85]

The most active organizers of migratory activity, however, formed new organizations—migration clubs. Created to take advantage of railroad group rates, the clubs constituted the organizational expression of the movement. Often based in existing social cliques, they served also to stimulate migration by permitting the migrant to be part of a group effort, thus easing the trauma of separation, the long journey, and perhaps resettlement as well. Most club leaders appear to have been men and women who owned property or businesses.[86]

At first, the clubs developed as a complement to the activities of labor agents. Where labor agents had been active in providing free passes, clubs often consisted of the families of men who had been recruited. Where agents' activities had been curtailed by white authorities, the clubs organized those who had not been among the lucky few to secure free passage. Some leaders reportedly told recruits that they had been authorized by a labor agent to form a "Tourist Club"; but characteristically, nobody ever actually reported seeing the agent, and it is likely that a few of these club leaders probably took advantage of the labor-agent folklore to sway those who were reluctant to leave without some indication that a job awaited them. Most clubs were formed at the instigation of a "captain"; few captains found that anyone had to be persuaded.[87]

To form a club, a man or woman would usually discuss the prospect with friends and neighbors and then arrange a convenient departure date. In many cases the leader would also contact friends in the North to receive the group. The size of clubs varied. In Jackson, Mississippi, most included forty to seventy-five members; in Hattiesburg, membership ranged from ten to eighty. Because the minimum number required for group railroad discounts was ten, nine members were sometimes compelled to contribute to the fare of an impecunious tenth associate; this practice further suggests the importance of group ties binding together club members. And, because of the sizable sums involved, the leader had to be someone trustworthy.[88]

Assembling large groups, making arrangements, and handling substantial amounts of other people's money, these club leaders tended to be individuals with status in their community. An Ellisville,

Mississippi, woman who "urged everyone to leave," and then organized a club and bought the tickets, owned two houses in town; her
husband appears to have been a businessman. In Hattiesburg, Mrs.
A. Holloway, who along with her husband owned five houses, organized a club of twenty-one. R. S. Horton, a Hattiesburg *Defender*
agent, barber and church deacon, led a group of forty. In some cases,
however, the migration upset former patterns of leadership. One Mississippi woman who organized a club was sufficiently prosperous to
own her own home, chickens, and a cow, but otherwise had no claim
to prominence. The local pastor opposed the movement, but she and
her followers ignored him.[89]

Whether those who showed friends and neighbors Chicago letters
and organized migration clubs were locally influential (as Charles
Johnson concluded during his Mississippi survey in 1917) or just
people who wanted to give others a chance to get in on a good thing,
they were not the Washingtonian educators or business leaders who
had been traditionally regarded as representatives of the black South.
The number of women involved is especially striking, given the overwhelmingly male character of the recognized regional leadership.
Abetted temporarily by the labor agents, these individuals organized
and promoted the Great Migration. The movement drew upon individual initiative, but it did not emerge full-blown among a disorgan-
ized, leaderless mass. Northern leaders provided information and
assistance. A few prominent black southerners encouraged the exodus, even if not always loudly. Most important, local activists—
Defender agents, club organizers, and others who played major roles
in the operation of the network—provided the movement with grass-
roots leadership. For the numerous migrants affiliated with clubs or
other groups, the decision to leave was facilitated by the knowledge
that they were not going alone. Indeed, sermons, community discussion and debate, and a "general feeling that it must be [the] best thing
since everybody was doing it," established the social context within
which most made the decision to migrate.[90] Black southerners ignored
the threats and admonitions of whites, as well as the reservations and
objections expressed by traditional leaders, and organized themselves and their neighbors to facilitate their journeys. Living in a society that sought to render them as dependent and powerless as
possible, they acquired a new source of power over their lives—
information that a better alternative not only existed but beckoned.
They used the information and the network to plan and execute
the process of their migration North, as well as to determine their
destination.

4

"Bound for the Promised Land"

Busy caring for her elderly mother in early 1917, an Ellisville, Mississippi, woman paid little attention to the "mild stir about the North." Her husband left for Chicago in March, but few others in town were "taking seriously" the rumors concerning the migration. In May, however, a friend breathlessly returned from New Orleans, buzzing with news of "the rush there to get out of the city." Telling her of the "great promise of the North," he reviewed the reasons people were giving for their departure. From her window she could see the northbound express trains "loaded with Negroes." She wrote to her husband, who confirmed that conditions in Chicago were "beyond belief." Unable to sell their property, she left anyway, organizing a club of twenty-six which accompanied her in mid-June. At the railroad station a policeman informed her group that they could not leave without permission. For the first time in her life she "talked back to a white person." Two days later she was in Chicago.[1]

However idiosyncratic, this woman's experience highlights salient features of the migratory process. Many other migrants were as cautious as she and did not leave until they had corroborated early rumors. Others left as soon as the first piece of information reached town. Some made careful plans, writing to friends, relatives, or social agencies in Chicago; others left in haste, pausing only to raise money to purchase a railroad ticket. Some families migrated together; others temporarily separated. If some migrants left without incident, thousands of others had to evade obstacles created by southern whites reacting to the threat to their labor supply. Many black southerners journeyed directly to the North; others sojourned in southern cities. Not all migrants asserted themselves as immediately or forcefully as did the Ellisville woman when she "talked back" to a southern policeman; but most did something during the voyage or soon after arrival in the North to certify, if only symbolically, their sense of renewed hope. Whether they moved out of the Jim Crow car after the train crossed the Mason-Dixon line or sat next to a white rider in a Chicago streetcar, the migrants—sometimes quietly, sometimes exuberantly— tested and welcomed their new status.

Many black southerners shared the Ellisville woman's uncertainty about the North. Despite the "sudden revelation of a new world" pictured by labor agents and rumors, the wisdom of an equally sudden decision to leave was questionable.[2] Many people were not prepared to abandon home and community until they could learn more about what the North might offer them. Where would they go? What would they do? Until they could secure answers, many cautious black southerners chose to stay home.

Some prospective migrants were not particular about where they went, as long as the destination was "any where but the south." Ready to go "anywhere north," one New Orleans man reasoned that "the worst place there is better than the best place here." Geography and rail routes helped many black southerners make a decision based on accessibility, and most moved due north. Yet such factors were hardly definitive: blacks leaving Bullock City, Alabama, selected seventeen different northern destinations in eight states. Even Canadian cities experienced an influx of black southerners during the Great Migration.[3] The availability of economic opportunities also influenced the choice, although jobs were available in most northern cities. The decision to go to Chicago, rather than to New York, Detroit, or one of many smaller northern communities, rested on a variety of factors, whose impact changed over time. The first from an area to leave for Chicago probably chose the city because of its position at the head of the Illinois Central and its particularly high visibility in the black South. Chicago's black baseball teams, its reputation as a center of black business enterprise, and its reputation based on visits from conventioneers, as well as mail-order catalogues which were found in homes in rural and urban communities, all complemented the monumental importance of the *Defender*. There were jobs in the city's mills and packinghouses, but there were jobs elsewhere too. Those who chose to go to Chicago went because they knew about those jobs and that particular city. This knowledge multiplied as migrants settled in Chicago. It is likely that eventually most black southerners who decided to go North—regardless of why they made that particular decision—chose a destination based largely on the presence of kin and townsfolk. George Ward, who migrated to Chicago from Laurel, Mis-

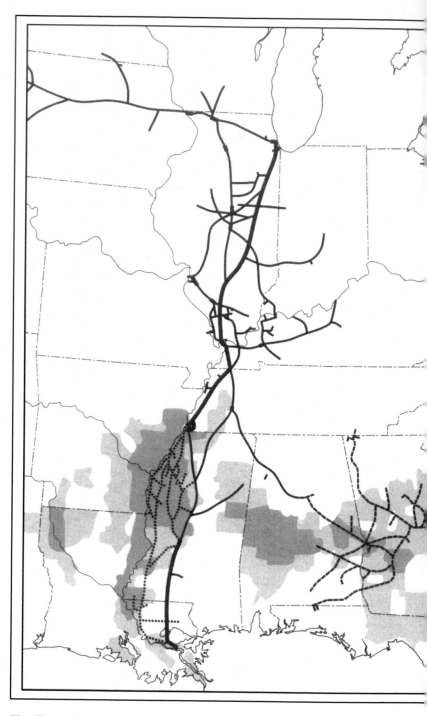

The Illinois Central Railroad system leading from the South to Chicago.

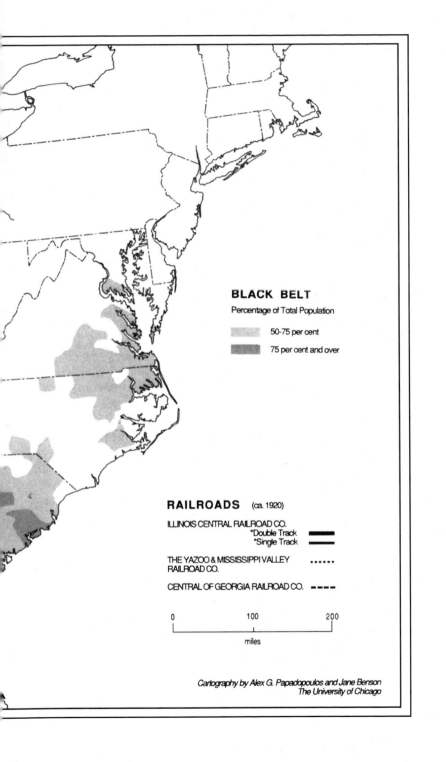

BLACK BELT

Percentage of Total Population

50-75 per cent

75 per cent and over

RAILROADS (ca. 1920)

ILLINOIS CENTRAL RAILROAD CO.
*Double Track
*Single Track

THE YAZOO & MISSISSIPPI VALLEY
RAILROAD CO.

CENTRAL OF GEORGIA RAILROAD CO.

0   100   200

miles

Cartography by Alex G. Papadopoulos and Jane Benson
The University of Chicago

sissippi, had relatives there and explained that "where there is the biggest bunch of birds that's where I go." However alien the city's landscape might be, it would at least have familiar faces.[4]

Drawing upon the information network that was bringing news South, prospective migrants made specific inquiries about Chicago. A few, planning to come North only after securing employment, placed advertisements in the *Defender*'s Situations-Wanted column. Others wrote letters in response to employers' advertisements. A man from Savannah, Georgia, said he would "come right way" only "if this application is satisfactory."[5] Chicago employment agencies advertising in the *Defender* made this process easier, stating in their notices what jobs were available and telling "out of town correspondents [to] enclose stamps for reply." Chicago's Bethlehem Baptist Association, which also advertised in the *Defender*, received "hundreds" of letters similar to that of Hattie L. Smith of Macon, Georgia, who was "planning to come to Chicago sometime this month providing that I can get an ans. from this I will thank you to advise me as to the price of board per week, in a nice place + also about work."[6]

Most people who sought institutional assistance wrote to the Chicago Urban League. During the first year of mass migration, the League received more than two thousand letters inquiring about the availability of jobs. Some merely asked what jobs were available; others stated a preference for certain types of employment and cited qualifications.[7] By writing letters to these institutions or to relatives and friends, prospective migrants substantiated rumors and made plans.

For some, however, not even positive replies to their inquiries were sufficient to induce them to pull up stakes. They had to see for themselves. Those who could afford it took advantage of special railroad excursion rates from Memphis and New Orleans. But even the majority who could not, relied heavily on the words of such travelers, along with the "scouts" who left small communities, "promising," as Charles Johnson observed in Mississippi, "to inform those behind of the actual state of affairs." Although Johnson referred to their actions immediately before leaving as "reckless," these men and women were acting cautiously, not leaving until pioneers had gone ahead to survey the terrain and make arrangements.[8]

Many migrants did leave "recklessly." Observers often exaggerated this phenomenon, but there is little doubt that some black southerners quickly made up their minds and departed hastily. In Mississippi, Johnson visited towns where drivers and teamsters had left wagons standing in the street. Similar departures occurred on farms, where men "left their fields half plowed."[9]

In most cases, decisions made on the spur of the moment seem to have been prompted by an urge to jump on the bandwagon, people having heard that "thousands of Negroes" were leaving the South at once. Clem Woods, who had been resisting the impulse to leave Mississippi, grew more restless with every departure. Finally, as a northbound train from New Orleans passed through town one night, a man yelled from one of the coaches, "Good-bye, bo, I'm bound for the promised land." Woods climbed aboard. In Brookhaven, Mississippi, a railroad section gang watched the trains pass through and dropped their tools "on the spot," not even bothering to collect their pay.[10] These departures might not have been as precipitous as they seemed. Many migrants had already pondered the decision and even made preparations, but were merely waiting for an opportune moment to depart. That was the case in Augusta, Georgia, where a *Defender* correspondent reported people "preparing to leave on 12 hours' notice," but waiting until they had first obtained leads on job opportunities.[11]

The time lag between a decision to leave and actual departure often depended upon how long it took to accumulate the cash to purchase a ticket. Passenger rates were two cents per mile at the end of 1916 and rose 34 percent over the next four years. In 1918, a migrant traveling via New Orleans had to raise approximately twenty dollars for a ticket to Chicago. Purchasing tickets was especially problematic for sharecroppers who, perpetually in debt to their landlords, could go years without seeing any cash. On one South Georgia plantation, two old men employed a traditional method of solving this problem— playing on a white man's paternalistic self-image. The landlord's paltry monthly allowance of twenty-five dollars for food and clothing made saving difficult if not impossible. Somehow, perhaps with the aid of labor agents, or by sending sons to work in turpentine or lumber camps and daughters to work in a nearby town, the families on the plantation had managed to depart. Old "Uncle Ben" and "Uncle Joe" were left behind to face the absentee landlord on his weekly visit. Sorrowfully informing the landlord of the other tenants' perfidy, Ben and Joe proclaimed their unending loyalty, pledged to care for the unworked crops, and requested money to fill some immediate needs. Impressed with their devotion and thankful that he could still rely on these faithful retainers, the landlord satisfied their request. As soon as he left, they headed North with their stake; their bags had already been packed.[12]

Most people managed to obtain their railroad tickets without recourse to manipulation of traditional racial roles. During the early days of the migration some were fortunate enough to encounter "pass riders"—labor agents who provided free transportation. When southern authorities curtailed the agents' activities and forced rail-roads to cease issuing free passes, migrants unable to afford regular fares began forming clubs and obtaining standard group rates. The size of these clubs and the elaborate arrangements their leaders made with the railroads indicate that the numerous migrants who joined them left neither thoughtlessly nor in haste.

Many dissatisfied black southerners, however, were unable to pur-chase a railroad ticket under any arrangement. George Thomas, who "wanted to better his condition but [recognized] that he never would have been able to leave if he had waited to get the money to ride on a passenger train," rode freight cars from Georgia to Chicago. This was hardly an alternative for most men and women. In desperation and hope they turned to the Promised Land for help. The *Defender*, the Chicago Urban League, and the city's churches were deluged with requests for railroad fares. A Pensacola, Florida, man wrote the *De-fender* that he "would leave tomorrow," if the newspaper could find him a job with a company that would "send me a transportation."[13] From Laurel, Mississippi, a man told the Chicago Urban League that "i am redy to come at once and i have not got money to pay our train fair and if you will send after us i will sure pay you your money back." Chicago's Bethlehem Baptist Association was asked to "kindly send me a ticket at once," and for "a suitcase to put things in."[14] Some of the requests came from people who had accumulated as much as they could, but not enough to make the trip. A Mississippian wrote from Brookhaven that he and his friends could leave "if the R.R. Co. would run a low rate excursion." A Texan who felt that "a man ought to help another when he try to help his self," wrote that he could pay half his fare and would work off the other half.[15] Such requests brought meager results, as these institutions could hardly afford such subsi-dies, and most Chicago employers found it more economical to re-cruit among migrants who had already arrived.

To raise money for train fare and a start in Chicago, some migrants tried to sell their belongings before they left the South. One Mis-sissippian, who had almost enough cash, sold some of his clothing to make up the difference. Young single workers, who might have found possessions an encumbrance, had to raise only a small sum, with only their own fares to consider.[16] Families, however, had to raise sub-stantially more if they intended to travel together. Those fortunate enough to own a house, or even a significant amount of furniture, often tried to sell it to pay for the trip. This was no easy task, as the magnitude of the movement could deplete the ranks of potential buy-ers, especially in such places as Carroll County, Mississippi, where the exodus was set in motion by whitecappers; there, migrants left behind all they could not carry, because few blacks remained to buy their property. Where whites sought to halt migration, they impeded the accumulation of cash by refusing to buy property from blacks.[17]

Whether a family sought to sell property to accumulate railroad fare or merely to recapture its investment, it suffered heavy losses. In Jackson, Mississippi, a man who had paid off seven hundred dollars on his one-thousand dollar house sold out for one hundred dollars. Gulfport homeowners sacrificed five-hundred dollar houses for one hundred fifty dollars. Some, unable to sell at all, either left their houses vacant or allowed them to be auctioned for taxes. At least one-fourth of the approximately fifty Mississippi migrants interviewed in Chicago by Charles Johnson in 1917 had been either unable to sell their property or had disposed of it at a substantial loss.[18] This property included both real estate and furniture. Frantic efforts to sell furniture in a depressed market enhanced the image of the migration as a movement based on unconsidered impulse. In one southern city, the second-hand shops began to run out of floor space, and people abandoned complete bedroom sets for only two dollars. A migrant from Decatur, Alabama, described the haste with which people left during the year preceding September 1917: "You could see hundreds of houses where mattresses, beds, wash bowls and pans were thrown around the back yard after the people got through picking out what they wanted to take along." They apparently did not even bother to try to sell what was left. Migrants reluctant to absorb such losses could leave personal property that could not be easily carried on a train in the care of friends or relatives. In Jackson, Mississippi, some migrants simply locked up their houses and left the key with neighbors.[19]

Many families resolved the problem of raising capital by having one member go North and subsequently send for the others. "The mens left first and the womens followed them," recalled James Turner of his home town in South Carolina during the Great Migration. This strategy not only eased the financial strain but permitted a cautious approach. "I am a maride man an hav a famly off 5," wrote one man asking the Chicago Urban League for transportation north; "if you cant sen for all send 2 one for me and my brother he live with me he is 18 yers old then i can arang for the rest after i get out there." A Pensacola, Florida, man intended "to come up there to see the place & then latter on send for family."[20] One Chicago black minister reported in March 1917 that "most of the arrivals now are men who have left their families behind until they can become settled." Numerous southern correspondents for the *Defender* reported subsequent reunions, in notices like the one from Hammond, Louisiana, stating that "Mrs. Viola O'neal left Sat. for Chicago to join her husband A. R." or, from Rome, Georgia, "Mrs. Gertrude Jones Dukis has gone to Chicago to join her husband."[21]

The apparent frequency of such separations led some black southerners to fear that the exodus was disrupting black family life. "C.V.B.," a *Defender* reader from Algiers, Louisiana, castigated men who left behind "a daughter here, a sister, wife or mother there, helpless and unprotected in this modern Sodom and Gomorrah, as far as the honor and virtue of Colored women is concerned." Temporary separation of nuclear family members, however, was nothing new to black southerners; married men and older sons had often performed seasonal labor away from home in turpentine and lumber camps. Furthermore, Charles Johnson's 1917 Chicago interviews and his field notes from his Mississippi investigation that same year corroborate other evidence that few people were left alone. In Promiseland, South Carolina, men left "their families behind in the safety and security they knew to be there until they were established in the cities," according to the historian of that community. This flexibility "afforded internal stability to families otherwise dislocated by radical change." A Louisiana migrant who wanted "to get my wife and children place until I can send for them," intended to "place them with my father over in Pass Christian Miss" until he could afford to bring them to Chicago. Aunts, uncles, parents, or in-laws were often stationed at each end of the migratory path, welcoming a family member entering Chicago or succoring those temporarily left behind in the South. Extended kinship ties not only facilitated migration, but helped to check whatever centrifugal pressures family division during migration might have produced.[22]

Some men deserted their wives and families; other families failed to survive the strain of migration. In some cases the departure of a husband or wife probably reflected already existing tensions. On the whole, however, Afro-American families—like those of immigrants from abroad—adapted their traditions to the demands of migration. The repeated *Defender* references to women leaving to join their husbands and the readiness with which families interviewed by Johnson temporarily separated and later reunited suggest that although departure split families apart, it hardly weakened ties. In the summer of 1917, a United States Department of Labor observer found a "consensus of opinion" in Georgia that the bulk of the migration comprised families going North to join men who had left during the previous year. Black family structure was not a victim of the

Great Migration; rather, its flexibility and strength anchored the movement.[23]

Not all migrants were willing to divide their families, even temporarily. A New Orleans man acknowledged that "having a wife and children to support [I] couldnt very well leave on a railroad pass as I hate to leave my family behind." Requesting free transportation, a Jacksonville, Florida, man promised that his wife and children also would work if someone could send enough for the whole family. Others writing for free transportation often took care to tell prospective employers or placement agencies of the qualifications of each member of the family.[24]

Whether they temporarily separated from families or traveled north with family intact, migrants often found it difficult to sever ties to their old homes. Until 1915, most southern black migrants had moved only short distances, usually to the nearest city or into an adjoining county, and thus had maintained connections to their former homes. Migration to the North, however, involved a more definitive separation. During arguments in gathering places in Mississippi communities, people questioned the wisdom of breaking up homes and abandoning land that had become productive only after "years of back-breaking toil."[25] Emmett Scott might have overstated blacks' devotion to "the sacred soil of the Sunny Southland, [where] his parents and relatives lie buried," but such attachments did complicate decisions to leave. Regardless of the oppression suffered there, the South had indeed been the home of black Americans for generations. More important than the land, however, were attachments to people. For this reason, perhaps, some men and women who were among the first to leave began "shying off" from their friends during the days preceding their departure.[26]

As the migration mushroomed into a mass movement, leaving one's community became not only easier, but almost imperative to many people who were emotionally or financially dependent on that community. "If I stay here I will go crazy," wrote "Mary B" in May 1917 to her friend who had already gone to Chicago. Like many others, she had seen her friends go North, leaving behind vacant houses and empty church pews. In Greenville, Mississippi, Charles Johnson found two hundred houses abandoned by migrants; in Jackson, two streets were completely deserted. Churches in Greenwood, Mississippi, lost a third of their members among the six hundred blacks who had left by autumn 1917. In Perry County, Mississippi, the school for black children did not open because the teacher had left for Chicago.[27] As familiar faces and institutions disappeared, many black southerners must have shared the sentiments of a woman in a small Mississippi town whose black residents had seen half their number leave within a year: "If I stay here any longer I'll go wild. Every time I go home I have to pass house after house of all my friends who are in the North and prospering. I've been trying to hold on here and keep my little property. There ain't enough people here I know now to give me a decent burial."[28]

Not only had friends and acquaintances departed, but new people had moved in, as blacks from the surrounding districts began to filter into cities and towns, sometimes to fill the migrants' jobs, but often as an initial stage on their own journeys north. In Chicago a Meridian woman received letters from back home reporting that life in Meridian was "dull," with nobody around anymore but "strangers," as "country people" were moving in. A woman in Jackson told her sister-in-law in Chicago that there was no one left except strangers from rural Mississippi and Alabama. The ties that bound these women to their communities had been broken by the migration.[29]

Black businessmen, dependent on their communities for financial survival, underwent similar experiences, as their customers abandoned them for the North. As early as April 1917, a Pensacola, Florida, barber decided to go to Chicago because "all the Trade is gone North & West." That same month an insurance salesman in Selma, Alabama, complained that "the great exodus of the colored people from the south has caused my work to lapse to an extent, so much so until I am unable to get a living out of it." Like the pastors who followed their congregations to Chicago, scores of black business and professional men followed their clientele.[30] The migration, clearly not dominated by "floating young men," as some have suggested, took its toll on the social fabric of southern black communities. Occupational and financial ties, no less than personal ones, weakened as the exodus altered the composition of those communities.

Despite the changes that had loosened ties to their communities, many migrants must have felt ambivalent about leaving. To the extent that they did, their final experiences in the South could easily have stiffened their resolve and reassured them of the wisdom of their decision. In towns and cities throughout the South, the sight of police trying to prevent departures dominated migrants' parting views of home. Greenville, Mississippi, police dragged blacks from trains. At Brookhaven, white authorities sidetracked a car for three days before letting it proceed. Thus, for many the final image of the South was not an emotional farewell from friends and relatives at the railroad station, but a traumatic encounter with a white South reluctant to lose its labor force. One group's last impression of its home in Georgia was the arrest of two hundred blacks waiting for the next northbound train in Savannah's Union Station.[31]

Before reaching a train station, many sharecroppers virtually had to escape from the plantation. Often held perpetually in debt by landlords who juggled accounts and made certain that a tenant's crop never brought more money than the landlord had advanced over the previous year, sharecroppers could not simply walk out on their obligations. Nearly all tenants were likely to be in debt to a landlord or merchant until "settlement time" at the end of the year. Whether or not a creditor kept books honestly, the departure of a debtor before the harvest was likely to leave a crop worthless in the field and an uncollectable debt secured by that same crop. "If he [a tenant] goes away," one planter remarked, "I just go and get him." Headed for Chicago, a sharecropper on Bill McGuire's two-thousand-acre Mississippi plantation managed to overcome the constant surveillance only by telling an overseer that he wanted to take his family to a circus.[32]

Even in towns and cities, blacks interested in northward migration had to take precautions. Like activists in the earlier Liberia movement, who masked intentions by giving emigrationist clubs such names as "the Young Men's Organization," those who met to debate or organize migration North exercised discretion. In Laurel, Mississippi, prospective migrants held secret meetings. In Lutcher, Louisiana, they would "whisper this around among our selves because the white folks are angry now because the negroes are going north." Black southerners who wrote to the *Defender* for information or assistance stressed confidentiality, many ending with the request, "Do not publish." Unwilling to disclose their plans, many migrants either left work without warning or gave their employers only a few hours notice. Not only could notification of an employer provide white authorities with clues regarding a possible mass departure, but it could be taken as an unacceptably aggressive statement of dissatisfaction. Even when whites did hear of an impending departure, some migrants would respond as tactfully as one Hattiesburg man, who masked his anger by carelessly musing that he just wanted to go, with no particular aim, and only to "see" the North.[33]

Since white attempts to stop blacks from leaving towns usually focused on the railroad station, migrants sometimes had to employ one final evasive tactic in order to leave. Twenty people leaving Macon, Georgia, avoided a confrontation with police by boarding the train seven miles up the track at Holden. Those leaving Greenville, Mississippi, walked twelve miles to Leland for the same reason. In Hattiesburg, where police thought they had outsmarted the migrants by keeping them away from the ticket office and then arresting anyone who tried to board a train without a ticket, blacks swung onto the train as it rolled out of town.[34]

Whether a migrant had walked miles to get to a railroad station, had evaded the harassment of police in the station and on the platform, or had met no obstacles at all and perhaps had even been seen off by friends, climbing aboard the train constituted a meaningful step toward a promising future.[35] The railroad itself had long represented to black Americans an opportunity for movement and change limited only by the seemingly infinite path of the tracks. In 1915, black laborers in Andalusia, Alabama, sang of its powers:

> When a woman takes the blues
> She tucks her head and cries;
> But when a man catches the blues,
> He catches er freight and rides.[36]

To teenager Langston Hughes of Kansas, who in 1915 would "walk down to the Santa Fe station and stare at the railroad tracks," the mystique even included a specific destination, as "the railroad tracks ran to Chicago and Chicago was the biggest town in the world to me, much talked of by the people in Kansas."[37] In addition, the elevated status of Pullman porters in black communities enhanced the railroad's importance as a symbol of upward mobility. Combined with the powerful image of the North as the Promised Land, the railroad assumed even greater significance. Its mythology harmonized with the migrants' dream of bettering their condition.

Departure was thus a difficult yet liberating process. Even as they left, some migrants shared Richard Wright's recognition that he "was leaving the South to fling myself into the unknown." The *Defender* reflected upon "black workmen [who] left the South with trembling and fear. They were going—they didn't know where—among strange people, with strange customs. The people who claimed to know best how to treat them painted frightful pictures of what would befall the migrators if they left the land of cotton and sugar cane."[38] Despite the uncertainties many, like Wright, expected that in Chicago they "could live with a little less fear." Migrants riding the Yazoo and Mississippi Railroad one Friday morning in February 1921 were readily reminded of the fear they were escaping, as the body of a black man swung lifeless from a tree alongside the railroad track. These migrants must have shared Gordon Parks' reaction as he left southern Kansas a few years later, aware that he was leaving behind "a doom. . . . For although I was departing from this beautiful land, it would be impossible ever to forget the fear, hatred and violence that Negroes had suffered upon it. It was all behind me now."[39]

Many migrants were unable to leave it all behind immediately. Although some journeyed directly to the North, others stopped in southern towns and cities. Blacks living on plantations might move to a nearby town after cotton picking ended in November or December and prepare to leave for the North in the spring. Many migrants, especially those living in areas served by the Illinois Central Railroad, were able to board Chicago-bound trains in the Deep South, but the majority had to make their way to a railroad hub such as Birmingham, New Orleans, Nashville, or Memphis. At Grand Central Station in Memphis, for example, a migrant headed for Chicago could transfer from any one of eight southern railroads to the Illinois Central.[40] In the Mississippi Delta, the migratory chain was lengthened by blacks from the nearby hill country moving onto plantations, to replace tenants who had gone to towns or directly to the North. Some of these "hill people," too, eventually would make their way north.[41] Thus, the longest trail might have started on a one-mule farm in the hill region and included stays of varying lengths in a plantation settlement, southern town, southern railroad center, and finally the North.

Migrants who tarried in a southern town or city usually did so because they could afford to go no farther. In the earliest stages of the exodus, when free passes were thought to be available in large cities, many migrants made their way to such places as Birmingham, Jackson, Memphis, or New Orleans in hopes of securing a free ticket to Chicago. Trying to arrange transportation at these points was considered by most to be safer than sending and receiving letters on a plantation or in a small village. With free transportation disappearing long before black southerners ceased believing in its existence, many found themselves stranded in cities, unable to proceed until they could accumulate enough money to finance the rest of the journey. Thousands of others were less naive, but considered a southern city—especially one in a border state—a convenient stopping place, either to earn enough to continue north or to learn the ways of the city and acquire some urban job skills.[42]

Work was not difficult to find in most southern cities, which had already begun losing their black labor force to northward migration. Hattiesburg, Mississippi, a large lumber center, and by 1917 the site of a United States Army cantonment, had been "almost depopulated of Negroes and repopulated again." Newcomers had little trouble finding jobs that would pay enough to allow them to follow the twenty-five hundred blacks who had already left the city for Chicago by late 1917. In Nashville, a convenient way station for migrants from most parts of the South, a severe shortage of young and middle-aged black males created job opportunities for even the most unskilled laborers; by June 1918, most of the city's black workers were recent arrivals from rural areas.[43]

For many the first move, entailing an intermediate adjustment to a southern city, rendered the final step less intimidating. Yet migrants probably learned little in southern cities that would be of much help in Chicago. Except in a few cities—notably Nashville and Birmingham—they could not secure jobs similar to those they would find in Chicago's packinghouses and steel mills. Even the border cities were sufficiently southern in their racial mores to offer no preparation for the impersonal, uncertain patterns of a northern city. In addition, most southern cities confined their black population to areas that were more rural than urban. Paved streets, running water, electric lights, sewers, and police and fire protection were either nonexistent or meager. The number of families with livestock suggests further the rural aspects of such neighborhoods. In small cities such as Pass Christian, Mississippi, where one observer noted that the railroad "does not disturb the country-like quiet," streets were unnamed and houses unnumbered. Even in larger cities in the South, blacks often lived amid what Monroe Work described as late as 1923 as "country conditions."[44]

Most northbound migrants, however, did not stay long enough to learn very much about the towns and cities that they regarded as little more than stopping points on the way to the final destination. Employers in border cities complained that black labor turnover far exceeded rates in northern cities, suggesting that many workers stayed only long enough to be able to leave. Most families who came from the surrounding countryside to Leland, Mississippi, to board the train, remained in town for only two or three weeks. The layover was even shorter for those migrants from rural Georgia and Alabama who bought tickets for Columbus, Georgia, and generally took the next train out, usually to Chicago. Southern cities offered jobs, but not freedom; even Cincinnati was considered "too southern" by many migrants who changed trains there en route to Chicago, Detroit, or Cleveland.[45]

Whether a migrant had stopped in a southern city or migrated directly to the North, a Jim Crow train provided a final reminder of what was being left behind. Limited to whatever space was available in the "Negro car," migrants often rode great distances standing in crowded aisles.[46] As a rule, these cars were attached either to the tender or baggage car, with the accompanying fumes and dirt, or to the end of the train. Even the more privileged migrants able to afford first-class Jim Crow fares suffered what Arthur Mitchell in 1919 described as "a horrible night ride. The colored women have one end of a smoker, separated from smoking white men by a partition that rises only part of the way from the floor toward the ceiling of the car. All of the smoke and fumes and some of the oaths come over."[47] Nor was there any place on the train (or in some of the stations) for black people to eat. Louis Armstrong, who came from New Orleans to Chicago in 1922, later recalled that "colored persons going North crammed their baskets full of everything but the kitchen stove." People were crammed as well. Mary Fluornoy, traveling to Chicago from Anniston, Alabama, found it difficult to breathe: "You couldn't get no air. . . . It was crowded." Nevertheless, migrants did all they could to maintain their spirits, including chalking on the side of the railroad cars such slogans as "Farewell—We're Good and Gone," "Bound for the Promise Land," and "Bound to the Land of Hope."[48]

As their trains sped northward, migrants looked forward to their first opportunity to put aside the way of life symbolized by the very conditions they experienced during the trip. Seventeen-year-old Matthew Ward from southwest Tennessee hoped that he would be able to see the Mason-Dixon line, which he and his traveling companion had expected to be marked by a row of trees. Although he was disappointed, he moved into another car when someone told him they were crossing into the North and searched until he found a seat beside a white man. A party of migrants from Handsboro and Gulfport, Mississippi, celebrated the event by enjoying a meal in the dining car. Others were more demonstrative. While crossing the Ohio River, many migrants prayed and sang songs of deliverance. A woman from Hattiesburg claimed that the atmosphere changed as they crossed the river and the air was "lighter," allowing her to breathe more easily. Having crossed what the *Defender* referred to as the Styx, migrants felt that they were embarking on a new life. In honor of the occasion, one group of men stopped their watches.[49]

As the train approached Chicago, the migrants' hope and excitement began to mix with awe, trepidation, and sometimes disappointment. Most railroad routes passed through the steel towns lying south and east of Chicago, offering initial views dominated by the gray pall that usually hung over the mills and the rickety houses of Gary and South Chicago.[50] To those arriving at night, the sight could have been particularly impressive and disorienting, as the fiery smokestacks never rested, denying the natural rhythms of night and day that ruled agricultural labor.

Finally the train rolled into one of Chicago's railroad depots. Migrants fortunate enough to have someone to meet them might have been unsettled by the crowds, but were soon reassured by the sight of a familiar face. The same network that stimulated and facilitated

A family arriving in Chicago from the rural South (source: CCRR, *Negro in Chicago*, 92).

migration by sending information South now assisted migrants upon their arrival. "Let me know what day you expect to leave and over what road, and if I don't meet you I will have some one there to meet you and look after you until I see you," wrote one woman to a member of her former church in Mississippi. Some migration clubs timed their departures so as to arrive in Chicago on a Sunday, when a working person would be able to come to the station.[51] Members of these clubs not only could count on someone to guide them through their first hours in the city, but could enjoy the comfort of numbers as well.

Those migrants who were not met at the train by a friend were immediately faced with the problem of finding their own way, usually to the South Side. A redcap at the Illinois Central station later recalled the confusion evinced by many of the newcomers, who had little idea of where they were going. "They knew somebody in Chicago. The only directions they had were when you get to the station you go two blocks this way or go this way, things like that." One migrant remembered being "completely lost. . . . I was afraid to ask anyone where to go." Louis Armstrong, arriving from New Orleans in 1922, was

Illinois Central Railroad Station, Chicago (courtesy of the Illinois State Historical Library).

terrified when he was unable to locate his friend Joe Oliver in the crowd at the station:

> I saw a million people, but not Mister Joe, and I didn't give a damn who else was there. I never seen a city that big. All those tall buildings. I thought they were universities. I said, no, this is the wrong city. I was fixing to take the next train back home— standing there in my box-back suit, padded shoulders, double-breasted wide-leg pants.[52]

Those without someone to meet them had to look elsewhere for assistance. At the Illinois Central terminal, city and station police were highly visible, with one usually near the track, another "on the floor," and another just outside the station. In addition, at the top of the stairway leading to the waiting room a neon sign advertised the services of the Travelers Aid Society, whose representatives sat at the table underneath the sign. Until June 1917 only white women represented Travelers Aid, and it is unlikely that many male migrants, accustomed to restrictive southern etiquette regarding black men approaching white women, took advantage of its services. After 146 black arrivals at the Illinois Central terminal approached the table in March 1917, however, the aides who worked there and two black social agencies agreed that a black representative was needed.[53] Although "unfavorable to such an innovation" in April 1917, the Travelers Aid Society board of directors two months later agreed to work with the Chicago Urban League and appoint a "Colored Assistant" at the Illinois Central. At Dearborn Station, where agents faced a similar influx of black migrants, Travelers Aid retained its exclusively white presence.[54]

Although Travelers Aid dealt with blacks only reluctantly and rather gingerly, a black porter at the Illinois Central station recalled that its representatives were often "very helpful" to migrants who seemed lost. Some white Travelers Aid agents had difficulty understanding the migrants' southern accents, one of them complaining condescendingly that the migrants could not speak or understand English. In such cases, black porters and doormen assisted, and often supplanted, the agents. Both white and black Travelers Aid assistants referred people with problems either to the Urban League or to the black branch of either the Young Men's Christian Association or Young Women's Christian Association.[55] Thus, migrants who received an institutional introduction to Chicago were welcomed by black institutions during their first hours in the city.

Whatever their problems immediately upon arrival, migrants experienced a series of shocks as they emerged from the railroad station. Some had not brought along warm clothing and received a chilling introduction to Chicago's climate, which could be daunting in the early spring when migration tended to peak.[56] Like the characters in Alden Bland's *Behold A Cry*, many newcomers gazed at the immense structures, the concrete and iron materials which seemed everywhere, and the swift motion of people, automobiles, and trolleys. Richard Wright was taken aback by the "towering buildings of steel and stone" and by elevated trains which occasionally shook the ground. The screeching of streetcars and honking of horns augmented the awesome sights. Scurrying residents seemed oblivious not only to their environment, but to other people as well, and their "clipped speech" was incomprehensible to Wright.[57]

The urban landscape was not only disorienting; it was exciting as well. Migrants generally headed straight for Chicago's famous South

Side ghetto, where the bright lights and commotion introduced them to the rhythms of their new home. Langston Hughes recalled the thrill of his arrival in 1918: "South State Street was in its glory then, a teeming Negro street with crowded theaters, restaurants, and cabarets. And excitement from noon to noon. Midnight was like day. The street was full of workers and gamblers, prostitutes and pimps, church folks and sinners."[58] The Chicago *Whip*, a black newspaper, agreed with Hughes' assessment, describing the district as a cosmopolitan "Bohemia of the Colored folks," where "lights sparkled, glasses tinkled," and one could find bootblacks and bankers dressed in finery. The center of activity, the heart of "The Stroll," was Thirty-fifth and State streets, where crowds of people milled about day and night. Looking east from the busy corner, a newcomer with an eye for the symbolic might have compared past and future, as five blocks away the Plantation Cafe's bright neon sign suggested dissonant images of the rural South and urban North.[59]

Unfortunately the crowds, lights, and attractions could also be dangerous to a naive migrant fresh off the train. On his first night in town, James Parker of Alabama picked up an eighteen-year-old girl at Thirty-fifth and State, and they spent the evening cabaret-hopping. The next morning Parker awoke in a hotel room, with neither the girl nor his money in sight. James Hill from Burnette, Texas, also arrived in Chicago "with plenty of cash in his jeans." Some "old friends," scenting a free night on the town, offered to show him the bright lights. Not only did he foot the tabs, but unaccustomed to city dangers, he repeatedly displayed the wad of bills he was carrying. At the end of the night he was relieved of his remaining $102.60 by three muggers.[60] An even more naive rube walked into a grocery store and handed the owner a twenty-dollar bill, telling him that he would return for it in a few hours. The police recovered his money, making him more fortunate than the numerous newcomers who fell victim to pickpockets preying on the crowds at busy street corners.[61]

Even before they experienced the excitement and perils of State Street, however, migrants confronted what had been on their minds ever since they had contemplated the journey—the absence of the hated southern racial code. In the railroad station, Richard Wright searched for the familiar FOR WHITE and FOR COLORED signs.

> It was strange to pause before a crowded newsstand and buy a newspaper without having to wait until a white man was served. And yet, because everything was so new I began to grow tense again, although it was a different tension than I had known before. I knew that this machine-city was governed by strange laws and I wondered if I would ever learn them.[62]

Migrants exiting train station in Chicago (courtesy of Special Collections, the University Library, University of Illinois at Chicago).

Migrants reacted to this sudden change in racial protocol in diverse ways. Many, perplexed like Wright, avoided racial contact, and tried to continue old patterns of cautious behavior. On the streetcars, these men and women sat towards the rear, with other blacks; in stores they asked merchants "can a Colored man buy this or that here."[63] Such fears were hardly irrational. Chicago had its own racial rules, but they were unwritten and ambiguous. An imaginary "dead line" separating the South Side's "Black Belt" from an Irish neighborhood symbolized the problem; to cross it could have violent consequences for the transgressor. Teenager Langston Hughes painfully learned that lesson when he ventured to explore the city his first Sunday in town. "Over beyond Wentworth," he "was set upon and beaten by a group of white boys, who said they didn't allow niggers in that neighborhood."[64]

Other migrants quickly set out to test and assert their newly attained rights. These individuals deliberately sat next to whites on the streetcar, if only to prove to themselves that freedom was real. Coming from a region where a black person's sole privileges were described by one observer as "ter pay his taxes and ter git out o' de road," many migrants wasted so little time learning and testing the new rules that the normally militant *Defender* chided them not to "mistake privilege for right."[65] Most migrants, however, were prob-

The Plantation Cafe (courtesy of the Chicago Historical Society).

ably more tentative. A Mississippi man moved to the front the first time he boarded a streetcar but "would not sit beside a white person at first." One woman recalled that when she boarded a streetcar for the first time and saw black people sitting alongside whites, "I just held my breath, for I thought any minute they would start something. Then I saw nobody noticed it, and I just thought this is a real place for Negroes."[66]

Part 2

5

"Home People" and "Old Settlers"

Black southerners arriving in Chicago generally knew where to go once they walked out of the train station. Like their counterparts in New York who asked in Pennsylvania Station how to get to Harlem, most black migrants to Chicago upon alighting at the Illinois Central terminal requested directions to the South Side or to State Street. People whose friends, relatives, or townspeople had preceded them sought out specific addresses; those who had no idea where to go were likely to be directed to the South Side. Whites would assume that all blacks "belonged" in the ghetto; blacks would reason that bewildered newcomers might obtain assistance from black institutions while avoiding the danger of straying into hostile white neighborhoods. The logic of such advice suggests the significance—if not the visibility—of Chicago's color line, as well as the importance of various aspects of community within black Chicago. Shaped by both the circumscribing influences of the white city that surrounded it and the demands of the migrants and "Old Settlers" who inhabited it, the emerging "Black Metropolis" on the South Side divided along lines of class, region, and even age. But it remained a community nevertheless, unified by the implications of racial taxonomies.[1]

In 1910, 78 percent of black Chicagoans lived on the South Side in a narrow strip of land known to whites as the Black Belt. Beginning at the edge of an industrial and warehouse district just south of the Loop (Chicago's central business district), black Chicago stretched southward along State Street for more than thirty blocks, remaining only a few blocks wide except at its northern end. The 1910 census counted 34,335 black residents in this growing ghetto, which was expanding slowly along its southern and eastern boundaries. Another 3,379 black Chicagoans lived on the West Side, while most of the remaining 6,389 lived in smaller enclaves in Englewood, the Near North

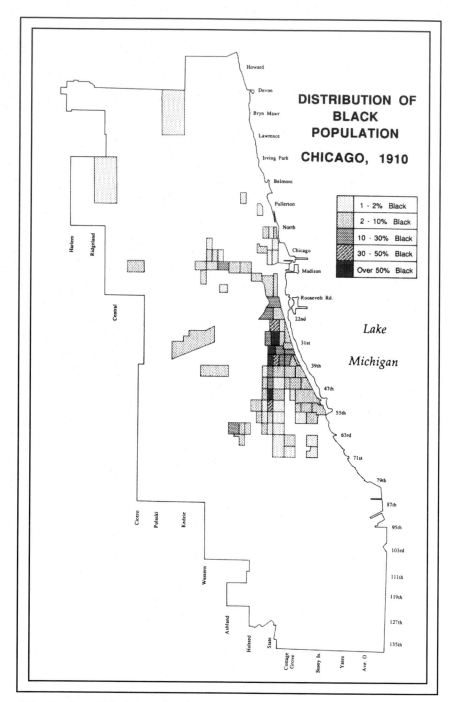

Distribution of black population in Chicago, 1910 (by census tract). Adapted from Allan H. Spear, *Black Chicago: The Making of a Negro Ghetto, 1890–1920* (Chicago: University of Chicago Press, 1967).

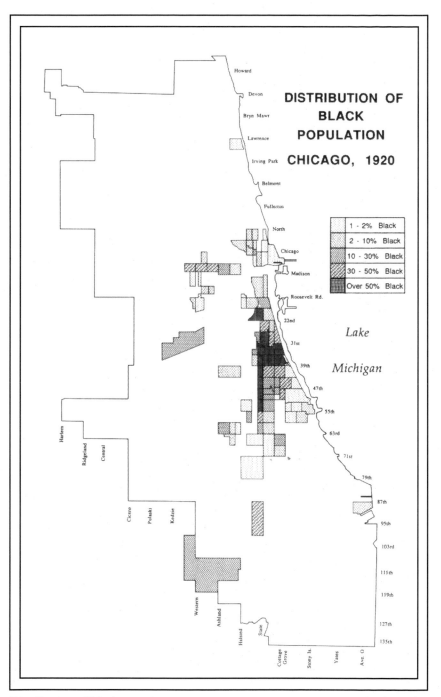

Distribution of black population in Chicago, 1920 (by census tract). Adapted from Allan H. Spear, *Black Chicago: The Making of a Negro Ghetto, 1890–1920* (Chicago: University of Chicago Press, 1967).

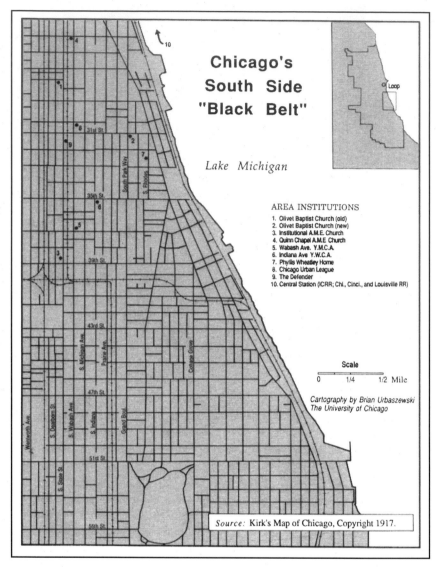

The South Side Black Belt and prominent institutions.

Side, and scattered other districts. Only 1,427 lived on the city's North Side. Because of the lingering presence of some whites in black neighborhoods, especially those on the edge of the Black Belt and the smaller enclaves, many black Chicagoans lived in what might loosely be called an integrated setting; but with black people virtually restricted to certain areas of the city, the housing market was actually segregated.[2]

This residential pattern had evolved during the previous quarter century, when Chicago's black population had increased from 6,480 in 1880 to 44,103 in 1910. As late as 1898, only slightly more than one-fourth of Chicago's black residents lived in precincts in which blacks constituted a majority of the population; more than 30 percent inhabited precincts at least 95 percent white. Yet black enclaves were already emerging, mainly on the South and near West Sides. Ward statistics understate this concentration of the black population, as blacks often occupied only a small sector in each ward. This consolidating trend accelerated along with black migration. Few white neighborhoods had ever accepted with equanimity the purchase of property by even a "respectable" black family, even before migration reached a level that might have remotely threatened whites with the specter of "invasion." As the black population began to increase, whites became still less likely to tolerate a black neighbor and more actively began to resist black settlement in their neighborhoods.[3]

At the same time, black institutional development contributed to the growing vitality and self-consciousness of the emerging black neighborhoods, making them attractive to blacks who preferred avoiding white people and their prejudices. What one historian of Detroit's black community has called the "push of discrimination" and "the pull of ethnocentrism" combined to impel black newcomers toward the ghetto. Exclusion aside, many migrants sought their first homes in areas populated by other blacks, where they could be more comfortable and find familiar institutions. This dynamic of choice and constraint, heavily influenced by economic factors, resembled the experience of European immigrants to Chicago during this period, but the differences were significant. Unfamiliarity with English made the ethnic neighborhood essential for many Europeans; blacks had no comparable imperative. White immigrants tended to live near workplaces; blacks dispersed in service occupations could not, and when they did obtain industrial employment they were excluded from neighborhoods adjoining Chicago's major industries. European newcomers lived near others of their nationality but usually in an ethnically diverse neighborhood that could hardly be described as a ghetto. Whether middle or working class, black Chicagoans were less likely than members of other ethnic groups to share public space across ethnic but within class boundaries. More than any other group, black Chicagoans occupied neighborhoods defined by permanent characteristics. Neither cultural assimilation nor economic mobility promised significantly wider choices.[4]

The color line separated more than residences. State legislation prohibiting racial discrimination in schools, municipal services, and public accommodations was seldom enforced, and except on the streets and in the streetcars, blacks and whites seldom mingled. Black children attended schools with whites, but only because by 1915 the emerging ghetto was still neither compact nor homogeneous enough to enable the Board of Education to draw district lines that would go beyond merely assuring that as few schools as possible would have black students. Municipal institutions often segregated black clients or discriminated in the provision of services. Most voluntary associations and private institutions simply excluded blacks, thrusting on the community the dilemma of accepting segregation or doing without such institutions as the YMCA. On the whole, in 1915 black Chicagoans lived among black neighbors, sent their children to predominantly black schools, and were excluded from most establishments catering to whites.[5]

Blacks occupied a similarly limited place in Chicago's booming economy. Fewer than one black male in twenty—and virtually no black females— worked in an occupation that might be described as managerial, professional, or proprietary; even many of these operated marginal businesses. Most workers were unskilled, and few worked in industry. If Chicago was the "City of the Big Shoulders," with an economic base of heavy industry, construction, and transportation, black workers found themselves relegated to marginal roles. White immigrants from southern and eastern Europe had to accept the worst jobs in the city's industries, but blacks lacked access even to those positions. Sharing the racial attitudes of other Americans, industrialists in Chicago and other northern cities saw no reason to hire blacks when they had thousands of white immigrants to fill their factories. Blacks were considered to be useful as strikebreakers on occasion, but were generally discharged once the strike ended. Industrial managers drew upon a series of commonly held assumptions about work habits and aptitudes of various "races," and if most Eastern European groups suffered from images that kept them in unskilled positions, at least they were white. Where foremen controlled access to industrial jobs, black workers lacked access to the networks of community and kin that were central to recruitment patterns. Chicago and other northern cities offered mainly service jobs to blacks, and between 1900 and 1910 the number of black servants in Chicago increased by six thousand, nearly half the city's increase in black population during that period. Men were likely to work as porters, waiters, servants, janitors, or elevator operators; two-thirds of all employed black women in 1910 were either servants or hand laundresses, with most of the others performing some other type of service.[6]

Despite this apparent homogeneity, however, black Chicago—

like other urban black communities—was divided along class lines. Severely truncated at the top, this class structure rested less on wealth or contemporary white definitions of occupational status (except at the highest levels) than on notions of "refinement" and "respectability" maintained by the upper and middle classes. The few professionals, some with professional connections to the white community, tended to dominate the highest rungs of the ladders, with businessmen close behind. Postal workers, Pullman porters, and servants employed by Chicago's wealthiest white families and best hotels constituted much of the solid middle class, which at its margins could also include other workers with stable incomes and some education. Stable income was at least as important as accumulated wealth, an uncommon phenomenon in the black community. "Respectability" frequently depended upon property ownership, membership in the appropriate organizations, and leisure habits. Church, club, or lodge activities conferred as well as signified status; symbols of respectability could include affiliation with one of the larger Baptist or African Methodist Episcopal Churches, a YMCA membership, or a Masonic identification card. Upper-class blacks, who considered themselves "refined" rather than merely "respectable," joined Episcopalian, Presbyterian, or Congregationalist churches, entertained according to specific rules of etiquette, and socialized only within a limited circle of acquaintances.[7]

Until the late nineteenth century, this upper class—largely businessmen with white clientele and professionals who had won the respect of their white colleagues—dominated black Chicago's leadership and resisted attempts to organize alternative institutions catering to blacks. To do so, they argued, would imply their acceptance of segregation. This elite not only opposed racial segregation in principle, but also feared its likely impact on their own social lives and institutional relationships. Disdaining association with blacks who lacked their refinement, members of this thin upper stratum recognized that segregation would force their social life inward toward the black community, rather than outward as they hoped.[8]

Between 1900 and 1915 a new leadership emerged in black Chicago, one with an economic and political base in the black community. The emergence of the physical ghetto coincided with widening racial discrimination in Chicago and other northern cities, which forced blacks to make decisions circumscribed by their exclusion from a variety of social and economic institutions. Increasing separation opened new opportunities for business, professional, religious, and political leadership, and by the first decade of the twentieth century, a new middle class had begun to replace an older elite unwilling to sacrifice integrationist principles and therefore wary of separate black institutions and a ghetto economy.[9]

This new generation of black editors, politicians, business people, and ministers would dominate Chicago's black institutions during the Great Migration and construct the foundation of what by the 1920s would be known as a Black Metropolis. The southern origins of these prominent figures perhaps contributed to their continuing influence on newcomers. Robert Abbott, raised outside Savannah, Georgia, visited Chicago in 1893 as a member of the Hampton (Institute) Quartet performing at the Columbian Exposition. He returned four years later and in 1905 founded the Chicago *Defender*. Louis B. Anderson, born in Petersburg, Virginia, was also drawn to Chicago by the fair; by 1919, he was not only an alderman, but also Mayor William Hale Thompson's floor leader in the City Council. Born in Alabama, Oscar DePriest traveled to Chicago from Kansas in 1889 and worked his way up from a house painter to election as Chicago's first black alderman in 1915. Thirteen years later he would climb even higher, as the first black congressman elected from a northern district. Reverend Archibald J. Carey, like DePriest the child of ex-slaves, came from Georgia in 1898 to serve as pastor of Quinn Chapel, the city's largest African Methodist Episcopal Church. Such notables, provided an image—and a self-image—of a prewar generation of migrants who built institutions, shaped a newly self-conscious black community, and dominated Chicago's growing black middle class.[10]

Adapting Booker T. Washington's doctrines of racial solidarity and self-help to the northern city, these business leaders and politicians deemphasized the fight for integration and dealt with discrimination by creating black institutions. Between 1890 and 1915 they established a bank, a hospital, a YMCA, an infantry regiment, effective political organizations, lodges, clubs, professional baseball teams, social service institutions, newspapers, and a variety of small businesses. The growth of the black community promised to multiply growing political influence and economic activity. Like Abbott, whose newspaper was partly responsible for the popularity of Chicago as a destination for black southerners, Chicago's black politicians and entrepreneurs saw the migrants as a source of votes and customers.[11]

Growth, however, also implied diversity, and neither the "old" nor "new" leadership in black Chicago was prone to tolerate those who did not measure up to their standards. The *Conservator*, Chicago's first black newspaper and the voice of prominent leaders in the late nineteenth century, frequently criticized "the seamy side" of black Chicago during the 1870s and 1880s. The *Defender* picked up the mantle in the twentieth century, with complaints about newcomers and degeneration even before the Great Migration. Both newspapers couched these criticisms within the context of appeals for improvement, providing lessons for proper behavior while chiding lower-class blacks for giving the race a bad image.[12] George Cleveland Hall, a prominent physician and personal friend of Booker T. Washington, typified the attitudes of many of his contemporaries. He served in official capacities in the NAACP as well as the Washingtonian National Negro Business League and later became one of the founders of the Chicago Urban League. In 1904, Hall voiced the attitudes of middle-class black Chicago concerning the need—and yet the impossibility—of maintaining the distance between classes in the black community:

> Those of the race who are desirous of improving their general condition are prevented to a great extent by being compelled to live with those of their color who are shiftless, dissolute and immoral. . . . Prejudice of landlords and agents render it almost impossible for [the Negro] to take up his residence in a more select quarter of the city . . . no matter . . . how much cultivation and refinement he may possess.[13]

Most black Chicagoans before the Great Migration, however, neither possessed Hall's "cultivation and refinement" nor lived "shiftless, dissolute and immoral" lives. Laboring long days in menial occupations, they returned home tired. Women, especially, spent most of their waking hours working, as they had to combine traditional household chores with other employment. Nearly half of all black women in Chicago in 1910 worked outside the home (compared with slightly more than one-fourth of white women), and among poor families the proportion was even higher. Most of these people had migrated from the South and had found that whatever skills or hopes they carried with them, service occupations provided the only possibility of employment in Chicago. Their leisure activities offered respite from their backbreaking, low-status jobs. Enthusiastic worship and lively nightlife attracted the scorn of much of the middle class, but such activities already were central elements of what St. Clair Drake and Horace Cayton would later call "the world of the lower class" in black Chicago. By 1904 (if not earlier), the storefront churches later to be associated with the Great Migration had already begun to appear along State Street. Less spiritually inclined workers found release in petty gambling, the fellowship of the numerous saloons along the State Street "Stroll," or boisterous parties. By 1914, the rent party (later made famous in Harlem) had been improvised to leaven the struggle for subsistence with sociability and relaxation.

These comforts drew upon the familiarity and relief of a black world; on the "Stroll," observed a black essayist in 1915, "for a minute or so one forgets the 'Problem.' It has no place here. It is crowded aside by an insistence of good cheer." [14]

As earlier migrants from the South to Chicago, some of these black workers numbered among the letter writers who helped to stimulate the Great Migration. In some cases, they formed the core of the kin and community networks vital to the initial adjustment of newcomers to urban life. Most, however, had not come from the Deep South states which provided the majority of migrants during the war years. On the whole, their relation to the Great Migration and their interactions with the migrants are difficult to discern. The migrants competed with these laborers for the limited supply of working-class housing available to blacks, and this group suffered from the rapid increase in rents which resulted from the impact of migration on the demand for cheap housing in the ghetto during the migration. Differences would also emerge over the issue of unionization in the packinghouses, with newcomers approaching labor organizations more warily. The greatest tensions, however, as well as the major nexus of institutional assistance, lay between the migrants and Chicago's black middle class. Dependent on the growth of the black community, the middle class had more to gain from the migration than did the lower class. But, in its concern for respectability and community image, the middle class also had the most to lose.

It is difficult to determine what kind of reception migrants expected from this community. Most probably anticipated a warm welcome. Much of what they knew about Chicago had been filtered through sources that emphasized race consciousness and individual and racial accomplishment. Class tensions and divisions within the black community seldom found their way into the *Defender*. Similarly, information from friends and relatives who only recently had arrived in Chicago highlighted instead the contrasts between South and North, rural and urban. Accustomed to middle-class disdain for poorer blacks, informants were unlikely to mention class tensions in letters extolling the wonders of the Windy City. Based on the information at their disposal, black southerners preparing to go to Chicago could logically envision a black community that was self-sufficient, fiercely militant, and eager to assist those of "the Race" in flight from southern oppression. Accordingly, many wrote hopefully to the *Defender*, Chicago Urban League, and Bethlehem Baptist Association for train fare, suitcases, and prearranged employment and housing. Chicago's black institutional leadership could not provide these resources, but it did offer useful assistance and services. The same network that had stimulated and facilitated migration could now smooth adjustment. As migration increased, the other part of the network—community and kin—would prove most useful to newcomers during their first days in the city.

This informal network helped many migrants to solve their first problem upon arrival—shelter. Earlier migrants, having provided essential information, and sometimes funds, to family and community members who followed them to Chicago, now supplied a different resource, as they helped newcomers find suitable temporary quarters. Frequently, they took friends, relatives, and former townsmen into their homes as lodgers. Women undertook the greatest part of this burden, continuing to play the connective and leadership roles that they had peformed as visitors, correspondents, and club organizers. Some of these women did not need the extra rent money; but they felt obliged to assist friends and relatives whom they had encouraged to come North.[15] Newcomers "stopping" at such houses not only secured interim housing, but spent their first few days in Chicago in a familiar social setting. The "lodger evil" frequently decried by reformers, who worried that households with too many adults threatened family morality, was also a crucial adaptive mechanism based on family and community ties. Given the economic strains on the urban black family, lodging could actually enhance family stability by permitting women to earn money while remaining home with their children.

Migrants arriving without such contacts, or whose friends either lacked the resources to help them or had themselves come to Chicago too recently to be useful as guides, had to rely on more formal channels in their initial search for housing. Some, especially women concerned about their vulnerability "in a large city by self among strangers," as one New Orleans woman put it, wrote ahead inquiring about housing or live-in domestic work. Generally even those whose request was as simple as that of Hattie Smith of Georgia, who wished to board in "a nice place," could not get an institution to work out an arrangement in advance. Newcomers who had believed rumors about agencies on State Street that would provide homes and furniture were equally disappointed.[16] There were, however, agencies that could help migrants find temporary shelter. This could be critical for migrants who arrived penniless, or, like Edwina Brown and a Mrs. Holly, were stranded at the train station when the people they expected to meet them failed to appear. These young women, like many others in their predicament, were sent by Travelers Aid representatives to the black YWCA branch. Many young men, arriving destitute after riding freight trains north, ended up in a courtroom, where at least one judge—Daniel P. Trude—regularly referred them to the Chicago Urban League.[17]

Although it distributed thousands of cards inviting any "Stranger in the City" to visit its office "if you want a place to live," the League did not operate any housing facilities. But it could provide institutional assistance by referring homeless migrants to appropriate institutions or offering them its "certified lodging list." During the 1916–17 crest of migration, for example, it could send indigent men and women to Walters AME Zion Church, which stayed open day and night to "succor those of our people" who had recently arrived. Single people who had some funds but were alone in the city and reluctant to seek a private lodging house might be sent to such agencies as the YMCA, YWCA, Phyllis Wheatley Home, Club Home for Colored Girls, or Julia Johnson Home for Working Girls, most of which were established after 1910 in response to needs created by migration.[18]

It was fortunate that there were some black institutions to which migrants could turn in their search for interim lodging arrangements upon arrival, as they were denied access to the standard alternatives available to other newcomers to Chicago. Most lodging houses in the city, including the Salvation Army's Reliance Hotel, YMCA Hotel, Christian Industrial League, Dawes Hotel, and probably the Municipal Lodging Houses, turned blacks from their doors, despite stated policies of accepting anyone who could pay except "inebriated" applicants. Even those hotels sufficiently nonexclusive to accept the patronage of "quiet" drunks, rejected blacks. Indeed, these institutions, like the Travelers Aid Society, could avoid dealing with blacks by referring them to the Urban League, using that organization—which defined itself as a "clearinghouse" for social service work among blacks—as a dumping ground for an undesirable clientele.[19]

Even black institutions, however, accepted transients only on an emergency basis, and few alternatives beckoned to newcomers. Single people might stop at one of black Chicago's hotels, such as the Pullman, which offered a range of accommodations at fifty cents to one dollar per day. At C. K. Smith's, all but the most impoverished migrants could afford the fifteen to twenty cent charge for a bed for the night.[20] By 1917, a migrant in search of more comfortable quarters could secure a room at the Idlewild Hotel with steam heat and hot water, at weekly rates of four dollars "and up." Although the number of hotels catering to blacks increased from six in 1917 to eleven in 1921, these establishments could not satisfy the demand. The Chicago Commission on Race Relations reported that between 1915 and 1920, "hundreds of unattached men and women" roamed the streets of Chicago's black neighborhoods until well after midnight looking for rooms.[21]

Thus, those who could not rely on old acquaintances or other connections to provide temporary shelter had to conduct a seemingly futile search for housing. The greatest wave of migration during 1917 and 1918 coincided with a virtual halt in new housing construction in Chicago, exacerbating a shortage shaped by the dual housing market. A summer 1917 survey of realtors supplying housing for blacks counted 664 applicants for the 97 listed units. Only 50 of the hopefuls found accommodations. The situation did not improve; in July 1920, the *Defender* lamented an unprecedented "home famine."[22] New arrivals quickly recognized that they would have to begin their new lives with less space and less privacy than they had envisioned. The Brown family, although less hard pressed financially than most migrants, squeezed three adults and one child into a single room during their first few weeks in Chicago. In 1917 such rooms cost approximately three dollars per week, four to five times the rates in Mississippi towns, and were nearly always regarded as temporary. Renting by the week, a family could continue its search for more desirable quarters and move at any time.[23]

If housing constituted one measurement of "bettering one's condition," Chicago was at best a flawed Promised Land. Migrants moved into houses and apartments in some of the city's most deteriorated neighborhoods. Among Chicago's decaying inner districts— many of which had been marked for extinction as residence areas by the city's planners—only those inhabited by blacks showed population increases between 1910 and 1920.[24] But Chicago did seem to offer many migrants—especially those who arrived before 1919—better homes than they had left behind in the South. Although many newcomers never escaped the dilapidated dwellings located west of State Street, others somehow managed to secure more space, if only temporarily. Even the ramshackle houses on some of the worst blocks were, if nothing else, frequently quite roomy, especially relative to what had been available in the South. In some cases, however, migrants had to close off rooms to reduce heating costs in drafty old frame houses. A more popular alternative was to take in lodgers, which while easing the adjustment process by perpetuating kinship or community ties, could also cause overcrowding and tension.

Observers disagreed as to the extent of overcrowding in the South Side ghetto, partly because few could agree on a meaningful standard. Generally, white reformers considered one room per person a reasonable ratio and agreed that two people per room represented crowding. The city's largely unenforced legal minimum for sleeping

Plantation home of black southerners who subsequently migrated to Chicago (source: CCRR, *Negro in Chicago*, 80).

room specified a parsimonious four hundred cubic feet for adults and two hundred for children. By any yardstick, however, Chicago housing compared favorably with the southern dwellings occupied by blacks. Migrants from towns or farms in the South had probably lived in crude cabins of perhaps three or four rooms. In such homes it was not unusual for as many as five members of a family to sleep in a single room. Traveling through Mississippi in 1917, Charles Johnson found "a stock accommodation: a two room cabin for a family in which they cook, sleep, eat and rear their children." A survey of North Carolina rural housing found cabins of three rooms—or smaller—that left inhabitants open to the vicissitudes of even the relatively mild climate. "Hot in the summer . . . [and] . . . almost impossible to heat" in the winter, these homes invariably had leaks that left floors damp after storms.[25] If many migrants ended up in Chicago flats without hot running water, even cold tap water had been unavailable in their southern homes, which had probably lacked plumbing or sewerage connections. The housing available to black newcomers to Chicago ranked among the worst in the city, but utili-

Homes occupied by black families, South Chicago (source: Adams, "Present Housing Conditions in South Chicago," 64).

ties that were routine in Chicago had been a luxury in plantation cabins and even in many southern towns. A Floridian who was "not particular about the electric lights" could hardly have been aware before leaving the South that in Chicago a dangling light bulb characterized even the dingy "kitchenette." Although migrants would soon grow dissatisfied with their substandard housing, most found homes that seemed better than what they had left behind in the South.[26]

Although most migrants moved frequently after locating in Chicago, their ability to improve their housing facilities was limited. The small black ghetto expanded rapidly in 1917, but resistance soon formed along its eastern and western borders. The ghetto expanded mainly to the south during the war, but it did so slowly and along a narrow corridor. Because landlords could extract higher—and rapidly increasing—rents from blacks excluded from the city's general housing market, recently "opened" blocks frequently commanded rates beyond the financial resources of most migrants. Black Chicagoans who moved into more expensive homes left behind buildings to be filled by newcomers; but this process did not create nearly

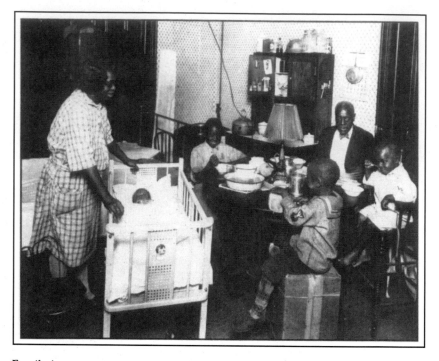

Family in one-room apartment in Chicago (source: Wilson, "Chicago Families in Furnished Rooms," 35).

enough vacancies to meet the demand. By 1919, despite a surplus of housing in other parts of Chicago, including working-class neighborhoods west of the ghetto, a severe housing shortage plagued black Chicago. This crisis contributed to the outbreak of the bloody race riot that year.[27]

The interaction of discrimination and rapidly rising demand for housing not only fueled racial tensions and frustrated migrants' hopes of progressively improving their living conditions; it also structured the physical environment of blacks already resident in Chicago and contributed to their concerns over the impact of the Great Migration. Although most black Chicagoans recognized that the exodus from the South and the entrance into the industrial economy represented a step forward for black America, they were not necessarily eager to see the newcomers become their neighbors. Some of these Old Settlers tried to avoid the social consequences of the Great Migration by fleeing from neighborhoods affordable to newcomers. Housing discrimination, however, left most of the city inaccessible even to the few blacks whose incomes should have provided a wide range of alternatives. A handful of middle-class black Chicagoans, mainly Pullman porters and City Hall employees, bought homes in Morgan Park, approximately ten miles southwest of the South Side ghetto. Their attitude toward the newcomers is suggested by their reaction to the news that migrants were beginning to rent apartments in their small community: they objected that the influx would depress property values and "render the neighborhood less desirable." Unlike white immigrants and their children who similarly worked to accumulate the resources to move to a "better" neighborhood, most black Chicagoans struggling for security, respectability, and an environment suited to raising children found their ambitions stymied.[28]

Although only a few hundred Old Settlers tried to escape the impact of the Great Migration by fleeing to Morgan Park, their reaction to the migrants suggests anxieties not uncommon among middle-class black Chicagoans. More frequently, they tried to insulate themselves by moving further south along the narrow strip that defined the gradually expanding South Side Black Belt. But the migrants inevitably followed. What was the middle-class edge of the South Side ghetto in 1917 had become a central part of that district by 1920. High rents and large houses in such areas inhibited, but could not prevent, their gradual transformation. Newcomers unable to afford large houses but wanting extra space or income frequently rented these buildings and took in lodgers. In addition, landlords—black and white—learned that they could increase profits by dividing a comfortable four-room flat into four "kitchenettes" by installing a gas burner in each room and renting to poor families by the week. Although newcomers tended to cluster in the older neighborhood west of State Street and north of Thirty-fifth Street, and the proportion of migrants decreased as one moved south, no black neighborhood lacked a significant number of migrants. Caught in the vise of the dual housing market, the middle class could not escape. One black professional man, who moved from Thirty-seventh Street to Fifty-first Street trying to keep ahead of the newcomers, complained in 1927 that "the same class of Negroes who ran us away from Thirty-seventh Street are moving out there. They creep along slowly like a disease."[29]

Few middle-class black Chicagoans, however, would have gone so far as to liken the migrants to an army of infectious germs. Most received the newcomers ambivalently. "They didn't seem to open-arm welcome them," recalled one black Chicagoan, "but they seemed to welcome them."[30] Although the *Defender*, Urban League, and other major institutions in black Chicago had encouraged the exodus from the South and virtually invited black southerners to relocate in their city, the men and women who dominated these institutions also perceived a potential threat in the influx. Fearful that the migrants, with their rural southern manners, would disrupt the community and embarrass the race, middle-class black Chicago tried to protect its respectability by instructing newcomers in acceptable forms of behavior. Many migrants, in turn, sought to maintain their self-respect and way of life by forming their own institutions—mainly churches—and networks of associations. And many, especially the younger men and women who constituted the bulk of the newcomers, adapted too easily to urban life, noisily crowding the streets, night clubs, dance halls, and "cafes," to the chagrin of the more staid Old Settlers.

Whether more concerned about the welfare or the behavior of southerners new to their community, black Chicagoans could draw on only a limited fund of existing institutional resources to deal with problems posed by the influx. Even before the Great Migration, the *Defender* had justifiably rebuked the city's black leadership for insufficient attention to the development of social service and welfare organizations. The community did raise funds for the Phyllis Wheatley Association's home for stranded women, the Jane Dent Home for Aged and Infirm Colored People, Provident Hospital, the black YMCA, and two settlement houses, but few of these institutions existed primarily to serve the poor. One of the settlement houses, Frederick Douglass Center, according to one of its founders in 1906 was "not organized to do slum work in what may be called the black belt of Chicago, but to be a center of wholesome influences," where middle-class whites and blacks might become acquainted. The Wendell Phillips Settlement on the West Side, along with two attempts by churches to organize settlement activities, focused more sharply on the poor. But the small Phillips Settlement struggled to stay open; the Trinity Church Mission expired when its founder, Reverend Richard R. Wright, left the city a few years after its founding in 1905; and much of Institutional AME Church's settlement program lasted only a decade longer. Most social welfare institutions dependent mainly on black support struggled along on marginal budgets. Among these, only the Negro Fellowship League and the Phyllis Wheatley Association specifically oriented their activities toward newcomers.[31]

The Wheatley Association, founded in 1896 as a women's club, changed its orientation in 1906 to aid female migrants. Its home for stranded newcomers grew out of a concern that respectable black women arriving in Chicago often encountered difficulty in finding appropriate jobs or housing and "were going astray by being led unawares into disreputable homes, entertainment and employment." Emphasizing its home's "culture" and "refined" atmosphere, and able to assist only a few women at any given time, the Wheatley Association embraced a narrow clientele.[32]

The Negro Fellowship League embodied a greater ambition. Created in 1910 by Ida B. Wells-Barnett, the League maintained a lodging house, an employment agency, and a reading room with southern as well as northern newspapers. In 1917 the organization stationed a representative at the Illinois Central depot to give "proper information and protection" to migrants, but Travelers Aid and the Chicago Urban League quickly pushed the Fellowship League out of this role. The lodging house, whose fifteen-cent per night fee made it affordable to most newcomers, if not to the "man farthest down" whom Wells-Barnett sought to reach, had closed in 1913, and the Fellowship League itself expired in 1920. Unable to attract contributions or interest among the "leading colored citizens," Wells-Barnett argued that these worthies disdained rubbing shoulders with the redcaps, elevator operators, rag-pickers, and State Street "elements" whom she defined as her clientele. This was no doubt true. But given her marginal place in Chicago's less confrontational black leadership, her feminism and refusal to take a back seat to male leadership, and her apparently abrasive personality, other factors contributed at least as much to the Fellowship League's demise. Probably most important, as Wells-Barnett later recognized when she criticized middle-class black leaders for their greater interest in organizations with closer ties to whites than her Fellowship League had cultivated, was competition from institutions with greater access to white resources. The establishment of first the black YMCA, and then the Urban League, diverted the funds available from white philanthropists and black businessmen.[33]

From its inception in 1911, the YMCA branch constructed explicitly for black Chicagoans was a source of considerable pride to large segments of the black community. The *Defender*, never reluctant to exaggerate, likened its founding to the Emancipation Proclamation and placed its chief benefactors—Julius Rosenwald of Sears, Roebuck and banker Nathan W. Harris—alongside John Brown, Charles Sumner, and Abraham Lincoln in its pantheon of white allies.[34] Opposed by some of the old-line leadership as a segregated institution, the Wabash YMCA attracted criticism from others as elitist. The Chicago *Whip* charged it with catering primarily to the "black Blue Stockings or better styled cod fish aristocracy of the race." More pointedly, Wells-Barnett argued that its steep membership fees prevented it from "reaching the boys or men who were farthest down and out." A "full senior" membership did, in fact, cost ten dollars, but a "social senior" member could use many of the building's facilities for only two dollars per year in 1915.[35] Moreover, Armour & Company, and probably other stockyards firms as well, paid membership fees for their employees after one year of service. Published membership figures fluctuated, and the organization probably inflated them. In 1913 it claimed 2,000 members; two years later its executive director privately set the number at 1,000; in 1919 the *Defender* reported 1,961; and only one year later, it had fallen to 675. By 1921 it had climbed to 1,411.[36] Few southern migrants stayed in its dormitories, and those who did tended to resemble the "leaders of the Mobile Young Men's Progressive Club" who made the Wabash YMCA "their headquarters" when they arrived in Chicago in 1917. Even this group, however, included stockyards workers. Laborers also participated in glee clubs, baseball leagues, and other leisure activities designed to compete with the temptations of State Street. Implicitly through its wholesome recreational programs and explicitly through meetings that often accompanied such programs, the Wabash YMCA provided a podium for white industrialists and black middle-class leaders who wished to address a small minority of newcomers who could be enticed through its doors.[37]

The centerpiece of both black and white efforts to assist and influence the newcomers was the Chicago Urban League, which provided the bulk of the services most important to recent migrants. Established five years after its parent organization's founding in 1911, the Chicago chapter immediately focused on the "adjustment or assimilation" of the city's black migrants.[38] Countless migrants knew of the organization; publicity in the *Defender* had given it a reputation as "the society in Chicago that cares for colored emigrants," and it received thousands of letters from black southerners preparing to migrate northward. Within eight months after its office opened in March 1917, seven thousand individuals had received some form of assistance. By 1919, the League could count more than twenty thousand people passing through its doors (not including repeat visits) in a twelve-month period, and statistics for the following year indicate that nearly half had "been in the city less than six months." Most of these clients were looking for work, and more than half of the applicants were placed each year, with the proportion higher during the war. In the areas of employment, housing, social work, and relief, the Urban League quickly emerged as the leading social agency in the black community.[39]

The League could accomplish as much as it did largely because of its ability to attract contributions from white philanthropists and employers, due in part to its extensive connections to Chicago's white social service establishment. But considering the narrow economic base of black Chicago, which had a miniscule business and professional class, the black contribution was meaningful. Although blacks provided only 10 percent of the League's 1917 budget of three thousand dollars, three-fourths of all contributions came from the 155 black men and women who gave small donations. By 1919, blacks were able to raise three thousand dollars themselves, and more than twice that amount the following year, when they provided 17 percent of the total budget. That hundreds of blacks gave between one and ten dollars to the League suggests that people who had little gave what they could. In a community in which post-office employees were considered solidly middle class, and the social arbiter was a clerk for the Pullman company, this represented no small commitment.[40]

If many of the middle-class social clubs and their members continued to ignore the poor except for occasional contributions to charity and frequent moralizing about respectability, the Great Migration did stimulate social welfare activity on the part of black Chicagoans. Considering the limited financial resources of Chicago's black institutions and the widespread poverty in the community even before the influx of newcomers, black Chicago demonstrated a considerable commitment to aiding new arrivals. The Wheatley Home expanded its facilities and its fundraising (although it still found itself unable to accommodate all those it wished to help), and a variety of smaller, similar homes for women were established. The Wendell Phillips Settlement expanded its program, although its slim budget continued to limit its reach. It and two women's clubs established day nurseries for black working women and their children, a service apparently not even contemplated in black Chicago until the Great Migration. A few of the larger churches sustained substantial programs which included limited assistance in finding homes and jobs. These and scattered other congregations also provided direct assistance to the poor, sometimes extending aid to nonmembers. The Wabash YMCA and a newly established black branch of the YWCA helped a small number of newcomers find homes and jobs. During the hard times after World War I, churches, clubs, businessmen, and other organizations all tried to cope with the rapidly expanding need for social services, relief, and temporary shelter. Much of this activity was coordinated by the Urban League. With most white charitable organizations and social institutions unwilling to accept black clients, and even some municipal facilities inhospitable, Chicago's black community assembled its meager resources to assist the newcomers.[41]

Chicago's black establishment encouraged and assisted migrants partly out of sheer self-interest. Politicians, businessmen, and newspaper publishers recognized that the newcomers represented voters, customers, readers, and a potential population boom which could swell the prestige of black Chicago both in the city and in black America. Editor Robert Abbott foresaw the *Defender's* influence growing along with the exodus it spearheaded and the community it represented. Indeed, by 1918, the *Defender* was able to sell 137 display advertisements, an increase of 93 percent over the premigration figure three years earlier.[42] But this self-interest transcended the personal ambitions of individual politicians and entrepreneurs; it included a racial component. The *Defender* voiced the hopes of much of black Chicago's business community and political leadership when it emphasized the progress that the migration could bring to the race. Cognizant of the direction of the American economy, Abbott proclaimed that participation in the industrial sector of the economy constituted the linchpin of success for any ethnic group in the United States. "Our entrance into factories, workshops and every other industry open to man places us on an entirely different footing," the editor declared; "We become a factor in the economy to be reckoned with."[43] The relationship between individual accomplishments, community prosperity and power, and racial progress placed the migrants at center stage.

This optimism put a great burden on the newcomers. "IF YOU DO WELL YOU WILL SERVE NOT ONLY YOURSELF BUT THE ENTIRE RACE," the Urban League told them. Conversely, failure would discredit the race; "respectable" black Chicagoans recognized that even if they could avoid living among migrants they would still be associated with them. If some Old Settlers reacted like the "Old Philadelphians" who "secretly hoped that whites would recognize that they were different from the southerners and treat them accordingly," most more realistically appreciated the importance of race as a category central to white social attitudes. Like German Jews who in the late nineteenth century feared that the influx of their coreligionists from eastern Europe would endanger their marginal but substantial foothold in gentile Chicago, black Old Settlers considered themselves vulnerable to stereotyped images dominated by visibly outlandish newcomers. It was essential to organize the community to handle the problem before it grew so large as to overshadow the community's respectable core. "We are our brother's keeper, whether we like it or not," the *Defender* reminded its readers. "It is our duty, if resolved to a selfish duty, to guide the hand of a less experienced one, especially when one misstep weakens our chance for climbing." The socialization of the migrants represented a "trial" for the race, and Chicago's black leadership was not about to permit the test to proceed without its intervention.[44]

Chicago's black middle-class residents assumed that the migrants had to be guided and controlled from the moment they stepped from the train. Mechanisms of social control in the South—church, lodge, gossip, and established customs—were weaker in Chicago, according to one Urban League official, and the migrants were thus more susceptible to dissolution and "disorganization." Ida B. Wells-Barnett lamented that migrants were first attracted to State Street, where "not a single uplifting influence" competed with the saloons, poolrooms, and cabarets.[45] The attractions of State Street and the old vice district at the northern end of the Black Belt threatened the migrants' moral fiber and sobriety as well as the reputation of the community. For if the newcomers fell easily into degeneracy as many Old Settlers feared—and whites expected—they would reflect poorly upon the race. They also would be unable to serve as efficient industrial workers or respectable citizens. By inculcating restraint, the Old Settlers hoped to protect the migrants' souls and pocketbooks, while preserving the community's honor.

The Urban League and the *Defender*, assisted by the YMCA, the larger churches, and a corps of volunteers, fashioned a variety of initiatives designed to help—and pressure—the newcomers to adjust, not only to industrial work, but to urban life, northern racial patterns, and behavior that would enhance the reputation of blacks in the larger (white) community. The *Defender* repeatedly published exhaustive lists of "do's and don't's," calling attention to examples of unacceptable behavior:

Don't use vile language in public places.
Don't act discourteously to other people in public places.
Don't allow yourself to be drawn into street brawls.
Don't use liberty as a license to do as you please.
Don't take the part of law breakers, be they men, women, or children.
Don't make yourself a public nuisance.
Don't encourage gamblers, disreputable women or men to ply their business any time or place.
Don't congregate in crowds on the streets to the disadvantage of others passing along.
Don't live in unsanitary houses, or sleep in rooms without proper ventilation.
Don't violate city ordinances, relative to health conditions.
Don't allow children to beg on the streets.
Don't allow boys to steal from or assault peddlers. . . .

Don't be a beer can rusher or permit children to do such service.
Don't abuse or violate the confidence of those who give you employment.
Don't leave your job when you have a few dollars in your pocket. . . .

The Urban League, through such activities as "Strangers Meetings," leafleting, and door-to-door visits, advised newcomers on their duties as citizens: cleanliness, sobriety, thrift, efficiency, and respectable, restrained behavior in public places. Under the League's auspices, for example, hundreds of club women visited the homes of migrants in 1917, offering "messages emphasizing the necessity of being orderly citizens, efficient working-men and good housekeepers." Perhaps expressing greater confidence to a white audience than he would privately among others of his race and class, Dr. George Cleveland Hall predicted that newcomers would "rapidly adjust themselves to their changed surroundings if they are reached by the proper people and get the right tip."[46] Under the tutelage of the respectable citizens of black Chicago, migrants were to become urbanized, northernized, and indistinguishable from others of their race. At the very least, they would learn to be as inconspicuous as possible.

This campaign exposed cultural conflicts generated by tensions along lines of age, class, and region. "Respectability," the badge of middle-class status in black Chicago, defined the standards to which migrants were held, and manifestations of southern culture—clothes, food, accent—drew both attention and reproof. So also did boisterous leisure activities undeniably urban and not specific to any region. The middle-class sensibilities of the men and women who spoke for black Chicago's newspapers, Urban League, clubs, and churches resembled those of settlement house reformers and others who sought to compete with streets, saloons, and other loci of popular culture for the souls and leisure hours of lower-class youth.

Mostly young men and women, the newcomers indulged in forms of public behavior characteristic of young urbanites, frequently antagonizing churchgoers with their apparent repudiation of conventional morality and attraction to the "gay life." They hung out on street corners, threw loud parties, dressed in the latest risqué fashions, and enjoyed the bright lights of the city's night life. Like the black alderman who wanted to "forbid loitering on street corners," community leaders objected to the tendency of young men and women to converse loudly, in language not entirely within the bounds of genteel respectability. Spending evenings in dance halls, and "dancing in a rareback fashion entirely too close to her partner to be anything other than VULGAR," aroused the *Defender's* ire as quickly as wearing tight or "abbreviated clothes." Young blacks could make a better impression on whites and improve themselves by par-

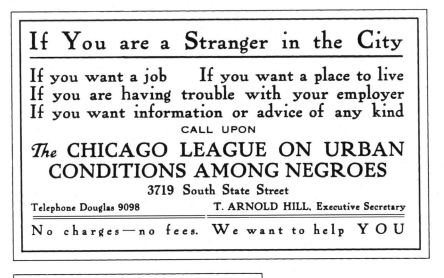

If You are a Stranger in the City

If you want a job   If you want a place to live
If you are having trouble with your employer
If you want information or advice of any kind

CALL UPON

The CHICAGO LEAGUE ON URBAN
CONDITIONS AMONG NEGROES

3719 South State Street

Telephone Douglas 9098   T. ARNOLD HILL, Executive Secretary

No charges—no fees. We want to help YOU

SELF-HELP

1. Do not loaf. Get a job at once.
2. Do not live in crowded rooms. Others can be obtained.
3. Do not carry on loud conversations in street cars and public places.
4. Do not keep your children out of school.
5. Do not send for your family until you get a job.
6. Do not think you can hold your job unless you are industrious, sober, efficient and prompt.

   Cleanliness and fresh air are necessary for good health. In case of sickness send immediately for a good physician. Become an active member in some church as soon as you reach the city.

Issued by

Card distributed by the Chicago Urban League (courtesy of Special Collections, the University Library, University of Illinois at Chicago).

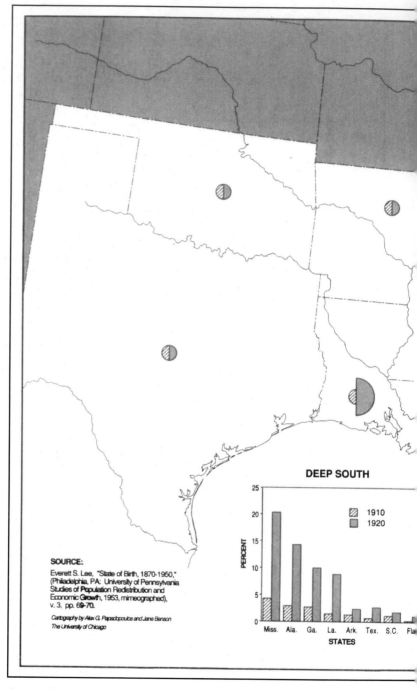

DEEP SOUTH

SOURCE:

Everett S. Lee, "State of Birth, 1870-1950,"
(Philadelphia, PA: University of Pennsylvania
Studies of Population Redistribution and
Economic Growth, 1953, mimeographed),
v. 3, pp. 69-70.

Cartography by Alex G. Papadopoulos and Jane Benson
The University of Chicago

State of birth of black Chicagoans, 1910–20.

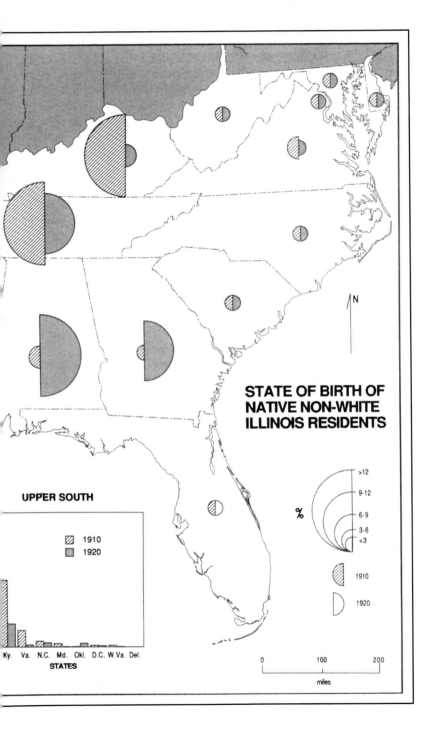

STATE OF BIRTH OF NATIVE NON-WHITE ILLINOIS RESIDENTS

%

>12
9-12
6-9
3-6
<3

1910

1920

UPPER SOUTH

1910
1920

Ky. Va. N.C. Md. Okl. D.C. W.Va. Del.
STATES

N

0   100   200

miles

taking in the "wholesome recreation" available in community centers, churches, and the YMCA and YWCA.[47] The propensity toward less acceptable forms of leisure activity probably had little to do with regional origins, but the conclusion that migrants were a large part of the "youth problem" was not unreasonable. The migrants were, on the whole, considerably younger than the adult black population already living in Chicago. Moreover, young blacks in Chicago were likely to be migrants, while older blacks were likely to have arrived before 1910. Four-fifths of all black Chicagoans in 1920 between ages twenty and thirty-four had arrived in the city since 1910, while less than half of those older than forty-five were newcomers. The importance of bright lights and leisure opportunities had been central to migrants' image of Chicago as a "freer" environment than the rural or small town South.[48] It seemed logical to the older, settled residents that recent arrivals would be particularly susceptible to the temptations of city life because of their unfamiliarity with its dangers and their supposedly undeveloped sense of self-discipline.

Much of what offended and embarrassed those concerned with maintaining standards, however, was identifiably southern. The Deep South origins of the wartime era migrants distinguished them not only from native Chicagoans, but also from those who had arrived earlier, usually from the Upper South. The differences were obvious to black Chicagoans: there was no mistaking the regional provenance of streetside barbecue stands and such icons as watermelon and head rags. Old Settlers grew particularly upset when newcomers publicly displayed their southern backgrounds. Both the *Defender* and the *Whip* castigated women who were "frequently seen in their boudoir caps, house slippers and aprons around the corner in the grocery store," or who appeared in public wearing a head rag. "We are not in the Southland and there is no mark of servitude that must be placed on a man or woman of color in these climes," the *Defender* informed migrants who wore overalls and aprons downtown, on streetcars, and to places of amusement. An Urban League leaflet was equally stern, demanding that the migrants pledge "I WILL REFRAIN from wearing dust caps, bungalow aprons, house clothing and bedroom shoes out of doors."[49]

To an extent, these lectures represented more than mere condescending admonitions. Many migrants did indeed have to adjust to different standards of dress and cleanliness in public, because in the South whites expected blacks to be dirty and poorly attired. Women who distressed Ida B. Wells-Barnett by coming to employment offices wearing "boudoir caps" had merely dressed as their former employers in the South would have expected. To travel to work wearing any-

Leaflet distributed by the Chicago Urban League (courtesy of the
Smithsonian Institution).

thing but work clothes could brand a black southerner as "uppity."
In Chicago, Old Settlers told that same worker that public appearance
should not reveal one's work activity because "servitude" was no
longer assumed. Even the seemingly straightforward issue of rudeness on streetcars was related to southern culture and involved a form
of adjustment on the part of migrants. Southern blacks were not by
nature rude, W. E. B. Du Bois explained, but had learned that any
politeness toward a white woman could easily result in "the most
outrageous misconstruction." Indifference, bordering on sullen hostility, was a safer attitude on streetcars in the South.[50] Old Settlers
hoped to teach the migrants how to earn the respect of whites, as
opposed to the southern imperative of alleviating whites' fears of the
"uppity nigger."

Unlike socially secure settlement-house workers, who valued the
folk music, art, and material culture of their European immigrant clients, Chicago's black middle class could see little redeeming value in
southern black folk culture. Symbolizing the dependency and degradation of blacks in the rural South, it had no place in the modern

northern city and only confirmed white stereotypes, thereby tarnishing the image that Chicago's black community wished to project. Although the image of the "golden age" of race relations before the migrants arrived, as later recalled by some Old Settlers, represented a view distorted by time and open conflict, black Chicagoans had worked long and hard to attain what civil rights they had won. Many feared that the already tenuous racial peace in Chicago would dissolve as whites reacted against crude peasants unaccustomed to the proper exercise of those rights. Kathryn Johnson, the associate editor of the *Half-Century*, a black middle-class women's magazine published in Chicago, feared "an aggravation of the segregation problem which has been so prevalent with us since Mr. Wilson became president. Many of those who are coming will be imprudent and will take their newly found liberty for license." A member of one of "the first colored families in Chicago" worried about what "to do with all of these Negroes from the South coming in here? They look terrible. They sit down on the street car beside white people and I am sure that there is going to be trouble." When trouble came, in the form of a race riot in 1919, many longtime residents blamed the migrants. One native Chicagoan insisted in 1927 that until the Great Migration "we had been accepted as equals." Even the *Defender*, the champion of the exodus, commented (inaccurately) that "there was absolutely no friction until the advent of a handful of undesirables who 'felt their oats' and cut loose upon the slightest provocation."[51]

It was not that the Old Settlers objected to the migrants exercising such rights as sitting where they pleased on streetcars. Indeed, many Old Settlers feared that southerners supposedly accustomed to meekly submitting to whites would fail to assert their rights and thereby indicate that blacks were by nature docile. Migrants had to learn the crucial distinction between exercising rights and what the *Defender* called "bad deportment," which reflected poorly on the race. Social class and "respectability" lay at the heart of the issue. Civil rights aside, for example, stockyards workers were instructed not to sit next to "women who are elegantly attired," especially if the laborers had not changed their clothes and washed before leaving work. The *Searchlight*, another black newspaper, agreed, accusing migrants of "forcing on us here in Chicago a condition similar to the one down South" by boarding the streetcars after work still wearing dirty dresses and overalls. Newcomers were also censured for loud talking, rudeness to conductors, and other streetcar conduct that showed "low breeding." Neither Chicago's black newspapers nor the Urban League ever tired of lecturing the migrants on proper streetcar manners. On the streetcars, migrants were most likely to be seen by middle-class whites, whose respect the black bourgeoisie were fighting so hard to win.[52]

Not all of the Old Settlers' criticisms and lectures grew out of their fears that the newcomers would embarrass the black community or jeopardize the economic benefits promised by the cash generated by new industrial jobs. Unlike their white immigrant counterparts, middle-class black Chicagoans could not move so far away as to encounter the less refined newcomers only when attending churches that remained in the old neighborhood. Even those citizens who lived in the "best" black neighborhoods usually still lived in the ghetto and conducted much of their business, religious, associational, and leisure activities among the migrants. Old Settlers disliked this constant contact, considering the transplanted southerners dirty, crude, and generally unpleasant. This distaste went beyond a class division, with many middle-class migrants failing to win acceptance. It was difficult to cease being southern sufficiently to meet standards set by the northern bourgeoisie. One club which accepted a number of newcomers regretted its liberality when new members suggested that the club sell chitterlings to raise money. Longtime working-class residents drew distinctions between serving in respectable white homes and toiling in factories. Although Chicago's black establishment promoted black employment in the packinghouses, steel mills, and other industries, some prominent members of the community deemed certain service work more respectable. Even those longtime residents too poor to keep moving south ahead of the migrants disdained mingling with their "crude neighbors" from the South. Migrants could not measure up to the standards of behavior demanded by the Old Settlers, unless they not only left their overalls and dirt at the plant, but also jettisoned all remnants of their background.[53] Hostility toward most things southern thus came to symbolize and exacerbate class tensions within black Chicago, but also drew upon notions about "respectablity" that crossed class lines.

The reactions of migrants to these messages varied, especially according to class. Middle-class migrants sought acceptance into Chicago's black bourgeoisie and shared its attitudes toward street life, boisterous behavior, and the trappings of lower-class life. They no more wished to be associated with southern rural culture than did the Old Settlers. At least one newcomer worried not only about what her new neighbors might think, but also made certain that "friends back home" would not open their weekly *Defender* and discover her name among those reprimanded for unacceptable behavior.[54]

Other newcomers, however, found the lessons condescending and either unnecessary, unwelcome, or impractical. Many had heard it all before; the Chicago Urban League's sermons on thrift, hygiene, and work habits differed little from the message emanating from Tuskegee. In Chicago, however, women encountered increased pressure to attend to the proper care of their homes. Many, especially those from rural areas, were in fact unaccustomed to the imperatives and standards of urban housekeeping. But the problem had less to do with race or geographic origins than with class. As one investigator discovered during the winter of 1919–20, working-class black women were as concerned as their white counterparts about "good housekeeping." Working-class women in general found it difficult to live up to standards set by middle-class women living in homes with proper plumbing facilities, more time for housework, and perhaps even a maid. More likely than whites to work outside the home, black women had even less time than whites facing similar obstacles. Residents of slums described by one investigator as plagued more by "bad repair" rather than the alleged "filth," recognized that admonitions could easily blame the victim. In any case, cleanliness was nobody's monopoly. The Mississippi woman who wrote home, "Honey, I got a bath tub" needed no instruction on the virtues of washing.[55]

Misdirected criticism extended beyond the home. Black stockyards workers were, on the whole, more conscientious than their white coworkers about showering and changing clothes before heading home. Most white workers, of course, lived near the packinghouses and did not have to ride the streetcar, where black workers—unable to eradicate the stockyards stench—attracted criticism for carrying home the aroma from their workplaces. Similar reproofs about disorderly conduct on streetcars led one newcomer from Mississippi to complain that "the whites act just as disorderly on cars as the Negroes. . . . Nothing is ever said."[56]

Migrants most actively resisted attempts to change aspects of their everyday life. Despite the pleas of Old Settlers to "give us more grand opera and less plantation melodies," the migrants did not leave their cultural baggage at the train station. "It's no difficult task to get people out of the South," the Chicago *Whip* remarked, "but you have a job on your hands when you attempt to get the South out of them."[57] Although they brought with them fewer "plantation melodies" than their fearful neighbors imagined, migrants did carry to Chicago a form of music equally disliked by many Old Settlers—the boogie-woogie, which probably had its origins in the Mississippi Delta and was closely related to southern revival music. Newcomers also continued to sing southern blues and work songs. One recently arrived huckster probably infuriated many staid Chicagoans with his products as well as his tone:

Water-mel-lone, jes' like from down home; rosten' ears, tatoes-
tatoes-tatoes; nice ripe toma-toes; tommy—tommy—tomatoes;
o-o-o-ochree and dry ingyuns.[58]

Continuing to sing, sell, eat, and dress as they had "back home,"
migrants retained cultural ties with the South. Many sustained these
links by occasionally visiting kinsmen who had stayed behind. It was
a relief to have left behind that region's oppression, but even years
after coming North, many migrants retained a certain ambivalence
about what came to be called "down home." Richard Wright, even
before leaving the South, recognized what Chicago's Old Settlers
would reluctantly learn: "I knew that I could never really leave the
South, for my feelings had already been formed by the South, for
there had been slowly instilled into my personality and consciousness, black though I was, the culture of the South."[59]

Along with retaining some of their southern customs, migrants
also established their own institutions in Chicago. Many southern
business and professional people followed members of their community to Chicago, hoping to retain their patronage. By 1919, approximately two-thirds of all black-owned businesses in Chicago
were operated by what the *Whip* called "newcomers" and an Urban
League spokesman called "migrants." Appealing to the newcomers'
affinity for "down home" cooking, Ira Guy and R. L. Mason opened
the Southern Home Cooking and Southern Lunch Room restaurants, while another establishment advertised "Good Things to Eat:
Southern Cooking." Other businesses, such as Robert Horton's Hattiesburg Shaving Parlor, appealed to more specific loyalties. Even
newcomers from regions sending relatively few migrants to Chicago
could find continued identification with their southern roots, at the
Florida East Coast Shine Parlor or the Carolina Sea Island Candy
Store.[60]

Such establishments sometimes formed the core of a neighborhood
dominated by migrants from a particular area. Horton's Hattiesburg
Shaving Parlor, for example, lay in the middle of a colony of more
than 150 families from Hattiesburg and its environs. Also located in
this five-block stretch along Rhodes Avenue were the Mississippi
Coal and Wood Company and other small businesses owned by Mississippians. "We people from Mississippi stick together—I guess it's
because they made us stick together down there," explained one
woman from Meridian. Another former Mississippian, referring to a
different enclave, later recalled that her family had lived for eleven
years in a "rough and rowdy" section of Federal Street, because "they
were home people you know and we thought we could feel protected

living near them." By living among fellow southerners, migrants could ease their adjustment to urban life, while sustaining familiar relationships and habits.[61]

Migrants also created more formal institutions that brought them together with others from their former homes. By 1921, newcomers from at least nine southern states could join clubs comprising natives of their home state. Many of these clubs met regularly or held social affairs. Frequently dominated by men and women who had migrated to Chicago before the Great Migration, the clubs also sometimes served as sources of organized support for black politicians, many of whom were among those earlier migrants. They also informed migrants of the location of business and professional men from their home state and urged "home loyalty." Although some clubs, such as the Tennessee Home League, which invited "all Tennesseans" to its meetings, professed to welcome all newcomers from the appropriate state, most resembled the Arkansas Club, which set "respectability" as the "prime requisite" of membership. "We don't want it so that just any old Tom, Dick, and Harry can get in," explained one member. To those who did join, the state clubs both perpetuated loyalties to one's birthplace and helped to integrate the newcomer into black Chicago's social and political life.[62]

The most important institutions founded by the migrants were their churches. At first, the city's established black churches exerted special efforts to recruit newcomers, and thousands of migrants readily accepted the invitations. During 1917–18, each week's *Defender* carried messages from churches claiming that "newcomers are welcome," "strangers welcome," or "everyone is welcome and made to feel at home." Some of the larger churches, led by Olivet Baptist and Institutional AME, viewed the newcomers as a challenge to their expanded programs, which included such services as employment bureaus, housing directories, and day nurseries. Others offered guidance, dynamic preaching, or "good singing."[63] The migrants responded enthusiastically. Olivet, which soon claimed to be the largest Baptist church in the world, added more than five thousand new members between 1916 and 1919. Arriving from Alabama in 1922, Mary Fluornoy went to Olivet her "first week here. We couldn't get in. We'd have to stand up. I don't care how early we'd go, you wouldn't get in." Smaller congregations grew as well. Walters AME Zion more than tripled its membership in three years, counting 351 newcomers by 1919. Such increases were not unusual, as men and women coming from towns and rural areas where ministers passed through only once or twice each month to preach in crude buildings were impressed even with Chicago's more modest institutions.[64]

The enthusiasm, however, was often temporary. Many migrants felt distinctly uncomfortable in Chicago's churches, because of both the size of some congregations and the style of worship acceptable to their ministers and laity. Migrants, especially those from the rural South, were accustomed to services accompanied by improvisational singing, "shouting," and other forms of active participation and demonstrative enthusiasm. These men and women reacted coolly to the intellectual sermons of such ministers as Reverend William Braddan of Berean Baptist Church, who refused to hold revivals and prohibited standing in his church during services. Even at such places as Walters AME Zion, where migrants apparently worshipped as they pleased, they could hardly be unaware that the pastor, Reverend W. A. Blackwell, considered "singing, shouting and talking being the most useless ways of proving Christianity." Most Chicago ministers permitted traditional "enthusiasm," and many of the most respected among them even matched southern preachers at driving a congregation to an emotional pitch. But these ministers generally did so only as a concession to some of the older members of the congregation and as an attempt to appeal as widely as possible; they also devoted a part of the service to a more sober sermon, which some migrants found uninspiring. One woman, who had joined Olivet when she arrived in Chicago, later recalled that she "couldn't understand the pastor and the words he used." She soon realized that "I couldn't sing their way. The songs was proud-like." She left to join a smaller church. Indeed, in most of the major churches, the majority of Old Settlers considered "the old time religion" preferred by this woman and many other migrants to be outdated, unrefined, and embarrassing. One group of migrants from rural Alabama and Georgia told an interviewer in 1917 that they needed a church "where they can sing without appearing strange, and where they can hear somebody else pray besides themselves." A newcomer from Slidell, Louisiana, felt similarly uncomfortable at Pilgrim Baptist Church, because "nobody said nothing aloud but there were whispers all over the place." Religious practice in such an atmosphere was not the communal experience that many southerners expected on Sunday mornings.[65]

Migrants not only objected to the general atmosphere and style of worship characteristic of Chicago's "old line" churches, but also found that they did not receive the individual recognition to which they were accustomed. One woman left the first church she joined because it was "too large—it don't see the small people. . . . The preacher wouldn't know me, might could call my name in the book, but he wouldn't know me otherwise. Why, at home whenever I didn't come to Sunday School they would always come and see what was the matter." This experience especially offended men and women who had been influential members of their churches back home. In response, some chose to organize their own congregations, frequently joining with former townsmen or other dissatisfied migrants seeking an alternative. A church founded by a small group of migrants provided an additional link to their southern backgrounds and to other newcomers. Some churches comprised mainly men and women who had worshipped together in the South and had either come North with their pastor or had sent for him after they arrived. Others, like Christ Temple Mission, which called itself a "Branch of Christ Temple Church, Jackson, Miss.," reconstituted themselves under new ministers. In some cases migrants finally managed to establish a struggling storefront church by finding a minister from their home state who could augment the membership by attracting others from a different part of that state. In this way, Monumental Baptist Church grew from a small "prayer band" into an "Alabama" church. Generally launched as storefronts (as most of the established churches had been earlier), many of these churches eventually grew to rival older institutions.[66]

This process of joining churches, splitting off, and starting new institutions was part of the adjustment process for many newcomers. By first entering large churches, newcomers could receive assistance in finding jobs and homes, meet other southerners, and perhaps glean useful information from announcements during services. Eventually migrants could decide whether to leave the large church for a more intimate congregation or try a different—but established—church. Chicago offered a seemingly endless variety, not only of denominations but of styles and sizes. A migrant could choose from among large churches like South Park Methodist Episcopal which had been organized by fifty Mississippians before the exodus and had grown to twenty-five hundred by 1919; any of the "old line" churches dominated by middle-class Old Settlers and featuring intellectual sermons on topics of social and political relevance; small churches such as St. John AME, which promised "old time religion"; revival tents; "rescue missions" offering services every night; and eclectic sects like the Church of the New Jerusalem, where the pastor "preached from a deck of cards." On the whole, migrants tended to stick with traditional denominations, although by 1919, twenty Holiness storefront churches presaged a trend which would increase that sect's membership to one-fifth of all black churchgoers within the next decade. Many migrants probably moved around a great deal, becoming what some ministers scornfully called "church tramps." One woman later recalled that "[Although I] was raised Baptist, when I came here I didn't like their services so I went from church to church, but they was all the same." Another migrant went from the Come and See Baptist Church to the Hope Well Baptist Church, and finally gave up and organized the New Galilee Baptist Church.[67]

This kind of shopping around would have been impossible for most migrants before they came to Chicago. Rural villages and towns in the South generally supported at most one church of any given denomination; considering the importance of the church to community life, the limitation was significant. In Chicago options were circumscribed by attitudes of Old Settlers, but migrants exercised considerable discretion over which church community they joined. Experimentation not only facilitated their adaptation to urban Chicago, but was in itself a form of adaptation.[68]

As a mode of adaptation to the new environment, choosing a church—or starting a new one—symbolized the hopes of many migrants. Migration not only had increased the number of available options; those options included the chance to adjust to the urban North while still retaining aspects of one's southern cultural heritage. In addition, many could realistically look forward to "bettering their condition" either by joining a more prestigious church or by organizing and leading a new congregation. And all this took place within institutions controlled by blacks, relatively insulated from oppressive race relations. "I goes every Sunday and Wednesday nights to prayer meeting," remarked one migrant who belonged to Olivet Baptist Church, "just to thank God that he let me live to go to a place of worship like that, a place where my people worship and ain't pestered by the white men."[69]

It is not surprising that a migrant might express in such a manner one aspect of the church's importance in her life. Olivet was dominated by Old Settlers—although not the elite of black Chicago—but it was still a black institution. Indeed, religious life in black Chicago suggests the complexity of the relationships between migrants and the city's established black community. If many migrants felt alienated from Chicago's black religious institutions, others remained within the large churches. The hostility that existed in individual churches along lines of class and geographic origin was partially bridged by the fact of membership in a single institution and the leadership of the minister. The divisions both within and between churches existed alongside a significant degree of cohesion based upon identification as part of Chicago's black community and its institutions. Although the fissures were significant, they were neither as deep nor as wide as the gap separating white and black. Migrants found a black community that seemed snobbish and condescending at times; but nevertheless the established community and the migrants shared one thing which set them all off from the rest of Chicago—race.

6

"Don't Have to Look up
to the White Man"

Migrants' expectations of northern race relations varied widely, partly according to the level and sources of information at their disposal. Images rooted in the days of the underground railroad and fertilized by continuing sectional debate and interregional communication led many black southerners to expect that northern whites would not share the racist attitudes that dominated the white South. According to one rumor that spread into southern Mississippi, "northern people had said that southern people were not treating colored folks right and wanted to move them all North." One family from Texas expected to encounter "no discrimination" in Chicago. Negroes, they had heard, "could go where they pleased without the embarrassment of being hindered because of their color."[1]

Hopeful but less naive migrants tempered such optimism with the wisdom of experience. Few black southerners interpreted their own experience or their region's history in a manner that would lead them to trust white people. Nor did they necessarily want as much contact with whites as many white Chicagoans feared. There is little evidence that black southerners coming to Chicago were especially interested in integration per se; most were more concerned about legal protection, political rights, and access to the paths to security or mobility. Because segregation implied inequality, racial integration could both guarantee and symbolize full participation in American society. In some aspects of everyday life, many newcomers looked forward to freedom from whites; they evinced little desire to attend integrated churches or spend leisure time with white people.

Optimism and caution coexisted within the context of an image of white Chicago that was often cloudy, and probably inaccurate when it was clear. Coming from a region whose population was largely of either African or British descent, black southerners had been exposed to little information likely to inspire a mental construction of Chicago's ethnic mosaic. Roughly one-third of the city's white residents had emigrated from Europe, and three-fourths had at least one parent who had been born abroad. From Germany, the ethnically diverse Austro-Hungarian and Russian empires, Ireland, Scandinavia, and Italy, immigrants had settled in Chicago and reshaped the city's cultural landscape. Even within the borders of the Second Ward, home to half of the city's black population in 1920 and the most accessible source of housing for newcomers, the white minority included a representative melange. The 15,031 whites included 5,771 immigrants and 6,893 of foreign or mixed parentage, with Jews, Irish, Scandinavians, Italians, and Germans most numerous among the foreign-born, followed by Canadians, Greeks, and Poles.[2]

If most migrants arrived prepared to adapt familiar categories of race to their new environment, most white Chicagoans were disposed to evaluate the potential impact of migration within the context of similar broad preconceptions. Such expectations depended heavily on perceptions about race and the dynamic of migration. Despite considerable variation according to class, neighborhood, ethnicity, and political affiliation, white reactions to the influx generally reflected widely shared assumptions about the passive role of blacks in the migration process in particular and in economic and political processes in general.

A small group of employers, Republican politicians, and block-busting realtors encouraged the movement precisely because of these assumptions. These individuals, who had little contact with blacks, had something to gain and perceived little potential impact on their everyday lives. Realtors active on the fringes of the ghetto eyed the substantial income opportunities offered by blockbusting. A group of Republican politicians, whose black lieutenants in the ghetto presided over a sophisticated vote-getting apparatus, regarded the newcomers as a large and manipulable bloc of voters. Employers recognized that the migration could solve their acute labor shortage. If blacks proved to be good workers and fit into the stereotypical anti-union mold, they also would help solve the more chronic problem of union agitation.[3] Few other white Chicagoans, however, looked upon the migration so optimistically.

Chicago's major white newspapers, which both reflected and shaped public opinion, pitied black southerners but viewed with pessimism and fear the onrush of ignorant, degraded, and helpless refugees, objects of the overwhelming social and economic forces emphasized by contemporary observers as causes of the Great Migration. This perspective logically induced an analytic framework dominated by a "Negro problem," or the need for black newcomers—like the white immigrants before them—to "adjust." Adaptation on the part of the city's institutions or its white population did not seem to be an issue. Characteristics of the migrants as either individuals (the most liberal perspective) or as southern Negroes, rather than the limitations structured by class relations and racism, defined the problem. Racial oppression was considered a southern disease, and the Chicago *Tribune* had no difficulty ridiculing blacks and referring to them as a threat to the city's health and morals, while repeatedly decrying southern racism and calling for reform south of the Mason-Dixon line. Complacency about race relations in Chicago combined with a view of the migrants as hapless but degraded victims to leave many whites at once sympathetic to blacks in general and threatened by the implications of black migration to Chicago in particular.[4]

Even the minority of whites who transcended this perspective were likely to view the influx with trepidation. Recognizing that prevailing racial attitudes in Chicago would shape the Great Migration's threat to civic order, the *Jewish Daily Courier* feared that whites would react violently. It is not unlikely that its self-image as a spokesman for a group that was neither black nor white, but rather stood "between them," permitted the Jewish newspaper to extend its critique of southern racial violence to a recognition of the implications of northern racism. Until the 1919 race riot, however, few other white Chicagoans expressed such concerns. Whites disagreed about how to meet the threat posed by the influx of blacks, but whatever the proposed solution—violent confrontation, prophylactic reform, or pressure on newcomers to return South—it was the migrants who were dangerous.[5]

Condemnation of southern racial policies, juxtaposed with a condescending hostility towards the debased victims of those policies and an ambivalence towards them as migrants, had firm roots in Chicago's past. Chicago's vociferous abolitionists, abetted by judges who openly flouted the 1850 fugitive-slave law, had given Chicago a reputation in southern Illinois as a "nigger-loving town" before the Civil War. Yet the city's white residents had seen no need to let their opposition to slavery interfere with their equal distaste for black people. Like their counterparts elsewhere in the North, antebellum black Chicagoans were segregated, disfranchised, and restricted to a narrow range of occupations. During the quarter-century following the Civil War, state laws removed most of the legal barriers to full citizenship for blacks, permitting them to vote (three years after blacks had secured that right in the reconstructed southern states), serve on juries, and testify against whites. The Illinois legislature also

banned school segregation (1874) and segregation in public accommodations (1885; tightened by amendment in 1897). These laws,
however, were seldom enforced, and convictions—when obtained—
usually resulted in token fines. Like most other white Americans,
Chicago's white residents had already imbibed racist values and beliefs which transcended legal niceties as influences on patterns of race
relations. Longtime black residents would later nostalgically recall the
nineteenth century as a period of interracial amicability, but a shifting
color line had always defined a series of boundaries.[6]

The legend of a golden age of race relations in nineteenth-century
Chicago cannot be discounted. A few black professionals and servants in wealthy white homes enjoyed cordial relationships with
whites, in some ways analogous to what a historian of black Louisville has called "polite racism." Although less circumscribed than
their contemporaries in that border city and more inclined to agitate
for integration and equality, Chicago's black elite could realistically
recall paternalistic relationships with whites from this period, as well
as romanticize what were usually patronizing friendships. Overt racial conflict seldom flared. On the whole, blacks were essentially invisible to most of white Chicago, constituting only 1.3 percent of the
city's population in 1890. Racial hostility began to escalate along with
black migration in the 1890s, as the black population more than doubled to 30,150 (1.9 percent of the total population). Like other northern cities, Chicago in the early twentieth century experienced what
Ray Stannard Baker described in 1908 as a rapid increase in "race
feeling and discrimination." This does not, however, imply a change
in direction so much as a consolidation of previously less coherent
tendencies.[7]

By the time of the Great Migration, Chicago was a divided city,
characterized by Richard Robert Wright a decade earlier as more segregated than any other northern metropolis.[8] Wright's evaluation—
even if exaggerated—appropriately directs attention to the countless
barriers separating black Chicago from the rest of the city, even if it
discounted the significant ethnic divisions crucial to an understanding of Chicago's social terrain. Recurrent nativist editorials in the
Defender and similar complaints by black spokesmen angry about
the relative treatment accorded blacks and "foreigners" indicate that
black Chicagoans were well aware of the presence of immigrants and
their role in the city's economy. But blacks generally ignored more
specific implications of ethnicity in their perceptions of "white Chicago." Sources generated from the black community suggest little
cognizance of seething hostilities pitting Irish against Italian, Norwe-
gian against Irish, or Pole against Lithuanian, German, or Jew.[9]

Of most immediate significance to the lives of black residents were the fault lines that separated them from others in the city and divided their own community. Class distinctions and hostilities set off most blacks from a significant portion of the white population, culturally, socially, and economically, while also dividing the black community itself. At the same time, popular ideas about racial differences influenced patterns of interaction (or lack thereof) characterizing work, play, prayer, learning, charity, habitation, and other aspects of everyday life. Where whites perceived racial distinctions to be most significant or most threatening, they sought separation or exclusion. Where differences mattered less, or in the case of certain forms of night life made association with blacks perversely desirable, contact was more likely. The Great Migration changed the configuration of these patterns only slightly. But its numerical impact magnified and multiplied them, while exacerbating previously less salient spatial, political, and occupational conflicts.

Largely unaware of the specifics of Chicago race relations, migrants tended to place what they did know within a context shaped by their experience in the South. They knew little of the city's ethnic diversity and even less of the tensions dividing various white ethnic groups, tensions exacerbated during the Great Migration by the conflict across the Atlantic. Black southerners preparing to go North thought about "the difference between north and south," as one explained, and their expectations were inextricable from such comparisons. A young man who had "never ben in the north no further than Texas," had heard "how much better the colard people are treated up there than they are down here." On the whole, therefore, expectations were likely to be fulfilled at some level, given both the qualitative and quantitative differences between North and South. Even after race riots revealed the force of racial hostility in Chicago and other northern cities, migrants who had sought relief "from the Lynchman's noose and torchman's fire," felt only a limited sense of disillusion. In addition, many migrants had from the beginning tempered images of greater freedom with traditional wariness of whites, to fashion expectations that were at once naively optimistic and realistically modest.[10]

Much of what they found in Chicago confirmed whatever optimism migrants might have had about the meaning of race in the northern metropolis. The mounting racial conflict that finally culminated in a riot in 1919 cannot obscure certain aspects of Chicago race relations central to the initial perceptions of black southerners arriving during and immediately after World War I. Levels of agitation, however much they varied during the half-century preceding the

Great Migration, reflected a degree of fluidity or at least a certain lack of definition. Moreover, most white Chicagoans cared as little about Negroes as they cared for them, a distinct improvement from the perspective of people accustomed to the southern obsession with racial control. Chicagoans might have been equally committed to white supremacy, but without the threat of a significant black population "the preoccupation with the issue of race" so essential to southern culture in the early twentieth century was unnecessary, if not irrelevant, in Chicago. At the same time, however, limitations and imperatives structured by ideas about the meaning of race at least indirectly affected nearly all aspects of black life. Black newcomers encountered a city "free from the outward signs of 'segregation,'" as one perceptive white reformer observed in 1913, but also a city where racial labels interacted with the class structure to limit options and define patterns of social interaction.[11]

The "outward signs of segregation" mattered much to migrants from a region where such signs delineated a caste system defined and legitimized by legal institutions. The absence of Jim Crow laws— indeed, the statutory prohibition of racial discrimination in most aspects of public life—suggested that Chicago at the very least lacked a public ideology of racial dominance. Although discrimination circumscribed black life in Chicago and interacted with the material circumstances of most migrants to relegate them to the worst housing and least desirable employment in the city, the color line was not ubiquitous. Nor did it reflect the public values embodied in the laws of the state and city.[12]

On the streetcars and occasionally elsewhere, the differences transcended the symbolic, as blacks and whites were accorded roughly equal treatment and not segregated. One of the few arenas of frequent and involuntary public interaction across lines of both race and class, the streetcars tested some of the implications of integration: longtime black residents feared that ill–mannered newcomers would cause the race to "fail," and migrants marveled at the seeming unconcern of white riders. The stereotypical anonymity of the urban environment, symbolized to Richard Wright by the white man on the streetcar whose "mind fastened upon some inward thought," apparently unconcerned about the black rider sharing his seat, could seem liberating to newcomers from the South. Given conventional racial attitudes in Chicago, most whites probably found it distasteful to sit next to a black person. Rather than publicly insulting a black seatmate, however, a white rider would silently bear the discomfort and perhaps complain later to other whites. It was, after all, within that black individual's rights (even if some whites wished to abolish those

rights) to take that seat, and objection promised a commotion unlikely to resolve the issue. If some white Chicagoans avoided streetcar
lines popular among blacks or stood rather than take an empty seat
next to a black rider, the tacit nature of the insult required neither
response nor acceptance and therefore differed qualitatively from
southern protocols. Despite frequent racial incidents in Chicago during the 1910s, there is little evidence of confrontation on the streetcars
during that period.[13]

Interactions in such public arenas as streetcars epitomized meaningful differences between northern and southern race relations.
Even if white Chicagoans shared the racial prejudices of white southerners, and most probably did, they seldom aggressively displayed
those attitudes in impersonal contacts with blacks. Asked why he felt
greater freedom in Chicago, one newcomer commented that blacks
were not "compelled to say 'yes ma'am' or 'yes sir' to white people,
whether you desired to or not." Whatever their racial attitudes,
northern whites did not—and could not—constantly try to strip
blacks of their self-respect, dignity, and pride. A black person "was
not counted in the South," observed one migrant, drawing a contrast
with Chicago. Another described the ability to "go anywhere you
want to go . . . don't have to look up to the white man, get off the
street for him, and go to the buzzard roost at shows." The symbols of
racial caste which permeated everyday life in the South were harder
to find in Chicago: "a man could feel more like a man."[14]

Black southerners also could leave behind much of the fear that
had so permeated their lives in the South. "We collord people are
almost afraid to walke the streets after night," explained a Palatine,
Texas, man ready to head north.[15] If, as one historian has recently
argued, a black "woman or girl in the South found herself in danger
of being attacked whenever she walked down a country road," and
had even greater trepidations about the intentions of male employers,
Chicago at least did not so readily accept the inherent legitimacy of
"white men's persistent violation of black women." Black southerners
who had been North remarked on the significance of the "fear of mob
violence" as a distinctive aspect of southern black life, and newcomers to Chicago noticed the difference. Bert Jones, who arrived in 1917,
later recalled that a Negro did not have to be afraid to "rub against a
white person or something. . . . You didn't have to be afraid to sit
down beside one, or you didn't have to stay in a position of being
on your P's and Q's." Recalling southern communities prepared to
lynch a black man for accidentally brushing against a white woman
while running to catch a train, migrants could easily appreciate the
contrast.[16]

But if black southerners enjoyed "greater freedom and independence" in Chicago, as nearly all affirmed to interviewers from the Chicago Commission on Race Relations, it was not because whites had rolled out the red carpet—or any carpet at all. The *Daily News* noted in 1916 that "every year Chicago welcomes, by the thousand, her old southern friends who 'summer' by the lake," but the welcome was clearly reserved for those southerners who were white.[17] Black southerners were greeted with headlines blaring "NEGROES ARRIVE BY THOUSANDS—PERIL TO HEALTH" and "HALF A MILLION DARKIES FROM DIXIE SWARM TO THE NORTH TO BETTER THEMSELVES." During 1916 and 1917, Chicago's three major daily newspapers (the *Tribune*, *Daily News*, and *Herald Examiner*) published forty-five articles on the exodus from the South. Most of the reports dramatically overstated the volume of migration; many, especially in the *Herald-Examiner* and *Tribune*, evoked images of hordes of blacks inundating the city, bringing their disease, vice, and low standards of living. According to the Chicago Commission on Race Relations, half of all articles on "racial matters" printed by these newspapers during 1916–17 either ridiculed blacks or focused on violence, black criminals, or vice. The *New World* generally ignored blacks, although a 1913 reference to "pickaninnies" was unlikely to foster positive images among its readers. Only the *Daily News* was inclined to portray blacks favorably, even winning praise from the *Defender* on one occasion.[18] Had they paused at the railroad station to pick up a local daily newspaper, black newcomers might have found their exuberance slightly chilled by what they read.

Despite considerable variation, this exaggeration, fear, and disdain defined the general tone of white response to the Great Migration, except for the many Chicagoans who simply paid no attention because they neither lived nor worked near blacks. Chicago's white population shared many—if not all—of the attitudes found among southern whites. Public opinion surveys taken in 1921 indicate that white Chicagoans considered blacks minimally educable, emotional, "unmoral" (as opposed to immoral; apparently they lacked moral standards), sexual, prone to sex crimes, larcenous, and malodorous. Newspaper articles, even when presented without explicit editorial comment, reinforced such images. Whether focusing disproportionately on vice or issuing well-intended pleas for official attention to problems of disease in the Black Belt, white journalists clearly characterized the black newcomers in terms familiar to white readers. References, however innocent, to "QUEER SCENES" at train stations, "pickaninnies," and rural habits that the *Defender* criticized but white newspapers ridiculed, provided additional confirmation to whites certain about the nature of civilized culture and its accoutrements. A streetcar line which served a district once inhabited by whites but now overwhelmingly black became known to white Chicagoans as the "African Central," and it is not likely that the term "African" connoted anything except an image of primitive or savage culture.[19]

What many whites feared was that the thousands of victimized, rural, uneducated, and racially inferior (whether culturally or genetically) newcomers would have difficulty "adjusting." This imperative had confronted previous black newcomers and white immigrants, and in the latter case had aroused such concern that restriction and Americanization movements had emerged. But the magnitude of the problem this time set it apart from earlier black migration, and the particular population involved distinguished it from European immigration. As usual, a failure to adapt would have social rather than merely individual implications, and what little most white Chicagoans knew about black Chicago defined potential implications of the influx.

Chicago's white daily newspapers had little difficulty identifying those implications. Almost immediately, the issue of public health infused reporting of the sudden influx of black southerners. The *Daily News* pointed out that the overcrowded housing dominating the "environment" to which the migrants would have to adjust posed a serious threat to the "city's health." Although intended to stimulate preventive measures, the warnings also elicited fears grounded in popular ideas about blacks. The *Tribune*'s references to a "peril" less ambiguously aroused readers who read of health commissioner John Dill Robertson's concerns about "an epidemic of contagious diseases, especially tuberculosis." As one public health nurse later recalled, "no longer could the Negro health situation be left into the background as it was a threatened menace to every one."[20]

Concerned that blacks displayed "a childlike helplessness in the matter of sanitation and housing," the *Tribune* was even more worried that "they have almost no standard of morals." Early reports of the Great Migration appeared soon after or even simultaneously with news of crackdowns on vice in the South Side Black Belt and black involvement in the corruption surrounding the "vicious resorts" raided by police. In January 1917, headlines publicized the arrest of black alderman Oscar DePriest for his alleged role in gambling, graft, and vice. Even in the relatively restrained, almost evenhanded coverage sometimes found in the *Daily News*, whites read about black corruption and vice at the same time they learned about the dramatic increase in the city's black population. The *Tribune*, which proclaimed DePriest "KING OF THE BLACK BELT" and headed exposés on vice in black neighborhoods with such phrases as "DRINK AND GAMBLE," communicated the message with greater gusto. It did not matter that the concentration of vice in the Black Belt owed more to public policy and selective law enforcement than to black proclivities; blacks forced to live in its midst could not escape its odium. That a large proportion of the clientele was white did not mitigate blacks' responsibility so much as render their disorder all the more threatening to public (i.e., white) morality.[21]

Here indeed lay the rub. White reformers, however much they opposed vice in principle and in practice, apparently found one particular kind of vice resort especially dangerous: the infamous "black-and-tan" where "white and colored patrons mingled in intoxicated revels," according to the blue-nosed and blue-blooded Committee of Fifteen. Equally opposed to cabarets, gambling, and vice, and never unwilling to warn newcomers against temptation, Chicago's black newspapers justifiably criticized white "pseudo Good Samaritans . . . [whose] attack is not made on CABARETS, but on BLACK AND TAN CABA-RETS," and social workers who "throng the Morals Court" in their outrage over interracial immorality. During the 1916 grand jury investigations of vice and corruption, the State's Attorney's office invariably asked whether interracial dancing was in evidence. The "mingling of white and black customers" seemed to attract attention even from whites generally less concerned about the immorality of night clubs and bawdy houses. If the popularity of black-and-tans and ghetto entertainments in general, not only in Chicago but in other northern cities as well, reveals much about tensions and attitudes among the white clientele, the exaggerated reaction to these clubs suggests what many reformers feared about the Great Migration. Whether they agreed with Graham Taylor that blacks were "depraved," or like Jane Addams lamented blacks' "lack of inherited control," they recognized that black Chicago was not isolated from the rest of the city. It had to be regulated, reformed, and stabilized. This required social institutions aimed at inhibiting "social disorganization" and agencies offering relief to families on the margins.[22]

Until the Great Migration, Chicago's renowned social service institutions had paid little attention to blacks or the impact of racial discrimination. Excluded from most private agencies and often provided inferior service by public institutions, black Chicagoans did not have access to the range or quantity of social services available to white immigrants. Most of what was available had to be provided by financially marginal black institutions. Black neighborhoods contained few, if any, orphanages, day nurseries, old-age homes, clinics, public baths and relief stations. Even some institutions located in or near the ghetto refused to accept black clients.[23] These policies rested on a combination of hostility towards blacks, fear of immigrant reluctance to use interracial facilities, and priorities. Reformers interested in Americanization were unlikely to think about serving the black newcomer who, as the *Defender* and other black spokesmen liked to remind whites more sympathetic to European immigrants than blacks, "needs no Americanization." Indeed, for many white reformers this was part of the problem, given uncertainty about the desirability of black entry into the mainstream.[24]

Despite widely shared assumptions about the existence and usefulness of racial categories, however, Chicago's white reformers differed in their attitudes towards blacks. An especially sympathetic and pluralistic minority, dominated by the women associated with Hull House and the University of Chicago Settlement, shared Edith Abbott's opposition to segregated facilities and insistence on enforcing laws requiring public institutions to accept blacks. Jane Addams, proud of her abolitionist heritage, was among the founders of the NAACP and wrote of the "chains" of racism, forged not only by southern racism but by northern indifference as well. Louise De-Koven Bowen recognized that even if blacks and white immigrants faced many similar problems, racial discrimination distinguished the black experience, with the "children of the negro" limited in ways unknown to the children of white newcomers. Sophonisba Breckinridge even went so far as to advocate "welcoming" black newcomers from the South. But these women, and the few men who shared their recognition of the significance of black poverty and racial discrimination, generally remained involved in activities oriented towards white immigrants, even after continued black migration and the expansion of black neighborhoods placed Hull House and other settlements within walking distance for many blacks. While Abbott, Addams, Bowen, Breckinridge, Mary McDowell, and a handful of others served on committees concerned with racial issues, wrote about the black ghetto, and criticized discrimination (usually privately), they tended to accept conventional assumptions about black cultural inferiority and the dangers of racial integration. Bowen's apparent ignorance of the significance of her failure to capitalize "Negro" symbolized a more general unawareness of black perspective. Their compassion and interest, however exceptional for its time and place, had little impact on the black community, race relations, or the lives of black newcomers.[25]

Most white reformers in Chicago were neither hostile to nor especially interested in black people. If the social gospel that underpinned much of the progressive social impulse grasped what one historian has called "the tenet that not only individuals but entire communities committed sin or won salvation," few reformers included racism among the social or individual sins of modern American society. Industrialization and urbanization occupied the conceptual focus of the social gospel's analysis of social problems, relegating racism to a background distorted by a dominant view of black inferiority. Social workers, slightly more sensitive than most other progressives, perceived a problem, but until the Great Migration defined it as rural, southern, and a matter for agricultural reformers. Race relations, black poverty, and related issues, W. E. B. Du Bois told Chicago's exclusive, white City Club, had "to do with some one on the outside . . . there is always that feeling of remoteness, the feeling that it is not their problem."[26]

The Great Migration began to push Chicago's white officials, reformers, and institutional leaders to think about the implications of both the increasing black presence and the place of blacks in the city's social and economic structure. During the war years much of "the burden of caring for this newly transplanted population was left entirely to the colored citizens of the city," according to the Women's City Club, but some "mainstream" agencies, especially the United Charities, did maintain offices open to blacks and located within the Black Belt. The "Negro problem" after all, had become inescapable. Migration was exacerbating overcrowding and therefore family "disorganization" in the ghetto, while bringing in people easily tempted by leisure activities dangerous to the city's moral order and racial integrity. Increasing racial violence, culminating in a riot in 1919, magnified the threat and convinced many reformers and philanthropists of the need for social services and "wholesome" institutions in the ghetto.[27]

Regardless of when they became interested in black clients, many social service professionals and other reformers found to their chagrin that newcomers shied away from their doors. Social workers complained that blacks did not take advantage of services, and black Chicagoans appear to have been especially wary of such programs as the United Charities aid for "dependent children of the juvenile court." Recent migrants ineligible for Cook County relief because of insufficient length of residence appear to have been reluctant to turn to United Charities. Less likely than whites to report tuberculosis cases, blacks did not use available medical facilities, perhaps because of the exclusively white staffs at such institutions as Cook County Hospital. Unlike similarly suspicious white immigrants, blacks feared neither the religious tone nor—with some exceptions—the assimilationist cultural imperialism that infused many progressive-era service institutions. But they had difficulty trusting white reformers, were often sensitive to the racist attitudes of even well-intentioned reformers, and were hostile to attempts by white and black reformers to change their leisure habits.[28]

It was difficult for white reformers to understand their inability to reach blacks. The answer was embedded in the problem itself: few white Chicagoans were able to look at Chicago from the perspective of black newcomers or even to recognize the importance of doing so. The city's social work establishment, with its various umbrella organizations and bureaucratic structures, was lily-white. The Chicago Council of Social Agencies, for example, typically included no blacks on its executive committee, and from the minutes of its meetings one might surmise that the city had no black people, or at least no blacks who needed social services. Black middle-class leaders tended "to withdraw from participation in organized social work" according to one black woman who did maintain ties. Participation, moreover, seldom led to considerable influence over policy, leaving whites still "somewhat at a loss in dealing with the colored people."[29] Reform and charity controlled by whites and rooted in varying combinations of paternalism, sympathy, racism, and a drive for social control stood distant from the needs and sensibilities of black men and women who had come to Chicago to seize control over their own lives.

Most philanthropists, city officials, and social service professionals thought they could address the issue of social service and wholesome leisure in the ghetto by developing a system of parallel public and private services located in the Black Belt. Municipal agencies or white philanthropists would decide what blacks needed, build facilities, provide resources, determine policy, and oversee administration if necessary. Black leaders deemed reliable and competent by white standards would deliver services, and the black institutions created in the process would act as training grounds for community leadership. Black managers and board members would provide responsible (i.e., middle-class) community input, indigenous leadership, and a useful visage of black control. If successful, this program would both discourage blacks from insisting on their statutory right to access to unfriendly public agencies located outside the ghetto and foster the growth of a viable network of private black institutions.[30] This model extended even to the Catholic Church, in the form of Archbishop George Mundelein's announcement in 1917 that St. Monica's parish would "be reserved entirely for the colored Catholics of Chicago." Blacks could attend other churches, but given Mundelein's objection to the formation of "national" parishes and the exclusion of black children from St. James School at 29th and Wabash, the *Defender's* charges of Jim Crow were not unwarranted. Mundelein's justification of his policy partly on the grounds of the desirability of fostering black leadership not only confirms the exclusion of blacks from leadership in integrated parishes, but places him within the mainstream of Chicago's reform community on the issue of institutional separatism. Most significantly, the ideal describes much of the attractiveness of the Chicago Urban League. The League's articulated mission as a "clearinghouse for social service work among Negroes" reflects not only its self-image as a leading force in the black community, but also its usefulness to white agencies seeking a morally and professionally defensible procedure for referring black clients elsewhere.[31]

"Elsewhere" was where most white Chicagoans hoped blacks would go, and most whites who lived in neighborhoods adjoining the already overcrowded South Side Black Belt agreed with the assessment of one neighborhood association that "there is nothing in the make-up of a Negro, physically or mentally, which should induce anyone to welcome him as a neighbor." Whites living in "changing" neighborhoods along the fringes of the Black Belt feared that their neighborhoods would become "tainted," and charged that the migrants constituted an "undesirable" element. The Chicago Real Estate Board reflected the sentiments of many white Chicagoans when in 1917 it first proposed explicit segregation of housing by race and then petitioned the City Council to pass an ordinance prohibiting further migration of "colored families" to Chicago until such time as the city could work out "reasonable restrictions" sufficient to "prevent lawlessness, destruction of values and property and loss of life." Even the *Tribune* dismissed the exclusion ordinance as unconstitutional. Such agitation continued, however, as the perceived threat multiplied along with the volume of migration.[32]

It was mainly middle-class blacks who wished to live in white neighborhoods. Homeowners living in the middle-class neighborhoods south and east of the gradually expanding South Side ghetto, therefore, confronted the greatest possibility (and occasionally the reality) of black neighbors. Vowing that "they shall not pass," upper- and middle-class whites living east of Cottage Grove Avenue punctuated their rhetoric with meetings, rallies, threats against wavering realtors, and fifty-eight bombings between 1917 and 1921.[33] The targets, middle-class blacks such as banker Jesse Binga rather than newcomers from the South, exemplify the true nature of the "threat"— Old Settlers who were themselves unhappy with their new neighbors in the Black Belt. The racial integrity, rather than the class basis, of such neighborhoods as Hyde Park, Kenwood, and Woodlawn was at risk. If the problem of "neighborhood" within the black community rested on class antagonisms with a regional component, the tensions on the South Side as a whole turned largely on racial divisions.

Neither more nor less willing than middle-class whites to share turf or institutions with blacks, working-class whites responded even more protectively when faced with the possibility of black neighbors. The commonality of class position between white workers and most blacks stimulated competition rather than engendering unity. Largely a function of the distribution of economic and political power in Chicago, this competition fed upon white workers' fears that the migration would undermine the little security and power they had attained. White working-class homeowners, many of whom had poured all their earnings into heavily mortgaged houses, "viewed the prospect of Negro neighbors as a catastrophe equal to loss of their homes," as one historian has noted. Institutional investments and the proximity of jobs in these neighborhoods exacerbated sensitivity to racial "succession." With blacks more likely to be able to afford homes in their neighborhoods than in more expensive districts on the other side of the Black Belt, working-class whites felt especially vulnerable. The perceived threat of "invasion" grew with the level of migration—or at least with the level of exaggeration in both the press and popular discourse.[34]

Unlike the middle class, working-class European immigrants and their descendants living near the Black Belt lacked the resources to use sophisticated methods (such as restrictive covenants) to exclude blacks from their neighborhoods or to move to another section of the city. So they used force. The Black Belt could expand only to the south and east, partly because of the level of violence encountered by any black who tried to cross Wentworth Avenue at the western edge of the ghetto. Given the assumption among white residents that it was impossible to share a block with black residents, constant vigilance became the price of neighborhood protection—the turf had to be defended by whatever means necessary.[35]

The line separating blacks from white working-class immigrants divided not only competitors for space but political opponents as well. Political participation was important to the migrants, who like many other Americans considered the right to vote central to their status as citizens. In the South the ballot box had symbolized not only racial proscription and white monopoly of formal authority, but also the inextricable relationship between class and racial proscription in the form of the poll tax. In some southern communities, the few blacks who could vote considered their franchise a status symbol. Robert Mays, who came to Chicago from Slidell, Louisiana, in the early 1920s, proudly recalled years later that "I am a standing voter,

I've been voting ever since I first came to Chicago. I voted in Slidell—I and Lijah Lewis, a preacher, were the only two Negroes in Slidell who could vote." For the vast majority who had not been able to vote in the South, the ballot box in Chicago was what one political scientist later called "one of the badges of [their] changed life." When questioned during the early 1920s about their political participation in Chicago, numerous migrants regaled interviewers with tales about the various devices used to disfranchise them in the South, implicitly emphasizing the relevance of past exclusion to the meaning of their new status as voters.[36]

It was easy for migrants to appreciate, if not overestimate, their significance as political actors in the city. Candidates targeted appeals directly at migrants from specific states. On Sundays many ministers opened their pulpits to politicians—black and white. Twice each year, at primaries and general elections, the Republican machine in the ghetto worked hard to bring migrants to the polls, certain that they could count on the southerners to maintain their loyalty to the party of Lincoln and the faction within it that paid most attention to black voters.[37]

This steadfast adherence not only to the Republican Party, but to one particular faction in that party, positioned the migrants in direct conflict with the working-class whites who lived west of Wentworth Avenue. Immigrants, especially Catholics, exercised what little power they had through the Democratic Party. To many migrants "Democrats" was a contemptuous euphemism for "white people." To make matters worse, the black community was a bastion of support for Mayor William Hale Thompson, who had earned the hatred of many of Chicago's Catholic immigrants for his nativist rhetoric and anti-Catholic slurs. Thousands of European immigrants and their families on the South Side would have agreed with the assessment of one Bohemian newspaper that Thompson was "the most despicable mayor Chicago has ever had." Overwhelmingly, black Chicagoans thought otherwise.[38]

"Big Bill" had been courting black voters since his first aldermanic campaign in 1900, when he arranged for Adelbert H. Roberts, a black politician, to make one of his nominating speeches. By then he had already forged a friendship with Reverend Archibald J. Carey, who remained a political ally until the AME bishop's death in the late 1920s. Both Carey and editor Robert Abbott of the *Defender* went so far as to compare Thompson with Lincoln, and black voters provided "Big Bill" with the margin of victory in either the primary (1915) or general election (1919 and 1927) in each of his victorious mayoral campaigns. To the annoyance of immigrants who competed with blacks for recognition as well as jobs at city hall, Thompson rewarded his supporters. By 1919, Thompson's city hall was known to many of his white enemies as "Uncle Tom's Cabin" because of the unprecedented number of black appointees. To blacks, the controversial politician was a hero for appointing blacks to city jobs and for recognizing such black politicians as Louis B. Anderson, who was his floor leader in the City Council. Like other Chicagoans, blacks received mostly "a whole lot of bad government" from Thompson. But both recognition of individual politicians and the symbolic importance of black patronage won the appreciation of migrants proud of their new political rights and influence.[39]

Thompson's reelection in 1919 fueled racial political antagonisms and confirmed some of the fears of immigrants concerning the harmful effects the influx of blacks would have on their power and status. In an atmosphere already charged with wartime ethnic tensions, the five-way contest among the controversial mayor, a Catholic Democrat, another Democrat running as an Independent, an Irish Labor Party candidate, and a Socialist aroused emotions across the city. Thompson's close victory in the April general election followed an acrimonious, mudslinging campaign marked by racial and religious slurs. Although "good government" forces in the city opposed Thompson because of his tolerance of vice and corruption, one of the major issues on the South Side was race. Symbolism cut two ways. To many white immigrants, especially on the South Side, Thompson was not only anti-Catholic, but a "nigger-lover." Blacks constituted only one of many identifiable blocs whose margin for Thompson exceeded his citywide plurality; but one Democratic newspaper proclaimed immediately after the election "NEGROES ELECT BIG BILL," thereby fanning flames of racial hatred that had scarred the campaign. Further migration of blacks could only enhance the power of black Republicans at the expense of white Democrats who represented the white working-class wards on the South Side.[40]

White workers viewed the workplace as a similarly competitive arena. Before 1916, blacks had been hired by Chicago industrialists only during strikes, and few white workers had much experience working side-by-side with blacks. A record of black strikebreaking in Chicago, exaggerated by white workers prone to ignoring the greater role of white scabs in nearly every instance, led many of those workers to view an influx of blacks into industry as a threat to their nascent organizing campaigns during World War I. A black foothold in industry also meant competition for jobs once the war ended, soldiers returned, and production declined. Some migrants found that white butchers in the packinghouses would "do almost anything to keep them from learning."[41]

Given the existence of these tensions, it is not surprising that incidents of violence plagued Chicago race relations and that the violence increased as the black population grew and competition intensified. Black workers were occasionally assaulted as they passed through white working-class neighborhoods on their way to jobs at the stockyards. Inside the packinghouses, wildcat strikes and racial confrontations frequently stopped just short of violence. Fears related to competition for housing heightened, and between 1917 and 1919 whites threw twenty-four bombs at houses owned by blacks who had attempted to push too far outside the boundaries of the Black Belt. Even public parks were dangerous for blacks, especially at night, when white youth gangs defended public space against racial "contamination." Usually allied with ward politicians, these ethnically organized "athletic clubs" enrolled young men who provided muscle on election day and fought to preserve the racial integrity of their neighborhoods when necessary. Certain that Mayor Thompson could not be relied upon to protect white Democrats and Catholics against the black horde, the "clubs"—especially Ragen's Colts—took this responsibility upon themselves. Migrants, even if they had not yet read threatening signs posted west of Wentworth, quickly learned that "the Mickeys" (many blacks mistakenly assumed that all the white gangs were Irish) would pounce upon vulnerable blacks who entered their territory. The police offered little protection, occasionally joining the aggressors or initiating their own attacks on blacks.[42]

Racial violence in Chicago increased dramatically beginning in 1917. When East St. Louis, Illinois, erupted in a race riot in July of that year and neither the militia nor the police provided adequate protection to black citizens, black Chicagoans began to fear similar outbursts in their city. Some urged blacks to arm themselves for protection, and as violent attacks on blacks multiplied between 1917 and 1919, preparations for self-defense seemed increasingly sensible.

Returning black soldiers added an especially explosive element to these racial tensions. Although Chicago's black community expressed pride in its representatives in the military and gave its own "Fighting Eighth" Infantry a hero's welcome, black soldiers otherwise found the same chilly reception received by black servicemen in other American cities. Despite the vicious discrimination they had endured at the hands of the United States Army, black soldiers arrived home expecting that their patriotism would yield some improvements in the conditions of black Americans. Indeed, this hope had induced support for the war effort from such spokesmen as W. E. B. Du Bois, who had advised blacks to "close ranks" behind the war effort in order to demonstrate to whites the loyalty and contributions which blacks could offer their country. In Chicago, young black men who in 1917 had accepted the counsel of community leaders to put aside "all the injustices for the time being," returned two years later already angered by "their harsh treatment in the Army, both at home and in France." In no mood to accept either petty harassment in parks by white youths or the reluctance of many employers to hire them, these veterans contributed to a growing spirit of resistance within the black community.[43]

In the spring of 1919, rumors began to spread through Chicago's black community that whites were planning an antiblack campaign even bloodier than the race riots in Springfield in 1908 and in East St. Louis. After two and one-half months of scattered violence, white and black youths clashed three times in mid-June, with whites apparently the aggressors. Ragen's Colts were especially active, but less organized white mobs also attacked blacks. By the end of June, many blacks believed that whites were planning to celebrate Independence Day with an invasion designed to drive blacks out of the city. Despite the threat, the fears it engendered, and the antagonisms it amplified, few migrants decided to return South.[44]

July 4 came and went without incident, but three weeks later the city shook in a paroxysm of racial violence touched off by the murder of a black teenager whose raft had floated too close to a "white" beach on the South Side. From July 27 until July 31, black and white Chicago battled in the streets, and occasional attacks punctuated the uneasy calm for another week. By August 8, twenty-three blacks and fifteen whites lay dead, and at least 537 other Chicagoans had suffered injuries. The police were unable—and in most cases unwilling—to suppress the violence; only a timely rainstorm and the belated assignment of the Illinois National Guard to Chicago's city streets restored order. Race relations in Chicago had reached a nadir, and many in the city—both white and black—blamed the rapid decline on the Great Migration.[45]

Some newcomers were sufficiently disillusioned to return home. "Hays," who had arrived from Alabama in 1918, decided that whites had "made it so warm" for blacks that he was better off elsewhere, and boarded a train to Kentucky soon after the riot. Despite southern employers' efforts both before and after the riot to recruit in Chicago, and the cooperation of the Chamber of Commerce, the *Tribune*, and federal agencies, Hays' reaction was unusual. Only 219 blacks left Chicago during the week following the riot, and more arrived in the city than departed. The few who left headed for other northern cities. "If I've got to be killed, I would rather be killed by my friends," observed one man when asked whether the riot had stimulated any desire to return South. Migrants interviewed by the Chicago Commission on Race Relations indicated that they still considered Chicago a place where they could "feel free," and most affirmed that they were continuing to advise friends to come to Chicago.[46]

Most migrants probably took in stride the disillusionment accompanying the riot because they did not consider whites to be their friends. As one black Louisianian had observed in 1917, the black southerner migrating North hoped to find "the peaceful way of living. He goes for a right to his rights; a right to live in peace and harmony unmolested by those he does not care to be with socially or domestically."[47] "Those" were white people. There is little evidence that blacks fled the South because they wished to mix with whites in northern cities. Rather, they sought to share equally in the privileges of citizenship and to have access to all institutions open to whites, including workplaces, political institutions, public services, and schools. Whites were most significant to blacks in those arenas where it was impossible to avoid them and their institutions—the workplace and the school.

7

"Eny Kind of Worke"

"I was scared to death. I had never seen anything like it in my life," recalled Leroy McChester of his first day in a steel mill near Chicago. The sixteen-year-old from Brinley, Arkansas, was not unusual in this regard. Only a few migrants—those who had worked in Birmingham's steel mills or in the largest saw mills in the Gulf states—had any idea of what heavy industrial production involved. Most of those with factory experience knew only of sawmills in open-sided sheds, of small cottonseed-oil mills and cotton gins, or of steam laundries, docks, or railroad yards. Work often took place either outdoors or with much movement in and out, with blacks relegated to such outside, nonmechanical tasks as hauling, driving wagons, lifting, and unloading.[1] Chicago factories, on the other hand, were big, noisy, smelly, and stuffy. Newcomers had to adapt to working indoors in buildings which could be oppressively hot, chillingly cold, inadequately ventilated, or poorly lit. In most industries, work regularly proceeded at what must have seemed like a breakneck pace to men and women accustomed to the uneven tempo of agricultural labor or work in southern sawmills and other light industries. Although plantation agriculture could require great effort and rapid pace, especially at harvest time, it did not prepare migrants for an environment structured by the rhythm of a whirring machine or conveyer belt.[2]

Unfamiliar or not, factory jobs were what most migrants expected to secure upon arrival. Few viewed such employment as either permanent or immiserating; instead they approached industrial Chicago positively, as a step out of a quagmire and onto a path leading eventually to new vistas. In Hattiesburg, Mississippi, blacks who had caught migration fever spoke of packinghouses in their musings about a future in Chicago. Although some migrants, like those who expected free housing, harbored unrealistic expectations kindled by labor agents and by information from friends and relatives who had inflated their own achievements, most entertained modest short-term hopes. Even craftsmen who preferred to find work at their trades readily stated their willingness to accept any employment. "I am a painter by traid but i will & can do eny kind of worke," wrote one man just before leaving Florida.[3]

Such flexibility was essential, as the glaziers, painters, carpenters, bricklayers, pipe workers, and other skilled craftsmen who left their jobs in the South had little chance of continuing their trades in Chicago.[4] It was not unusual for a bricklayer from Mississippi, unable to find work on a construction site, to turn to the packinghouses. Chicago's powerful building trades unions excluded black workmen, shutting them out of employment in most trades at which blacks had acquired skills in the South. One member of a southern local of the Wood, Wire and Metal Lathers' International Union learned when he arrived in Chicago that even a union card was of little help; the Chicago local refused to accept his transfer.[5] Although they frequently blamed their discriminatory hiring practices on employee prejudices, employers were often equally unwilling to accept skilled or train unskilled black workers. Only in foundries, where work was heavy and often hot and which many blacks came to with experience gained in the South, did migrants find semiskilled and skilled positions immediately upon arrival.[6]

Many migrants with business and professional experience had similar difficulties trying to continue in their former lines of work. Businessmen, with the meager capital they brought north, found it difficult to compete with the resources of stores in the Loop or even with the storekeepers in the ghetto. Teachers, because of discriminatory hiring practices and sectional disparities in educational standards, were immediately disappointed if they sought positions in Chicago schools. The stiff requirements for teacher certification in Chicago, which required an education equivalent to a Chicago high school diploma for elementary school teachers and a college degree for high school teachers, barred most migrants from even applying.[7] Throughout the South many black teachers had little more education than their pupils. These men and women, and even those with advanced training in the grossly inferior southern schools, could not teach in Chicago schools. Like one woman who went from a Virginia classroom to a Chicago laundry, a glue factory, and then a garment shop, many turned to the city's factories.[8] In general, black newcomers in search of white-collar employment were likely to share the experience of Mississippian Corneal Davis, who went to Chicago after his discharge from the army. "It was hard to get a job, oh real hard," he later recalled. "Real hard, real hard, real hard. And it was double hard, triple hard for a colored to get jobs."[9]

Most migrants arrived without any skills transferable to Chicago's urban-industrial economy. When asked what her former employment was, one woman from Pecan Point, Arkansas, answered, "What did I do? Lawd I chopped and picked cotton." Most migrants had similarly inadequate training. Of all gainfully employed black southerners, 63 percent were listed by the 1910 census as agricultural workers, and the proportion was even higher in the states that sent the most migrants to Chicago (e.g., 81.2 percent in Mississippi). On a national level, both an NAACP survey and a quantitative study undertaken during the 1920s concluded that the Great Migration drew primarily from the rural areas of the South.[10] Both the Chicago Urban League and the Chicago Commission on Race Relations characterized the migrants as farmers, and even those migrants who came from "towns" probably came from communities with an employment structure dramatically different from what they would find in Chicago.[11]

Lacking industrial and urban experience, migrants also tended to have few educational resources. A third of all blacks in the rural South were judged illiterate within the liberal definitions of the census in 1910; an exaggerated complaint from a draft board in the heart of Chicago's ghetto in 1919 branded 95 percent of the registrants as "almost illiterate." Although those black southerners who chose to come North—like most migrant populations—were likely to be better educated than those who stayed behind, they were still poorly educated by northern standards.[12] Inadequately educated and inappropriately trained, most migrants had few options in the Chicago job market.

Unqualified for all but the most unskilled labor, most newcomers nevertheless expected to find jobs easily and quickly. A black YWCA official in Chicago observed in 1917 that many believed "that if they could only get here a means of livelihood would immediately present itself." Such expectations were not unrealistic during the war years, although the availability of work fluctuated during the following decade. Black men willing to start at the bottom were usually able to fulfill short-term expectations. "A Negro could always get a job in the stockyards," a railroad porter recalled many years after the Great Migration; "They could go to the stockyards any day of the week and get a job." At one large meat-packing firm, the number of black employees increased from 311 in January 1916 to 3,069 two years later. By 1918, between ten and twelve thousand black men and women traveled daily to the stockyards.[13] Taking into account high turnover rates, one historian has estimated that by the end of World War I most black men in Chicago "had working experience in a meat packing establishment." Interviews and surveys conducted in 1917 agreed that a "large majority" of the migrants had found work in the packinghouses. For them, the bottom rung on the ladder of success was the bloody, slippery floor of a killing room.[14]

Only the steel industry employed Chicago's black newcomers in numbers comparable to meat packing. "They were hiring day and night," recalled Leroy McChester. "All they wanted to know was if you wanted to work and if you had a strong back." Illinois Steel's black work force increased from 35 in 1916 to 1,209 three years later. At U.S. Steel's Gary Works, to which many black Chicagoans commuted, the number rose from 407 in 1916 to 1,295 by 1918. When steel firms hired large numbers of black strikebreakers during the 1919 strike, the black proportion of the work force increased further. By 1920, the census counted 4,313 black Chicagoans working in the iron and steel industries, an increase of 4,093 in a decade. Most other black male industrial workers were scattered among food-products industries other than meat packing (primarily the Argo Corn Products Company), the Pullman Car shops, steam laundries, and a few tanneries.[15]

Two other types of work were readily accessible to black men in Chicago during the Great Migration: unskilled nonindustrial labor and service. Approximately nine thousand black men (one-fifth of the city's employed black males) were counted by the 1920 census as unskilled laborers working outside "manufacturing and mechanical industries." Most of these men were listed as laborers, porters and helpers in stores, draymen, teamsters, and expressmen. Another 11,514 black men occupied service positions, mainly as porters "not in stores," waiters, servants, janitors, and sextons. With the number of servants increasing by only three thousand during the decade, it appears that newcomers moved more readily into industrial positions than into service occupations similar to those occupied by black Old Settlers.[16]

Female migrants, on the other hand, were likely to be consigned to unskilled service occupations, although Chicago was one of the few cities in which fewer than half of all employed black women (43.9 percent) were classified by the 1920 census as servants or hand laundresses. The census counted 2,608 black women in Chicago's factories (12.6 percent of employed black women), but the number was probably significantly higher during the war. One employer, considered typical by a Department of Labor official, remarked in 1919 that he had hired black women "solely on account of the shortage of labor. . . . As soon as the situation clears itself no more colored help will be employed." [17] Wartime labor shortages prompted 170 Chicago firms to hire black women for the first time. Although the list of firms was dominated by hotels, restaurants, and laundries, it also included garment, mattress, button, box, tobacco, and sundry other factories. The packing industry was probably the greatest single employer of black women during the war. There and elsewhere in industrial Chicago, black women from the South confronted problems of adaptation to industrial work initially similar to those faced by their male counterparts. [18]

Migrants trying to find any job on their own could easily meet with frustration. Few employers advertised in the *Defender* until 1919, with steel mills and packinghouses notably absent from the newspaper's Help Wanted columns. A number of garment factories advertised for black women, but applicants for these positions would sometimes unwittingly walk into labor conflicts. [19] Enterprising newcomers who pounded the pavement on their own or answered advertisements in white newspapers risked immediate rejection. Two men applying for an advertised job at Chicago Shipbuilding Company were told "we have nothing whatever for colored men to do." A Mississippi migrant who relied on a friend's help was more fortunate; his friend met him at the train and brought him to a stockyards firm hiring laborers. Many migrants found positions through this type of personal referral, which was frequently an extension of the same network that had facilitated the migratory process. These connections did not, however, serve blacks as effectively as they had the European immigrants who preceded them to Chicago. [20]

In the black community, an institutional matrix exercised considerable influence in the placement of black job-seekers. Those without friends or relatives able to assist them could turn to a private employment agency, a public employment service, a social agency, or a minister. Private agencies advertised in the *Defender* and were therefore known to many newcomers, with one employment agency even remaining open Sundays and nights for migrants particularly eager to obtain their first positions. By 1917 at least six agencies, nearly all located within a ten-block area on State Street, catered to black Chicagoans. Others opened nearby during the next decade. Although limited in scope by the tendency of employers to include only domestic and laborer positions in Black Belt listings, these agencies did steer newcomers toward employers willing to hire blacks. Owned mostly by black entrepreneurs, the agencies could also command the trust of migrants. Neither black newspapers, nor the Chicago Commission on Race Relations, nor investigations by reformers indicate that migrants expressed dissatisfaction with these agencies, even though many charged applicants (rather than employers) for placement services and rates appear to have been rather high compared with agencies elsewhere in the city.[21]

For many urban workers the public employment bureaus established during the 1910s offered an alternative to private agencies. Although federal and state employment offices often listed mainly unskilled, poorly-paid positions, they did provide their services without charge and carried whatever prestige governmental institutions possessed in working-class neighborhoods. Like most social agencies, however, both the Illinois State Employment Service and the United States Employment Service (USES) looked to the needs of white Chicagoans before assisting black job seekers. The state agency's Chicago division, the Chicago Free Employment Office, did not open a branch in the black ghetto until 1920, and with that branch designated "colored," blacks apparently were unwelcome at other offices. Similarly, the USES occupied locations inaccessible to blacks, and when it did open a Chicago office usable by black workers it made certain to designate it "colored." Employers could thus choose whether they desired black or white applicants and distribute their listings accordingly.[22]

The USES began working through an organization staffed by blacks in June 1918, when the Chicago Urban League agreed to operate its employment bureau as a branch of USES.[23] The League had opened an employment bureau catering especially to newcomers in March 1917 and was a logical destination for a newcomer in search of employment. Already known to many migrants, it actively recruited clients by arranging to have Travelers Aid and League representatives at railroad stations distribute cards advising migrants to visit the Urban League for assistance in employment and other matters. More than 10,000 applicants, most of them recently arrived from the South, filed into the employment bureau in 1918, with 6,861 finding positions. The following year the League placed 12,285 men and women in jobs.[24]

Although the Urban League was by far the largest employment agency for black Chicagoans, other black institutions offered similar services. The Wabash Avenue YMCA placed five hundred men in 1916; given its close ties to stockyards firms during the following decade, it was probably able to help newcomers secure jobs there. The organization's vocational section submitted contradictory reports, but apparently assisted fifty to one hundred men each month by 1919. The YWCA maintained no "organized employment agency" but helped one hundred women (of 232 applicants) find jobs in 1917.[25] The Negro Fellowship League operated a small employment office until 1920, as did two black churches. At many storefront churches, ministers supplemented their income with factory jobs and served both employer and congregants as informal employment agents. By helping newcomers to find jobs, these institutions also became potential mediating forces between employers and black workers.[26]

Migrants who used employment agencies—private or "free"— thus experienced their first adjustment to new patterns of labor relations before setting foot in a factory. Employment agencies did not exist in the rural South and were scarce even in the cities. Few migrants had ever had a formal interview. Yet if the whole procedure was new, it was not altogether unwelcome. The well-dressed black men and women sitting in swivel chairs behind the desks at the Chicago Urban League interviewed each applicant, and although perhaps condescending to the migrants, treated them with greater respect than had white foremen, planters, and gang bosses in the South.[27] The interviewers themselves seemed to confirm migrants' notions regarding chances for success and respectability in the North. At the YMCA, YWCA, churches, Negro Fellowship League, and most of the private agencies, newcomers also dealt with black interviewers. Not until they showed up at the workplace did most migrants encounter the all-too-familiar racial pattern—white men gave the orders and black men and women obeyed.

Most newcomers—especially males—were sent to the stockyards. Although by the 1920s an employment service might send a worker to the packer's personnel department, during the war laborers were hired in the manner noticed by an observer in 1910:

> There would be a long row out in front of the employment office as a rule anywhere from 200 to 1,000 men. . . . The employment agent would look over the group generally and pick out those who seemed to be the sturdiest and best fitted to do the unskilled work. So far as I could see there was no bargaining and discussion about wages, terms of employment, or anything of that sort. Just the employment agent would tap the one he wanted on the shoulder and say "Come along."[28]

The agent would then take the new worker to the employment office, which at Armour & Company acted as a "labor clearing house" for all departments. Other packinghouses had similar procedures, as did large companies in other industries.[29] A migrant applying for work had to deal with a bureaucrat— an employment manager—who had played little if any role in the southern black experience. In the South, a tenant farmer or laborer generally struck a personal agreement with a prospective landlord, employer, or foreman.[30] At this point in the

Men waiting outside Chicago Urban League employment office (courtesy of Special Collections, the University Library, University of Illinois at Chicago).

process a newcomer in Chicago might well have wondered for whom he was working after all.

Once hired, a worker was handed a time card and assigned a number—one's identity in the workplace. Packinghouses, steel mills, the Pullman shops, and other employers of black migrants paid and monitored their employees according to check number, and even outside the plant managers referred to an employee as "check number such and such." Even the most rationalized corporate-owned plantations in Mississippi would never have used such a method; as one federal investigator noted in 1913, planters did not deem "the Negro" sufficiently intelligent to operate under such a system.[31]

If becoming a number could be disorienting, the physical surroundings in Chicago's large plants were likely to exacerbate anxieties. In the packinghouses, migrants encountered familiar slaughtering procedures, but the work was intricately subdivided and the meat intended for an unseen marketplace. The process took place in factories vastly different from the farms on which black southerners had for years been slaughtering hogs. In buildings crammed too close together, workers breathed foul air, endured extreme temperatures, and toiled under dirty skylights or unshaded electric light bulbs. All the while, the surreal cacophony of bleating, bellowing animals, squeaking pulleys, and clanging machinery assaulted their ears.[32]

Although conditions in packinghouses varied from firm to firm,

Job-seekers being interviewed at Chicago Urban League employment office (courtesy of Special Collections, the University Library, University of Illinois at Chicago).

black workers generally endured the worst any company had to offer. Most black men worked in the killing floors, cold storage areas, and loading docks. Amid hot temperatures and without ventilation, men in killing gangs stood on wet, slippery floors, as grease, cold water, and warm blood flowed at their feet.[33] In the beef casing room, where temperatures reached 115 degrees Fahrenheit, one reformer reported that "ceilings are low, the artificial light bulbs unshaded and inadequate to illuminate the room. The few windows provide a bit of natural light only for a bench of workers seated beneath them. The majority of workers in this room are Negro men." Black men laboring in the cold storage areas did not have to endure the heat; temperatures there ranged from 30 to 38 degrees. Beef luggers, who carried meat from the cooler to the loading area, had to bear continuous cold because carcasses loaded at room temperature might "sweat." It was easy for a migrant to get a job as a beef lugger; most white men refused to do it.[34]

Relegated to positions left vacant by white women during the wartime labor shortage, black women toiled in some of the most noxious rooms in the packinghouses. The most unfortunate among them landed in the beef casing, beef tallow, mutton tallow, hog-killing, casing, packing, hog head, bone, and hair departments. Barred from the less unpleasant tasks of canning and wrapping, black women spent their days inspecting, washing, grading, and measuring casings; cutting bungs; washing chitterlings; packing and trimming fat; and trimming lungs, hearts, kidneys, ovaries, paunch, snouts, and tongues. In the packing rooms these women wore coats to keep warm. In the trimming rooms at one medium-sized firm the only ventilation came from opening the outside doors, a harsh alternative during the winter when these rooms were already cold. In this company's "newer" building, trimming room ventilation consisted of a door to another room.[35]

The packinghouses were not only unhealthy, they were dangerous, especially to inexperienced newcomers. The tools used in the killing and dressing of livestock—knives, saws, cleavers, and axes— posed obvious hazards, especially during speedups. Even workers not handling blades could suffer injuries, like the burns sustained by five black women at Morris & Company, when a pipe "suddenly burst" in the stuffing room where they worked. Jack Carroll, a recent migrant from Tennessee, painfully learned of such dangers when he was scalded by hot water from an Armour & Company vat. An inexperienced beef lugger who made the mistake of carrying a right beef quarter on his right shoulder, instead of his left, would soon comprehend the reason behind the recommended method: the sharp, ragged edges of the bone frequently cut luggers who had not turned the bone away from their bodies. Migrants working in steel mills encountered even more danger. In the year ending in June 1917, approximately one of every eight steelworkers in the United States was injured on the job.[36]

If work environments could be alien, noxious, and dangerous, the work process itself required an even greater adjustment. The meatpacking industry, while containing elements of rural production in terms of its focus on slaughtering, epitomized the transition required of newcomers to industrial work. After the refrigerated railroad car widened the distribution market during the 1870s, economies of scale provided a strong incentive to mechanize production and standardize tasks. A burgeoning national market strengthened the position of the largest firms, facilitating the accumulation of capital to develop and implement new technologies. By the turn of the century six large companies dominated the industry, slaughtering 89.5 percent of federally inspected cattle east of the Rocky Mountains in 1906.[37]

These firms, especially such industry giants as Swift and Armour, conquered local markets by underselling smaller competitors. Centralizing operations in massive complexes like those at Chicago's Union Stock Yards, the "big six" drastically cut costs by mechanizing and rationalizing production. During the last two decades of the nineteenth century, slaughtering and dressing of livestock achieved a level of efficiency unprecedented in American industry. Conveyers carried carcasses around the killing floors, and a series of chutes routed casings, bones, organs, and other byproducts to appropriate departments. Every part of an animal was turned to some profitable purpose; in 1920 a one-thousand-pound steer could be expected to yield 41 byproducts weighing 225.5 pounds, plus 137 feet of casings. The packers, according to a packingtown cliché, used "everything about the hog except the squeal."[38] This rationalization of production, made possible by the "disassembly line," involved a division of labor so intricate that "from the pen to the cooler," 126 men participated in the slaughtering of a single hog. At one medium-sized Chicago firm, the 157-man beef-killing gang included 78 distinct occupations, two-thirds of which were designated common labor. Although the tasks were less mechanized than those in other departments, individual efforts bore little relevance to a finished product; management had reduced work to a series of tedious, repetitive motions.[39]

It was this very standardization and subdivision of tasks, so unlike the farm work to which many migrants were accustomed, that made meat-packing jobs readily available to unskilled newcomers. Packinghouses relied more heavily on unskilled and semiskilled workers than did most other industries and demanded only that a worker be willing to repeat a simple motion at progressively higher speeds. Most operations required only one or two days of training; some, only a few hours. A new man assigned to the cattle-killing gang might start as a foot skinner, easily learning the three simple cuts and skinning motion. A woman sent to the sausage room could quickly grasp the fundamentals of cutting or tying links. The processes were so easy to learn that at Swift & Company, a new employee was briefly instructed by an experienced hand, watched the operation being performed a few times, and then began working.[40] Much of southern farm labor was equally tedious and repetitive, but an agricultural worker performed a variety of tasks. Whether factory work might be considered easier or harder, it involved greater standardization and a more minute division of labor, even compared with plantations run on a gang system.

Once newcomers learned how to perform the required operations, they faced the more difficult challenge of adapting to the pace. Packinghouse laborers, remarked Upton Sinclair, "worked with furious intensity literally upon the run." Not only did migrants have to work faster than they had in the South, but the tempo was set by a machine regulated by the employer. "If you need to turn out a little

more," a Swift & Company superintendent explained, "you speed up
the conveyers a little and the men speed up to keep pace." In departments unconnected to the assembly line, a pacemaker, the fastest
worker, would determine the clip of such tasks as stuffing sausages
or cutting links. Anyone who could not keep up was discharged.[41]

Other industries in Chicago required similar adjustments. If steel
production involved a familiar pattern of intense effort punctuated
by brief spells of relaxation between tasks, the mills also required
workers to time their efforts to a mechanized and subdivided process.
Shop floor supervision, bureaucratic personnel policies, and systematic work incentive programs resonated poorly with the work experience of most migrants. Even laundries, an important source of
employment for black women, were characterized by a division of
labor comparable to a modern factory. A woman might spend hour
after hour, day after day, only pressing cuffs, yokes, or sleeves, folding shirts, or wrapping clothes. Often running more than one machine (up to eight), these women worked at a pace comparable to
factory operatives in production industries.[42]

Like other laborers new to industrial work, most migrants had
work habits unsuited to the fast, unbroken routine of a northern factory. Not only was southern farm labor largely nonmechanized, but
workers who could not work as quickly as others were often simply
designated as "half-hands," and retained at reduced compensation.
Although speed was essential at harvest time, spells of furious effort
alternated with a slower tempo. Cotton cultivation, for example, was
characterized by what one planter called "a series of spurts rather
than by a steady daily grind."[43] Where workers did have to sustain a
regular pace—hired labor on some plantations, railroad-tie layers,
dock hands, construction gangs, sawmill laborers, and turpentine
crews—a work song set the rhythm. Men laying railroad ties set a
cadence to their efforts with songs like "Raise the Iron":

> Down the railroad, um-huh
> Well, raise the iron, um-huh
> Raise the iron, um-huh[44]

Unlike a machine, such songs were highly flexible. The song
leader, who set the tempo, could alter rhythm and lyrics when necessary. Jazzman Big Bill Broonzy recalled that during his days laying
railroad ties in Mississippi between 1912 and 1915, a man who wished
to relieve himself would signal the leader, who would "sing it to the
boss." Upon the boss's nod, he would sing, "Everybody lay their bar
down, it's one to go." When the worker returned from the bushes the
leader would start the crew up again with "All men to their places

like horses in their traces."[45] It would not be quite so easy to halt a conveyer belt of carcasses in a Chicago packinghouse or to interrupt the fabricating process in a steel mill.

Using songs to synchronize their work rhythms, black southerners simultaneously helped the time to pass more quickly. The songs relieved the tedium of constant labor, and even men who worked alone would sing. Muddy Waters, who grew up in Mississippi in the 1920s, later remarked that a man would sing even to a mule. Southern employers encouraged singing, because it reinforced their stereotype of carefree blacks and presumably stimulated greater intensity. Employers' requirements for gang leaders—a strong voice, rhythm, and the ability to improvise—suggest that work songs enhanced both regularity and flexibility. In the northern factories, however, black southerners accustomed to singing would have to learn not only not to sing, since singing was considered disruptive by efficiency experts, but to replace the song leader's and their own voices with the hum of a machine.[46]

Industrial time demanded not only adaptation to a faster, more continuous pace, but to greater regularity in attendance. Except for Louisiana's sugar plantations, with their "unmechanized but coordinated" gang labor, southern farms tended to be small and "loosely held together by the supervision of landlords and suppliers of credit." To be five minutes late during cotton-picking season meant working faster to catch up, but to be tardy at a factory could upset an entire production line. Black southerners' hours of work had depended as farmers and rural laborers not upon the clock, but upon the sun, the calendar, and the vicissitudes of a crop. The workday had lasted from sunup to sundown, with compensation based on either a daily wage or a share of the crop. Daily patterns of labor revolved around tasks to be completed rather than the passing of a certain amount of time at a work station. Flexibility existed when a task had to be performed within a span longer than the number of days required to complete it. For instance, on a one-horse farm in the Black Belt region of Alabama or Mississippi, planting required five man-days and had to be done between April 1 and April 10. Allowing for inclement weather, a farmer usually had six and two-thirds days within which to schedule this chore. Even on a tightly supervised plantation, a farmer could plant an acre less than recommended on a given day and catch up on the next. Such adjustments would not be possible in a factory, unless it was the manager controlling the machines who wished to alter the pace.[47]

Over the course of the year, a black rural southerner's time orientation was fixed by the demands of the cotton crop. Although work began with January plowing, intensive labor did not begin until May, when thinning, weeding, and chopping dominated the farmer's waking hours. This heavy schedule continued into June and early July with fertilizing and hoeing. August was a month of picnics, barbecues, camp meetings, and other forms of rural leisure, usually involving large gatherings. Slack time ended in September; picking then would occupy the lives of most black southerners well into November. During such periods of intense labor as chopping and picking times, schools shut down and ministers discouraged their followers from engaging in excessive outside activity. When the cotton and perhaps a small corn crop required little attention, a farmer could not rest completely; such miscellaneous tasks as ditch digging, wood cutting, fence and tool repairing, and other maintenance made continuing demands on his time. Further, with farm incomes inadequate for the support of a family, many men secured "outside" work whenever possible. One observer calculated that these activities, added to days spent on a crop, totaled a work year only a few weeks short of that of a continuously employed industrial worker. But the cycle allowed some variety and a degree of flexibility. Discussing the demands of the crop cycles, sharecropper Ned Cobb emphasized the importance of performing a task "on time," but it was a time determined not by man but by God. No foreman or supervisor could accelerate the pace by tuning a machine. "You can't start His time, you can't stop it." [48] Whether or not they had worked harder or longer than they would in Chicago, migrants were not accustomed to the total regulation of life by inflexible time sequences unconnected to the rhythms of their physical environment.

Along with providing some diversity and leeway, the patterns of southern agriculture engendered the development of leisure activities that would be inappropriate to the industrial-time framework of Chicago. On a day to day level, a farmer could relieve his toil with the occasional social affairs which interrupted the tedium of rural life. On occasion sharecroppers would take full days off and turn weddings and funerals into prolonged social occasions, especially during seasons of less intensive labor in August and between Christmas and Valentine's Day. In Chicago, however, industrial employers, worried about filling places in a continuous production process, would be less tolerant of such spontaneous and unilaterally declared "holidays." [49]

Many migrants initially found it difficult to adjust to the new demands on their time. When asked whether he had gone to work every day, one newcomer who had complained about losing his job responded, "Goodness no, I just had to have some days of the week for pleasure." At the Nachman Spring-Filled Mattress Company, only

payday attracted the entire work force, with attendance usually drop-
ping to 50 percent the following day. Saturday production often suffered the same malaise. "Saturday is not a national holiday," one
black community leader reminded the migrants. When they did show
up for work, many migrants had difficulty arriving and leaving "on
time," a concept often interpreted differently in rural areas regulated
by the rhythms of sunup and sundown. Employers' complaints
about attendance and lateness do not appear to have stemmed only
from assumptions about racial characteristics; they often carefully differentiated between northern and southern blacks, noting that only
the latter failed to show up every day. Although black southerners
had always worked hard, they were accustomed to more flexible
schedules.[50]

Closely related to the problem of attendance was continuity. Employers complained that the migrants changed jobs frequently, and
reports breaking down turnover rates by race corroborate these complaints. In early 1919 meat-packing firms reported a weekly turnover
rate of 7 percent among blacks, as opposed to 5 percent overall. In
steel mills the six-week rate for blacks was 29 percent, compared with
19 percent for white steelworkers.[51] High turnover, however, was
hardly peculiar to black workers in the 1910s. The Bureau of Labor
Statistics estimated annual turnover rates of 115 percent in American
factories in 1913–14, and eminent labor economist Paul Douglas
considered 300 percent per year to be "quite common in normal times
for many of our larger and smaller industries." Whatever differences
did exist between black and white workers in Chicago rested partly
on demographic factors: the migrants were overwhelmingly young,
single, and unskilled, characteristics which generally correlate with
transiency.[52]

Observers, black and white, generally agreed that black newcomers readily changed jobs and attributed turnover to the seasonal
and distasteful nature of most stockyards jobs held by blacks, the
migrants' unfamiliarity with industrial labor, and their sudden encounter with an array of industrial opportunities. Ignorant of standardization in meat-packing and steel-production processes, some
newcomers moved from one plant to another, expecting qualitative
variations between experiences in different plants.[53] But a complete
explanation runs deeper, and relates to the circumstances of the Great
Migration and the complex relationship between southern experience
and northern conditions.

Many migrants were accustomed to changing employers frequently, and by definition those who left the South for Chicago
were among the most restless. In the rural South, both whites and

blacks moved often, impelled by a search for better land and a more reasonable landlord. Seasonal employment off the farm, seldom discouraged by landlords confident that their laborers would return, contributed even more to the migratory habits of black southerners. During slack seasons, black men traveled to towns or cities where they might work a few months in railroad yards, cottonseed-oil mills, fertilizer plants, or warehouses. The temporary nature of such employment left little reason to remain with one employer, and day labor was characteristically mobile. Women, usually employed as domestics, also were restless; lacking any other leverage or protection in labor relations, their only method of altering conditions was to change employers. As a rule, working conditions for black southerners owed less to standardized procedures than to personal relations, so a dissatisfied worker had good reason to leave for a new job.[54]

Conditions in Chicago enhanced the impulse to change jobs. The expansive wartime labor market made it easy to find an initial job and then move on. Arriving with little or no money, migrants took the first job they found but recognized that it would be worthwhile to stay alert to better opportunities.[55] Those who commuted to jobs in Argo, Pullman, Burnside, and the steel towns east of Chicago soon learned that local housing for blacks was scarce (virtually nonexistent in Argo, Pullman, and Burnside), and took positions closer to the South Side ghetto as soon as possible. The 600 percent annual turnover rate for black workers at Inland Steel in Indiana Harbor is hardly surprising; many of its black workers commuted ninety minutes to and from work each day.[56] Racial discrimination did not have to occur at the workplace to have an impact there.

Unfair treatment on the shop floor also motivated many migrants to quit their jobs. Black workers at companies that complained of high turnover observed that many employees had left because foremen discriminated against blacks in the distribution of overtime and in advancement opportunities, while treating them with "unreasonable exactness." At one large packinghouse, an executive admitted that one forelady "doesn't like colored girls. They have to be superefficient to get along with her and must cater to all her moods." Because of this forelady, who considered blacks "lazy and saucy," he had "let go" many black women. "Prejudiced and pugnacious foremen," argued an official of the Chicago Urban League, were making it difficult for newcomers to adapt to industrial labor.[57]

To some extent, the failure of migrants to remain at one job long enough to suit their employers reflected their understanding that Chicago meant not only freedom from the oppression of the South, but freedom to explore new opportunities and new attractions. For some southern sharecroppers it had been difficult to change employers at will. "Mr. Dorsey," a migrant from rural Georgia, remembered how his father had been cheated by a landlord and his whole family had "felt themselves wronged but helpless." In sawmill and turpentine settlements, personal industrial relations, the symbolic implications of conflict between a black employee and a white boss, and the power of employers meant that a worker who had quit under hostile circumstances would have to move elsewhere to find another job.[58] In Chicago, only union activism was likely to place a worker on a blacklist. The easiest way to deal with an objectionable foreman at Armour was to go next door and apply at Swift. Changing jobs thus constituted an extension of migration itself, with movement remaining a metaphor for freedom.

Migrants welcomed not only the liberty to change jobs at will, but also the wherewithal to do so. Southern employers retained control over their black labor force partly by keeping it economically dependent. Landlords kept tenants in debt; sawmill owners paid wages in scrip. The whole system, observed W. E. B. Du Bois after visiting rural Georgia, rested upon blacks' lack of independence and cash. Chicago employers, however, paid in cash. Men and women accustomed to living on credit could be tempted by cash in the pocket to quit working until they again needed money. "Don't leave your job when you have a few dollars in your pocket," the *Defender* admonished migrants. In the South, withdrawal from the labor market invited prosecution. The "Chain Gang Blues" articulated the consequences:

> Judge gave me six months
> 'Cause I wouldn't go to work.

In the North only economic necessity could force anyone to work. Nothing could require a black worker to remain with the same company.[59]

Celerity, punctuality, regularity: taken together, these attributes characterized an efficient industrial operative. A migrant who wanted to make it in industrial America had to learn to be efficient. And in the late 1910s Chicago employers depended on the migrants' efficiency in their quest to fill the mounting orders which promised huge wartime profits.

Chicago industrialists hoped for, but hardly expected, efficiency from their new work force. They knew little about black workers, having previously employed them in significant numbers only temporarily as strikebreakers. In 1910 only 357 black men worked in the stockyards, and 37 more in blast furnaces, rolling mills, and iron foundries. Only 46 black women worked in factories of any kind. Industrialists considered "colored help" inefficient and relied on the thousands of Europeans augmenting the labor force each year. Even when immigration began to taper off in 1915, many employers first looked to other sources of labor. One Chicago railroad decided to start track work early because "the American hobo caught in the spring of the year will work," and expected to fill other needs with Mexicans. Commonwealth Edison hired white women before filling vacancies with blacks. "The Negro," declared the *New Republic* on the eve of the Great Migration, "gets a chance to work [in the North] only when there is no one else." Industrial managers knew as little about Afro-America in 1916 as the migrants knew about northern factories.[60]

Once the wartime labor shortage forced them to consider hiring black labor, industrialists approached the venture as temporary, or at best as an experiment. Sharing popular notions regarding "Negro character," most assumed that the migrants were lazy, unreliable, and slow.[61] "Negro character," steel managers read in the *Iron Trade Review* in 1917, made for poor industrial workers. What is more, they were told that only the most unreliable, footloose types had come North. Accordingly, a 1917 survey of five hundred Illinois firms employing at least fifty blacks each reported that only half intended to retain black workers any longer than necessary.[62] Black workers would have to convince these employers that they could do the job.

Employers who did envision the migrants in their permanent work force usually evaluated their potential within the context of traditional assumptions about "racial efficiency" and the particular characteristics of individual racial and ethnic groups. Opportunities in steel mills, for example, could be both created and limited by theories about the superior ability of blacks to withstand heat. In 1923 the personnel manager for National Malleable Castings, which had been employing blacks in its Chicago plant for five years, still viewed "the Negro" as "constituted temperamentally quite different" from other workers, and requiring closer supervision and more careful treatment.[63] Significantly, he did not dismiss the viability of black industrial labor, but rather assumed it required different management techniques. Employers more confident about the potential of both black workers and the efficacy of the free labor market maintained an evolutionary view of racial traits. The *New Republic* reflected such cautious optimism in 1916:

> On the average he [the Negro] is probably not yet so efficient or so tenacious as the white man. We must combat certain racial virtues and vices. Yet from what we know of how ability responds to

opportunity, and of how the Negro has advanced under almost impossible economic and social conditions, we cannot but draw hopeful conclusions.[64]

The emerging science of industrial management faced a new task— molding men and women stereotyped as slow, lazy, ignorant cotton pickers into efficient operatives, able to work according to an enforced routine. This stereotype partly shaped the response of employers to the Great Migration. Assuming that white southerners knew how to "handle" black workers, some managers logically sought to draw on that experience. Writing in *Iron Age*, one steel manager suggested that the migrants would be "best controlled by a white man from the South." A Chicago NAACP official noted in 1927 that as black southerners had entered Chicago, white southerners had entered alongside them, and many had procured supervisory positions in big plants, "relying on their boasted knowledge of the Negro and 'how to handle him.'"[65] Relying on southern whites' "expertise," however, did not require hiring a southern foreman. One stockyards executive who complained that the warm weather was inducing his black employees to become lazy, told an investigator that "the only way to get work out of him [the Negro] is the way they got it out of him in the South—with a whip."[66]

Few, if any, managers took this route. Contemporary theories regarding industrial relations both reflected and reinforced management's confidence in its ability to manipulate workers more subtly and even to reshape their personality and culture. Although many manufacturers resorted to strict work rules as a means of enforcing discipline, others either replaced or supplemented the regulations with such low-key tactics as lectures or incentives. Swift & Company explicitly rejecting coercion, stressed the importance of harmony on the shop floor and the value of enlightened, diplomatic, and reasonable foremen. There and elsewhere, managers adapted various components of welfare capitalism programs to what they perceived as the specific needs and psychology of black workers. After all, welfare capitalism was oriented towards inculcating loyalty, and among the commonly held stereotypes of black workers was that they were loyal.[67]

Most employers of large numbers of migrants recognized that they could most effectively shape the work habits of migrants by seeking the advice and aid of black Chicagoans who shared their objective of creating an efficient black work force. They did not have to look far for such assistance. Black Chicago's Old Settlers considered the prosperity of migrants essential to their business and professional interests. They also knew that industrial positions had provided stepping stones for other ethnic groups who had arrived recently but seemed to be moving past blacks on the economic ladder. Given the importance of prejudices regarding black work habits and aptitudes, black leaders considered it imperative that the migrants perform creditably in Chicago's factories. The *Defender* summed up the perspective of Chicago's black establishment: "Our entrance into factories, workshops and every other industry open to man places us on an entirely different footing; we become a factor in the economy to be reckoned with. . . . We are on trial." Later, black sociologist St. Clair Drake and journalist Horace Cayton commented that to much of black Chicago, the migration was a "step toward the economic emancipation of a people." For that emancipation to yield substantial fruit, the migrants would have to prove their mettle, and the Old Settlers shared employers' concerns regarding the handicaps southern work culture had placed upon the newcomers.[68]

Two organizations provided contexts within which employers and Chicago's established black leadership could work together to modify the migrant's work habits—the Chicago Urban League and the Wabash Avenue YMCA. The latter blatantly served the interests of the packers, while the Urban League tried to steer a tortuous middle course among employers, black employees, and Chicago unions. Both, however, considered it their duty, in the words of one Urban Leaguer, to develop "in the worker's mind her personal responsibility to become a regular and efficient employee and of showing her the requirements and standards of satisfactory service."[69]

The Wabash Avenue YMCA enjoyed a close relationship with many Chicago employers, and in 1916 its program turned increasingly toward "industrial work." The focal point of this joint effort to mold black migrants into a loyal, tractable, efficient labor force was the company-based "Efficiency Club." Five packinghouses, International Harvester, Corn Products Refining, Pullman, and National Malleable Castings sponsored these clubs and strongly encouraged black employees to join, in some cases upgrading a man's "work rating" if he attended. George Merritt, president of the Armour Efficiency Club, and also a member of the Wabash YMCA Committee on Management, was a foreman; the idea was thus reinforced that members would receive favorable treatment and that participation might be a key to upward mobility. Purportedly designed to instill "a sense of responsibility on the part of the industrial worker and sympathetic understanding and good will on the part of company officials," the clubs offered employers an opportunity to recruit loyal shop floor leadership.[70]

Swifts' Premiums baseball team (source: CCRR, *Negro in Chicago*, 292).

Whatever "sympathetic understanding and good will" emerged on the part of company officials had little to do with their interaction with workers in the efficiency clubs. Apparently workers generally listened while managers and YMCA officials lectured. Meetings, held in the YMCA auditorium, often were training sessions, focusing on "Progress of the Negro in the Packing Industry," "Electricity and its Use in the Yards," or "Refrigeration." Workers apparently attended these meetings in large numbers. During the first nine months of 1920, for example, attendance totaled 5,394, an average of 142 at each session. Years later, A. L. Jackson, the branch's executive director during the war, claimed that efficiency club membership had reached "four or five hundred." In 1919, the efficiency clubs were sufficiently influential among workers for the meat packers to use them to urge black employees to return to work after the race riot.[71]

Employers turned to the YMCA for a variety of activities characteristic of welfare capitalism programs. Under its auspices they established glee clubs, choral societies, baseball leagues, orchestras, and job-training programs. Many of the programs enjoyed considerable popularity among black workers. The Morris & Company Glee Club, organized in 1917, often drew crowds of four hundred men and women to its concerts at the YMCA. The industrial baseball league, formed in 1918, attracted 10,107 fans the following year to its 56 games between such teams as the Swifts' Premiums and the Armour Star Lambs. Although the Chicago Federation of Labor attacked it as a tool of the meat packers, and the packers did indeed pay the salary of a YMCA "extension worker among Negro employees," the organization saw its role as facilitating relations between blacks and industry. Lectures on such topics as "Why Leave a Job?" served the interests of both employers and middle-class black leaders interested in the socialization of black workers. YMCA officials also organized meetings at which industrial managers listened to the ideas of black leaders, providing a channel of communication useful to both groups.[72]

Like the YMCA, the Chicago Urban League sought to help the migrants adjust to new conditions, but the League sometimes fought to change those conditions as well. "We have tried to fit the workers to the jobs and the jobs to the workers," the League stated in 1919. Urban League officials served employers by screening applicants, exhorting newcomers to adopt industrial values and work habits, and providing consultants when problems developed involving black workers. At the same time, they pushed employers to hire more blacks and open new—especially skilled and supervisory—positions to blacks. Equally important, they used their credibility among industrial managers to improve conditions and combat on-the-job racism. Reluctance to hire black foremen, for instance, diminished when the Urban League suggested that such action would increase productivity by reducing conflict. The organization's task was to maintain a careful balance: it had to convince industrialists to hire blacks and help managers mold those workers into a productive labor force, but at the same time it wanted to protect inexperienced black migrants against exploitation on the job.[73]

This dual role could best be performed by maintaining a strong influence at the workplace, along with trying to control the placement of black workers. Employers of black labor grew accustomed to consulting the League whenever problems arose with black workers. Between November 1919 and October 1920, for example, sixteen firms asked advice on such problems as turnover, inefficiency, and racial tensions. The League usually sent a representative to confer with management over problems resolvable through administrative action and then worked with the migrants themselves. League officials cooperated in sponsoring welfare and training programs but also lectured company officials and foremen on such topics as "How to Handle Negro Labor." After Urban Leaguer William Evans delivered a series of such addresses at International Harvester, relations between foremen and black workers improved considerably. In other cases the League provided a firm with a black "welfare worker," who became responsible for industrial relations problems involving black workers. For her article in *Opportunity* describing her work as a personnel administrator at Montgomery Ward and Nachman Spring-Filled Mattress Company, Helen Sayre of the Chicago Urban League chose a revealing title—"Making Over Poor Workers."[74]

Concurrent with advising industry, the League sought to increase the migrants' efficiency on the job by attempting to inculcate values of punctuality, zeal, regularity, and ambition. Charles Johnson of the National Urban League described the general approach to this task as "the recreation of the worker." Transforming migrants into productive industrial laborers, he argued, required "a reorganization of the physical and mental habits which are a legacy of their old experience." A card distributed to black factory workers by the Detroit Urban League epitomized the message that Chicago's branch conveyed as well:

WHY HE FAILED
He watched the clock.
He was always behindhand.
He asked too many questions.
His stock excuse was "I forgot."
He wasn't ready for the next step.
He did not put his heart in his work.
He learned nothing from his blunders.
He was content to be a second rater.
He didn't learn that the best part of his salary
   was not in his pay envelope—SUCCESS.[75]

Although it did not serve employers as unstintingly as did the YMCA, the Urban League could not ignore its dependence on industrialists. The League had only as much influence over working conditions as employers would grant, based on its expertise and ability to deliver. More important, its budget relied heavily on contributions from stockyards firms, Julius Rosenwald of Sears, Roebuck, a few steel companies, and International Harvester. As the League demonstrated the usefulness of its services during the war years, corporate contributions increased. In exchange for these funds and for continued corporate cooperation with the League's placement office, the Urban League transmitted the shibboleths of efficiency to transplanted black southerners. It even organized some of its programs around employers' complaints based on racial stereotypes. When an employer told the League he would not hire blacks because they were habitually late, the League lectured migrants on punctuality. To the extent such inadequacies could be ascribed to the workers' southern backgrounds rather than to their race, the Old Settlers in the Urban League shared some of the prejudices. Some lessons were, in fact, appropriate, although not always for the reasons assumed by employers or Urban Leaguers. It was necessary and helpful to lecture migrants on ambition, for instance, not because black southerners lacked ambition, but because they were accustomed to keeping such impulses to themselves; in the South black ambition was labeled arrogance. By preaching ambition to the migrants and informing employers that only incentives would nourish such ambition, the League characteristically served three masters: it advised industrialists and helped them to increase productivity; it improved conditions for migrants; and it took a step toward eliminating one manifestation of the newcomers' behavior which so annoyed black Chicago's Old Settlers.[76] All of its actions seemed to serve the black community in general, because every successful black worker could open the door to a few more, as the race gained a reputation for efficiency.

Whatever the initial skepticism of Chicago industrialists, the migrants responded to the demands of the workplace. By the early 1920s time and efficiency problems began to recede. An Interchurch World Movement study, using piecework earnings as a yardstick, found productivity among black and white workers approximately equal. A 1920 survey of 137 employers of blacks in Chicago found 118 satisfied with their work: 34 of 47 manufacturers claimed that black workers were as efficient as whites, and most employers praised blacks' reliability and efficiency. Employers of large numbers of blacks sung the migrants' praises almost unanimously: 29 food-products and iron and steel producers, employing a total of 11,297 blacks, reported black labor "satisfactory," while only 6 companies in those sectors, employing 179 black men and women, found them "unsatisfactory." A meat packer and steelmaker, both of whom had reported problems during the war years, found absenteeism among blacks equal to or less than among white workers. In 1924 a mattress manufacturer who had sought Urban League assistance in dealing with problems of time discipline could boast of attendance and punctuality records above 95 percent. A field agent for the Phelps Stokes Fund corroborated these results, finding employers "highly satisfied" with black workers. Few employers complained of continued recalcitrance in matters of work discipline. Those who did tended to agree with the managers at Argo Corn Products Company, who listed such problems as turnover, "shiftlessness," and irresponsibility, but admitted that efficiency varied directly with a worker's length of stay in the North. Others who continued to complain did so in the face of contradictory statistics. More typically, a foundry superintendent revealed both his ignorance of how hard blacks had worked in the South, and his satisfaction with their performance in his plant: "The Negro up here from the South never heard of working six days a week and being on time. . . . But with a little persistent effort and showing him that it is necessary he soon learns the system the same as the others."[77]

The Chicago Commission on Race Relations concluded that despite the handicap of a rural background rendering them "ill-fitted for the keen competition, business-like precision and six-day week routine," the migrants had "succeeded in Chicago." The *Defender* agreed, ceasing to exhort blacks to greater efficiency. By 1920, editor Abbott no longer considered it necessary to convince employers to hire unskilled blacks, and casually referred to "the recognition of the efficiency of our workers" by Chicago employers.[78] Most migrants had worked for six—often seven—days a week for much of their lives. Their accomplishment lay in adapting to factory time discipline and convincing white industrialists that they could do the job.

The migrants adapted quickly to the new culture of work because they had come to Chicago eager to learn. Labor historians in the United States and abroad have shown how industrialists often resorted to forms of coercion against a recalcitrant and resistant work force unwilling to abandon traditional patterns of work.[79] In the case of black newcomers, at least, that was unnecessary in Chicago. The young men and women who journeyed north had already rejected some southern social and cultural patterns. The industrial future represented opportunity to them. It conferred prestige as well:

> I used to have a woman that lived up on a hill
> I used to have a woman that lived up on a hill
> She was crazy 'bout me, ooh well, well, cause
> I worked at the Chicago Mill.[80]

The young were not alone in their eagerness to jettison the ways of the past. With bitter recollections of life in the rural South, and memories of sharecropping and perpetual debt gainsaying any golden age on the countryside, few migrants felt committed to old work habits. They had come to Chicago for more than jobs and high wages; they sought a new way of life and considered their factory jobs a first step. Upon arrival and hiring, they wanted to do the "right thing" in their new environment. The Urban League and YMCA owed their effectiveness to the eagerness of newcomers who requested their assistance and accepted their advice.

To an extent, the migrants' achievements had the effect the Urban League had envisioned. One manufacturer, considered typical by T. Arnold Hill, industrial secretary of the Chicago Urban League, declared that he was "so pleased" with the black women he had hired that he planned to expand and wanted the League to recruit more workers for his shop. At a conference of Chicago industrialists, representatives from Armour, Argo Corn Products, International Harvester, Morris, and Yellow Cab unanimously expressed satisfaction with black workers and declared that they would not reduce their black work force. By the end of 1919, Hill could confidently report that because they now considered blacks as efficient as whites, a number of firms intended to maintain a ratio of three whites to one black.[81]

The Urban League's program, however, was not an unqualified success. Black workers had grasped a foothold, and some had even stepped firmly onto the ladder. But few would climb. If most Chicago industrial employers tended to agree with one industrial relations specialist's call for his colleagues to "revise our estimate of the negro, [because] the past two years have wrought in him a change and the orthodox ideas on negro psychology must be revised to fit," blacks still suffered from assumptions about their natural limits. What Charles Johnson described as a "vicious circle" plagued black operatives. Originally channeled towards positions considered most appropriate to their strength and endurance, they found that a positive attitude and satisfactory performance only further convinced employers that they had a particular aptitude for such occupations. The Chicago Commission on Race Relations found in 1920 that "employers frequently expressed the belief that Negroes are incapable of performing tasks which require sustained mental application." Where it was acknowledged that blacks were capable of filling better jobs, limitations often stemmed from other problems related to race. At Swift and Armour, for example, managers defended a rule prohibiting blacks from handling finished products by pointing to the need to avoid offending plant visitors.[82] Finally, constant effort by management to deskill production processes, an important force in the creation of the very semiskilled positions that migrants perceived to be the door to advancement, narrowed the corridors of mobility within the blue-collar world, as skilled jobs continued to be eliminated. "Progress" for the race would be primarily horizontal during the 1920s: the opening of more low-level jobs and the retention of a substantial proportion of those jobs when layoffs struck.

The disinclination of employers to extend their seemingly progressive employment policies to the arena of promotion was not initially self-evident to either the Urban League or optimistic black newcomers. But the stated intentions of industrialists to maintain a specific racial ratio suggests an underlying purpose that helps to explain why some doors were opened wider than others. Black workers constituted an essential element in the timeworn tactic of maintaining an ethnic mix in order to perpetuate mutual distrust among workers and thus inhibit unionism. Empire Mattress Company President M. Van Gelder told the Urban League that he had increased the number of blacks on his payroll because those he had first hired were good workers, and he contrasted them with his immigrant employees, who had "assumed an insolent air of independence and became unreasonable in their demands." Another Chicago business executive commented that not only had there been "great changes in the characteristic of the Negro as a laborer since he has come into Industry," but that blacks "were loyal in times of stress."[83]

8

"The White Man's Union"

On July 6, 1919, members of Amalgamated Meat Cutters and Butcher Workmen of North America Local 651 gathered at the local's State Street office for a parade and rally. Two miles away, in the shadows of the Chicago stockyards, another group of packinghouse unionists prepared for a march to the same mass meeting. The two groups—one black, the other white—had intended to merge and walk the final ten blocks together, but police officials warned that racial tensions were too high to risk a joint march. Threatened with revocation of their permit, union leaders agreed to abandon plans to have white and black unionists demonstrate their brotherhood by parading along State Street through the heart of black Chicago. Reluctantly the Stockyards Labor Council segregated parades to a rally designed largely to "interest the colored workers at the yards in the benefits of organization."[1]

After approximately two thousand union members converged on a playground at the western edge of the Black Belt, three blacks and four whites addressed the throng. "It does me good," roared Jack Johnstone, secretary of the Stockyards Labor Council, "to see such a checkerboard crowd. . . . You are all standing shoulder to shoulder as men, regardless of whether your face is white or black." Other speakers, however, knew that self-congratulation for interracial solidarity was premature. John Kikulski, addressing his countrymen in Polish, urged them to abandon their prejudices and cooperate with their black coworkers. Charles Ford, a black organizer, reminded both groups that if they continued to wrestle with each other they would all remain in the dirt, mired in perpetual battle and mutual degradation. And while his very presence implied support for the union, T. Arnold Hill of the Chicago Urban League also warned that "if he and his colleagues were expected to advise the colored workers to join the union, they expected the union men themselves to be fair toward [black] workers."[2]

This episode suggests many of the obstacles impeding the Stockyards Labor Council's attempts to organize black workers during and immediately after World War I. Union leaders recognized that they had to dissolve suspicions separating black and white workers. Furthermore, they had to convince Chicago's black leadership of their sincerity and their strength. With thousands of black and white workers parading together through the ghetto, organizers had hoped that this demonstration would show to black Chicagoans how unions could be vehicles for racial harmony. At the same time, white marchers were to have recognized that black workers could be organized, that there was black community support for the union, and that they should therefore cease regarding blacks as a "scab race." But the same racial hostility that the union sought to overcome gave the packers an opening which they used to cripple the rally's effectiveness.

Moreover, some black leaders played their usual ambiguous role, fearing the consequences of the march at a time when racial tensions had made a riot seem not only possible, but imminent. Black politicians probably cooperated with packinghouse officials to influence police officials. The *Defender* ignored the event. The Urban League representative who spoke at the rally refrained from either attacking the packers or explicitly endorsing the union; what support he did offer was qualified by a reference to past discrimination. Finally, a turnout that compared unfavorably with most Stockyards Labor Council rallies suggests that organizers had neither attracted as many blacks as they hoped nor convinced white members of the demonstration's importance.[3] But the march and rally did take place; black and white workers did mingle; the black community did show considerable interest in the event; an influential black leader did aid the union by agreeing to speak; and the union was able to showcase two black organizers. The Stockyards Labor Council had attracted the interest of many black workers and was continuing to present its case to thousands of others.[4]

Eventually the Stockyards Labor Council lost its battle to organize the packinghouses, partly because it failed to win sufficient support among black workers, especially the recent migrants from the South. Although many blacks joined, most had dropped out by 1921, when a disastrous strike finally crippled the five-year organizing drive. Union leaders lamented that the migrants were ignorant about unionism and had been difficult to reach because Chicago's black leadership had adamantly and effectively opposed unionization. But the issue was more complicated. Many Chicago black leaders, like the numerous workers who had joined the union temporarily but lost interest, vacillated, waiting to see which side was a more valuable ally to the race. As for the migrants, their presumed lack of understanding of union principles was less important than their history, their ideas about industrial society, and their perceptions of the dynamics of social relations. To most union men the conflict clearly turned on class interests. But to blacks, both migrants and community leaders, race was the central concept; unionism had to prove its efficacy as a solution to a racial problem.

Few migrants who worked in Chicago's factories could avoid decisions relating to strikes and unions. Black southerners entered a city with a long history of bitter labor strife at a time when workers sought to take advantage of wartime conditions to build or rebuild unions. Seventy-one strikes wracked Chicago during 1916, compared with twenty-five the year before. When Pullman car cleaners walked out in March 1916, the company sought replacements among blacks. At garment shops, a wool warehouse, and International Harvester, a black newcomer in 1916 could easily secure a job by crossing a picket line.[5] Such opportunities would continue to arise, and similar—perhaps more complicated—decisions faced blacks already employed by firms undergoing organizing drives. During the next five years, packinghouses, steel mills, garment factories, hotels, restaurants, laundries, and lamp shade factories all experienced strikes, and all either employed blacks prior to the conflict or recruited them as strikebreakers.[6]

When confronted with picket lines, union organizers, and employer propaganda and pressure, most black workers eschewed strong commitments to unionization. They did so for a variety of reasons: union racism, antiunion leadership within the black community, unfamiliarity with trade unionism, and intimidation by employers. The interaction and impact of these factors turned on the experiences and goals migrants brought with them to Chicago. They made decisions based on what they had learned in the past, what they were learning at the time, and what they hoped for in the future. Black workers from the South ultimately rejected union appeals because they analyzed the situation in racial rather than class terms. This analysis was a logical extension of both their migration experience and the liberal world view embodied in the meaning of the Great Migration.

Because the meat-packing companies employed a sizeable plurality of black workers at any given moment and the unions attempting to organize their plants actively recruited black workers, the five-year campaign to unionize the stockyards affords special insight into the

attitudes of black newcomers to Chicago. The Great Steel Strike of
1919, which attracted more attention nationally and has since served
as the apotheosis of the era's labor conflict, is less interesting in this
context. Unlike the Stockyards Labor Council, the National Committee For Organizing Iron and Steel Workers made no special efforts to
organize blacks and did little to try to convince them that previous
patterns of discrimination would be abandoned. Predictably, blacks
remained largely outside the organization, although many in Chicago
and elsewhere participated in the walkout on the first day of the Great
Strike. The packinghouses, more than the steel mills, provide a setting that affords an opportunity to understand how black workers
from the South regarded their place in American industrial society.[7]

The Stockyards Labor Council, a consortium of thirteen craft
unions formed by the Chicago Federation of Labor, launched its
organizing drive in September 1917. To preempt the traditional employer tactic of promoting unskilled nonunion men to skilled positions and introducing thousands of strikebreakers, labor leaders
modified traditions of organizing along exclusive and divisive craft
lines. Instead they organized all workers into the Stockyards Labor
Council, and later parceled them out to appropriate unions claiming jurisdiction, mainly the Amalgamated Meat Cutters and Butcher
Workmen (AMC&BW).[8]

Packinghouse workers responded slowly at first, but after three
months of mass meetings, parades, automobile rallies, and smokers,
approximately 40 percent of Chicago's stockyards workers had joined
unions.[9] When national leaders of the AMC&BW called a strike and
industry representatives refused to negotiate, the federal government
intervened to stabilize what it considered an essential wartime industry. On December 25 packers and unions signed separate agreements
(allowing employers to avoid even implicit recognition of the union)
with the President's Mediation Commission, prohibiting strikes and
lockouts during the war and providing a mechanism for binding arbitration. When the arbitrator, Judge Samuel B. Alschuler, issued his
first award in March 1918, increasing unskilled minimum hourly
wages from 27.5 cents to 32 cents and providing a basic eight-hour
day with ten hours' pay and premiums for overtime, the union
claimed its first victory. Membership soared. In November 1918,
62,857 packinghouse workers nationwide paid dues to the AMC&BW,
twice the total recorded in January of that year.[10]

Under the umbrella of the Alschuler administration, industrial relations in the packinghouses settled into a relative calm during the
year following the initial arbitration award. Packinghouse executives
even began to speak directly with union officials. Such contacts,

however, remained informal, and without recognition as bargaining agents the unions' position remained tenuous, dependent on the federal government's willingness to compel employers to negotiate. With Alschuler's mandate due to expire as the government dismantled war machinery in 1919, union leaders sought a new agreement without the federal middleman—a contract. Unwilling to grant this crucial principle but not yet prepared to fight, packers offered only to renew the existing arrangement until one year after the signing of the peace treaty. The AMC&BW's national leadership, despite opposition from the more radical Stockyards Labor Council, agreed in June 1919 to renewal.[11]

The Stockyards Labor Council responded to the decision to renew the agreement by mounting a massive organizing drive. In violation of the Alschuler accords, unionists carried the campaign inside the packinghouses, refusing to work with nonunion men. Throughout June and July 1919, spontaneous walkouts interrupted production in departments not "one hundred percent" union. These stoppages exposed the Achilles' heel of Chicago's stockyards unions—racial hostility and black cynicism about unions.[12]

Ostensibly, the June-July 1919 wildcat strikes had nothing to do with race. "I can get along with these colored fellows . . . that have the [union] buttons on," testified union committeeman Louis Michora after a walkout in Wilson & Company's dry-salting department. It was the others who bothered him. "I cannot stand working with them. The colored fellows won't obey our orders and they won't get along with us." After listening to another union official at Wilson, Alschuler agreed that "it is not a question of color at all." Robert Bedford, a black shop steward on that company's cattle floor, insisted that blacks and whites in his department usually got along quite well; both union and nonunion factions included members of each race. The packers, he charged, had introduced racial hostility into the situation in the person of Austin "Heavy" Williams, whom they had hired to buttonhole black newcomers and discourage them from joining the union. "This Williams is the leader of some men to raise a line of prejudice, and show the white man, the colored man is not with him, and show the colored man, the white man is not with him."[13] Whatever the hopes of black and white union activists, race was an issue, and stockyards employers would do all they could to dramatize it.

The racial tensions central to the wildcat strikes in 1919 demonstrated that recent migrants represented the balance of power in the stockyards. "Northern" black workers—men and women either born in the North or resident there before 1916—joined unions in proportions comparable to white workers, with perhaps as many as 90 percent signing up. It was the migrants who seemed to be troublesome. These "new men," explained Bedford, were "from one part of the country, and . . . stand solidly together, and you cannot do anything with them." Frank Custer, another black steward and like Bedford a "northerner," registered a similar complaint, accusing Wilson & Company of "taking my race up from Texas, using that as a big stick."[14] The outcome of the organizing drive rested largely on how migrants reponded to Robert Bedford, Frank Custer, Heavy Williams, and others who competed for their allegiance. Some became loyal unionists; others, implacable scabs. Most fell somewhere in between—uncertain, flexible, and trying to discern the extent to which blacks could expect a square deal from one side or the other.

For some migrants the choice was obvious, because they had belonged to unions in the South. Black dockworkers in New Orleans had begun organizing as far back as 1872, and even the men who broke a screwmen's strike in the 1890s had become union members by 1903. Subsequently the Industrial Workers of the World had organized black longshoremen in New Orleans and Galveston. Black carpenters and bricklayers belonged to craft unions in many southern cities. During the first decade of the twentieth century in the Birmingham district, at least eight thousand black workers belonged to trade unions, mainly the United Mine Workers, even if only for a short time. Black unionists from Mobile, Montgomery, Selma, Anniston, Birmingham, and other Alabama cities served as delegates to the Alabama Federation of Labor convention in 1903. "As strikers," recalled Oscar Ameringer of his experience organizing black brewery workers in New Orleans in 1906–7, "there could be no better." Like the seven hundred black "helpers" who struck railroad shops in Marshall, Texas, during a wage dispute in October 1916, these men, their families, and their friends were familiar with the advantages and the meaning of unionization.[15]

Rural black southerners also understood the value of collective action. The bloody riot near Helena, Arkansas, in 1919 was provoked by a meeting of an organization of sharecroppers.[16] Some ten thousand to seventeen thousand black men had belonged to the Brotherhood of Timber Workers, which organized in 1910 and conducted a series of strikes in the southern woods between 1912 and 1914. Many of these men might also have carried an Industrial Workers of the World red card, since the Brotherhood affiliated with the IWW in 1912. Like the sawmill laborers who had participated in Knights of Labor strikes in Mississippi in 1889 and 1900, these men traveled frequently, many of them living in farm settlements as well as in labor camps. Through them, individuals with more limited experiences learned about organization and strikes. A broader source of organizing lore lay among the sixty thousand blacks who had joined the Knights of Labor in the 1880s, when black local assemblies were formed not only in southern cities but in smaller communities as well. The Colored Farmers Alliance, even if its claim of one million members was an exaggeration, also left a considerable legacy of collective protest in the rural South after it disintegrated in the 1890s.[17] Much of this activity took place in parts of the South that later sent large numbers of migrants to Chicago and involved sectors employing the mobile young men most likely to migrate and end up in packinghouses.

Migrants predisposed toward unionization, however, were a small minority. Most black southerners, if they knew much about unions, had learned to be suspicious of organized labor. Georgia's labor leaders, notes one historian, "as a whole were conservative, Protestant, Democratic, and Ku Klux Klannish."[18] In southern cities where craft unions had attained some power, white craftsmen frequently excluded black competitors and pushed nonunion black workers out of all but the least desirable jobs. The Amalgamated Association of Iron and Steel Workers in Birmingham in 1905 demanded as a condition for a strike settlement that management "discharge all the niggers." Where black carpenters, bricklayers, painters, and blacksmiths had such a secure foothold that their strikebreaking potential could not be ignored, unions organized them into separate—and powerless—locals. Whether a union blatantly excluded blacks or merely demanded the elimination of the wage differential which induced employers to hire blacks, the effect was the same. Successful union organization meant that black craftsmen lost their jobs.[19]

Other than American Federation of Labor craft unions, only the railroad brotherhoods gained significant strength in the early twentieth-century South, and these organizations left few doubts as to the relationship between unionization and race. The brotherhoods refused to admit blacks, and union victories often had dire consequences. "Since the White has organized a Union," complained one Illinois Central shop laborer in Memphis, "it is simply bad the way we are treated." During the fifteen years preceding the Great Migration, white workers on southern railroads staged a series of strikes protesting the employment of black firemen and demanding that blacks be either replaced or denied seniority rights. In response, black railroad men formed associations which combined benevolent functions with attempts to "guard against attacks upon colored railway employees." The Association of Colored Railway Trainmen, for example, appealed to the United States Railway Labor Board to invalidate a 1919 agreement between the white brotherhoods and the Illinois Central and Yazoo and Mississippi railroads, which limited the opportunities of black employees. The experiences of black railway men suggested not only that white unions could mean trouble for blacks, but that black unions existed to fight white organizations in addition to (or even rather than) the employers. Given the importance of railroad men in the communication network through which black southerners learned of the North and its opportunities, their battles with white unions might well have informed the predilections of many migrants.[20]

The overwhelming majority of migrants had been neither members of unions in the South nor victims of racial discrimination by white unions. They knew about unions because of the experiences of family and friends, or through stories about organized resistance to landlords and employers, or, more likely, through general accounts of how unions kept the black man down. Many were ignorant of unions and strikes. "They didn't have no unions where I comed from— ain't nothin' there anyway but farmers," one migrant remarked two months after his arrival in Chicago. He had not joined because "these other folks been here longer than me; they ain't joined and I reckon they know more about it than me."[21]

The "other folks" at the workplace could include the Robert Bedfords and Frank Custers. In the community, however, other voices spoke loudly. Like most prominent Afro-Americans at the beginning of the twentieth century, Chicago's black leadership did not eagerly embrace the labor movement. Several factors underlay these generally antiunion sentiments. Individuals educated at Hampton Institute, Tuskegee, and their offshoots had imbibed the bootstraps attitude toward capitalism taught at these schools: individual effort, hard work, and moral virtue fostered improvement, and group advancement rested on individual achievement. The philanthropic captains of industry who funded these and other black institutions were not only friends of the race, but role models. Where educational philosophies differed from the Washingtonian schools, racial radicalism was more common than economic radicalism. Whatever their disagreements on racial strategies, Kelly Miller of Howard University and Booker T. Washington of Tuskegee Institute could agree that blacks should distance themselves from trade unionism. During the prewar years, W. E. B. Du Bois was one of the few nationally recognized black leaders who sought cooperation with the American Federation of Labor. Among most others, whether they emphasized the role of a "talented tenth" black vanguard or vocational education for the masses and gradual upward mobility, bourgeois values dominated economic ideas.[22]

The policies and actions of the AF of L reinforced these antiunion tendencies while repelling black leaders more receptive to unionization. As in the South, unions in the North often excluded or discriminated against blacks. Many national union constitutions specifically barred blacks from membership. For years, AF of L President Samuel Gompers had tried without success to convince affiliates that blacks outside the labor movement represented a potential strikebreaking threat which could be neutralized only by inclusion within the organizations. But only a handful of national unions, led by the United Mine Workers, appreciated the logic. Precluded by the Federation's structure from forcing a union to alter rules or practices, Gompers abandoned the debate. By 1900, he was recommending instead that the AF of L organize black workers into separate "federal locals." These locals, affiliated directly with the federation rather than with the union of their trade, were virtually powerless. They institutionalized and legitimated the exclusionary policies of the national unions.[23]

By World War I, Gompers had become a symbol to black Americans of union racism. AF of L actions that showed insensitivity toward black Americans, including the 1917 convention's rejection of a resolution condemning racial discrimination, were consistent with Gompers' proclivity for relating racist anecdotes in testimony before government commissions and in the *American Federationist*.[24] Although some union leaders, especially those who dominated the Chicago Federation of Labor, advocated more liberal policies, it was Gompers whose statements received the most publicity and who was regarded as the spokesman for American labor. Like white workers and union leaders who knew of no black leaders other than Booker T. Washington, and therefore considered blacks implacably proemployer, black leaders and workers accepted Gompers' statements and AF of L policies as definitive.

Black Chicagoans had plenty of evidence that corroborated images of the labor movement as racist and antagonistic to their interests. Pullman porters and other trainmen had considerable experience with the railroad brotherhoods, and the powerful building-trades unions dominated occupations that some black workers sought to enter. When blacks in Chicago thought of unions, they generally had in mind these organizations. Until black workingmen found jobs during a 1900 strike, construction unions had, by one means or another, excluded them from the industry. Chicago locals refused to honor blacks' union cards from out-of-town locals, and those unions willing to accept black members did so only to control their employment. Upon receiving a black craftsman's initiation fee, a business agent would studiously ignore him when requests for workers came in from contractors. Even after the 1900 strike forced the building-trades unions to take black workers more seriously, generally only black hod carriers, bricklayers, plasterers, and asphalt pavers were able to secure the union card essential for most employment. Logically, the *Defender* concluded in 1915 that "as things stand the labor unions are his [the black worker's] worst enemies for they deny him an opportunity to earn an honest living." [25]

If highly visible railroad and construction unions provided a general notion of how unions operated and how their quest for power could limit black economic opportunities, the waiters' union supplied a specific incident which convinced black Chicagoans that even a union claiming to represent them fairly could not be trusted. In 1903, black and white workers struck the Kohlsaat restaurant chain. The AF of L union of cooks and waiters counted twenty thousand members in Chicago, two thousand of them black and organized into a separate local. Black strikers later insisted that the union double-crossed them after seven weeks, when it extracted a favorable settlement from management and demanded as part of the agreement that the black waiters be dismissed. Sometime during the conflict, the charter of the black local had been revoked. Although the facts of the incident became even more confused as the years passed, black Chicagoans were still referring to it twenty years later when asked their attitudes regarding unions. Milton Webster, a black union organizer, observed in 1927 that the affair had exerted a decisive influence, predisposing black workers to distrust unions. Employers were, as one black legislator put it, "more kindly toward colored labor." [26]

Packinghouse firms, like other employers, had long relied on ethnic and racial divisions in their battles against organized labor. In 1886, faced with a surge of agitation among workers of mainly native white, German, Irish, English, and Scandinavian backgrounds, employers began hiring large numbers of eastern and southern Europeans—all contemptuously labeled "Poles" by the experienced men. Poles, Bohemians, Slovaks, Ruthenians, Magyars, Serbs, Croatians, Slovenes, and Syrians entered packingtown during the following decades. When workers walked out in sympathy with the American Railway Union in 1894, packers continued to capitalize on ethnic jealousies and introduced blacks into the equation. Though numerically insignificant, blacks provided yet another obstacle to working-class unity in the stockyards. In response to a strike ten years later, the packers again used the racial "weapon," immediately hiring approximately ten thousand black strikebreakers. Although nearly all blacks were laid off after the 1904 strike (only 365 remained in 1910), employers kept the threat visible. Dennis Lane, secretary of the AMC&BW, described the packers' strategy in 1915: "They will put a big burly negro on one side and a white man on the other, and let them battle it out for supremacy; that is their method of arriving at efficiency." [27]

The strategy was not ineffective. The 1904 strike seemingly confirmed what many white packinghouse workers had already decided in 1894: blacks were a "scab race." During the earlier strike a group of white workers had drawn a graphic representation near the entrance to the stockyards. A white newspaper described the black laborer hanging in effigy: "A black face of hideous expression had been fixed upon the head of straw and a placard pinned upon the breast of the figure bore the skull and cross bones with the words 'nigger-scab' above and below in bold letters." [28] The "hideous expression" reflected traditional American notions that blacks were less than human. The association of "nigger" and "scab" articulated the growing belief that blacks were different from other strikebreakers and had an inherent propensity to break strikes.

Chicago's white workers believed they had ample evidence of that propensity. During the bloody strikes in southern Illinois coal mines in the 1890s, the role of black strikebreakers received considerable publicity in Chicago. Locally, in addition to the packinghouse conflicts, blacks helped to break strikes of building tradesmen (1900), teamsters (1905), and even newsboys (1912). The conflation of labor and racial hostility became increasingly common. During the long, bitter, and violent teamsters strike, whites for the first time attacked blacks who were not strikebreakers. Union men wielding rocks told one black union member who insisted that his employer was not involved in the strike that being a "nigger" was enough to earn him a beating. A school principal, whose pupils refused to attend while black scabs delivered coal to the building, supported their actions "if the dirty niggers deliver coal at this school." He failed to mention that the black deliverymen were strikebreakers—because they were black, that was simply assumed. [29]

Whites exaggerated the degree and impact of black strikebreaking. Many black workers struck along with their white colleagues in both the 1904 packinghouse strike and the teamsters dispute a year later. Moreover, with as many as five thousand jobseekers—mostly whites—appearing at the stockyards gates each morning, employers hardly needed to "import" as many blacks as the strikers imagined. The image of "trainloads" of as many as fourteen hundred blacks arriving at the stockyards was surely an exaggeration, inspired by the sense of inundation felt by white workers accustomed to seeing only white faces in packingtown. The teamsters strike provoked unprecedented racial violence, although less than 15 percent of the strikebreakers were black. In each case white strikers singled out only one ethnic group—blacks—as the enemy of the labor movement. To many white Chicago workingmen, "nigger" and "scab" had become virtually interchangeable, as the overwhelming reality of color dwarfed all other characteristics of the anonymous men and women who crossed picket lines.[30]

If previous experience with black strikebreakers had convinced white packinghouse workers of the impossibility of organizing blacks, some of Chicago's farsighted labor leaders had learned a different lesson. Organizing blacks was "imperative," argued William Z. Foster, who preceded Jack Johnstone as Secretary of the Stockyards Labor Council. By 1917 blacks constituted one-fourth of the stockyards labor force, and Foster knew that "a place had to be made in the movement for every negro in the packing houses." But creating places for black workers was only half the battle; to fill those places, unions had to convince black workers that they were sincere. The task was formidable. Because discriminatory policies could jeopardize the whole campaign, "we didn't want any Jim Crow situation out there," recalled John Fitzpatrick, chairman of the Stockyards Labor Council and president of the Chicago Federation of Labor.[31]

Unfortunately, neither the Stockyards Labor Council nor its parent organization, the Chicago Federation of Labor, could influence the membership policies of the international unions whose locals constituted the Council. Nor could it overturn exclusionary or discriminatory decisions made by locals. Although the AMC&BW had always admitted blacks and claimed to treat blacks and whites equally, some locals did discriminate, and one national official reportedly advocated keeping "the niggers out of the stock yards." Other packing industry craft unions were even more troublesome, some excluding blacks entirely.[32]

The solution was to create an AMC&BW "miscellaneous" local headquartered in the Black Belt. Unlike most stockyards locals, which comprised workers who performed a given task (cattle butchers, beef boners, canners, etc.), Local 651 served a particular neighborhood, a euphemism for its racial constituency. Although unusual, this structure was not unique: many white unskilled laborers also belonged to locals similarly organized along community lines, and a number of locals conducted business in a foreign language, necessarily attracting an ethnically homogeneous membership. Moreover, blacks were not limited to a single local. They technically could join any of the approximately forty AMC&BW locals organized by the Stockyards Labor Council and indeed could be found in perhaps as many as thirty-seven of them. Yet most "gravitated" to Local 651, which became known as the "colored" local. Foster later argued that blacks preferred their own local where they could make independent decisions, and a white organizer of "English speaking women" in the stockyards claimed that blacks preferred "their own local meeting with their own officials in charge." These claims are consistent with other evidence of working-class black preferences for controlling their own institutions. But there is no other evidence of black men or women requesting this arrangement, which was not altogether different from the generally resented—and powerless—AF of L federal local.[33]

Local 651 was launched with a "monster meeting" on November 24, 1917. That same month the *Butcher Workman*, which until late 1917 had either ignored blacks or stereotyped them as scabs, boasted that a two-hour strike protesting "the unwarranted brutality of a foreman toward a colored employee" had brought in seventy-eight new members. Charles Johnson noted the stockyards unions' "more favorable attitude" and observed that "for the first time Negroes have begun to join freely." Progress, however, was slow. Both John Riley, the main black organizer in the yards, and Irene Goins, a black member of the Women's Trade Union League and organizer of black women, reported frustration in 1918. No membership data exist, but dues payments to Local 651 suggest tremendous fluctuation and little commitment. Only in three months did Local 651 make per capita payments on more than one thousand members, reaching a maximum of 1,715 in November. Local 213, the black women's local formed in March, generally hovered more consistently around the 160 mark.[34]

With racial division the greatest impediment to union solidarity, the Stockyards Labor Council targeted black workers when it stepped up its organizing drive in mid-1919. Union leaders renewed efforts to convince blacks that they were welcome in the union and worked to soften the hostility of white members. Irish readers of the *New Majority*, the official newspaper of the Chicago Federation of Labor, learned that Local 651 had passed resolutions and signed petitions supporting Irish independence. In their *Butcher Workman*, packinghouse workers read about Local 651's G. W. Downing, profiled in the newspaper's front page series, "Who's Who in the A.M.C. & B.W. of N.A." The article took care to mention that Downing had always been a union man, belonging to the Street Pavers' Union before joining the

Amalgamated. Both newspapers printed articles by black organizers reminding blacks that "the Negro's great opportunity" was to work in the packinghouses and to join the union. "There is no discrimination in the Amalgamated Meat Cutter and Butcher Workmen Union," declared Mrs. G. W. Reed, wife of one of the nine black organizers on the union's payroll between 1917 and 1922. The parade and rally on July 6, 1919, was an important part of this drive to breach racial barriers and arouse black enthusiasm.[35]

These efforts appeared to produce results. "A. K. Foote, Secretary of Local 651, was singing the blues a few days ago," observed Riley in late June, "but now he has a smile so broad that it is almost impossible to believe that such a change could come over a man. In the mornings at 7:30 we find applicants waiting to be signed up and every night until 9 and 10:30 a steady stream of humanity rolls in and out of the office." In July an "elevated train committee" of black union members maintained the momentum, buttonholing laborers at transfer points between the stockyards and the South Side ghetto. By July, Local 651's per capita payments to the International indicated 2,213 members in good standing, and Local 213 held steady at 160 women.[36] These figures are not inconsistent with most observers' estimates that approximately six thousand blacks belonged to Chicago's stockyards unions at some point. The six thousand figure probably includes many workers who had not paid dues recently but were still listed on union membership rolls. Many black workers testified during the Alschuler hearings that they had joined the union and dropped out soon after. The apparent statistical discrepancy suggests the pattern of black union membership: black workers joined readily, but let their dues lapse just as freely. They were interested in unions, but not committed to them.[37]

This cautious ambivalence angered white unionists. Black workers seemed to reap the benefits of the Alschuler arbitration award, without sharing either the risks or the costs of union pressure that secured it. In June 1919, whites received an ominous reminder of the threat posed by blacks when the hair spinners at Wilson, members of a union not covered by the Alschuler agreement and comprising white workers only, called a strike and were promptly replaced by nonunion blacks.[38] The spate of walkouts in June and July reflected the mounting anger toward black nonunion men. Blacks often stood among the union men refusing to work, but the offending nonmember was almost invariably black. Many white workers continued to perceive blacks as a scab race—with exceptions—while many nonunion blacks construed the refusal of union men to work with them as a racial insult and an attempt to prevent them from working. Accustomed to southern patterns, migrants especially were likely to interpret the dispute as a racial issue. In this context, they bristled at the suggestion that white workers could control their access to jobs.

Tension in the stockyards combined with competition over housing and political influence to set the stage for the 1919 race riot. Emphasizing conflicts over space, the *Defender* downplayed industrial conflict "because most of the laborers of our group have become unionized, thus doing away with the occasion for friction along those lines." The Chicago Commission on Race Relations, while more conservative in its estimates of black union membership, agreed that the riot had not arisen out of conditions involving the workplace. Yet 41 percent of the clashes had taken place in the stockyards district, a part of Chicago to which blacks traveled for only one reason—to work. Labor issues were, at the very least, major contributors to the hostility. Undoubtedly, the riot was a blow to unionization. The racial antagonisms it exposed and the suspicions it confirmed solidified barriers between black and white workers and facilitated employers' efforts to manipulate racial divisions and compete with the unions for black workers' loyalty.[39]

Stockyards employers moved quickly to turn the riot to their advantage. With support from the commander of the militia and the chief of police, they set plans for blacks to return to work under guard on August 4. Union leaders immediately protested that violence would be impossible to prevent: in a racially charged atmosphere, employers intended to reassemble a workforce of mutually hostile blacks and whites wielding knives, cleavers, and other lethal tools. Justifiably, they charged that the plan was little more than a subterfuge for what the packers had wanted all along—to bring in thousands of nonunion blacks under the protection of the state militia, a tactic well known to Chicago's embattled labor movement. If the packers persisted in their folly, the Stockyards Labor Council promised to call a strike until the situation had cooled sufficiently for black workers to return to the stockyards without military protection. The packers temporarily abandoned their scheme, probably because a fire in a Lithuanian neighborhood rekindled the racial tinderbox. But the union had been forced into the position of appearing to deny blacks the opportunity to work, a situation all too familiar to migrants and other black Chicagoans.[40]

When blacks did return to work on August 7, accompanied by police and militia, white unionists promptly walked out and later that day announced a mass meeting to call a strike for a union shop. Nonunion black workers would have to join or lose their jobs.[41] Once again, two different historical traditions inspired two different interpretations of the same series of events. To Chicago's white unionists, nonunion workers entering a plant under the protection of troops was a provocation, understood within the context of a half-century of class conflict marked by bitter strikes, injunctions, and armed protection of strikebreakers. To black workers from the South, the troops offered protection from whites trying to deny them their right to earn a living as free and equal citizens.

With the militia withdrawn on August 8 and the AMC&BW opposed to a strike on the grounds that it would violate the arbitration accords, the one-day walkout was not extended. Stockyards unionists continued their efforts to organize black workers, but the task was now virtually impossible. Even black union men were suspicious of white residents of the stockyards district. The week after the riot Local 651 petitioned the mayor to provide an armed escort for its members "to the end that we can reach our places of work and not be menaced or intimidated by any group of people who are seeking our employment by trying to place the entire race in a discreditable light." This request for "protection" coincided with the protests of white unionists against militia presence; even union membership could not bridge a distance defined by race.[42]

Along with identifying white union men as aggressors in the riot, many blacks perceived that the employers rather than the unions offered them emergency assistance. Aid funneled by the AMC&BW to Local 651 during the riot received no publicity in black newspapers. One black worker claimed that it was the union's fault that blacks were forced to stay home during the riot while whites went to work. He also complained that the union paid whites fifty dollars (twenty-five if single) if their houses had been burned during the conflict, while black members whose houses had been destroyed received nothing. "That's why I won't join. You pay money and get nothing." In 1920, a black worker who had moved from the packinghouses to a box factory observed that, "if a thing can't help you when you need help, why have it," and concluded that "unions ain't no good for a colored man."[43]

Stockyards employers, on the other hand, not only made visible moves (if perhaps for cynical reasons) to return blacks to their jobs, but also provided food assistance to the South Side during the riot. A black redcap later recalled that "Armour, Swift sent truck loads of meat into that district, otherwise some of those people would have starved." The *New Majority's* arguments that the packers' actions had caused the riot either went unheard or resonated poorly in the Black Belt.[44]

If, as the *New Majority* declared, the period immediately following the riot was the "acid test" which would determine "whether the colored workers are to continue to come into the labor movement or whether they are going to feel that they have been abandoned by it and lose confidence in it," the results were hardly encouraging. Local 651's per capita payments declined sharply toward the end of 1919, and by December had fallen to a total of two hundred dollars, indicating eight hundred paid-up members. Five months later, only half of these remained. Local 213 fared even worse, forwarding payments in only two of the first five months of 1920, although its decline might be attributable to layoffs of black women.[45] Johnstone claimed in January that Council locals included approximately two thousand black members, but even that inflated figure was accompanied by the lament that "we ought to have 10,000." In August of 1920 the AMC&BW acknowledged its failure, declaring the proportion of organized black workers "insignificant," and criticized the "unconcern and often resentful attitude" of black workers. "The colored members and organizers have done all in their power to interest their people, but have failed," concluded the AMC&BW District Council's statement.[46]

The *New Majority*, however, remained optimistic and in March 1921 claimed that "thousands of negro workers" numbered among the twenty-five thousand workers attending a rally protesting wage cuts. This claim was probably for the benefit of white workers. Fearful of renewed racial violence likely to widen the distance between black and white workers, the *New Majority* continued to try to convince whites that blacks were neither their enemies nor instinctively anti-union. The newspaper's coverage of a bitter coal strike in West Virginia that year omitted any mention of the black strikebreakers who had been recruited there. Frequent articles appeared on organizations of black waiters, cooks, and Pullman porters. And in an attempt to show all readers the unity of black and white workers against their common enemies, the *New Majority* criticized the Chicago *Tribune* (a favorite target of the *Defender*), which "never misses an opportunity to throw the hooks into negroes, Irish freedom and labor."[47]

With the packers establishing employee representation plans, cutting wages, and agreeing in March, 1921, to only a six-month extension of the arbitration agreement, union leaders recognized that a showdown was imminent. And if some workers and AMC&BW officials had hoped in 1919 that intimidation and impending layoffs would reduce the black presence in the stockyards, they now realized that black workers still held the key to the success of the organizing drive begun four years earlier. In November the *Butcher Workman* abandoned its recent tone of impatience with black workers, declaring "without question that the colored workers in the packing plants in Chicago at last are thoroughly aroused as to the imperative need of constructive organization activity."[48]

Nothing could have been further from the truth. In December 1921, membership in Local 651 stood at 112, with only 49 in good standing. Confident of the loyalty of black workers, employers announced wage cuts in November, hoping to provoke a strike. Union weakness went beyond inability to win the allegiance of blacks. The packers had chosen their hour wisely, and the conflict erupted during a period of widespread unemployment and at the beginning of winter. Yet, announcing the walkout which began on December 5, 1921, AMC&BW President Cornelius J. Hayes declared that "it does not matter if the packers try to hire scabs to take the places of union men. . . . They cannot run the plants on scab labor alone."[49]

Hayes was wrong. Although packinghouses slaughtered only one-fourth of their customary run and probably processed no byproducts, they secured enough strikebreakers to remain in operation. One Urban League official estimated that of the approximately five thousand replacements, at least half were black. One large company doubled the black proportion from one-sixth to one-third of its payroll in January 1922, while another increased its ratio from one-fourth to one-third.[50] Morris & Company made no secret of its strategy: as soon as the strike began, it opened an employment office in the black ghetto. Union men returned defeated in early February. Unlike earlier packinghouse strikes, however, this one did not end with a dismissal of black strikebreakers. During the next five years, blacks retained approximately 30 percent of stockyards jobs. "We took the Negroes on as strike-breakers in 1921 and have kept them ever since in order to be prepared for any sort of outbreak," explained the president of one small stockyards firm.[51]

The failure of the AMC&BW and the Stockyards Labor Council to attract and retain black members critically weakened the five-year organizing campaign. Union leaders could not dislodge suspicions and hostilities which both divided black and white workers and impelled black community leaders to advise black workers to keep up their guard. T. Arnold Hill of the Urban League, who considered the organizers sincere in their intentions toward black workers, found a "general attitude on the part of Negroes that the trade union movement is not earnestly seeking to get Negroes to join it." As Hill astutely observed, "It is not the facts that actuate one's opinions but conceptions of what he believes to be facts."[52] White and black workers inhabited worlds separated by different traditions and by prejudices and competition which fed upon each other. Outbreaks of violence only reinforced each group's image of the other as implacably hostile.

Labor leaders refused to accept the blame for their inability to dissolve this atmosphere of mutual suspicion and antagonism. They had recognized the problem from the outset and felt that they had made every effort to win the support of blacks. The AMC&BW had hired nine black organizers; both the *Butcher Workman* and the *New Majority* had encouraged racial cooperation and proclaimed a policy of nondiscrimination. Union officials, claimed Foster, had worked especially hard to handle "very carefully" the grievances of black workers. "If the colored packing house worker doesn't come into the union," the *New Majority* had declared in 1919, "it isn't the fault of the Stock Yards Labor Council." [53]

Whose fault was it? When the AMC&BW and the Stockyards Labor Council split in 1919 over tactics and personality conflicts, Council leaders accused the AMC&BW of impeding efforts to organize blacks. Hurled amid the heat of mutual recriminations, however, such charges hardly amounted to a significant indictment. Union leaders did admit to a problem of racial prejudice among the white rank-and-file, but they took pride in their campaign for racial tolerance within the movement. They did not believe that members' racial attitudes had discouraged blacks from joining, especially after the creation of Locals 651 and 213, which permitted black unionists to control their own affairs. Proud of their enlightened racial policies and outreach to black workers, Chicago union officials located the problem in the black community. "Every effort has been made to organize the colored workers in the Stock Yards and elsewhere," insisted organizer John Kikulski and Chicago Federation of Labor Secretary Ed Nockels. Union leaders had "offered them the same chance as the white man or woman, but the negroes were guided by their ministers and the YMCA, who were under the influence of the packers and big interests." After the riot the Chicago Federation of Labor leveled more specific accusations: packers "subsidized negro politicians and negro preachers and sent them out among the colored men and women to induce them not to join unions." Black organizer Charles Dixon agreed, adding editors to the list of culprits. Because of this "propaganda" in the black community, William Z. Foster complained, union organizers were "afraid to go around to some of these saloons and poolrooms." The task, he concluded, had been impossible. From the beginning, "the firm opposition of the negro intelligensia" had created a barrier. "It made no difference what move we made, there was always an argument against it." Black workers, he concluded, were "constitutionally opposed to unions." [54]

The behavior of black workers during the organizing drive, however, suggests that Foster's evaluation of their "constitution" was simplistic. Although many never were receptive to the union message, the common pattern of joining and then permitting dues to lapse suggests that many black workers did weigh the advantages of membership. The "negro intelligensia," by which Foster meant Chicago's black middle-class leadership, not only lacked unanimity, but frequently expressed opposition that was less than "firm." Stockyards Labor Council spokesmen had rejected the ideology of racial exclusion, but they shared with other whites the inclination to generalize about "the Negro." They assumed that "the Negro," especially "the southern Negro," either lacked the intelligence or experience to make an informed decision or was a victim or tool of employer manipulation. "The Southern negro," lamented Fitzpatrick, "is different. We figure that his slavery days ended at about the time that he came up here to work in the Packing houses." They underestimated the ability of both the migrants and the black bourgeoisie to evaluate unionism rationally, according to standards different from those familiar to white union leaders—standards shaped by the overwhelming reality of racial discrimination as part of a historical experience. Black workers asked whether unionism was "good for the colored man"; black leaders asked whether it would benefit the race.[55]

Although most prominent black Chicagoans recognized the complexity of the issue, some readily and unequivocally cast their lots with the industrialists. Richard E. Parker, a shady entrepreneur, provided an easy target for unionists who emphasized the role of a hostile black leadership. At the beginning of the organizing drive in 1917, Parker distributed handbills warning black workers to "BEWARE THE STOCKYARDS UNION. . . . Do Not Join Any White Man's Union; Save Your Jobs." Speciously claiming in March 1920 that his American Unity Welfare Labor Union represented six thousand black workers, Parker increased his estimate to thirty thousand a year later. With black stockyards workers never numbering more than fifteen thousand, Parker's second claim was ridiculous, and although his earlier statement was at least within the realm of possibility, there is no evidence that his "union" ever enrolled more than a handful of members or that his newspaper, the *Negro Advocate*, attracted a significant readership. Considered inconsequential by black leaders, Parker received little or no attention from the black press until his arrest in 1922 for practicing law without a license. He probably had some propaganda value to packers and perhaps recruited some black workers for them. Moreover, he seemed important enough to whites to attract publicity in Chicago's daily newspapers and in Associated Press dispatches.

The *New Majority* took the trouble to refute statements he printed and perhaps unwittingly conveyed to white workers the mistaken impression that he was a figure of some significance in black Chicago.[56]

Equally antiunion, but far more influential than Parker, was the Wabash Avenue YMCA. The obligation of the YMCA, emphasized the branch's *Official Bulletin*, "is understood to be to *change men. Not primarily to change the existing social or industrial order.*" A. L. Jackson and George Arthur, executive secretaries between 1916 and 1922, considered "plant loyalty" an essential lesson to be learned by black workers "recently from the South."[57] Recreational activities fostered goodwill and identification with the company name, as workers became not only employees but members of the Armour Glee Club or Swifts' Premiums baseball team. On a less subtle level, YMCA social events often included speeches by company officials. Members of both the Armour and Morris glee clubs interrupted "socials" in 1920 to endure lectures from company representatives, who addressed a total of 442 workers at the two functions.[58] Efficiency Clubs, the centerpiece of the antiunion drive in the YMCA, were, according to one black union steward, billed as unions. Workers who showed up at meetings were bombarded with information designed "to try to undermine" bona fide stockyards unions. Employers found these clubs sufficiently effective that they revived them during the CIO organizing campaigns in the 1930s.[59]

A reliable and fertile source of leadership cadre, the YMCA did not directly reach the mass of black workers. Many of its officers, such as A. L. Jackson, who was educated at Phillips Andover Academy and Harvard, were nearly as removed from black working-class life as were white managers. The YMCA, however, exerted significant influence as a major community institution and a focal point of antiunion sentiment. Its clubs associated with local employers attracted up to 250 men at meetings and even more at the social gatherings. Even if most of its members were not workers, and whether they were is uncertain, those workers who were active in the Efficiency Clubs and similar activities were active propagandists on the shop floor. The YMCA offered employers an ideal facility for the recruitment of potential antiunion leaders, and once employers unilaterally established "employee representation" plans—company unions—the YMCA helped them to select the right black men for the plant representation boards.[60] By 1923 the Wabash YMCA had established joint programs with eleven plants, mainly in steel and meat packing. Executives from Swift, Armour, Wilson, Hammond, Morris, Brady Foundry, National Malleable Castings, the Illinois Central Railroad, and Sears, Roebuck regularly attended special dinners and advised Wabash YMCA officials and volunteers on membership campaigns. More than any other institution, the YMCA deserved the abuse that union leaders later heaped on the black middle class.[61]

The black branch of the Young Women's Christian Association maintained a lower profile. Although packers funded efficiency clubs and worked with the organization to operate a summer camp on land owned by Swift, the Indiana Avenue YWCA did not actively discourage union membership. Seeking broader ties than her male counterparts, Irene Gaines, who headed the Industrial Department, was a member of the Women's Trade Union League and attended meetings regularly. Gaines did not, however, publicly advocate unionization, and her datebook reveals no other activities relating to unionism. Her participation in the WTUL enabled her to maintain ties with the white reformers; black women and the struggling Indiana Avenue YWCA needed whatever allies they could find among Chicago's influential reform community. She faced little pressure to oppose unionization, because relatively few black women worked in the stockyards and the packers contributed only minimal funds to her organization. In addition, the national YWCA body did not share the antiunion orientation which characterized the YWCA. The Indiana Avenue YWCA, therefore, remained neutral except for whatever loyalty might have been fostered by the summer camp and occasional company picnics.[62]

Whatever its intentions, the Indiana Avenue YWCA had little impact on black attitudes towards unions. The organization's Industrial Department, organized in late 1920, had only 360 members by the end of the following year. "The industrial women as a group are harder to reach," observed one branch official. The industry-sponsored summer camp had a poor reputation and failed to attract as many working women as expected, even though many employers paid the expenses of their employees.[63]

As part of their campaign for the loyalty of black workers, employers had another line of communication to black workers through a more indigenous institution—the black church. An integral part of the urban black community, as well as a source of cultural and institutional continuity for many migrants, the church remained central to the lives of many working-class black men and women. A few of the largest churches operated employment bureaus, the most active of which placed 268 people in 1919, and ministers at storefront churches sometimes "recommended" members to employers. More important, most black church services were sermon-oriented, making the minister a critical source of information to congregants. When union men attended fifteen black churches one Sunday during the 1921 strike and heard fourteen ministers urge workers to ignore the strike, they had good reason to be alarmed.[64]

A few black ministers were prounion, allowing organizers to speak on Sunday, permitting their churches to be used for meetings, or even preaching on "the benefits of unionization." These included Lacey Kirk Williams and John F. Thomas, who occupied influential pulpits at Olivet and Ebenezer Baptist churches. There is no evidence that Williams exerted significant effort in the interest of unionization, although both steel and packinghouse organizing were discussed at his church. Thomas qualified his endorsements by cautioning worshippers to resist the message of the IWW and other advocates of "revolution." Among ministers at the largest churches, only James Henderson of Institutional AME Church was willing to assist labor leaders in their efforts to secure meetings with black ministerial alliances.[65]

To the extent that they thought about labor unions, pastors at most of Chicago's large black churches tended to agree with AME Bishop Archibald J. Carey, that "the interest of my people lies with the wealth of the nation and with the class of white people who control it." This class of whites doubtless included Philip Armour, Gustavus Swift, Cyrus McCormick, H. H. Kohlsaat, and George Pullman, whose substantial contributions had rescued Carey's Quinn Chapel from foreclosure at the turn of the century. Carey remained a friend and political ally of packinghouse entrepreneurs and other industrialists. When black organizers tried to build the Brotherhood of Sleeping Car Porters in the mid-1920s, Carey opposed even this race-conscious movement. Other churches had similar ties to industrialists. Trinity AME Church received liberal donations from the Swift and Armour families during the early years of the twentieth century and responded by housing black strikebreakers during the 1904 strike. When the 1920–21 depression left many black Chicagoans unemployed, Swift generously supplied Trinity's relief drive. One South Side minister overnight recruited three hundred black women to break a 1916 strike by hotel chambermaids, while still another regularly secured strikebreakers to replace members of the International Ladies Garment Workers Union. Pastors at struggling storefront churches often needed the income they could secure as labor agents for employers seeking scab labor; one clergyman reportedly earned approximately two dollars for each worker he supplied. At churches so poor that their spiritual leaders supported themselves with outside jobs, labor trouble at the minister's workplace offered not only the opportunity to earn an employer's gratitude but also to assist unemployed members of the congregation. Black churches provided employers who had little other contact with black Chicago a means of communication to potential strikebreakers; but it is not clear that they represented either a unanimous or deeply committed voice opposed to union membership.[66]

Black newspapers, which rivaled ministers as sources of leadership in the black community, addressed unionization more directly and more frequently. Again, however, any imputation of either unified or firm opposition contradicts the evidence. Newcomers who read black newspapers received a message whose consistency lay less in specific advice than in a general tone which was likely to resonate well among an audience particularly attuned to the dynamics of race in American society.

Only two newspapers unequivocally and consistently opposed unions or encouraged strikebreaking. One of these was Parker's *Negro Advocate*, whose vicious denunciations of the stockyards unions attracted little attention from blacks. A somewhat more significant newspaper, the *Broad Ax*, only occasionally mentioned either unionism or local organizing campaigns. Its position was summarized in a column by a local black lawyer who described labor organization as when "15% of the laborers have unionized or banded themselves together to control the labor market to the exclusion of 85%, and 100% of those who employ labor."[67] But these journals neither represented nor influenced significant segments of black Chicago.

The *Defender*, which had won the trust of many migrants even before they left the South, was the most influential newspaper in black Chicago. Its apparent inconsistencies reflected the ambivalence many black leaders felt toward unions. Some editorials advised black workers to join unions; others recited the virtues of company loyalty. The *Defender*'s fluctuating position defies neat categorization: it praised the concepts of trade unionism and collective bargaining; opposed strikes; considered AF of L unions discriminatory, and left-wing unions too radical; advised blacks to join unions if they would be treated as equals; and considered strikebreaking legitimate, especially during periods of high unemployment and as a means of entry into industries from which blacks had been previously excluded. It recognized that employers had not always dealt fairly with blacks, but preached business values and remained wary of antagonizing the men who controlled jobs and philanthropic purses.[68]

Part of this ambiguous position had been worked out before the Great Migration. Between 1910 and 1916, the *Defender* seldom mentioned specific labor issues, but criticized unions generally for being either discriminatory or unreasonable. Editorials occasionally castigated capitalists for "using" blacks in battles against unions, but union discrimination was the more constant theme. An employer who "refused to turn off his colored help when requested by the unions" earned praise. The newspaper insisted that blacks would join unions if admitted, and "would stick" with an organization for better or for worse; but this insistence reflected less a conviction that blacks should join unions than an argument that they should be able to join unions. The distinction is crucial. Racial exclusion and discrimination anywhere fell under attack in the *Defender*, and wherever an existing union seemed to benefit workers, the *Defender* argued that black workers had a right to its protection. Most of the *Defender*'s analysis pertained to closed shops, especially in the building trades. But the "race paper" said little about whether blacks in nonunion industries should join the battle to secure a contract. If anything, the newspaper suggested that employers could be trusted to run plants efficiently and treat blacks equitably.[69]

The Great Migration and the packinghouse organizing campaign forced the *Defender* to confront the issue of whether a black worker should accept an invitation to join a union that as yet had delivered nothing. Two issues had to be evaluated: the union's sincerity regarding its racial policies, and its power to be a more valuable ally to the race than philanthropic employers had been. On the first issue, the *Defender* had too often complained about union policies to accept readily the Stockyards Labor Council's declarations of goodwill. "B-E-W-A-R-E," the *Defender* advised; "this movement must be met with thought and consideration, but above all, guard yourself. Remember the waiters, the railroad engineers, the firemen, etc. . . . Whatever ye sow, so shall ye reap, and perhaps the unions will sow their corn different hereafter, but it is a big PERHAPS."[70]

The *Defender*'s editorials continued to sound this cautious tone but soon began also to acknowledge the advantages of unionization. In February 1918, the newspaper for the first time declared that blacks should join a union, but only if that union clearly lacked any vestiges of racial discrimination. Unionization received the most comprehensive treatment to date in the *Defender*'s columns in April 1919. Reviewing the labor movement's record of discrimination, the newspaper remarked that blacks had "justifiably" opposed organized labor. But in the past five years union leaders had changed their policies and recognized that black membership was essential to the survival of their organizations. Since "capital has not played square with us . . . it has simply been a matter of choosing between two evils." It was now time to "accept the olive branch" if labor offered it. Although reminding readers of past union discrimination, an April 1920 editorial concluded that "a noticeable change" had occurred, and "the experiment of unionizing should be tried." In October, the newspaper advanced to the position of blaming discrimination on employers and celebrated collective bargaining as the road to equity and fairness. "We cannot too strongly urge the wisdom and importance of our workmen joining labor unions whenever and wherever it is possible to do so," declared the *Defender* in its most unqualified endorsement of unionization.[71]

Yet it would be a mistake to conclude that the *Defender* had embraced an industrial analysis entirely compatible with trade unionism. Educated at Hampton Institute, editor Abbott admired industrialists, their ideas, and their ideals. He opposed anything that smelled of economic radicalism. In the same article in which he labeled corporations "soulless," and unions and strikes an essential counterforce, Abbott lamented that "a handful of disgruntled workers have it within their power to make hundreds of thousands of innocent people suffer. . . . Harmony must prevail." Here lay the heart of the *Defender's* position. Particularly sensitive to restrictions on economic opportunity, Abbott was wary of any institution that might narrow a black worker's right to work. Schooled in nineteenth-century liberal economics, he firmly believed that the interests of labor and capital were harmonious, rather than opposed. "Labor," he declared, "is helpless without capital, and vice versa. The two must go hand in hand, and when there is dissension and a parting of the ways not only the parties directly concerned suffer, but the entire public is affected." Most important, Abbott wanted to know how blacks would be affected by a particular dispute.[72]

Much of the *Defender's* position on the relationship between blacks and unions rested on Abbott's vision of opportunity. Sharing the hopes of migrants who had come to Chicago to better their condition, Abbott had encouraged the union movement because he thought it would increase the race's economic opportunities and political power. Like all other issues, unionization was evaluated on the basis of whether it would "advance the race." As unions in the steel mills and packinghouses gained strength between 1918 and 1919, it appeared that they could wrest significant benefits for both black and white workers. Abbott worried that a union victory might result in the elimination of blacks from these industries, unless they had influence in the organizations.

As the 1921–22 strike approached, the essence of this pragmatism was revealed. Despite continued attacks on union discrimination, the *Defender* had been advising blacks in the stockyards to join the unions for nearly four years. Although it had criticized the spontaneous strikes of 1919 because they violated a sacred contract, the newspaper had not returned to the proemployer perspective it had held before 1917. But as the strike began in 1921, Abbott sensed that the union would lose and recognized that blacks were in a powerful position as the most readily available strikebreaking force. In addition, the 1920–21 depression had impressed upon the black community the fragility of the wartime economic gains. Now was the time to solidify the foothold black workers had acquired in Chicago's basic industries. Reacting opportunistically, the *Defender* suddenly stopped praising unions and issued an implied endorsement of strikebreaking, announcing in the middle of the strike that "when the smoke of battle is cleared away from the stock yards we hope the packers will be true to their promise and stand by the black workers who came to their assistance in a crisis." Six months after the stockyards strike ended, the newspaper continued in the same vein, declaring in an editorial on a coal miners' dispute that "strikes at best are stupid."[73]

Although the *Defender* repeatedly shifted its stance and usually qualified its pronouncements, antiunionism emerged as the dominant sentiment. In 1918, Abbott's editorials began to advise workers to consider union appeals, but his newspaper could still run a cartoon showing a black man threatened by a mob that included Jim Crow legislation, cruelty, yellow journalism, barbarism, and labor unions. News columns ignored organizing campaigns in steel and meat packing even as editorials commented on the issues involved. The newspaper did not even mention the numerous organizing activities and street debates that took place in neighborhoods inhabited by black workers. Abbott's continuing attacks on union racism, concurrent with his advice to join unions and insistence that blacks were good union men, suggest that some of his prounion rhetoric was aimed as much at the unions as at black workers. Abbott fought racism wherever it existed, and he knew that unless blacks lost their reputation as a scab race, potentially powerful unions could severely limit their economic opportunity. But as soon as it became clear that loyalty to the union required participation in a decidedly risky strike, and that employers—not unions—controlled jobs in heavy industry, he dropped the unions quickly and easily.[74]

The *Defender's* rhetorical ambivalence and tacit hostility contrasts sharply with the attention the stockyards campaign received in the somewhat less influential Chicago *Whip*, which was founded in 1919 and quickly become the city's second-ranked black newspaper. Devoting a much larger proportion of its space to labor issues than did the *Defender*, the *Whip* even carried a regular column by organizer John Riley. Union rallies in the black community—ignored by the *De-*

fender—were advertised and then reported in the *Whip*, frequently on the front page. Although the editors also advised blacks to join unions "only when to their advantage," they unequivocally declared membership in the stockyards and steel unions to be "to the Negro's advantage." But by the time of the 1921–22 packinghouse strike, the *Whip* had joined the *Defender* in ignoring the union campaign and meetings called by black organizers. Perhaps by then its editors had decided that black workers were not joining the unions and that union activities were therefore of little interest to readers. As Local 651's membership dwindled, newspaper coverage of union affairs declined accordingly.[75]

The complaints of union leaders regarding the hostility of the black press probably applied mainly to the *Defender*. During the crucial period in the summer of 1919, the *Whip* assisted the stockyards unions by publicizing meetings and printing articles by unionists denying that race discrimination existed in the unions. At the same time the *Defender* was praising the concept of unionism but criticizing stockyards locals that "break with impunity on the slightest provocation any or all of the agreements."[76]

It is unlikely that either newspaper's treatment of packinghouse unionism was directly influenced by employer pressure. Although the *Defender* carried employment advertisements for butchers in late December 1921—positions which were probably replacements for strikers—there is no indication that packers had ever purchased advertising space in the newspaper until then. Subsequent events suggest that the *Defender* reacted more reflexively to pressure from within the black community than from influential whites. After initially opposing A. Philip Randolph's attempt to organize black Pullman porters during the mid-1920s, Abbott soon reversed his policy, partly because of declining circulation. But Abbott was acutely aware of the packers' largesse toward black institutions, and he avoided harsh criticism even when he concluded temporarily that unionization was in the race's best interests. He also unfailingly praised the antiunion YMCA as a beneficial racial institution, probably because he did not care about its position on unionization.[77]

What is most salient about these influential black voices, linking them to a broad consensus in the black community that was imperfectly understood by white unionists, was that they considered strikebreaking thinkable, even when not practicable or desirable. The scab represented an unambiguous evil to white unionists, but to many blacks strikebreaking had to be considered seriously—even if rejected. Where the *Butcher Workman* considered the strikebreaker "a two-legged animal with a corkscrew soul—a waterlogged brain, a combination backbone made of jelly and glue," the *Defender* saw instead a man who faced starvation, and reminded readers that "self-preservation is the first law of nature."[78] The means of self-preservation was more of an open question than it seemed to white union leaders certain that black editors were tools of industrial interests.

Both the *Whip* and the *Defender* were primarily race newspapers and evaluated issues accordingly. Because the principle of unionization was secondary to the specific question of what stockyards unions could do for the black community, the editors could change their minds easily, depending on the power equation in the stockyards and the level of interest in the black community. When Abbott became convinced that the packers would win, he abandoned all attempts to maintain good relations with the unionists. When the *Whip* reached the same conclusion, its editors—who were younger than Abbott and less steeped in capitalist values—simply dropped the issue entirely.

One black institution could not dispose of the unionization question so readily—the Chicago Urban League. Because of its active role as an employment service for black workers, it had to take a position on whether to refer applicants to struck plants. Like the *Defender*, the Urban League commanded special influence among migrants. Not only had innumerable prospective migrants written to it from the South, but thousands of newcomers had obtained either a first job or some other form of assistance from the League. In 1919 alone, fourteen thousand blacks found jobs in Chicago through the Urban League and more than 20 percent of Chicago's black population used the League's services at least once. Although its patronizing and didactic attitude toward migrants tended to discredit its advice on some matters, its counsel on economic issues carried weight.[79]

The National Urban League declared its official position on unionization at a conference in Detroit in 1919. Written by Horace Bridges, a founder and officer of the Chicago affiliate, the memorandum stood as "the standard of our action here in Chicago." Referring to "the grinding of the Negro between these upper and lower millstones" of capital and labor, the League accused both employers and unions of impeding racial progress. Unions either ignored black workers or actively excluded them from labor markets; employers hired blacks but discriminated against them with regard to wages and chances for advancement. The solution to the problem lay in collective action. Where white unions did not discriminate, black workers should join and participate in collective bargaining. If excluded from a union, they should form their own organization and bargain with both the employer and the white union. The manifesto advised black workers to accept jobs as strikebreakers "only where the union affected had excluded colored men from membership."[80]

Strict adherence to these principles implied support for the packinghouse campaign. The AMC&BW lacked a history of racial exclusion, and both it and the Stockyards Labor Council had hired black organizers, something the Urban League had repeatedly requested of the AF of L. Between 1917 and 1919 the League established and maintained cooperative relations with stockyards organizers. In February 1918, League representatives joined officials of the Illinois Federation of Labor at a meeting held under the auspices of Local 651, designed to explain to black workers the benefits of joining the AMC&BW. By October 1919, the *New Majority* felt sufficiently confident of the League's support that it looked forward optimistically to the Detroit conference. It was not disappointed with the conference's resolution on unionism, labeling it "a solution to the problems of the colored race."[81]

The prounion flavor of the Chicago Urban League is attributable mainly to its executive secretary, T. Arnold Hill. Hill had come to Chicago in December 1916, as an organizer for the National Urban League and had intended to stay only long enough to put the Chicago organization on its feet. Instead of the projected one month, Hill remained for eight years. Other than his speech at the July 6 rally, he seldom expressed himself publicly in Chicago on the subject of unionization, but unless his perspective changed radically after he left Chicago to become industrial director of the National Urban League in 1925, Hill hoped to see black workers organized into unions. Between 1925 and 1927, he worked actively with A. Philip Randolph, James Weldon Johnson, and others to develop a working relationship with the AF of L, pledging "active cooperation" with the Federation's Executive Council. Unlike the statements of Robert R. Moton, Emmett Scott, and many other black leaders within and outside the Urban League movement, Hill's protestations of amity toward the labor movement were genuine, rather than merely gestures designed to maintain good relations. His private correspondence, especially letters to former associates in Chicago's black community, confirm that he considered unionization the only solution to the black worker's insecurity in the industrial labor force.[82]

Hill was not the only influential black leader associated with the Chicago Urban League who was inclined to encourage migrants to join unions. George Cleveland Hall, a prominent physician instrumental in the branch's formation, was an honorary member of the AMC&BW, and he noted in 1918 that unionization of black workers would contribute to the eradication of racial prejudice as well as to black industrial advancement.[83] Charles Johnson, research director of the League until the Chicago Commission on Race Relations "borrowed" his services in 1920, recognized that because of the class position of the overwhelming majority of blacks, alliances with employers were less useful than "harmonious relations" with white workers. William Evans, the League's industrial secretary, declared unequivocally—but privately—in 1920 that "the best interest of colored men in the Yards in my belief is in union organization."[84]

Despite individual prounion inclinations and the official positions of both the National Urban League and the Chicago branch, powerful forces precluded outright support of the stockyards unions. As middle-class professionals and entrepreneurs, these and other black leaders had more ties with employers than with union leaders. Hall, chief of surgery at Provident Hospital, could hardly afford to alienate the Swift family, some of whom sat on his board of trustees there. More important, the Urban League itself depended on employers' contributions and cooperation with the League's job placement office. Whatever their assessment of the long-run interests of black workers, the League's leadership recognized that for the immediate future institutional survival depended on the goodwill of wealthy contributors. As Bridges later explained, the encouragement to join unions was "a statement that we wanted to make clear-cut and unambiguous, yet not needlessly provocative."[85]

Until 1919, the risks of quiet, moderate support for the Stockyards Labor Council seemed slight to Hill and other sympathetic Urban League officials. Their strategy could appeal even to more cautious members of the community, who were equally aware of the implications of the tight labor market: employers were unlikely to repeat old patterns and dismiss black workers, even if they joined a union and thus became as "troublesome" as whites. Indeed, although stockyards firms contributed heavily to the Chicago Urban League, they exerted minimal pressure on the issue of unionism.[86] Employers probably assumed that if a showdown arose, they would already have a supply of black workers, many of whom seemed resistant to unionization, if only because blacks were by nature "loyal." If necessary, a contributor could exert leverage on the Urban League at the crucial moment.

Having established smooth relations with employers, League officials recognized the importance of dispelling the old "scab race" image. After riots erupted in East St. Louis in 1917, largely because white union men considered black workers a threat, it seemed apparent that black workers could help ensure racial peace in Chicago by joining with white workers rather than fighting them. In addition, the stockyards unions seemed likely to gain a contract, and workers remaining outside the union could lose their jobs and would almost certainly forfeit any opportunity for advancement. "The skilled trades," observed Evans, " . . . are well tied up with unions."[87] With employers controlling unskilled jobs and unions potentially controlling skilled ones, the safest path avoided offending anyone. The Urban League continued to serve employers by screening black job applicants and assisting in programs designed to help migrants adjust to factory discipline. At the same time, the organization cooperated with unions by advising workers to join. As long as the stockyards remained peaceful, the League could straddle the fence, even if it leaned slightly to the left.

The Chicago Urban League discarded its careful balancing act sometime before the 1921–22 strike. Its decision cannot be dissociated from the League's increasing dependence on donations from packers and other major employers. By 1919, meat-packing interests were donating $3,600 per year to the Urban League, fully one-fifth of the League budget. The reasons for these generous gifts are suggested by their immediate decline after 1922: by then unions in steel and meat packing had been decisively defeated.[88]

But it was more than dependence on the packers' money that led the Urban League to ignore its guidelines and provide strikebreakers to at least two packinghouses in December 1921. The 1919 riot had demonstrated the persistence of white workers' racism, despite the good intentions and sincere promises of leaders of the Stockyards Labor Council. Moreover, the postwar depression had forced the League to recognize the tenuous nature of the employment gains about which it constantly boasted. During the depression, blacks had lost a number of skilled positions in both the steel mills and stockyards, and the unions had done nothing to protect them. The strikes in both industries offered opportunities to regain those jobs. Instead of resting its decision regarding strikebreakers on a union's record—which would have ruled out sanctioning strikebreaking in the stockyards—the League now measured an employer's record. Companies that had hired blacks before the strike were assisted in their recruiting efforts in the black community. It is unknown whether Hill supported the shift. The League's spokesman during this period was Evans, who considered the strike "a chance for occupational advancement to colored men which was accepted." Insisting that neither he nor the League opposed unionism—only "white unionism" which excluded blacks—he attacked the strike as unwise and left little doubt that opportunism was the order of the day.[89]

Although its financial ties and middle-class perspective certainly influenced its posture and limited its options, the Urban League also must be understood in terms of a world view dominated by the category of race. Like Abbott at the *Defender*, black Urban Leaguers looked first to the interests of the race, and middle-class values interacted with but did not determine the substance of their race-consciousness. "The League is not opposed to unionism," explained an unidentified spokesman (probably Evans), "but is interested primarily in the welfare of colored workers."[90] By 1921, it was clear that employers controlled the jobs and the money, and while managers could not be trusted to treat blacks equitably in matters of promotion, unions were no more trustworthy and had less to offer. Alliances with unions were a wartime luxury and ironically, perhaps even a wartime necessity in some cases. They lasted only so long as they did not require blacks to make the commitments and take the risks demanded by a strike. Given the psychological and material relationships between migration and jobs, such risks were unacceptable both to middle-class black leaders and to hopeful and ambitious newcomers.

Even during the war, however, the Urban League inhibited unionization of black workers, albeit unwittingly. The League and other black institutions performed functions that rendered unions redundant for many black workers. "If you are having trouble with your employers," instructed Urban League cards distributed to newcomers, "call upon the Chicago League on Urban Conditions Among Negroes." A black worker with a complaint about a foreman could go to the Urban League, whose representative would usually discuss the problem with a plant official. The Urban League, observed one white social worker, "furnish[ed] the leadership usually furnished by the federation." By providing grievances procedure with direct links to management, the Urban League and the YMCA appropriated a crucial function of a trade union, and they did it within a black institutional matrix.[91]

Formal positions on unionization aside, Chicago's black institutional and commercial world inhibited the organization of its working class into unions. Unlike Back-of-the-Yards, garment districts, and neighborhoods surrounding the steel mills, Chicago's Black Belt bore no special relationship to a particular industry. Its institutional development had preceded the entrance of its population into industry, and its culture was structured by neither the rhythms nor the social relations of a set of similar workplaces. Black workers had to be organized either outside the community or away from the immediacy of the workplace. The process of organizing white workers in Packingtown, which according to one historian, "took on the atmosphere of a Baptist camp meeting" at the height of the campaign, contrasted sharply with the task of stirring up enthusiasm among black workers, who had to be collared on train platforms and in streetcars.[92] Black workers in unionizing industries were less likely to attend union meetings after work partly because they had to travel home; in nearly all cases they did not—and could not—live in the factory neighborhood.

Once a strike began, black and white working-class communities experienced the conflict differently. In Back-of-the-Yards, the 1921 strike was a community event. Women hurled bags of paprika at policemen. Crowds stoned homes of strikebreakers. Pastors, businessmen, lodges, and even neighborhood bankers donated provisions to strikers. Without overstating the level of community support for strikers in such neighborhoods, it is clear that unions were neighborhood—and often ethnic—institutions. In the Black Belt, however, they were external to the community, seeking support both from workers and from middle-class leaders whose neighborhood orientation competed with unions, rather than enhanced the process of mobilization.[93]

Unlikely to become a part of the black community, unions had even less chance of being perceived as external institutions that—like schools—were self-evidently beneficial and amenable to incorporation into Afro-American tradition. Their burden was inescapable in this context. They had to demonstrate that they were interracial institutions, able to offer blacks access to opportunities and power—access that was central to both the Great Migration itself and its support among northern black leaders. But the unions seemed to most blacks to be white institutions, primarily interested in the welfare of white workers. Many black men, disillusioned with the AMC&BW, complained that although black butchers received equal treatment in the stockyards, where the union needed their support, they found their union cards useless in organized shops elsewhere. Black unionists, concluded one black workman at Wilson & Company, were "damn fools," and "nothing but a lot of white folks' niggers." The Chicago Federation of Labor ironically identified the problem when after the riot it defensively claimed that "Labor has done everything in the stockyards and held out its hands to the negro and established organizations and invited the negroes into the white men's unions." Justifiably proud of their invitation and their unconventional racial policies, white labor activists could not understand why black workers remained wary.[94]

The *New Majority* unwittingly reinforced the same image of the movement. Like most American newspapers, the newspaper of the

Chicago Federation of Labor printed racist anecdotes, usually in dialect. Perhaps unaware of how offensive such items were, the *New Majority* in a single issue published both an article praising the NAACP for its battle against racial discrimination in the South and an anecdote about Caesar, "an old darkey."[95] The *New Majority* never capitalized the first letter of "Negro"; to many black Americans this involved a question not of grammar, but of respect and recognition. References to black strikebreakers in Gary as "a bunch of colored ex-crap shooters" hardly dispelled suspicions about labor's racial attitudes. If unionists could justifiably criticize the *Defender* for omitting news about union activities, blacks could with equal justice point out that the *New Majority* mentioned race relations and black workers only when they posed a threat to a unionization campaign. Once the steel and packinghouse drives had ended by 1922, blacks all but disappeared from the pages of the *New Majority*. Reading union newspapers in the stockyards hardly encouraged blacks to place faith in the white organizations.[96]

White organizers did little better. Leaders of the Chicago Federation of Labor and its subsidiary, the Stockyards Labor Council, lacked the overt, conscious, and malicious racism displayed by Gompers, most leaders of craft unions, and most other Americans. Indeed, Evans considered them "inclined to be fair to Negro workers."[97] Nevertheless, they could neither jettison traditional notions of racial characteristics nor completely understand the meaning of race to black migrants from the South.

John Fitzpatrick was an especially tragic figure. During the late 1910s and 1920s, Fitzpatrick regularly and conscientiously sought to organize black workers into Chicago unions without racial discrimination. Black leaders in Chicago, who were familiar with his record, warmly praised him for his efforts. But when Fitzpatrick described to Judge Alschuler how packers had manipulated a succession of ethnic groups, he demonstrated his inability to transcend the racial ideology of his generation. As soon as one group began to organize to seek a redress of grievances, "that nationality has been ousted; then another nationality is brought in and used, and in turn they are exhausted and thrown out and another one, and so on, until they got down to,—well, the very lowest." This was the black southerner, whom he described as "hopeless, oppressed, and discouraged."[98]

Fitzpatrick was only partly right. The migrants were indeed oppressed, but were hardly hopeless or discouraged. Nor were they as ignorant or as passive as other white union leaders suggested. Most black leaders—even those opposed to or wary of unionism—were not "tools of the packers," and most migrants made their decisions carefully and even ambivalently, according to criteria that the white unionists apparently did not understand.

Such misapprehensions not only led union leaders to misinterpret the actions of black workers, but also suggest the reason for their inability to unite black and white workers: between white unionists and many blacks there existed a chasm unbridgeable by union rhetoric and the realities of class conflict. As Abram Harris, a black economist, observed in 1925, "a few Marxian epigrams" would not sway black workers whose "experience and tradition" suggested an independent course.[99] Migrants recalled their experience with white working-class competition and their tradition of individual relationships with both "good" and "bad" employers (or landlords qua employers). Also, their immediate goals and the optimism implicit in most decisions to migrate defined a faith in the ideology of industrial capitalism that they shared with the black leadership. Unionization was one possible method of bettering their condition, and many migrants flirted with it; but it did not appear to be the most effective way to obtain and retain good jobs. Its risks, magnified by a perception of unions as oriented toward the priorities of white members, included losing whatever the newcomers had already accomplished by coming to Chicago and finding industrial employment.

Migrants who wished to better their condition in Chicago had to begin by finding work. Viewing the migrants' quests from the standpoint of a community defined by race, black institutions thought that the first step was to convince employers to hire increasing numbers of black workers. This emphasis on access led both black leaders and newcomers to ponder the implications of union exclusion of blacks from construction and railroad occupations. Industrial employers had recently changed their attitudes—or at least their promises—and were opening jobs to blacks. Employers were indeed prejudiced, but to many blacks these prejudices were best dealt with by convincing employers that black workers were efficient. This perspective even condoned strikebreaking, because replacing strikers offered blacks an opportunity to prove their competence to skeptical managers.[100]

Once migrants had secured jobs, and once black institutions began to think about protecting the footholds the race had secured in Chicago industries, unionization presented an attractive strategy. In the past employers had dismissed blacks after the end of a labor conflict; but if blacks participated in a union victory, they would be protected by the union—if the union could be trusted. Walter White of the NAACP, visiting Chicago after the riot, noted that migrants sought from the unions "binding statements and guarantees that cannot be broken at will." But the Stockyards Labor Council and the AMC&BW

could not convince the bulk of the migrants—even those who had joined, at least temporarily—that they were not white institutions. The riot cast even further doubt on the wisdom of trusting whites to protect black jobs. By the time of the 1921 showdown, it seemed unlikely that the union even had the power to protect its members.[101]

Given their failure to present themselves to blacks as genuinely interracial or interested in problems peculiar to black workers, stockyards unions had to appeal on the basis of wages and working conditions. Many migrants considered thoughtfully this chance to better their condition. But union organizers faced a formidable obstacle: the migrants' frame of reference. Unlike their white coworkers, they did not compare wages and hours in the stockyards in 1917 with conditions in 1914 and see stagnation in the face of employer prosperity. Instead, they compared their current situation with what they had recently known in the South and felt the sense of achievement reflected in the letters written back to the South. When the union did secure significant benefits through the Alschuler arbitration awards, migrants probably interpreted the process through the lens of their southern experience. The judge, rather than the union, had been the instrument of the changed working conditions. Furthermore, after Alschuler's decision had raised wages and cut hours, the migrants did not share the fears of white workers and black "northerners" who remembered the prewar conditions that would return once the threat of unionization had ended. Such fears had little relevance to black newcomers like the woman who decided that "Chicago was a real place for colored people"; she feared most of all a return to a different past, and knew that a job in industry protected her. "No indeed, I'll never work in anybody's kitchen but my own, any more," she vowed, "that's the one thing that makes me stick to this job."[102]

It was the relationship between their different past and their place in the northern industrial city—a heritage and consciousness unfamiliar to white workers—that led most migrants ultimately to reject unionization. As black southerners who had long been excluded from the economic mainstream, they felt that their new industrial jobs represented meaningful progress, rather than immiseration. Those dissatisfied with their new positions were likely to complain to other blacks, move on, or approach unionization cautiously, if at all. Even loss of faith in the promise of industrial society left many black workers uncertain that a union could do anything for them, given the dynamics of race. Two decades later, amid the more successful efforts by CIO unions to overcome racial barriers to organization, a black worker in Chicago explained this perspective to an interviewer: "Let's see what happens before we go into the union. We all get fired anyway. I don't see that it makes much difference. But I always think that it's best for us colored workers to wait and see what happens. We always get the short end of the horn anyway."[103]

Unions—at least those in the stockyards, steel mills, and other Chicago industries—were white organizations. As such, they were regarded warily by black migrants unaccustomed to fair treatment from white institutions. In the 1919 riot, unions lost whatever chance they had of demonstrating their sincerity, when white workers viciously attacked blacks in the streets because they perceived blacks as a group apart. Ironically, the white workers were not completely wrong; in some ways, black workers were different, especially the migrants. They had a different history and a different sense of their place in society. Because of that different consciousness, blacks trusted their own institutions and shared with those institutions and race leaders a set of priorities and assumptions unlike those of white workers. They were exploited, they perceived, not because they were workers, but because they were black. Advancing the race was more important than industrial democracy, at least in the short run.

9

"What Work Can I Get If I Go through School?"

If the industrial workplace promised opportunity to the young black men and women who migrated from the South, Chicago's school system apparently offered an even greater chance for their children. Many prospective migrants wrote of their intention to place their children in good schools, and education was central to the meaning of the Great Migration as a new departure for black Americans. If the immediate rewards of migration could be found in leisure opportunities, black institutions, voting, race relations, and factories, the future lay in the schools.

Like their grandparents and great-grandparents, who had rushed into the freedmen's schools immediately after emancipation, migrants to the urban North placed great faith in the power of education. Although officials at Tuskegee and similar institutions in the South might have overstated the argument that the availability of schools like theirs could prevent migration, they did identify one of the primary goals of many migrants: to place their children in good schools and perhaps even to go to night school themselves. Readers of the *Defender* had ample evidence that Chicago provided that opportunity. The newspaper frequently commented on educational facilities in Chicago and contrasted them to southern schools. Its boosterish articles celebrating everyday activities at Wendell Phillips High School on Chicago's South Side communicated to black southerners an image of a modern, integrated urban institution—an impression that in 1916 was essentially correct. One reader of the *Defender*, accustomed to southern standards, figured that Wendell Phillips was a college, and inquired as to the "best High school in Chicago," which he hoped to attend while working mornings and nights.[1]

It was unlikely that this—or any other—migrant would attend Chicago's best schools. Relative to those elsewhere in the city, schools in

Chicago's black neighborhoods tended to be old, poorly equipped, and by 1918, overcrowded. All ten Chicago elementary schools which by 1920 were more than 30 percent black (all of these were at least 75 percent black), had been built before 1900, with nine predating 1890. More than half of the city's "white" schools, on the other hand, were less than two decades old. Of the ten "black" schools, only six had bathrooms; three had neither an assembly hall nor a gymnasium; none had the separate gymnasium and assembly hall considered desirable by Chicago school administrators. Although the *Defender* disagreed, some black parents complained in early 1916 that the instruction their children received compared unfavorably with what was available in white schools. Only Wendell Phillips High School, built in 1904, offered full facilities. Despite that school's symbolic importance to migrants, few had children with sufficient education to attend a Chicago high school immediately upon arrival.[2]

Even Chicago's worst schools, however, could seem impressive to black newcomers from the South. Migrants from Georgia, where 85 percent of the schools attended by blacks operated in one-room buildings often without blackboards or desks, were unlikely to be disappointed when they walked into a Chicago school. Many southern counties did not provide funds for black schoolhouses; classes were taught either in whatever structures local blacks could afford to build or in buildings designed for other purposes.[3] The oldest school in the South Side ghetto—Moseley Elementary School, built in 1856—had cooking facilities, manual training equipment, and a gymnasium. Even the school's unwieldy forty to one student-teacher ratio still seemed low by southern standards. In Jackson, Mississippi, classes in the two black schools ranged from 75 to 125 pupils. Atlanta's ratio of sixty-five to one, which resembled statistics for rural Alabama, was little better. Many migrants were accustomed to raising children with only minimal access to any school. In Georgia, Alabama, and Louisiana, less than half of all black children under ten years old attended school at all in 1910; in Mississippi the proportion reached 55 percent. Among children ten to fourteen years old, attendance was only slightly higher, ranging from 45 percent in Louisiana to 71 percent in Mississippi.[4] Those who did attend school had had little hope of receiving more than a basic education. Few black southerners living in states that sent large numbers of migrants to Chicago lived anywhere near a high school they could attend; in 1915, Mississippi, Alabama, Georgia, and Louisiana had a total of six public secondary schools open to black students, and only two of these offered a full four-year curriculum. Private institutions, funded by religious associations or northern philanthropy, provided only widely scattered options. In

A black school in the rural South (courtesy of the Smithsonian Institution).

Chicago, migrants could look forward to their children graduating from elementary schools and attending Wendell Phillips High School, with its impressive drill companies, laboratories, shops, domestic science rooms, gymnasiums, and other modern facilities.[5]

Within the context of the experience of most migrants, therefore, Chicago's schools epitomized northern opportunity. State law prohibited segregation, and Chicago schools had been integrated formally since 1874. Although school officials took advantage of court rulings permitting them to gerrymander district lines, total racial segregation was impossible. Blacks were effectively excluded from most of the city's schools, but many of those into which they were "segregated" included a significant number of whites. As late as 1920, after four years of heavy migration had increased the concentration of Chicago's black population, every school attended by blacks had some white students. There were all-white schools in the city; but a migrant accustomed to Jim Crow schools could proudly write home that "I have children in school every day with the white children."[6]

Many adult migrants, eager to educate themselves as well as their children, soon learned that working people also had access to good

Moseley School in Chicago (source: CCRR, *Negro in Chicago*, 242).

schools. At Wendell Phillips Night School, adults could enroll in any elementary grade for the minimal fee of one dollar and in high school for two dollars (the fees were refunded if the student attended at least three-fourths of the classes). Most migrants entered in the elementary grades. With the night school catering mainly to blacks—it even offered Afro-American history and literature by 1920—there was no question that blacks were welcome in these evening classes, taught by regular day faculty. Newcomers from the South flocked into the school, with enrollment increasing dramatically soon after the first wave of migration in late 1916. Teachers reported an "unusual" eagerness to learn, and the school quickly grew into the largest night school in Chicago. By 1921, nearly four thousand black Chicagoans were enrolled, with an average nightly attendance of two thousand. The evening school was one urban institution to which the migrants had little difficulty adjusting; it offered direct and unconditional access to an institution that they considered central to their full participation in American society.[7]

Migrants needed even less encouragement to comply with the Illinois compulsory education law, a welcome contrast to southern policy. Many white southerners, especially in rural areas, still believed that blacks not only did not need education, but were ruined by schooling because it "unfits them for work." At some times during the year—especially cotton-picking season—planters wanted children in the fields and forced schools to close until the crops were in. Committed to an economy powered by an unskilled labor force, the South had little to gain from educating black children. What it had to lose were laborers who, if too well educated, might leave. Black southerners who wished to keep their children in school for nine months out of every year faced a task that was at best difficult and usually impossible.[8]

By contrast, Chicago not only offered comparatively good schools, but encouraged children to attend regularly for the full school year. The city's political and business elite, along with its vocal reformers, agreed on the essential social role of the city's schools for working-class children. Basic education could provide the socialization necessary for ready adaptation to industrial work discipline, the skills appropriate to a dynamic manufacturing economy, and the ideological integration to cope with what the *Tribune* called "the dangers of citizenship lacking in intelligence and self-respect." This imperative to socialize a working class that would otherwise be inefficient as well as socially volatile combined with humanitarian sympathy for youthful toilers, to stimulate considerable pressure in favor of schooling over child labor. Although school authorities did not enforce the section of the state compulsory education statute which required unemployed sixteen- and seventeen-year-old children to attend school, they did take seriously their obligation to require and encourage younger children to attend school. While southern black children were expected to work in the fields, taking time off for school when work was slack, northern black children learned from their teachers that few jobs existed for children and that the jobs available to uneducated adults were insecure. "Your job today is to go to school," children read in the bookmarks distributed in Chicago schools. To migrants, the message was clear: their children would get the education they had sought in coming North.[9]

School authorities hardly had to pressure migrants to send their children to school. Having been denied the opportunity for so long— or having available only minimal facilities—they grasped it quickly. For some parents, like George Wilson from Promiseland, South Carolina, enrolling children in the public schools was a source of considerable pride, a "first act as a city father." By 1920, 92 percent of Chicago's black children between the ages of seven and thirteen attended school; this figure surpassed not only the percentage of foreign-born whites but also the black percentage in Chicago before the Great Migration. Among children who were fourteen or fifteen years old, blacks attended schools in greater numbers not only than immigrants, but also than native-born whites of mixed or foreign parentage. As late as the 1930s, black overall school attendance was matched only by children of native whites. If one measure of adjustment to city life was the extent to which black parents discontinued the practice of putting their children to work as soon as the youngsters could contribute to the family economy, they shifted priorities quickly. Unlike immigrants, noted one observer, black families did not ask their children to help with the work many women brought home from factories. Child labor statistics indicate that blacks removed their children from the labor market during World War I. Few migrants would have disagreed with the *Defender's* reminder that "Education Will Force Open the Door of Hope Behind Which Is success." That the schools were run by whites did not threaten those hopes at first; only later would optimism wither under the recognition that education and skills would offer little advantage in a racist job market.[10]

But if youthful migrants welcomed the chance to secure the education denied to their parents, they quickly learned that northern schools welcomed them ambivalently at best. From the first day, they suffered indignities and embarrassment. Soon after they entered school, migrants previously educated in inferior southern schools learned that they were "retarded." Statistics from predominantly black schools in Chicago indicate that this designation applied to at least three-fourths of the children from the South, and the label had serious implications. Chicago school officials had developed an elaborate scheme to separate "backward" and "retarded" children from their peers ("backward" ranked above "retarded," which was in turn slightly above "defective" and "feeble-minded"). Many migrants were immediately ushered into "subnormal rooms," whose number doubled citywide between 1915 and 1924. Much of this growth was in overwhelmingly black schools, nearly all of which had such rooms by 1924. Only one secondary school, Wendell Phillips, had a "special division," which was created expressly to serve migrants. Children sent to these rooms not only suffered the indignity of being labeled "subnormal," but also encountered a curriculum consonant with their separate and subordinate place in the school. "Designed for a type of child who has little interest in and is unable to learn academic work," special divisions relegated newcomers to a ghetto that became increasingly isolated from the regular graded classrooms. During 1917–18, one-fourth of the children in these divisions citywide earned transfers into the mainstream; by 1925 the proportion had plunged to one-eighth. Unaware that white children in other elementary schools—especially in immigrant neighborhoods—were handled similarly, migrants could readily assume that they were being singled out, especially as many schools specifically referred to these rooms as being "for children recently arrived from the South."[11]

Because of limited space and rapid migration, the schools could relegate only a minority of recently arrived black children to the subnormal rooms. But other children did not escape similar indignities. Having been judged "retarded," most of these children had to enter Chicago schools in grades lower than appropriate to their age, in classrooms with younger children. Pupils who had received little or no education—especially those who had lived on plantations—frequently had to begin in the first grade, which embarrassed and insulted teenagers. Those who did have some schooling often resented what they considered a demotion, since they had attended a higher grade than the one they were required to enter in Chicago. Some students expressed their resentment through aggressiveness, others through timidity. A fifteen-year-old boy, who at five feet eight inches tall towered over the other children in his class, was afraid that girls would see him in a room with such small children. He left school rather than suffer this embarrassment. Discouraged, embarrassed, and resentful, many black children dropped out at fourteen, the minimum age to leave school. Others, however, preferred to stay, and parents frequently exerted pressure in this direction. The Chicago Commission on Race Relations observed in 1920 that one of the major reasons that there were more black than white children who were "retarded" was that black parents were more likely than whites to keep "over-age" children in school. The presence of many blacks in their late teens in the higher elementary grades testifies to this perseverance. But for many, the price of this commitment to the promise of education was a severe blow to their self-esteem.[12]

Along with the initial indignity of either relegation to a subnormal room or placement in a classroom with younger children, newcomers had to deal with the eternal childhood problem of adjusting to new schoolmates. Archibald J. Carey, Jr., born in Chicago in 1910, did not recall fights between "residents" and "newcomers," but he did remember considering the migrants "less cultured, more crude, more down-to-earth [in] dress, speech, [and] performance generally." Although the social distinctions Carey recalled from his years at the Doolittle School were as much class-based as geographically-oriented, children from the South did perceive hostility from children of Old Settlers. Ida Mae Cress, the daughter of a service worker at a hotel, looked down on the girl whose family boarded with hers as "real country-like." Even newcomers she liked, Cress later observed, had been separated by "social differences." Perhaps already self-conscious because of their scholastic standing and teachers' constant corrections of their speech, migrants sometimes reacted defensively. One teacher noted that northern children frequently insulted newcomers and that a child from the South often "meets a word with a blow." Observing that recently arrived children tended to be either too timid or too aggressive, teachers pointed to frequent fights as evidence of tensions between the two groups of black children.[13]

Dealing with white children could be even more difficult for the newcomers. Even before the Great Migration, race relations in Chicago's integrated schools had been characterized by what one historian has called "humiliating friction," and the influx of black migrants could only exacerbate tensions. Furthermore, some children came to Chicago without having had any contact with white children in the South. In the West Side ghetto, which had a smaller black population than its counterpart on the South Side, blacks frequently attended school with Jews, Italians, and Greeks, and thereby confronted an even more unfamiliar environment. The youngest children had the least difficulty adjusting to their peers, perhaps because the white children had not yet assimilated prevailing ideologies of race. At one integrated school, whose white students represented a multitude of eastern European nationalities, an observer from the Chicago Commission on Race Relations reported that children "played so naturally together that passersby frequently stopped to watch them."[14]

On the South Side, race relations varied according to the racial proportions in the school and the age of the students, with the most amicable relations occurring among elementary school children in overwhelmingly black schools—perhaps because the most virulently racist white parents pulled their children out of these schools. At Doolittle School, which was 85 percent black in 1920, all teachers except one white southerner agreed that children freely mingled in the classrooms and on the playground. But at Webster School, on the western edge of the South Side Black Belt and with a 30 percent black population, children played separately, usually on different playgrounds. Black children attending other schools along the Wentworth Avenue "dead line," also known as the "gang line," quickly learned to fear white boys who waylaid them on their way to and from school. Most migrants, however, attended the overwhelmingly black schools, where the outnumbered whites learned to get along with their black schoolmates. On the whole, the Chicago Commission on Race Relations concluded that race relations among children inside the elementary schools and on the playgrounds seemed quite acceptable. But as children grew older, tensions increased, and graduations from elementary schools usually brought requests from white parents and children that whites and blacks march separately.[15]

Not surprisingly racial separation and antagonism was most prevalent in the high schools. The few migrants who tried to enter a "white" high school immediately learned that they were unwelcome. In some cases transfers were suddenly revoked when school officials realized that the new student was black. Where administrators and teachers were willing to accept blacks, white students drew the line. Sixty blacks attempting to attend one technical high school were physically driven out by their white peers. At Wendell Phillips, whites either transferred out as black enrollment increased or excluded blacks from student activities, most of which they controlled. Despite some racial mixing on athletic teams, clubs generally remained whites-only. White students refused to admit blacks, and black students resisted forming their own clubs because doing so would imply an acceptance of segregation. With Chicago schools beginning to adopt John Dewey's notion of the high school as a training ground for citizenship—with a consequent emphasis on student participation in extracurricular activities—black students were relegated to the all-too-familiar role of second-class citizens.[16]

Segregated social organization within the school was possible partly because nearly all teachers and administrators were white, and many were no less racist than white students and their parents. No school had a black principal until 1928, and black teachers remained nearly as scarce until at least a decade after the beginning of the Great Migration. At the time of the first wave of migration in late 1916, even schools in the black ghetto had at most one black teacher. By 1920, blacks constituted half the teaching staff at only one of these schools. More typical were Raymond School (93 percent black students) with six black teachers out of forty, and Doolittle School (85 percent black) with only two out of thirty-three. Indeed, it was not unusual for schools with black children to have no black teachers, as some principals stood fundamentally opposed to hiring them. Justifications for this policy ranged from the inability of white teachers to "be intimate with colored teachers" to characterizations of black teachers as "cocky" or too eager "to seek positions in white schools." Voicing a common sentiment, one principal argued that "Negro children had no respect for Negro teachers."[17]

A more accurate generalization would assess the respect white teachers had for black students. Black children, according to one principal, frequently complained that teachers harassed them because of their race. Despite this principal's dismissal of such charges, these children had valid complaints. Although some teachers made genuine efforts to "recognize ability wherever they see it" and to teach their students to ignore racial distinctions, most of the white men and women who taught black children in Chicago shared the prevailing views on race and on the inherent inferiority of blacks in most things intellectual. One teacher characterized black girls as limited by a "low mentality," with the infrequent exceptions attributable to "white blood." Another, less certain as to the reason for the several "exceptions" she could cite, considered "Negro girls in general slightly retarded." She attributed this condition to their "early sexual development." Such logic was not unusual. Instructors ventured a range of reasons and explanations for the intellectual limitations of their black students, whom they considered either less moral, less self-disciplined and persevering, or more poorly trained at home than children of other "races," whose virtues and vices teachers catalogued equally freely. Most often, teachers simply contrasted black and white, arriving at conclusions similar to that expressed by the principal of an elementary school with a 70 percent black population: "The great physical development of the colored person takes away from the mental," she declared; "while with the whites the reverse is true. There is proof for this in the last chapter of Ecclesiastes." [18]

If biblical texts or the "common knowledge" provided by contemporary racial beliefs could not provide reliable evidence of the inferiority of black children, more modern thinkers in the Chicago school system could rely upon "scientific" evidence of racial distinctions among children. Unfortunately for black children, intelligence testing began its rise to popularity during World War I, and Chicago's teachers considered themselves among the most advanced practitioners of pedagogical science. A multitude of studies on the relationship between race and "intelligence" began to appear in educational and psychological journals, and with intelligence tests providing the evidence, they generally concluded that black children suffered serious limitations. Such assumptions not only influenced how teachers approached black children upon first meeting them, they also continued to affect how black children were treated in the classroom. A few white teachers, for example, told interviewers in 1920 that black children had to be "jollied along," as they would work only if schoolwork was presented in the guise of play. Not surprisingly, black children from the South frequently complained that Chicago teachers played with them rather than taught them. This perception might have owed partly to the migrants' unfamiliarity with Chicago's modern teaching methods; but it also reflects a classroom environment influenced by assumptions commonly held among teachers that black children were less ambitious, less self-disciplined, and less intelligent. "Negroes," concluded the principal of one school, "need a curriculum especially adapted to their emotional natures." [19]

To their credit, some teachers pointed to the importance of poor schooling in the South as a reason for the low scores of black newcomers in standardized reading tests. A few even recognized the influence of their colleagues' attitudes and low expectations on the classroom performance of black children. On the whole, however, white teachers had difficulty establishing rapport with blacks, and newcomers from the South were even further removed from their sensibilities. Even well-intentioned teachers considered the speech patterns of children from the South "undesirable" and "inaccurate." Many principals had difficulty discussing problems with black parents, whom they considered "uncooperative" and "antagonistic" because the parents complained of racial slights from teachers and students. Charles Perrine, principal at Wendell Phillips until 1920, was so insensitive to black community concerns and leaders that he guilelessly told Lacey K. Williams, pastor of Olivet Baptist Church, that black teenagers dropped out of school because they lacked ambition and were "temperamentally . . . fitted for special lines of work."[20]

Such insensitivity was molded into the curriculum. Fourth grade children heard their teachers tell them that the "typical" farm grew wheat, produced dairy products, and was owned by a farmer whose "boy and girl play and go to school"; to newcomers who thought they knew what farm life was all about, this farm must have seemed strange indeed. History and civics curricula similarly ignored the black experience. They were geared mainly toward instilling patriotism in children who could identify with heroes on "both" sides of a whitewashed Civil War, and toward Americanizing white foreigners.[21]

Black children, neither as numerous nor presumably as assimilable as immigrants, were simply not of major concern to Chicago educators. If Americanization was a central function of the public schools, black children constituted a special case. Even the subnormal rooms were not created for blacks, but rather had been crudely adapted to deal with them.

Black children, therefore, learned a white-oriented curriculum, from white teachers who were frequently prejudiced and almost universally unattuned to black culture, sensibilities, and concerns. Indeed, some black Chicagoans had long argued that perhaps even segregated schools might be desirable, because black teachers would have more positions in such a system. Even W. E. B. Du Bois agreed that there was, in fact, a serious dilemma, as integrated schools left black students in the unfortunate position of being taught by prejudiced whites and deprived blacks of any control over what the schools taught. For newcomers this could be a special problem, as they had come from a dual school system in the South, where black schools frequently had black teachers. Given their experience and the attitudes of many Chicago teachers, it is not surprising that many black children from the South tended to be timid and fearful at school.[22]

Under these difficult circumstances, recently arrived black children achieved mixed results. Compared with other schools in the city, predominantly black institutions had high failure rates, but by no means compiled the worst records. A 1918 survey ranking the 272 Chicago elementary schools according to the proportion of courses passed by students placed black schools at 87, 88, 215, 216, 218, 246, and 263. Clearly, many newcomers experienced considerable frustration and failure. At Raymond School, attended by a high proportion of migrants, nearly one-sixth of all pupils were not promoted in 1920. But if black students were failing in disproportionate numbers, the rates were lower than one might expect given their weak (or in some cases nonexistent) educational backgrounds and the discrimination within Chicago schools. By 1920, only 7.2 percent of all children failed to win promotion at the five predominantly black elementary schools whose records are available. And they did stay in school.[23]

As migrants reached the higher grades in school their tenacity encountered even more severe challenges. Along with the problems of discrimination and insensitivity in the classroom, they faced the recognition that education would not open the doors they had anticipated. Black students in Chicago had always known that a high school diploma meant nothing to most white employers if the holder of that diploma happened to be black; black high school graduates were usually offered the same manual positions open to their less-educated peers. According to a juvenile court official in 1916, the "truant colored boy" regularly responded to his arguments by asking, "What work can I get if I go through school?" This frustration was especially galling to students in integrated schools, who could expect after graduation to be shining shoes or cleaning floors for their white classmates.[24] One of the few quantitative analyses of the value of a high school diploma to blacks in a Northern city during this period found that despite their ambitions for white-collar employment, 56 percent of the graduates of a black girls' high school in Pittsburgh ended up as domestic servants. The most likely white-collar position was as a clerk in a gambling establishment. With its more diversified employment structure, Chicago probably offered black women slightly greater opportunity, but the difference was marginal at best. Not surprisingly, few blacks finished high school in Chicago, despite their tenacity in remaining in school well into their teenage years. Those who did were likely to agree with a 1940 United States Office of Education study which found that "the more schooling a black person achieved the more dissatisfied he was with his job." [25]

White Chicagoans who recognized the problem misinterpreted it. Some argued that black pupils were "incapable of mastering the subjects" emphasized in a liberal education and advocated "the Tuskegee type of education" along vocational lines. Even those more attuned to the impact of discrimination in the job market generally took essentially a different route toward the same policy. Because interference with the labor market was not an alternative, they reasoned, the solution lay not in increasing the range of work opportunities available to black high school graduates, but in making education for blacks more appropriate to accessible positions. Whether the problem was too few white-collar jobs for blacks or their alleged inability to master academic subjects, black students were supposedly wasting their time taking academic rather than vocational courses. This thinking applied especially to children relegated to subnormal rooms, where teachers were mainly concerned with inculcating "the habits of industry, punctuality, neatness, persistence, and ability to complete a piece of work assigned." The goal of this program, declared the superintendent of schools, was not to educate these children, but rather to teach them habits that would permit them "to attain social and economic competence." These habits were remarkably similar to those required of unskilled and semiskilled workers in industry. [26]

However much the public school system might have been structured by the imperatives of the city's labor market and the class interests of its appointed school board, its promise, illusions, and failures resonated in particular ways among black newcomers. Schools—apparently good ones—were available, and black children were encouraged to attend; such availability could easily confirm notions about the legitimacy of black citizenship in Chicago. But the ubiquitously separate category of "Negro education" had ominous implications. [27] "Social and economic competence" represented a euphemism for the limits whites placed on black achievement, limits defined in some cases by what whites thought blacks could do and in others by what whites permitted them to do. Either way, migrants found their advancement stymied by barriers defined by ideas about race and its ramifications. Access to Chicago's schools fulfilled initial goals, but newcomers and their children would learn that access was not enough.

Conclusion

When asked what they liked about the North, nearly all black new-comers interviewed by the Chicago Commission on Race Relations in 1920 mentioned "freedom." This freedom cannot be neatly defined; it meant different things to different people, as it had fifty years ear-lier at emancipation. For nearly all who left the South during the Great Migration, it embodied some combination of rights, opportu-nities, dignity, and pride. In Chicago, black men and women did not have to truckle to whites. They could vote, a right that symblized their full citizenship and the legitimacy of their participation in the affairs of the broader community. They could send their children to schools whose quality seemed guaranteed not only by the apparent political influence of black aldermen, but by the more tangible pres-ence of white children sitting alongside black pupils. They could work in factories, where they earned high wages, envisioned the possibil-ity of promotion, and made meaningful choices on the crucial issue of unionization. Significantly, black workers responded positively to the "industrial democracy" programs introduced by some of Chica-go's largest employers during the 1920s.[1]

Although many newcomers were disappointed by the failure of Chicago race relations to live up to their expectations, the 1919 riot ironically highlighted liberating aspects of the Great Migration, even as it demanded recognition of the ubiquity of racial confrontation. While southern racial violence usually resulted from a symbolic trans-gression of racial etiquette, Chicago's riot grew out of a competitive situation that suggested the importance of blacks in the city's political and economic life as well as in its housing market. Moreover, the riot revealed a black militancy that would have provoked either repres-sion or expulsion in the South: when whites attacked, blacks fought back, and the *Defender* kept score on the front page. Blacks endured the bulk of police violence and were more likely to be arrested than whites, but only a small minority of those who participated in attacks suffered retribution. Although some whites responded to the riots with race-baiting political rhetoric or calls for school segregation and action to curb migration, others reacted strongly against racial violence per se.[2] The appointment of an interracial commission to study the riot probably had little impact on the minds of most newcomers, but to a few it affirmed at least the official unacceptability of racial violence as well as the legitimacy of black participation in the public life of the city.

Underneath both the real and apparent freedom lay ominous forces invisible to most migrants. Black political participation and influence operated within a framework dominated by clientage relationships with white politicians. Despite their instrumental role in the election of Mayor Thompson, their pivotal position in a closely and bitterly divided Republican party, and the visibility of their aldermen and committeemen, black Chicagoans enjoyed only limited access to the resources of the metropolis. School integration, while attributable in part to whites' disinclination to enact de jure segregation, persisted mainly because the Board of Education had not yet been able to gerrymander districts efficiently. Integrated schools were doomed, their demise awaiting only continued black migration into a city committed to ghettoizing its black inhabitants. Continued industrial opportunity was attributable partly to the cynical manipulation of ethnic divisions by employers whose racial prejudices included images of blacks as loyal, but "incapable of performing tasks which require sustained mental application." Limits on advancement beyond semiskilled positions all too often complemented discriminatory layoff policies. But much of this would become apparent only later in the 1920s and the 1930s. Frustrations and conflicts at the workplace, racial violence, and various forms of exclusion and discrimination did indeed mark visible boundaries of Chicago as a Promised Land during and immediately after the Great Migration, but the barriers seemed neither as systematic nor as unbreachable as they had in the South. Because protocols were neither enshrined in law nor absolute, enough exceptions existed—and were well publicized in the *Defender* and from countless pulpits scattered across the South Side—to provide hope.[3]

Moreover, blacks enjoyed considerable autonomy in Chicago, permitting migrants to shape much of their own adaptation to urban life. This autonomy rested partly on the historic marginality of blacks to Chicago's economy and social ecology. Ironically, considering the vulnerablility of all workers to the fluctuations of the business cycle and the impulse among industrial employers during this period to tighten control over their work force, it also is attributable to characteristics of industrial employment: the impersonality of industrial relations, the separation of home and work, and the cash nexus. "I can quit any time I want to," commented a former Kentuckian who stayed at his job but valued his option to quit without legal recrimination, forfeiture of unpaid wages, or word spreading among employers about his work habits.[4] These distant employers, unlike landlords or merchants with a lien on the crop, neither pressured wives and children to work nor related social order and the availability of a work force to what blacks did outside the workplace. Welfare capitalism programs oriented towards nonwork hours tended to be channeled through black institutions like the YMCA and YWCA, and behavior modification campaigns originated from sources that were essentially nonthreatening. White reformers could safely be ignored, and even the advice of the black middle class seemed authoritative only when relations with the unfamiliar world of white institutions were at stake. No attempts to reshape behavior outside the workplace carried coercive implications.

To a considerable extent, the analogue of the separation of work and home was a distinction between the white world in which most migrants worked during the day and the black world to which they returned at night. On the South Side, recalled Mahalia Jackson, who arrived in the 1920s, a black worker "could lay down his burden of being a colored person in the white man's world and lead his own life."[5] In this black world, the migrants both adapted to urban life and retained styles and sensibilities rooted in southern, and often rural, culture.

The material basis of the black community's vitality, and of the ability of migrants and other black Chicagoans to build a social world within it, was the cash wage. Migrants, paid in cash, valued the freedom to spend or save according to their priorities and inclinations. Newcomers who had come from a sharecropper economy based on credit had little experience with a regular cash income. Labor in turpentine and lumber camps, where wages were paid monthly and often in scrip or some other form of credit at the company store, had been only slightly more likely to generate cash. Migrants who had lived in cities, especially women accustomed to supplementary employment and petty commerce, had handled cash, but generally less than even the meager wages of domestic work in Chicago. A pay envelope from a packinghouse, steel mill, or other factory provided still greater spendable income. The opportunities to spend that cash presented a terrain of freedom that was new (except for those migrants from the largest southern cities), tangible, accessible, and—if one so desired—not altogether removed from southern culture.

The rapidity with which migrants adopted urban leisure habits paralleled their ready adaptation to industrial work discipline. Embracing the emerging mass consumer culture more quickly and less ambivalently than European immigrants, they bought radios, frequented movies, attended baseball games, crowded cabarets and vice resorts, and patronized chain stores. On the whole, these tastes represent a break with the migrants' southern pasts. Few blacks in the South either attended movie theaters or owned radios, even in the largest cities. One survey of Detroit's black migrants found that hunting and fishing had dominated leisure time in the South, followed by "sitting down." Urban church and lodge activities provided the greatest source of continuity with southern patterns.[6] Yet the influence of the South on the streets of Chicago's South Side was unmistakable. The aromas of southern cooking, especially from the ubiquitous barbecue stands during the summer; the sounds of New Orleans jazz and Mississippi blues; styles of worship; patterns of speech: these were but the most obvious manifestations of the extent to which black southerners reshaped both their cultural heritage and their new environment.[7] In Chicago's Black Metropolis, newcomers adapted to urban life and helped to create an Afro-American urban culture.

The question is not whether southern culture persisted, but rather how it fit into an interactive process, influencing behavior on the one hand and undergoing change on the other. Southern culture and the selectivity, dynamic, and goals of the Great Migration interacted with material structure and the implications of racial discrimination to shape reactions to urban-industrial life in the North. Industrial work habits, for example, did not require rejection of values that migrants brought with them. Chicago's factories did, however, demand a reorientation of ideas about time, the organization of work, and labor relations. The enthusiastic response to Chicago's schools was shaped by both the history of black education in the South and ideas about the place of education in the attainment of the political and economic citizenship so central to the decision to migrate. That decision, and other choices migrants subsequently made in Chicago, represented at once an affirmation of traditional values, a rejection of certain southern institutions and economic activities, and an impulse toward membership in urban-industrial society.

The process of adaptation was shaped partly by the role that values central to mainstream American ideas about capitalism, mobility, democracy, and citizenship had played in the migration process. Black southerners had come North to partake in "privileges" that they perceived as "white" in the South, but theirs by right as American citizens. This perspective is central to the complex relationship between race and class consciousness among the migrants. Within the black community, they differentiated themselves from the black middle class. In the outside worlds of production, politics, and municipal institutions, however, conditions in Chicago resonated with their experience and their goals to dramatize the significance of racial categories. Voting, education, and employment lay within the realm of white society, and migrants perceived that obtaining their share of the perquisites, power, and opportunity seemingly offered by industrial capitalism entailed breaking racial barriers and overcoming racial prejudices.

Because they defined these arenas in terms of racial proscription or control, they perceived their interests in racial terms. Their children had received inferior and inadequate schooling in the South because they were black. Chicago's "integrated" schools provided better education apparently because blacks as a group had access to what whites had. Southern disfranchisement appeared as a racial proscription.[8] Once in Chicago migrants continued to equate "Democrat" with white hegemony and racial exclusion and "Republican" with the legitimacy of black participation, in a not-unreasonable analysis of Chicago political alignments at the time. One migrant even referred to higher wages, so often emphasized by analysts as the uncomplicated cause of the migration, in terms of the chance to "make a white man's salary up there." Schools, government, and jobs were accessible in Chicago apparently because its racial patterns differed from what the migrants had left behind in the South. That whites controlled this access only underscored the importance of racial categories and black unity. Assessing their interests within the context of their southern experience and the motivations underlying migration, black newcomers defined those interests largely in terms of continued access. Racial proscriptions, rather than structural characteristics of the city's economy, appeared to threaten that access or limit its efficacy. Therefore they and the black middle class seemed to share essentially identical interests when white institutions controlled resources. When the option existed, most migrants looked to black institutions, patronized black professionals, and, as Drake and Cayton explained, "enjoyed the city in situations where they didn't have to bother with white folks."[9]

Within the black community, the white world posed neither threat nor opportunity. There, differences among blacks, especially along class lines, could not be ignored, partly because class in the black community depended so heavily on activity in the very arenas in which blacks exercised the greatest autonomy: leisure and church. When migrants refused to blend inconspicuously into a cultural landscape defined by middle-class sensibilities and imperatives, black Chicagoans concerned about respectability and community standards became increasingly frustrated and angry. Their lectures, disdainful manner, and attempts to distance themselves from the newcomers often succeeded only in widening gaps and emphasizing anew the symbols of respectability and refinement that defined class in black Chicago. Inside the Black Metropolis, where whites exercised little overt institutional influence, class tensions emerged clearly and constituted a significant aspect of the migrants' sense of their separateness from others in the community.

The combination of faith in the promise of industrial capitalism, mistrust of the white people who controlled its institutions, divided loyalty to the city's black middle-class leadership, and inclination to enjoy free time without worrying about racial etiquette offers speculative insight into the nature of the most popular black mass movement to emerge after the war. When Marcus Garvey urged Afro-Americans to take pride in their heritage and racial identity, he addressed both the optimism of the migrants and their frustrations. Despite vocal opposition from much of the community's leadership, his Universal Negro Improvement Association attracted five thousand to seven thousand black Chicagoans into its ranks during the early 1920s. The size of Garvey's following in Chicago suggests that it had to have reached into the working class, and an organizer for the Communist Party later recalled that "new migrants" were well represented in the Garvey movement, along with small businessmen and a few unemployed professionals and intellectuals. Often portrayed as a manifestation of disillusion with northern cities, Garvey's popularity perhaps rested more on its relevance to the ideology of the Great Migration. His synthesis of free enterprise, assertive separatism, and optimism logically resonated with those migrants who had grown disillusioned in Chicago and located the source of that disillusion in the familiar context of racial proscription. Rather than forging a black consciousness among alienated masses, Garveyism drew upon ideas about the meaning of race that had been central to the Great Migration itself.[10]

What their early experiences in Chicago confirmed for many migrants was the potential of a variant of pluralism. Venturing North to share in both the process and the rewards of democracy and industrialism, they did not necessarily expect or wish to abandon their identity as black Americans. Indeed, they expected that what Chicago offered was an environment that would permit them to choose to interact with whites only in settings essential to economic and political citizenship. The political process, the workplace, and the school were the most important of these settings; to many, the decisions surrounding unionization turned on whether unions fell into a similar category. Whenever possible, migrants from the South chose to work through, participate in, and enjoy the fellowship provided by black institutions. It seemed possible to share in the American Dream while grafting that dream onto a black consciousness.

True pluralism, however, requires empowerment. Black southerners who moved to Chicago found themselves able to earn high wages and promotions into semiskilled jobs, vote for black aldermen and state representatives, send children to good schools, and enjoy the night life of State Street. In this very meaningful sense, migration had indeed permitted them to share in the perquisites of an American citizenship that they had defined within the context of a more circumscribed life in the South. But initial progress could not be translated into an ongoing process leading to full participation in the city's economic or political life. Neither the migrants nor Chicago's black leadership, which mediated their relations with white institutions, could penetrate networks of power in the city or mobilize sufficient resources to provide an alternate route based on an internal economy. Unionization, which in Chicago's packinghouses emerged as an unusually open proposition for black workers, might have offered security and access to power based on a class position that united most of the black community with a large proportion of white Chicagoans. But even the most well-intentioned white unionists understood little about black southerners and were as unwilling as other whites to accept blacks as equal partners except on terms defined by whites.

The dreams embodied in the Great Migration eventually collapsed under the weight of continued racial oppression and the failure of industrial capitalism to distribute its prosperity as broadly as the migrants had expected. The promise of the movement had required a freedom that could not be attained by crossing the Mason-Dixon line, finding a job in a factory, entering a voting booth, or going to school. As writer Ralph Ellison explained a quarter-century after the Great Migration, freedom would have to entail "a democracy in which the Negro will be free to define himself for what he is and, within the large framework of that democracy, for what he desires to be."[11] This is what many migrants expected to find at the northern end of the railroad line. What most would eventually recognize, however, was that there still remained a journey longer than the Great Migration and strewn with greater obstacles.

Appendixes

Appendix A Net Black Migration to Chicago, 1910–20, by Age

Age	Actual Black Population, 1920	Expected Black Population, 1920[a]	Net Migration, 1910–20[b]	Percent Increase[c]	Migrants as Percentage of Black Population, 1920
10–14	6,129	2,420	3,709	153	61
15–19	6,969	1,868	5,101	273	73
20–24	11,780	1,965	9,815	499	83
25–34	30,681	5,547	25,134	453	82
35–44	23,058	10,933	12,125	111	53
45–64	15,803	15,828	−25	0	0
65+	2,222	1,639	583	36	26
Total (Age 10+)	96,642	40,200	56,442	140	58

Sources

Survival ratios and method—Everett S. Lee, Ann R. Miller, Carol P. Brainerd, and Richard A. Easterlin, *Population Redistribution and Economic Growth, United States, 1870–1950* (Philadelphia, 1957), 15–25.

National population—U.S. Bureau of the Census, Thirteenth Census, 1910, 1:326.

Chicago population—U.S. Bureau of the Census, Thirteenth Census, 1910, 2:480; Fourteenth Census, 1920, 3:248.

[a] Estimated settled population computed using forward census survival ratios, converted to fit the age groups using the national black population breakdowns (1910) as a weighting device.

[b] Net migration (number of migrants) = actual 1920 population − expected population.

[c] Percent increase = Percentage by which the migrants increased the population size for each age group = Net migration ÷ expected population.

Appendix B State of Birth of Native Nonwhite Illinois Residents

Birthplace	1910 Population		Number of Nonwhite Migrants, 1910–20	1920 Population		1910–20 Migrants as Percentage of All Illinois Nonwhites, 1920	Distribution of Nonwhite Migrants to Illinois, 1910–20
	Number	Percent		Number	Percent		
Total	106,862	100.0	73,437	180,289	100.0	40.7	100.0
Illinois	36,070	33.8	8,393[a]	44,463	24.7	4.7[a]	11.4[a]
South	50,367	47.1	58,403	108,770	60.3	32.4	79.5
(Upper South)	(34,441)	(32.2)	(13,428)	(47,869)	(26.6)	(7.4)	(18.3)
(Deep South)	(15,926)	(14.9)	(44,975)	(60,901)	(33.8)	(25.0)	(61.3)
Rest of U.S.	20,425	19.1	6,641	27,056	15.0	3.7	9.0
Upper South							
Tennessee	15,309	14.3	8,692	24,001	13.3	4.8	11.8
Kentucky	13,315	12.5	3,164	16,479	9.1	1.8	4.3
Virginia	3,332	3.1	260	3,592	2.0	0.1	0.4
No. Carolina	1,178	1.1	586	1,764	1.0	0.3	0.8
Maryland	645	0.6	37	682	0.3	0.0	0.1

Oklahoma	0.1	138	481	619	0.3	0.3	0.7
D.C.	0.3	270	134	404	0.2	0.1	0.2
W. Virginia	0.3	230	66	296	0.2	0.0	0.1
Delaware	0.0	24	8	32	0.0	0.0	0.0
Deep South							
Mississippi	4.3	4,614	14,883	19,497	10.8	8.3	20.3
Alabama	3.0	3,208	10,466	13,674	7.6	5.8	14.3
Georgia	2.7	2,875	7,313	10,188	5.7	4.1	10.0
Louisiana	1.5	1,610	6,474	8,084	4.4	3.6	8.8
Arkansas	1.3	1,355	1,744	3,099	1.7	1.0	2.4
Texas	0.7	790	1,910	2,700	1.5	1.1	2.7
So. Carolina	1.2	1,231	1,406	2,637	1.5	0.8	1.9
Florida	0.2	243	779	1,022	0.6	0.4	1.1

Source: Everett S. Lee, "State of Birth, 1870–1950," University of Pennsylvania Studies of Population Redistribution and Economic Growth (Philadelphia, 1953), 3: 69–70 (mimeographed).
Note: State-of-birth data is unavailable for Chicago. Illinois data is likely to understate the Deep South component of black migration to Chicago, because of the proximity of downstate Illinois to the Upper South. Most black southerners who migrated to Illinois locations other than Chicago were likely to move to downstate communities, especially East St. Louis.
[a] Natural increase.

Abbreviations

1. Archives

CHS	Chicago Historical Society, Chicago
DuSable	DuSable Museum of African-American History, Chicago
Fisk	Special Collections Division, Fisk University Library, Nashville
JRL-UC	Manuscripts Division, Joseph Regenstein Library, University of Chicago
LC	Library of Congress, Manuscripts Division, Washington, D.C.
NA	National Archives, Washington, D.C.
UIC	Special Collections, the University Library, University of Illinois at Chicago
WNRC	Washington National Records Center, Suitland, Maryland

2. Manuscript Collections

CCRR Papers	Papers of the Chicago Commission on Race Relations, 1919–1920, Illinois State Archives, Springfield (microfilm)
IWP, "Negro in Illinois"	Illinois Writers Project, "The Negro in Illinois," a file of reports, interviews, and clippings compiled by the Illinois Writers Project of the U.S. Works Progress Administration during the late 1930s and early

	1940s. Vivian Harsh Collection, Carter Woodson Regional Library, Chicago
LSRM	Laura Spelman Rockefeller Memorial Collection, Rockefeller Archives, Tarrytown, New York
NAACP	Records of the National Association for the Advancement of Colored People, LC
NULR	Records of the National Urban League, LC
NULR-SRO	Records of the National Urban League, Southern Regional Office, LC
WCMC	Records of the Welfare Council of Metropolitan Chicago, CHS

3. Government Records

DNE-USDL, RG 174	Records of the Division of Negro Economics, in General Records of the U.S. Department of Labor, RG 174, NA
Files-USDL, RG 174	Files of the Chief Clerk, U.S. Department of Labor, RG 174, NA
FMCS, RG 280	Records of the U.S. Federal Mediation and Conciliation Service, RG 280, WNRC
MID File, RG 165	Files of the Military Intelligence Division, U.S. Department of War, General and Special Staffs, Entry 65, RG 165, NA
OFM-BAE, RG 83	Records of the Office of Farm Management, Bureau of Agricultural Economics, U.S. Department of Agriculture, Series 133, RG 83, NA
Service and Information Branch, RG 165	Records of the Service and Information Branch, U.S. Department of War, General and Special Staffs, RG 165, NA
WLPB, RG 1	Records of the U.S. War Labor Policies Board, RG 1, NA
Women's Bureau, RG 86	Records of the U.S. Women's Bureau, U.S. Department of Labor, RG 36, NA

4. Other Frequently Cited Sources

BW	The *Butcher Workman*

CCRR, *Negro in Chicago*	Chicago Commission on Race Relations, *The Negro in Chicago* (Chicago, 1922)
Johnson, "Draft," NULR	Folder marked "Migration Study, Draft (Final) Chapters 7–13" [1917], Box 86, Series 6, NULR, LC. These essays by Charles Johnson, drawn from the data he gathered in Mississippi and Chicago in 1917, formed the basis for a considerable portion of Emmett Scott's *Negro Migration During the War*
Johnson, "Interviews," NULR	Folder marked Charles S. Johnson, "Chicago Study, Migration Interviews" [1917?], Box 86, Series 6, NULR
Johnson, "Mississippi Summary," NULR	Folder marked "Migration Study, Mississippi Summary," in Box 86, Series 6, NULR
Migration Letters, NULR	Folder marked "Migration Study, Negro Migrants, Letters Fr.," Box 86, Series 6, NULR
NM	The *New Majority*
USDL, *Negro Migration*	U.S. Department of Labor, Division of Negro Economics, *Negro Migration in 1916–17* (Washington, D.C., 1919)

Notes

Introduction

1. Richard Robert Wright, *87 Years Behind the Black Curtain: An Auto-biography* (Philadelphia, 1965), 37–38. The following paragraphs are from pp. 38–39, 67; and Richard Robert Wright, "The Industrial Condition of Negroes in Chicago" (B.D. thesis, University of Chicago Divinity School, 1901), 5–6.

2. Richard Wright, *Black Boy* (New York, 1937), 181, 228.

3. Ibid., 228; Richard Wright, *American Hunger*, (New York, 1977), 1–3. For Wright's impressions of the migratory experience, see also his more rhetorical and stylized *12 Million Black Voices* (New York, 1941), 93, 98.

4. Emmett J. Scott, comp., "Additional Letters of Negro Migrants of 1916–1918," *Journal of Negro History* 4 (October 1919): 452; R. J. Bennett to Bethlehem Baptist Association, [March or April] 26, 1917, Box 6, Carter G. Woodson Collection, LC.

5. Johnson, "Interviews," 4, NULR; Frederick G. Detweiler, *The Negro Press in the United States* (Chicago, 1922), 75; U. S. Bureau of the Census, *Negroes in the United States, 1920–1932* (Washington, D.C., 1935), 55; William E. Vickery, "The Economics of Negro Migration, 1900–1960" (Ph.D. dissertation, University of Chicago, 1969), 173; Seth Scheiner, *Negro Mecca: A History of the Negro in New York City, 1865–1920* (New York, 1965); Nathan I. Huggins, *Harlem Renaissance* (New York, 1971), 21 and passim; George E. Haynes, "Negroes Move North, I" *Survey* 40 (May 4, 1918): 116; George E. Haynes, "Effect of War Conditions on Negro Labor," *Proceedings of the Academy of Political Science* 8, no. 2 (February 1919): 311; Charles S. Johnson, "The New Frontage on American Life," in Alain Locke, ed., *The New Negro: An Interpretation* (New York, 1925), 278; John M. Clark, *The Costs of the World War to the American People* (New Haven, 1931), 257.

6. Charles Johnson, "Stimulation of the Movement," 2, "Draft" NULR (emphasis in the original); CCRR, *Negro in Chicago*, 87; Johnson, "New Frontage," 278; "Anthony Overton," *Journal of Negro History* 32, no. 3 (July 1947): 394; Chicago *Defender*, February 20, 1915, January 27, 1917; Robert Peterson,

Only the Ball Was White (Englewood Cliffs, 1970), 112. For a map of the Illinois Central Railroad system, see insert in *Seventy-First Annual Report of the Illinois Central Railroad Company for the Year Ended December 31, 1920* (Chicago, 1921).

7. Interview with Milt Hinton, n.d., transcript, 18, Institute of Jazz Studies, Newark, N.J. (I am indebted to Theodore Panken for providing me with a photocopy.) It is difficult to estimate the volume of migration to Chicago during this period. The census statistics, when controlled for deaths and births, yield a figure of approximately 50,000 (61,000 between the 1910 and 1920 censuses), an estimate accepted by Allan H. Spear in his classic *Black Chicago: The Making of a Negro Ghetto* (Chicago, 1967). However, the 1920 census probably undercounted blacks, especially in cities, and because the 1910 census employed black enumerators, it is likely that its statistic is not as underestimated; therefore, the difference between 1910 and 1920 is probably understated. Observers unanimously offered figures higher than 50,000. According to Emmett Scott, "daily counts," probably by the Chicago Urban League, indicated that 50,000 migrants arrived in Chicago between January 1916 and June 1917 alone. The Chicago Urban League estimated at the end of 1919 that the city's black population had increased 75,000 since 1913; most of the increase would have occurred during the war. Others, including Charles Johnson, Mary McDowell, and Carl Sandburg, offered estimates of 1916–19 migration ranging from 65,000 to 75,000. Sandburg, who claimed that his estimates drew upon an exhaustive survey of forty local authorities, guessed that 150,000 migrants arrived in Chicago, with only 70,000 remaining permanently. His penchant for exaggeration, however, must be taken into consideration. See Otis Duncan and Beverly Duncan, *The Negro Population of Chicago: A Study of Residential Succession* (Chicago, 1957), 33; Spear, *Black Chicago*, 141; Emmett J. Scott, *Negro Migration during the War* (New York, 1920), 102; *Defender*, December 13, 1919, January 31, 1920; Charles S. Johnson, "Digest of Contributing Factors to Racial Outbreak July 29, 1919" [c. 1920], 1, typescript in Box 87, Series 6, NULR; Carl Sandburg, *The Chicago Race Riots July, 1919* (New York, 1919), 5, 10.

8. For distinctive applications of the ghettoization framework, see David M. Katzman, *Before the Ghetto: Black Detroit in the Nineteenth Century* (Urbana, 1973); Spear, *Black Chicago*; Kenneth L. Kusmer, *A Ghetto Takes Shape: Black Cleveland, 1870–1930* (Urbana, 1976); Gilbert Osofsky, *Harlem: The Making of a Negro Ghetto*, 2d ed. (New York, 1971); Gilbert Osofsky, "The Enduring Ghetto," *Journal of American History* 55, no. 2 (September 1968): 243–55. Different patterns of black community development can be found in Thomas C. Cox, *Blacks in Topeka, Kansas, 1865–1915: A Social History* (Baton Rouge, 1982); Douglas H. Daniels, *Pioneer Urbanites: A Social and Cultural History of Black San Francisco* (Philadelphia, 1980); and George C. Wright, *Life Behind A Veil: Blacks in Louisville, 1865–1930* (Baton Rouge, 1985). For reviews of this historiography, see Joe W. Trotter, Jr., *Black Milwaukee: The Making of an Industrial Proletariat, 1915–1945* (Urbana, 1985), 264–282, and Kenneth Kusmer, "The Black Urban Experience in American History," in Darlene C. Hine, ed., *The State of Afro-American History* (Baton Rouge, 1986), 91–122. The best study of a northern race riot during this period is William M. Tuttle, Jr., *Race Riot: Chicago in*

the Red Summer of 1919 (New York, 1970); its chapter on the Great Migration is probably the most evocative and insightful chapter-length treatment of the movement. See also Elliott M. Rudwick, *Race Riot at East St. Louis July 2, 1917* (Carbondale, Ill., 1964); David Levine, *Internal Combustion: The Races in Detroit, 1915–1926* (Westport, Conn., 1976). Trotter's *Black Milwaukee*, by focusing on class formation rather than ghettoization as the central process in Afro-American urban history, has moved outside what he calls the "ghetto synthesis" and drawn attention to migrants as the central actors in the process of "proletarianization." But the focus is still the community, rather than the migrants themselves, and the process is viewed from the perspective of community development rather than the experience of the migrants.

9. Peter Gottlieb, *Making Their Own Way: Southern Blacks' Migration to Pittsburgh, 1916–1930* (Urbana, 1987). The other major book-length historical study of the Great Migration, Florette Henri, *Black Migration: Movement North, 1900–1920* (Garden City, 1975), adds narrative detail and argumentative force to Emmett Scott's classic *Negro Migration*, upon which it draws heavily for its framework. Its premise, that the Great Migration prepared black Americans to be "New Negroes," reads the movement backward rather than forward.

10. Alain Locke, "The New Negro," in Locke, ed., *The New Negro*, 6; Leroi Jones [Amiri Baraka], *Blues People: Negro Music in White America* (New York, 1963), 96.

11. Leon F. Litwack, "The Ordeal of Black Freedom," in Walter J. Fraser, Jr., and Winfred B. Moore, Jr., eds., *The Southern Enigma: Essays on Race, Class, and Folk Culture* (Westport, Conn., 1983), 6. On the impact of northern racism, the business cycle, and class relations on northern urban black life, see Trotter, *Black Milwaukee*, and William J. Wilson, *The Declining Significance of Race* (Chicago, 1978). On the transformation of State Street into a corridor of housing projects, see Arnold Hirsch, *Making the Second Ghetto: Race and Housing in Chicago, 1940–1960* (New York, 1983).

Chapter 1

1. James D. Reese [to Chicago Urban League?], April 24, 1917, Migration Letters, NULR; Lynch quoted in *Colored Tennessean*, August 11, 1865, quoted in Gerald D. Jaynes, *Branches without Roots: Genesis of the Black Working Class in the American South, 1862–1882* (New York, 1986), 190.

2. "Immigration During September and October, 1915," *Monthly Labor Review* 2, no. 1 (January 1916): 10; "Work of Federal, State, and Municipal Employment Offices in the United States and of Provincial Employment Bureaus in Canada," *Monthly Labor Review* 5, no. 1–6 (July-December, 1917): 164, 372, 559, 728, 966, 1188; USDL, *Negro Migration*, 11–12; CCRR, *Negro in Chicago*, 83; *Iron Age* 99 (June 28, 1917): 1563–64. For a more systematic discussion of the inverse relationship between white immigration and black migration to northern cities, see Brinley Thomas, *Migration and Urban Development: A Reappraisal of British and American Long Cycles* (London, 1972).

3. Carter G. Woodson, *A Century of Negro Migration* (Washington, D.C., 1918), 169.

4. Montgomery *Advertiser*, quoted in CCRR, *Negro in Chicago*, 81; Scott, "Additional Letters," 424, 419, 421.

5. *Defender*, March 20, 1915, January 1, 1916, February 24, 1917, November 1, 1919; Scott, "Additional Letters," 437; CCRR, *Negro in Chicago*, 80–81, 366–67; USDL, *Negro Migration*, 22; United States Administrator for Adjustment of Labor Questions Arising in Certain Packing Houses, *Findings and Award* (February 15, 1919), 7–8, pamphlet in File 33/864, FMCS, RG 280; Johnson, "Interviews," 1, 4, NULR.

6. Emmett J. Scott, comp., "Letters of Negro Migrants of 1916–18," *Journal of Negro History* 4 (July 1919): 297, 313; Scott, "Additional Letters," 421, 425, 427. This sentiment is evident throughout both collections of letters.

7. USDL, *Negro Migration*, 11–12, 118; Scott, *Negro Migration*, 6; George E. Haynes, "Migration of Negroes into Northern Cities," *Proceedings of the National Conference of Social Work* 44 (1917): 495; Charles S. Johnson, "How Much of the Migration Was a Flight From Persecution," *Opportunity* 1, no. 9 (September 1923): 272–74; St. Clair Drake and Horace R. Cayton, *Black Metropolis: A Study of Negro Life in a Northern City* (New York, 1945), 99–100. Three often-cited Columbia studies reached the same conclusion. See Dean Dutcher, *The Negro in Modern Industrial Society: An Analysis of Changes in the Occupations of Negro Workers, 1910–1920* (Lancaster, Pa., 1930); Edward Lewis, *The Mobility of the Negro: A Study in the American Labor Supply* (New York, 1931); Louise V. Kennedy, *The Negro Peasant Turns Cityward: Effects of Recent Migrations to Northern Centers* (New York, 1930). See also Henderson H. Donald, "The Negro Migration of 1916–1918," *Journal of Negro History* 6, no. 4 (October 1921): 389–90, 410ff., for conclusion that the migration was economically motivated, based on his survey of migrations in general, which demonstrated that "the economic causes of migration are primal." A notable exception to this narrow framework is Clyde Vernon Kiser's insightful study of migration from St. Helena in the South Carolina Sea Islands to northern cities, especially New York. Rejecting the search for "one or two operative causes," he examined a variety of social, economic, and environmental factors, along with "changes and alterations in the personal attitudes of individuals." See Kiser, *Sea Island to City: A Study of St. Helena Islanders in Harlem and Other Urban Centers* (New York, 1932), 85–113. More recently, economic historians have employed the tools of quantification to argue that the "cause" of the migration was "economic." See Vickery, "Economics of Negro Migration"; Robert Higgs, "The Boll Weevil, the Cotton Economy, and Black Migration: 1910–1930," *Agricultural History* 50, no. 2 (April 1976). Both, most egregiously Vickery, dismiss "discrimination" as a "constant."

8. "Program of Work Adopted at the Informal Conference on Negro Labor Problems, Washington, February 17 and 18, 1919, as Approved by the Secretary of Labor," File 8/102, Files-USDL, RG 174; [George E. Haynes], "Matters of Record" [1917], 9, typescript in Box 184, DNE-USDL, RG 174; George E. Haynes, "Memorandum for the Secretary," May 7, 1918, File No. 8/102, Files-USDL, RG 174.

9. Johnson, "How Much of the Migration Was A Flight From Persecution," 272. Florette Henri reviews much of the sociological and historical literature in *Black Migration*, 51–59, and in contrast to most other analyses, sees

these studies as slightly overstating their case. For the quantitative studies, see Vickery, "Economics of Negro Migration," and Higgs, "Boll Weevil."

10. *Defender*, February 10, 1917; W. E. B. Du Bois, "The Migration of Negroes," *Crisis* 14, no. 2 (June 1917): 66.

11. Johnson, "How Much of the Migration Was a Flight From Persecution," 272–74; Scott, *Negro Migration*, 22; Johnson, "Interviews," 5, NULR; Sandburg, *Chicago Race Riots*, 26.

12. James Weldon Johnson to assorted newspapers, July 23, 1923, Box C-373, Group I, NAACP; Charles S. Johnson, "Negro Migrations" [c. 1926], 14, typescript in Folder 31, Box 167, Charles Johnson Papers, Fisk; Johnson, "Greenwood," part 2: 4–5, "Mississippi Summary," NULR. On nineteenth-century whitecapping, see Nell Irvin Painter, *Exodusters: Black Migration to Kansas after Reconstruction* (New York, 1977).

13. [Hugh M. Dorsey], *A Statement From Governor Hugh M. Dorsey as to the Negro in Georgia* (Atlanta, 1921), 13–14; T[homas] J. Woofter, "The Negro on a Strike," *Journal of Social Forces* 2, no. 1 (November 1923): 85. Defining whitecapping as a specific illegal activity on the part of white small farmers, William F. Holmes has argued that it was suppressed for good in 1906, but similar practices seem to have endured; see William F. Holmes, "Whitecapping: Agrarian Violence in Mississippi, 1902–1906," *Journal of Southern History* 35, no. 2 (May 1969): 165–185. John Dittmer has described the practice in Georgia's Upper Piedmont in *Black Georgia in the Progressive Era, 1900–1920* (Urbana, 1977), 26.

14. CCRR, *Negro in Chicago*, 85–86; Johnson, "New Frontage," 281; "The Exodus," *AME Church Review* 33, no. 3 (January 1917): 149.

15. Houston *Observer*, October 21, 1916, reprint in Box 86, Series 6, NULR. For comprehensive lists of "social" causes, see Scott, *Negro Migration*, 18–22; CCRR, *Negro in Chicago*, 84–86; Thomas J. Woofter, *Negro Migration: Changes in Rural Organization and Population of the Cotton Belt* (New York, 1920; reprint, New York, 1969), 121; Eric D. Walrond, "The Negro Migration to the North," *International Interpreter* 2, no. 20 (August 18, 1923): 628–29.

16. Wright, *Black Boy*, 147, 70; Wellborn Victor Jenkins to *Atlanta Constitution*, October 10, 1916, in Migration Letters, NULR.

17. For an insightful critique of both the "push-pull" framework and the separation of individual dissatisfactions from a general pattern of social relations, see Neil Fligstein, *Going North: Migration of Blacks and Whites from the South, 1900–1950* (New York, 1981), 65–66.

18. Johnson, "General," 1–2, "Mississippi Summary," NULR.

19. U.S. Bureau of the Census, *Historical Statistics of the United States, Colonial Times to 1970*, (Washington, D.C., 1975), part I: 95. Jack T. Kirby has observed that the Great Migration must be considered partly responsible for the direction and volume of the larger migration that followed, because it established "interregional networks of family and friends." See his "The Southern Exodus, 1910–1960: A Primer for Historians," *Journal of Southern History* 49, no. 4 (November 1983): 592.

20. *Defender*, October 18, 1916; E. Franklin Frazier, *The Negro Family in Chicago* (Chicago, 1932), 80.

21. Quoted in Lawrence W. Levine, *Black Culture and Black Consciousness:*

Afro-American Folk Thought From Slavery To Freedom (New York, 1977), 262.

22. Allan Kulikoff, "Uprooted Peoples: Black Migrants in the Age of the American Revolution, 1790–1820," in Ira Berlin and Ronald Hoffman, eds., *Slavery and Freedom in the Age of the American Revolution* (Charlottesville, Va., 1983), 143–44, 147–48, 151–53, 155; Richard Dunn, "Black Society in the Chesapeake, 1776–1810" in Berlin and Hoffman, eds., *Slavery and Freedom in the Age of the American Revolution*, 49–82; Richard L. Merrill and O. Fred Donaldson, "Geographical Perspectives on the History of Black America," *Economic Geography* 48, no. 1 (January 1972): 5–6; August Meier and Elliott Rudwick, *From Plantation to Ghetto*, 3d ed. (New York, 1976), 57–58. Richard Sutch's estimate of the volume of the domestic slave trade comes from Herbert Gutman and Richard Sutch, "The Slave Family: Protected Agent of Capitalist Masters or Victim of the Slave Trade?" in Paul David et al., *Reckoning with Slavery: A Critical Study in the Quantitative History of American Negro Slavery* (New York, 1976), 99. Robert Fogel estimates that 835,000 slaves were moved into the "western cotton states" between 1790 and 1860; see Robert Fogel, "Without Consent or Contract: The Rise and Fall of American Slavery" (preliminary draft, 1986), 105.

23. Ira Berlin, *Slaves Without Masters: The Free Negro in the Antebellum South* (New York, 1974), 135, 165ff.; Leslie Owens, *This Species of Property: Slave Life and Culture in the Old South* (New York, 1976), 85ff.; George Rawick, *From Sundown to Sunup: The Making of the Black Community* (Westport, Conn., 1972), 5; Spear, *Black Chicago*, 5. On the migration of blacks to northern cities after the American Revolution, see Gary B. Nash, "Forging Freedom: The Emancipation Experience in the Northern Seaport Cities, 1775–1820," in Berlin and Hoffman, eds., *Slavery and Freedom in the Age of the American Revolution*, 10. For a broad discussion of the migration of free blacks and ex-slaves to the North, see Woodson's classic *A Century of Negro Migration*, 18–60, 81–100.

24. Vernon L. Wharton, *The Negro in Mississippi, 1865–1890* (Chapel Hill, 1947; reprint, New York, 1965), 18–19; Leon F. Litwack, *Been in the Storm So Long: The Aftermath of Slavery* (New York, 1979), 30–36, 51–59, 132–35.

25. The quotations are from Jaynes, *Branches without Roots*, 74, 88. On "moving about" after the Civil War, see Wharton, *Negro in Mississippi*, 106; Litwack, *Been in the Storm So Long*, 296–97, 305, 308–10; Peter Kolchin, *First Freedom: The Responses of Alabama's Blacks to Emancipation and Reconstruction* (Westport, Conn., 1972), 4–6, 8–9, 22–23, 46–48.

26. The attempts by the Freedmen's Bureau to adjust labor supply to demand is discussed in William Cohen, "Black Immobility and Free Labor: The Freedmen's Bureau and the Relocation of Black Labor, 1865–1868," *Civil War History* 30, no. 3 (September 1984): 221–23. On the meaning of land ownership, see Edward Magdol, *A Right to the Land: Essays on the Freedmen's Community* (Westport, Conn., 1977), 17–18; Litwack, *Been in the Storm So Long*, 401; Kolchin, *First Freedom*, 22–23, 46–48; Roger Ransom and Richard Sutch, *One Kind of Freedom: The Economic Consequences of Emancipation* (Cambridge, Eng., 1977), 8.

27. Litwack, *Been in the Storm So Long*, 312–14; Howard N. Rabinowitz, *Race Relations in the Urban South, 1865–1890* (New York, 1978; reprint, Urbana, 1980), 18–24; Kolchin, *First Freedom*, 6, 10–11.

28. Rabinowitz, *Race Relations in the Urban South*, 3, 20–30; Litwack, *Been in the Storm So Long*, 192, 222, 316–18, 323–25; Kolchin, *First Freedom*, 7–8; Jaynes, *Branches without Roots*, 57–74. Neither urban migration nor interstate rural migration reached the level that southern whites indicated at the time. Even the proportionate increase in black city dwellers overstates the importance of rural-urban migration, given the small black urban population in 1860 and the fact that the overwhelming portion of freed people remained in rural areas. See Rabinowitz, *Race Relations in the Urban South*, for more of an emphasis on urbanization as an aspect of the social history of Reconstruction.

29. Leon F. Litwack, *North of Slavery: The Negro in the Free States, 1790–1860* (Chicago, 1961), 71–72; V. Jacque Voegeli, *Free But Not Equal: The Midwest and the Negro During the Civil War* (Chicago, 1967), 2, 4–8, 17–19, 65–67; Cohen, "Black Immobility," 223, 229–33; Litwack, *Been in the Storm So Long*, 308.

30. This interpretation of the Kansas Exodus relies heavily on Nell I. Painter's analysis of the movement's roots and impulse, as well as her emphasis on the importance of grass-roots organization. See Painter, *Exodusters*. See also Arvarh Strickland, "Toward the Promised Land: The Exodus to Kansas and Afterward, " *Missouri Historical Review* 69, no. 4 (July 1975): 376–79; and Magdol, *A Right to the Land*, 204–6. On the centrality of land ownership to the Exodus, see Painter, 66–68; Strickland, 379; Magdol, 208; and Norman L. Crockett, *The Black Towns* (Lawrence, Kans., 1979), 45–48. The relationship between land owning outside the South and citizenship is discussed by Crockett, 45, 78.

Reliable estimates on the volume of migration to Kansas are hard to come by. The most careful use of census data to calculate net in-migration can be found in Everett S. Lee, Ann R. Miller, Carol P. Brainerd, and Richard A. Easterlin, *Population Redistribution and Economic Growth, United States, 1870–1950* (Philadelphia, 1957), vol. 1, *Methodological Considerations and Reference Tables*, 87, which estimates a total increase during the 1870s of approximately 18,000. But this does not accurately count gross in-migration since it misses those who came and left. William Vickery, in "Economics of the Negro Migration," 180–81, 183, 185, 187, counts approximately 9,500 black Tennesseeans and Kentuckians migrating to Kansas in the 1870s and 6,176 blacks from Louisiana, Mississippi, and Texas during that same period. Topeka's postmaster estimated an influx of 15,000–20,000 black people in the year ending April 1, 1880 (Magdol, 207). Painter, after separating various emigration movements by the southern state in which they occurred, concluded that 9,500 black Kentuckians and Tennesseeans migrated to Kansas during the 1870s and that the actual Kansas Fever Exodus of 1879 "took some 6,000 Blacks from Louisiana, Mississippi, and Texas to Kansas in the space of a few months" in 1879 (Painter, 146–47, 184–85). This might be a slight underestimation, because Painter's reliance on state-of-birth data understates migration from these three states, given their importance as destinations for blacks migrating from states further east during the preceding decade. Assuming some continuation of migration in 1880, my estimate (10,000 plus 6,000, plus approximately 6,000) reflects an attempt to synthesize these calculations and is a conservative one. As Painter emphasizes, however, the point from the perspective of southern history is the excitement generated by the movement and the number of people who either considered emigrating or unsuccessfully tried to emigrate.

31. W. E. B. Du Bois, *The Souls of Black Folk* (Chicago, 1903), 3–4. The estimate of black migration to Oklahoma 1890–1910 comes from Vickery, "Economics of Negro Migration," 169. My discussion of the black towns in this and the following paragraph has drawn heavily on Crockett, *Black Towns*; see especially xi–xii, 1–40, 45, 78, 117; the quotation is from 78. See also Strickland, "Toward the Promised Land," 404–7, 410–12; Edwin S. Redkey, *Black Exodus: Black Nationalist and Back-to-Africa Movements, 1890–1910* (New Haven, 1969), 99–101; Meier and Rudwick, *From Plantation to Ghetto*, 248–49.

32. The quotation is from Martin R. Delaney, *The Condition, Elevation, Emigration and Destiny of the Colored People of the United States Politically Considered* (1852), quoted in Redkey, *Black Exodus*, 20–21. The figure of 12,000 includes 1,227 settled in Liberia by the Maryland Colonization Society; see William Cohen, *At Freedom's Edge: Black Mobility and the Southern White Quest for Racial Control, 1861–1915* (forthcoming), ms. p. 220. On the attitudes of antebellum free blacks towards emigration to Africa, see Berlin, *Slaves Without Masters*, 168. On Liberia schemes and Liberia "Fever," especially between 1890 and 1910, see Redkey, *Black Exodus*; see also August Meier, *Negro Thought in America, 1880–1915: Racial Ideologies in the Age of Booker T. Washington* (Ann Arbor, 1963), 63–66; George B. Tindall, *South Carolina Negroes, 1877–1900* (Columbia, S.C., 1952), 153–68. The importance of land ownership and political and economic freedom is discussed in Edwin S. Redkey, "The Flowering of Black Nationalism: Henry McNeal Turner and Marcus Garvey," in Nathan I. Huggins, Martin Kilson, and Daniel M. Fox, eds., *Key Issues in the Afro-American Experience* (New York, 1971), 2: 109. See also Painter, *Exodusters*, 138–41; for interest in migration to agricultural regions in Mexico, see Glenn N. Sisk, "Negro Migration in the Alabama Black Belt, 1875–1917," *Negro History Bulletin* 17 (November 1953): 32.

33. Tindall, *South Carolina Negroes*, 171–76; Donald, "The Negro Migration of 1916–1918," 395; William O. Scroggs, "Interstate Migration of Negro Population," *Journal of Political Economy* 25, no. 10 (December 1917): 1037; Meier, *Negro Thought*, 59–60. The quotations are from Sydney Nathans, "'Gotta Mind to Move, A Mind to Settle Down': Afro-Americans and the Plantation Frontier," in William J. Cooper, Jr., Michael F. Holt, and John McCardell, eds., *A Master's Due: Essays in Honor of David Herbert Donald* (Baton Rouge, 1986), 213–14. The most careful research on a "mini-migration" can be found in William F. Holmes, "Labor Agents and the Georgia Exodus, 1899–1900," *South Atlantic Quarterly* 79, no. 4 (Autumn 1980): 436–48; the quotation is from 445. While Nathans portrays migration into the Mississippi Delta as an ambitious move to a developing region, Robert Brandfon has viewed it as a movement of refugees "enticed" by labor agents and "drifting out of the worn-out lands to the east." See Robert Brandfon, *Cotton Kingdom of the New South: A History of the Yazoo Mississippi Delta from Reconstruction to the Twentieth Century* (Cambridge, Mass., 1967), 74. On migration to Arkansas, see Redkey, *Black Exodus*, 107–9.

34. Alfred H. Stone, "A Plantation Experiment," *Quarterly Journal of Eco-*

nomics 19 (February 1905): 285; Charles Johnson, "Peonage," 1, "Mississippi Summary," NULR; Litwack, *Been in the Storm So Long*, 303–4. On the commitment of ex-slaveholders to the plantation system, see James Roarke, *Masters Without Slaves: Southern Planters in the Civil War and Reconstruction* (New York, 1977).

35. Planter quoted in Charles Johnson, "Peonage," 2, "Mississippi Summary," NULR; sharecropper (Robert C. Smith), in Levine, *Black Culture and Black Consciousness*, 265. On peonage, see Pete Daniel, *The Shadow of Slavery: Peonage in the South, 1901–1969* (Urbana, 1972). Other forms of involuntary servitude are discussed in William Cohen, "Negro Involuntary Servitude in the South, 1865–1940: A Preliminary Analysis," *Journal of Southern History* 42, no. 1 (February 1976): 31–60; and Dittmer, *Black Georgia*, 72–89. On advances, see Dorothy Dickins, *A Nutritional Investigation of Negro Tenants in the Yazoo Mississippi Delta*, Mississippi Agricultural Experiment Station Bulletin no. 254 (1928), 11. The limitation on rented land is discussed in Booker T. Washington, "The Rural Negro and the South," *Proceedings of the National Conference of Charities and Corrections* 41 (1914): 123; and Howard A. Turner, "Mississippi Delta Planting Co." [1913], 8–10, typescript in Box 86, OFM-BAE, RG 83. For a suggestive discussion on some of the implications of the plantation system and the importance of control, see Jay R. Mandle, *The Roots of Black Poverty: The Southern Plantation Economy after the Civil War* (Durham, 1978); the relationship between freedom and control is analyzed in Jaynes, *Branches without Roots*, 109–15.

36. Gavin Wright, *Old South, New South: Revolutions in the Southern Economy since the Civil War* (New York, 1986), 65, 98; Woofter, *Negro Migration*, 102–3.

37. Jacqueline Jones, *Labor of Love, Labor of Sorrow: Black Women, Work, and the Family from Slavery to the Present* (New York, 1985), 111. Lawrence Levine analyzes the continuing migratory impulse and its cultural meaning in *Black Culture and Black Consciousness*, 263. The relationship between the refusal of blacks to accept roles prescribed by the "New South" and the origins of Jim Crow as a form of social control is insightfully suggested in Rabinowitz's *Race Relations in the Urban South*, 333–39.

38. W. J. Spillman and E. A. Goldenweisser, "Farm Tenantry in the United States," U.S. Department of Agriculture *Yearbook*, 1916 (Washington, D.C., 1917), 344; USDA *Yearbook*, 1923 (Washington, D.C., 1924), 592; Fligstein, *Going North*, 86–87.

39. Fligstein, *Going North*, 15. On the advance of the boll weevil, see for example, Lorenzo J. Greene and Carter G. Woodson, *The Negro Wage Earner* (Washington, D.C., 1930), 207; F. W. Farley, "Growth of the Beef Cattle Industry in the South," USDA *Yearbook*, 1917 (Washington, D.C., 1918), 329–30; M. B. Oates, "A Farm Management Study of Plantations in Northwest Louisiana" (1916), 7, typescript in Box 59, OFM-BAE, RG 83; Pete Daniel, *Breaking the Land: The Transformation of Cotton, Tobacco, and Rice Cultures since 1880* (Urbana, 1985), 7–9. Its impact on yields (by state) is summarized in USDA *Yearbook*, 1923, p. 801. Its impact on black migration is described by Johnson in "Vicksburg," 1, "Mississippi Summary," NULR, and analyzed more syste-

matically in Fligstein, 121–25. For a different view of the impact of the boll weevil, see Higgs, "Boll Weevil," 338–40, 345.

40. "A piece of doggerel from the cotton fields," quoted in George E. Haynes, "Negroes Move North, I," 118.

41. Howard A. Turner, "An Account of Runnymede Plantation" (1916), 2–3, typescript in Box 86, OFM-BAE, RG 83; Fligstein, *Going North*, 122–29.

42. Farley, "Growth of the Beef Cattle Industry in the South," 330; Glenn N. Sisk, "Rural Merchandising in the Alabama Black Belt, 1875–1917," *Journal of Farm Economics* 37, no. 4 (November 1955): 709; USDL, *Negro Migration*, 93. The centrality of the credit system to the structure of cotton agriculture is emphasized in Ransom and Sutch, *One Kind of Freedom*.

43. Daniel, *Breaking the Land*, 7–9, 18; Johnson, "Greenwood," 1, "Meridian," 1, and "Jackson, Mississippi," 5, all in "Mississippi Summary," NULR; Scott, *Negro Migration*, 15.

44. Johnson, "Interviews," 23, NULR; USDL, *Negro Migration*, 93; Daniel, *Breaking the Land*, 6.

45. Johnson, Untitled Section, 2, "Mississippi Summary," NULR; U.S. Bureau of the Census, *Negro Population, 1790–1915*, (Washington, D.C., 1918), 568; Spillman and Goldenweisser, "Farm Tenantry," 344; Charles S. Johnson, *The Negro in American Civilization: A Study of Negro Life and Race Relations in the Light of Social Research* (New York, 1930), 18–19; Howard A. Turner, "Bledsoe Plantation" (1913), 19, typescript in Box 86, OFM-BAE, RG 83. See also Dittmer, *Black Georgia*, 27. I agree with Rabinowitz, *Race Relations in the Urban South*, 334–39, that the refusal of succeeding generations of black southerners to accept their place had been evolving since the 1870s. The point here is the particular manifestations of youthful restlessness in the early twentieth century.

46. George F. King, ed., *King's Agricultural Digest* (Clayton, N.J., 1923), 55–56; Theodore Rosengarten, *All God's Dangers: The Life of Nate Shaw* (New York, 1974), 37–41, 72–80; Lester C. Lamon, *Black Tennesseans,1900–1930* (Knoxville, 1977), 127, 132–34; G. L. Morris to W. F. Cadwallader, April ?, 1923, and USDA Bureau of Crop Estimates, "Special Report of Field Agent [Texas] on Negro Migration" [April 13, 1923], both in folder labeled "Populations Movements (Negroes from South to North, April 1923)," Comments on Special Surveys, "Miscellaneous" category, Entry 90, U.S. Department of Agriculture, Bureau of Agricultural Economics, RG 83, NA; Kiser, *Sea Island to City*, 87–109. For a particularly insightful discussion of the relationship among the crop cycle, the life cycle, and migration, see Gottlieb, *Making Their Own Way*, 22–32. On the role of social and economic instability on the one hand and "comparative rigidities in the structure in the local community" on the other, in the roots of "the great 19th-century migrations," see Frank Thistlewaite, "Migration from Overseas in the Nineteenth and Twentieth Centuries" (1960); reprint in Stanley N. Katz and Stanley I. Kutler, eds., *New Perspectives on the American Past* (Boston, 1969), 2: 78–79.

47. George B. Tindall, *The Emergence of the New South, 1913–1945* (Baton Rouge, 1967), 162. For the argument that planters effectively curtailed competition for black labor, see Jonathan Wiener, *Social Origins of the New South:*

Alabama, 1860–1885 (Baton Rouge, 1978), 181–82, and Mandle, *Roots of Black Poverty*, 16.

48. U.S. Bureau of the Census, *Negro Population, 1790–1915*, 90, 93, gives the urbanization figures as 15.3 percent and 21.2 percent, but I have used the data in Hope T. Eldridge and Dorothy Swaine Thomas, *Population Redistribution and Economic Growth, United States, 1870–1950*, vol. 3, *Demographic Analysis and Interrelations*, (Philadelphia, 1964), 204, which more appropriately place Maryland, Delaware, and Washington, D.C., in the North; Elizabeth Rauh Bethel, *Promiseland: A Century of Life in a Negro Community* (Philadelphia, 1981),172. See also Woofter, *Negro Migration*, 102–3; John Bodnar, Roger Simon, and Michael P. Weber, *Lives of Their Own: Blacks, Italians, and Poles in Pittsburgh, 1900–1960* (Urbana, 1982), 31–33; Kiser, *Sea Island to City*, 87–109; Gottlieb, *Making Their Own Way*, 28–32. I am especially indebted to Gottlieb's work on the mobility of young black southerners as a prelude to the Great Migration.

49. These migration statistics include Maryland, Delaware, and Washington, D.C., in the North, and are taken from Eldridge and Thomas, *Population Redistribution and Economic Growth*, 3: 90. The "talented tenth" thesis was first presented in Woodson, *Century of Negro Migration*, 159–66; see also Drake and Cayton, *Black Metropolis*, 53.

50. Spear, *Black Chicago*, 59; Dittmer, *Black Georgia*, 166–67. Du Bois is quoted in the Savannah *Tribune*, March 8, 1902, quoted in Dittmer, 174. On post-rioting migration, see also Wright, "Industrial Condition of Negroes in Chicago," 5.

51. Elizabeth H. Pleck, *Black Migration and Poverty: Boston, 1865–1900* (New York, 1979), 53; Vickery, "Economics of Black Migration," 26; Kusmer, *A Ghetto Takes Shape*, 110–11. Gilbert Osofsky argues that the youth of these migrants contradicts the "talented tenth" thesis, but because the latter argument portrays the group as unusually well-educated or skilled, a youthful population would not necessarily contradict the thesis; see Osofsky, *Harlem: The Making of a Ghetto*, 20–21. Evidence from one oral-history project, however, indicates that small farmers constituted the bulk of Pittsburgh's pre–World War I black migrants; see Bodnar, et al., *Lives of Their Own*, 31. Smaller cities, because they tended to draw "secondary" migrants (Milwaukee's came from Chicago) drew upon an even more self-selecting base and therefore might have received a larger proportion of better-educated migrants; Joe W. Trotter in his study of Milwaukee argues that a "disproportionate number of educated mulattoes characterized" the black population moving to that city between 1870 and 1890, but describes the majority as "laboring class." See Trotter, *Black Milwaukee*, 8–9.

52. Washington quoted in "Memorandum (To be Used in the Urban League Industrial Campaign)" [1925], typescript in Box 4, Series 4, NULR, and in *Up From Slavery* (New York, 1903), 219; *Defender*, January 16, 23, 1915. See also Meier, *Negro Thought*, 100, 177. Robert Higgs has argued that the "investment" required for migration would have been imprudent, given the expense of information and travel. Ransom and Sutch more cautiously state that departure from the South was difficult because of the lack of information,

capital for relocation, and opportunities. Higgs, *Competition and Coercion: Blacks in the American Economy, 1865–1900* (Cambridge, Eng., 1977), 31–32; Ransom and Sutch, *One Kind of Freedom*, 195.

53. Cohen, "Involuntary Servitude," 59–60; Johnson, "Mound Bayou and Boliver Co.," 2, and "Clarksdale, Mississippi," 1, both in "Mississippi Summary," NULR; Lamon, *Black Tennesseans*, 128; Frank A. Ross, "Internal Migration and Local Migration" (1925), typescript in Folder 1035, Box 103, LSRM. The quotation is from Johnson, "General," 1, "Mississippi Summary," NULR.

54. "The Exodus," 149; Lamon, *Black Tennesseans*, 117; Rupert B. Vance, *Human Factors in Cotton Culture: A Study in the Social Geography of the American South* (Chapel Hill, 1929), 257. See also, Brandfon, *Cotton Kingdom*, 157, on the reluctance of plantation owners to sell land to tenants.

55. *Defender*, May 6, 1916; Letter to *Defender* (name withheld by request), April 28, 1917; Nashville *Globe*, July 23, 1909, quoted in Lamon, *Black Tennesseans*, 117–18; Rosengarten, *All God's Dangers*, 27. See also Rosengarten 192–93, 213; William C. Graves, et al., to George F. Peabody, November 25, 1918, Folder 14, Box 9, Julius Rosenwald Papers, JRL-UC; Robert Park, "The 'Money Ralley' at Sweet Gum. The Story of a Visit to a Negro Church in the Black Belt, Ala." [c. 1912], 11, typescript in Robert E. Park Papers, JRL-UC; Litwack, "Ordeal of Black Freedom," 15–18; Janet S. Hermann, *The Pursuit of a Dream* (New York, 1981), 228; and Dittmer, *Black Georgia*, 25.

56. Rupert B. Vance, *All These People: The Nation's Human Resources in the South* (Chapel Hill, 1945), 215, 242; U.S. Bureau of the Census, *Thirteenth Census, Bulletin, Age of Farmers, By Color of Operator, Character of Tenure and Size of Farm* (Washington, D.C., 1914), 14; Wright, *Old South, New South*, 120–21; Fligstein, *Going North*, 127; Scott, *Negro Migration*, 24–25.

57. Haynes, "Effect of War Conditions on Negro Labor," 305.

58. *Defender*, October 23, 1915, August 19, 1916, July 10, 1915.

59. Scott, "Letters," 298–99, 303, 306, 315, and passim; Scott, "Additional Letters," 439, and passim; Haynes, "Migration of Negroes into Northern Cities," 496. See also CCRR, *Negro in Chicago*, 80–84, 95–98.

60. Scott, "Additional Letters," 426.

61. Ibid., 428. On the importance of these perquisites of citizenship to emancipated slaves, see Litwack, *Been in the Storm So Long*, 547.

62. Washington, "Rural Negro and the South," 125; Thomas Jesse Jones, "Negro Education," in U.S. Bureau of Education, *Report of the Commissioner of Education, 1914* (Washington, D.C., 1915) 1: 420; Scott, "Additional Letters," 432–34.

63. Locke, "The New Negro," in Locke, ed., *New Negro*, 6.

64. CCRR, *Negro in Chicago*, 385; USDL, *Negro Migration*, 107. For the same theme, see the Oklahoma City *Black Dispatch*, October 10, 1919, quoted in Robert Kerlin, *The Voice of the Negro* (New York, 1920; reprint, New York, 1968), 63. A view of urban industrial life as a modern and promising alternative to dependency relationships in rural areas was, of course, hardly unique to northbound black southerners. A recent study of eastern European Jewish women observes that to emigrating Jews, "factories had a mysterious, almost

forbidden quality, in part because industrial jobs had been restricted mainly to gentiles." See Susan A. Glenn, "The Working Life of Immigrants: Women in the American Garment Industry, 1880–1920" (Ph.D. dissertation, University of California, Berkeley, 1983), 249.

Chapter 2

1. Wright, *Black Boy*, 221; Murphy quoted in George M. Fredrickson, *The Black Image in the White Mind: The Debate on Afro-American Character and Destiny, 1817–1914* (New York, 1971), 287. Howard Rabinowitz has insightfully suggested how the South dealt with the previous generation of young blacks who refused to accept their "place" in his argument that Jim Crow legislation represents "white fears generated by black resistance in word and deed at the end of the 1880s." See Rabinowitz, *Race Relations in the Urban South*, 333–39; the quotation is from p. 339. For a different interpretation, emphasizing the autonomous force of racism, see I.A. Newby, *Jim Crow's Defense: Anti-Negro Thought in America, 1900–1930* (Baton Rouge, 1965), 118–22.

2. Fredrickson, *Black Image in the White Mind*, 206–7, 285–87 (Grady quotation on p. 207); "How to Stop Migration," *Manufacturers Record*, reprinted in *American Fertilizer* 58, no. 12 (June 16, 1923): 68; Lieutenant Ray C. Burrus to Major John B. Reynolds, June 15, 1919, Box 413, Entry 359, Service and Information Branch, RG 165; "Letter intercepted by the Postal Censorship from 'Clarisse' to M. Propper," in memo from Major J. E. Spingarn to Major Walter H. Loving, July 25, 1918, File 10218–186, Box 3191, Entry 65, MID File, RG 165. See other correspondence in Boxes 3189–96 for southern wartime fears regarding subversion. For two contrasting views on antebellum southern "paternalism," see Eugene Genovese, *Roll, Jordan, Roll: The World the Slaves Made* (New York, 1974) and James Oakes, *The Ruling Race: A History of American Slaveholders* (New York, 1982).

3. Clark Wissler, "Report of the Committee on the American Negro," Hanover [N.H.] Conference, August 10–13, 1926, p. 4, Folder 1020, Box 101, LSRM; Washington, "Rural Negro and the South," 122. See also Mandle, *Roots of Black Poverty*, 69, 75. On the persistence of the southern planter class, see Wiener, *Social Origins of the New South*.

4. Montgomery *Advertiser*, quoted in "Negro Moving North," *Literary Digest* 53, no. 15 (October 7, 1916): 877. The *Literary Digest* noted that this was the "prevailing southern comment."

5. Columbia, S.C., *State*, quoted in Scott, *Negro Migration*, 156; Ray Stannard Baker, *Following the Color Line* (New York, 1908; reprint, New York, 1964), 59–60, 268; Bert J. Loewenberg, "Efforts of the South to Encourage Immigration, 1865–1900," *South Atlantic Quarterly* 33 (October 1934): 363–85; Rowland T. Berthoff, "Southern Attitudes toward Immigration, 1865–1914," *Journal of Southern History* 17 (August 1951): 336, 342, 355, and passim.

6. Montgomery *Advertiser*, quoted in "The Looking Glass," *Crisis* 13, no. 1 (November 1916): 23; Scott, *Negro Migration*, 154–56. On Texas and Mexican labor, see T. C. Jennings to Jesse O. Thomas, Sept. 9, 1920, "Labor" Folder, Box A-3, and George B. Terrell to Jesse O. Thomas, January 20, 1926, "La-

bor—Negro Migration" Folder, Box A-19, both in NULR-SRO; Mark Reisler, *By the Sweat of Their Brow: Mexican Immigrant Labor in the United States, 1900–1940* (Westport, Conn., 1976), 5, 78.

7. Lieutenant Ray C. Burrus to Colonel Arthur Woods, May 3, 1919, Box 600, Entry 352, Service and Information Branch, RG 165; Albon Holsey to Robert R. Moton, June 19, 1918, Box 1, Papers of Emmett J. Scott, Special Assistant to the Secretary of War, Records of the Adjutant General's Office, U.S. Department of War, RG 407, NA; *Defender*, August 28, 1920.

8. *Defender*, May 19, March 31, 1917; Johnson, "Greenville," 3, "Mississippi Summary," NULR; Scott, *Negro Migration*, 3; Woofter, *Negro Migration*, 63; "Exodus Costing State $27,000,000," *Journal of the American Bankers Association* 16, no. 1 (July 1923): 52.

9. Charles B. Johnson to William B. Wilson, Nov. 5, 1917, File No. 8/102, Files-USDL, RG 174. Macon *Telegraph* quoted in Scott, *Negro Migration*, 156. On labor supply, see U.S. Department of Agriculture, *Yearbook*, 1924 (Washington, D.C., 1925), 1121.

10. Alfred G. Smith, "Uncle Tom Moves Up North," *Country Gentleman* 89, no. 11 (March 15, 1924): 10; Lieutenant Robert B. Owen to Major William H. Kobbe, June 1, 1919, Box 413, Entry 359, Service and Information Branch, RG 165; [Frank B. Stubbs], "Memorandum of Southern Trip," November 3, 1923-December 5, 1923, Folder 1006, Box 99, LSRM.

11. Reprints of articles from the Nashville *Banner*, 1916, and Birmingham *Age-Herald*, December 2, 1916, Box 87, Series 6, NULR; Thornwell Jacobs, "South Benefits From Migration," *Journal of the American Bankers Association* 16, no. 3 (September 1923): 181–84; F. W. Gist, "The Migratory Habits of the Negro Under Past and Present Conditions," *Manufacturers Record* 85, no. 11 (March 13, 1924): 77–79.

12. Vicksburg *Herald*, August 19, 1916, reprint in Box 86, Series 6, NULR; P. O. Davis, "Negro Exodus and Southern Agriculture," *American Review of Reviews* 63 (October 1923), 404–7.

13. Ransom and Sutch, *One Kind of Freedom*, 171–76; Wright, *Old South, New South*, 122; Pete Daniel, *Standing at the Crossroads: Southern Life in the Twentieth Century* (New York, 1986), 11–13; Daniel, *Breaking the Land*, 91–109, 175–83. For reformers' advocacy of diversification and mechanization, see T. A. Cunningham to Atlanta *Constitution*, November 28, 1916, and Montgomery *Advertiser*, October 4, 1916, both reprinted in Box 86, Series 6, NULR; Howard L. Clark, "Growth of Negro Population in the U.S. and Trend of Migration from the South Since 1860. Economic Condition the Reason Negroes are Leaving South," *Manufacturers Record* 83, no. 4 (January 25, 1923): 63; John G. Van Deusen, *The Black Man in White America*, (Washington, D.C., 1938), 39–40; C. Vann Woodward, *Origins of the New South* (Baton Rouge, 1951), 176, 406–12.

14. "A Southern Business Man Approves Negro Migration," *Manufacturers Record* 84, no. 1 (July 5, 1923): 79; Nashville *Banner*, 1916, reprint in Box 86, Series 6, NULR; "Negro Migration as the South Sees It," *Survey* 38, no. 19 (August 11, 1918): 428.

15. Vicksburg *Herald*, August 19, 1916, reprint in Box 86, Series 6, NULR.

See also Nashville *Banner*, 1916, reprint in Box 86, Series 6, NULR; Clark, "Growth of Negro Population," 63; Editorials in these issues of *Manufacturers Record*: 83, no. 4 (January 25, 1923): cover; 83, no. 6 (February 8, 1923): 59–60; 83, no. 21 (May 24, 1923): 67; 83, no. 22 (May 31, 1923): 53; 83, no. 23 (June 7, 1923): 87–88; 84, no. 1 (July 5, 1923): 79; 85, no. 16 (April 17, 1924): 68. Many blacks shared a similar optimism concerning the more equal distribution of the American black population. Charles Johnson thought it would "release the South from its fear of numerical domination of Negroes." Johnson, "Negro Migrations" [c. 1926], 22, typescript in Folder 31, Box 167, Johnson Papers.

16. John Hope to W. T. B. Williams, October 10, 1917, W. T. B. Williams Mss., Hollis Burke Frissell Library, Tuskegee Institute, Tuskegee, Ala. (I am indebted to John Vernon for providing me with a copy of this letter); *The Christian Advocate*, February 22, 1917, reprint in Box 86, Series 6, NULR. *Times-Picayune* quoted in "Why the Negroes Go North," *Literary Digest* 77, no. 7 (May 19, 1923): 14. For a 1908 expression of a similar sentiment by a white educator who hoped that education would stimulate black migration to Africa, see M. L. Bonham, "Answer to the Negro Question: Education," *Education* 28 (April 1908): 507–10.

17. Johnson, "Efforts to Check the Movement," 1, "Draft," NULR; Scott, *Negro Migration*, 72; Clark, "Growth of Negro Population," 61; Southerner, "Exodus Without Its Canaan—But Not Without its Lessons," *Coal Age* 11 (February 10, 1917): 258; Baton Rouge *State Times*, quoted in Chicago *Whip*, November 6, 1920.

18. Boyce M. Edens, "When Labor is Cheap," *Survey* 38, no. 19 (September 8, 1917): 511; Montgomery *Advertiser*, October 4, 1916, reprint in Box 86, Series 6, NULR; Kingsley Moses, "Negro Comes North," *Forum* 58 (August 1917): 181. Two decades later a white resident in Indianola, Mississippi, similarly luxuriated in his tale of a trip to Chicago, where a black waiter not only responded to being called a "son of a bitch" by praising "the sweetes' words" he had heard since leaving the South, but assured the southerner that he stayed in the North only because of the opportunity to make money. See John Dollard, *Caste and Class in a Southern Town*, 3d ed. (New York, 1957), 177 (originally published in 1937).

19. Clipping from Atlanta *Constitution*, August 4, 1919, Box C-373, Group I, NAACP; Haynes, "Migration of Negroes Into Northern Cities," 496.

20. New Orleans *Times-Picayune*, December 15, 1916, reprint in Box 86, Series 6, NULR. "The Migration," *Crisis* 14, no. 1 (May 1917): 8, discusses the reaction of southern white newspapers.

21. Johnson, "Interviews," 5, NULR; Roi Ottley, *The Lonely Warrior: The Life and Times of Robert S. Abbott* (Chicago, 1955), 141–46; "Mississippi Freedom," *Survey* 44, no. 6 (May 8, 1920): 199–200. See also Scott, *Negro Migration*, 72–85.

22. Nashville *Banner*, November 4, 1916, reprint in Box 86, Series 6, NULR; New Orleans *Times-Picayune*, October 1, 1916, reprint in Box 87, Series 6, NULR. The isolation of the southern labor market is examined in Wright, *Old South, New South*, 65–80. On the continuity of patterns set by the

southern reaction to the Kansas Exodus, see Strickland, "Toward the Promised Land," 383–87.

23. J. S. Cullinan to W. B. Wilson, June 26, 1917; John T. Watkins to W. B. Wilson, July 14, 1917, both in File No. 8/102, Files-USDL, RG 174; T. R. Snavely to James Dillard [1917], File No. 13/65, Files-USDL, RG 174. Southerners were not the only people to charge that the migration was a conspiracy on the part of a group of northern whites. Democrats in Cleveland, Chicago, three cities in southern Illinois (East St. Louis, Cairo, and Danville), and elsewhere claimed that the Republicans had "colonized" blacks so as to inflate the Republican vote in 1916; see Kusmer, *A Ghetto Takes Shape*, 176; Rudwick, *Race Riot at East St. Louis*, 7–15; Chicago *Daily News*, October 17–19 and November 14, 1916.

24. *Defender*, August 12, 1916, April 6, 1918; USDL, *Negro Migration*, 62–63; New Orleans *Item*, March 23, [1917?], reprint in Box 87, Series 6, NULR. On the enforcement of Jacksonville's ordinance, see Jerrell H. Shofner, "Florida and the Black Migration," *Florida Historical Quarterly* 57, no. 3 (January 1979): 270–71. The origins of the various statutory prohibitions against the recruitment of labor in southern states is carefully detailed in Cohen, "Involuntary Servitude," 33–39.

25. *Defender*, September 30, 1916; Montgomery *Advertiser*, September 20, 1916, reprint in Box 86, Series 6, NULR.

26. Montgomery *Advertiser*, September 20, 1916, reprint in Box 86, Series 6, NULR; Johnson, "Labor Agents," 1, and "Efforts to Check the Movement," 1, both in "Draft," NULR.

27. New Orleans *Item*, March 23, [1917?], Box 87, Series 6, NULR; Richard W. Edmonds, "The Negro Exodus: Will It Be Permanent," *Manufacturers Record* 85, no. 16 (April 17, 1924): 77–78; "Exodus Costing State $27,000,000," 51.

28. Reprint of letter from an anonymous Mississippi minister to William Pickens, printed in Baltimore *Afro-American*, January 26, 1919, Box 86, Series 6, NULR; Johnson, "Greenwood," 2: 1, "Mississippi Summary," NULR.

29. Edward C. Niles to Warren G. Harding, June 12, 1919; John R. Shillady to Walker D. Hines, June 16, 1919; Max Thelen to Hines, June 21, 1919; Hines to Edward Chambers, July 3, 1919; W. T. Taylor to Hines, July 3, 1919; Walter White to Clyde B. Aitchison, July 27, 1920; all in File P 19–3, Box 114, File of the Director General, U.S. Railroad Administration, RG 14, WNRC; National Association for the Advancement of Colored People, *Tenth Annual Report for the Year 1919* (New York, 1920), 44; *Defender*, December 30, 1922; Johnson, "Jackson, Mississippi," 2, "Mississippi Summary," NULR.

30. Junius B. Wood, *The Negro in Chicago* (Chicago, 1916), 9; Scott, *Negro Migration*, 73; *Defender*, August 26, 1916; Johnson, "General," 1, "Mississippi Summary," NULR. The quotation is from Scott, "Additional Letters," 451. This kind of obstructionism was hardly new in the South. On the persecution of black southerners who announced plans to go to Africa, see Redkey, *Black Exodus*, 88, 112–13; on police dispersing departing groups of blacks from train stations during a migration from Georgia to Mississippi in 1899–1900, see Holmes, "Labor Agents," 445–46.

31. "Resolution Adopted by Agricultural Bureau of the New Orleans As-

sociation of Commerce, May 23, 1919," Box 413, Entry 359, Service and Information Branch, RG 165; John T. Watkins to W. B. Wilson, July 14, 1917, File 8/102; "Memorandum on Exodus of Negroes From the South," [1917], File 13/65; J. S. Cullinan to W. B. Wilson, June 26, 1917, File 8/102; all in Files-USDL, RG 174; Arthur Woods to Newton Baker, [April 22, 1919?], Box 600, Service and Information Branch, RG 165; William C. Fitts to War Labor Policies Board, May 18, 1918; F. R. Bissell [President of Texas Portland Cement Company] to Senator Morris Sheppard, November 7, 1918; Adams Calhoun to Felix Frankfurter, June 12, 1918, all in Box 31, WLPB, RG 1.

32. William C. Fitts to War Labor Policies Board, May 18, 1918; Memo titled "Harmful Newspaper Advertising," June 20, [1918]; Adams Calhoun to Felix Frankfurter, June 12, 1918, all in Box 31, WLPB, RG 1.

33. Johnson, "The Call of the North," 2, "Draft," NULR; U.S. Department of Labor *Reports of the Department of Labor*, 1917 (Washington, D.C., 1918), 79–80; Albon Holsey to Robert R. Moton, June 19, 1918, Box 1, Scott Papers, Department of War, RG 407.

34. William B. Wilson to Newton D. Baker, July 16, 1917, File 8/102, Files-USDL, RG 174. See also Wilson to J. T. Watkins, July 17, 1917, in same file. In general the Department of Labor's files during this period indicate that the department was an exception to the Wilson administration's hostility—or indifference at best—toward blacks. Secretary Wilson and Assistant Secretary Post seem to have been especially reluctant to accede to pressures to dissolve the Division of Negro Economics and to act positively to halt the migration. On attempts to convince Chicago black veterans to return South, see folder marked "Employment of Negro Ex-Servicemen," Box 600, Entry 352, Service and Information Branch, RG 165.

35. J. S. Cullinan to William B. Wilson, June 26, 1917, File 8/102, Files-USDL, RG 174; "Resolution Adopted by Agricultural Bureau of the New Orleans Association of Commerce, May 23, 1919," Box 413, Entry 359, Service and Information Branch, RG 165; William C. Fitts to War Labor Policies Board, May 18, 1918, Box 31, WLPB, RG 1.

36. [Felix Frankfurter?], "Memorandum for the Secretary," June 12, 1918, Box 31, WLPB, RG 1. For referrals, see J. S. Cullinan to William B. Wilson, June 26, 1917, File 8/102, Files-USDL, RG 174; "Resolution Adopted by Agricultural Bureau of the New Orleans Association of Commerce, May 23, 1919," Box 413, Entry 359, Service and Information Branch, RG 165; William C. Fitts to War Labor Policies Board, May 18, 1918, Box 31, WLPB, RG 1. On the activities of Woods, see Colonel Arthur Woods to Major John B. Reynolds, April 22, 1919, Box 600, Entry 352; Woods to Reynolds, May 9, 1919, Box 422, Entry 349; "Employment of Ex-Servicemen," Box 600, Entry 352; all in Service and Information Branch, RG 165. For complaints, see William C. Fitts to War Labor Policies Board, May 18, 1918; Adams Calhoun to Felix Frankfurter, June 12, 1918; both in Box 31, WLPB, RG 1.

37. "Weekly Reports of Activities Undertaken By State Councils: Activities Initiated By State Councils," February 11-September 30, 1918, folder marked "State Activities," Box 862, Series 15-A4, RG 62, Correspondence of the U.S. Council of National Defense, Field Division, WNRC; Unidentified

news clipping, June 30 [1917 or 1918], Series 6, Box 86, NULR. For southern manipulation of Wilson's "Work or Fight" order to force some blacks into virtual peonage, see NAACP press release, September 24, 1918, July–Sept. 1918 folder, Box C-319, NAACP; John D. Finney, "A Study of Negro Labor during and after World War I" (Ph.D. dissertation, Georgetown University, 1967), 203–6.

38. Scott, "Additional Letters," 412; *Defender*, August 9, 1919; Johnson, "Efforts to Check the Movement," 3, "Draft," NULR. See also Scott, "Letters," 334–35.

39. Bolton Smith to George E. Haynes, September 16, 1918, File 8/102, Files-USDL, RG 174; Macon *Telegraph*, quoted in "The Looking Glass," *Crisis* 12, no. 6 (October 1916): 291.

40. Montgomery *Advertiser*, [1917?], reprinted in Box 86, Series 6, NULR; "Voice of the Press on Migration of Negroes to the North," *AME Review* 33, no. 3 (January 1917): 130; Atlanta *Constitution*, quoted in Henri, *Black Migration*, 54; Atlanta *Constitution*, quoted in New York *Age*, December 14, 1916, clipping in Arthur W. Mitchell Papers, Folder 1, Box 1, CHS.

41. Scott, *Negro Migration*, 154–55; "Voice of the Press on Migration of Negroes to the North," 130; "The Looking Glass," *Crisis* 13, no. 4 (February 1917): 179–81. See also articles in folder marked "Migration Study, Newspaper Extracts, 1916–1917," Box 86, Series 6, NULR; Henri, *Black Migration*, 75; Scott, *Negro Migration*, 20, 59–60; "Will the South Lose by the Negro Migration Now Underway," *Manufacturers Record* 83, no. 21 (May 24, 1923): 68.

42. NAACP, *Tenth Annual Report for 1919*, 24; Woodson, *Century of Negro Migration*, 177; Atlanta *Constitution*, quoted in Ottley, *Lonely Warrior*, 164; Macon *Telegraph*, n.d., quoted in "The Looking Glass," *Crisis* 12, no. 6 (October 1916): 291; "Current Comment," *The Freeman* 7, no. 176 (July 25, 1923): 457. See also Atlanta *Constitution*, December 14, 1916, reprint in Box 87, Series 6, NULR.

43. New York *Age*, December 14, 1916, clipping in Folder 1, Box 1, Mitchell Papers; Homer W. Borst to George E. Haynes, June 27, 1917, Folder 10, Box 1, George Edmund Haynes Papers, Fisk; Johnson, "Greenwood," 2: 2–3, "Mississippi Summary," NULR.

44. Albany *Herald*, quoted in "Current Comment," *Freeman* 7, no. 176 (July 25, 1923): 457; Frank Andrews to Gov. Theodore J. Bilbo, June 26, 1917, "Migration Letters," NULR; USDL, *Negro Migration*, 25; "The Looking Glass," *Crisis* 12, no. 6 (October 1916): 291; Montgomery *Advertiser*, October 4, 1916, reprint in Box 86, Series 6, NULR.

45. W. W. Alexander, "The Negro Migration," *The Christian Index* 103, no. 23 (June 14, 1923): 6–8.

46. USDL, *Negro Migration*, 17, 23, 25; Johnson, "Greenville," 2, "Mississippi Summary," NULR; H. A. Turner, "Labor Management on some Plantations in the Yazoo-Mississippi Delta" (1916), 2, typescript in Box 85, Series 133, OFM-BAE, RG 83; Monroe Work, "Effects of the War on Southern Labor," *Southern Workman* 47, no. 8 (August 1918): 382; U.S. Department of Agriculture, *Yearbook*, 1925 (Washington, D.C., 1926), 1344.

47. Dittmer, *Black Georgia*, 191; Johnson, "Vicksburg," 5, "Mississippi Summary," NULR.

48. *Negro Farmer and Messenger*, May 5, 1917; Sisk, "Negro Migration in the Alabama Black Belt," 34; U.S. Bureau of Education, *Report of the Commissioner of Education*, 1919 (Washington, D.C., 1920), 197; Hastings Hart, "Rising Standards in the Treatment of Negroes" [1922], 2, typescript in Folder 4, Box 6, Rosenwald Papers.

49. *Advertiser* quoted in "The Looking Glass," *Crisis* 13, no. 4 (February 1917): 179; USDL, *Negro Migration*, 60; P. O. Davis, "Negro Exodus and Southern Agriculture," 401–4.

50. Hugh H. Ellis to Birmingham *News*, August 1, 1917, in Migration Letters, NULR; Houston *Post*, quoted in "The Exodus," *Half-Century Magazine* 3, no. 3 (September 1917): 9; New Orleans *States*, July 24, 1916, reprint in Box 86, Series 6, NULR. See also Nashville *Banner*, November 4, 1916, reprint in folder marked "Migration Study, Newspaper Extracts, 1916–1917," Box 86, Series 6, NULR. Other articles in this folder suggest similar sentiments.

51. Quoted in Locke, "The New Negro," in Locke, ed., *The New Negro*, 12.

52. See for instance, Montgomery *News*, [1916 or 1917], reprint in Box 86, Series 6, NULR; Atlanta *Constitution*, quoted in Henri, *Black Migration*, 54; Moses, "Negro Comes North," 185–86; Rev. John M. Moore, "The Migration of the Negro from the Standpoint of the South," *Eleventh Annual Meeting of the Home Missions Council* (January 1918): 24.

53. Johnson, "Jackson, Mississippi," 6, "Mississippi Summary," NULR.

54. Johnson, "Greenwood," 2: 2–3, "Mississippi Summary," NULR. See also *State Conference Issues Important Address to the Honorable Members of the State Legislature and the White Citizenry of Georgia* [Atlanta?, 1923?], 4–9; "Exodus Costing State $27,000,000," 51.

55. Memphis *Commercial Appeal*, October 5, 1916, reprint in Box 86, Series 6, NULR; "Governor McLeod of South Carolina on Negro Migration," *Manufacturers Record* 84, no. 12 (September 20, 1923): 77.

56. Clipping from Birmingham *Age-Herald*, March 21, 1917, Folder 1, Box 1, Mitchell Papers.

57. *Defender*, October 13, 1917; Johnson, "Greenwood," 2: 2–3, "Mississippi Summary," NULR.

58. Johnson, "Efforts to Check the Movement," 3, "Draft," NULR; Robert E. Jones to Robert E. Park, March 2, 1917, Box 10, Woodson Collection; Johnson, "Interviews," 5, NULR. Fear of blacks freezing to death in the North was not new. In 1801 Thomas Jefferson abandoned the idea of colonizing blacks on the northern borders of the U.S. partly because he "doubted that the black race would live in such a rigorous climate"; see Woodson, *Century of Negro Migration*, 10. On the 1917 East St. Louis riots, see Rudwick, *Race Riot at East St. Louis*.

59. USDL, *Negro Migration*, 36; "How the War Brings Unprophesied Opportunities to the Negro Race," *Current Opinion* 61 (December 1916): 404; *Defender*, April 20, 1918. On Darwinian aspects of white attitudes, see Fredrickson, *Black Image in the White Mind*, 228–55.

60. Johnson, "Mound Bayou and Bolivar Co.," 4, "Mississippi Summary," NULR; Johnson, "Efforts to Check the Movement," 3, "Draft," NULR; Chicago *Whip*, November 6, 1920.

61. Johnson, "Jackson, Mississippi," 6, and "Greenwood," 2: 2, "Mississippi Summary," NULR. On Perry Howard, see Neil R. McMillen, "Perry W. Howard, Boss of Black-and-Tan Republicanism in Mississippi, 1924–1960," *Journal of Southern History* 48, no. 2 (May 1982): 205–24.

62. "Editorial Column," *Negro Advocate* (New Orleans) 3, no. 9 (August, 1920): 1–3; *Defender*, August 19, 1916; Unidentified Council of National Defense memo to Southern State Councils, n.d., "Negroes" folder, Box 859, Series 15-A4, Records of the Council of National Defense, RG 62, WNRC; Atlanta *Constitution*, April 24, 1917, clipping in Monroe Work Clipping File, Hollis Burke Frissell Library, Tuskegee Institute, Tuskegee, Ala. (I am indebted to John Vernon for a copy of this clipping). See also Kelly Miller, "The Farm the Negro's Best Chance," *Manufacturers Record* 90, no. 5 (August 5, 1926): 96–97; Memphis *Commercial Appeal*, 1917, cited in "The Exodus Train," 8, IWP, "Negro in Illinois" (I overlooked this particular document and am indebted to William Tuttle for providing me with a photocopy of it); folder marked "Migration Study, Newspaper Extracts, 1916–1917," Box 87, Series 6, NULR; Speech by Robert Moton, reported in *Negro Farmer and Messenger*, May 5, 1917.

63. Letters regarding Secretary of Labor Wilson's appointment of an advisor on "Negro labor," in late February 1918, File 8/102a, Files-USDL, RG 174; Finney, "Negro Labor," 141–42; *Defender*, April 5, 1919.

64. *Defender*, April 5, 1919; CCRR, *Negro in Chicago*, 88–89.

65. Montgomery *Advertiser*, October 4, [1916 or 1917], reprint in Box 87, Series 6, NULR; *Negro Farmer and Messenger*, October 21, August 12, October 7, November 18, 1916; February 10, May 5, 1917.

66. Speech by Isaiah J. Whitley, Mt. Vernon, Alabama, September 19, 1916, quoted in Montgomery *Advertiser*, September 20, 1916, reprint in Box 86, Series 6, NULR; *Negro Farmer and Messenger*, October 7, 1916; J. D. Davis to Columbus, Ga., *Enquirer-Sun*, December 17, 1916, in Migration Letters, NULR; Percy H. Stone, "Negro Migration," *Outlook* 116 (August 1, 1917): 520–21.

67. Jacksonville *Times-Union*, August 6, 1916, quoted in Shofner, "Florida and the Black Migration," 269; "Resolutions, etc. of Negro Bodies," 1–2, reprinted from Montgomery *Advertiser*, December 11, 1916; New Orleans *Times-Picayune*, December 9, 1916, both reprints in Box 87, Series 6, NULR; Johnson, "Interviews," 5, NULR; *Defender*, October 21, 1916. See also Dittmer, *Black Georgia*, 190–91. For opposition to migration voiced by Dr. J. H. Mason, president of the Colored Alabama Baptist State Association, see Birmingham *Age-Herald*, September 25, 1916, reprint in Box 86, Series 6, NULR.

68. *Negro Population*, 568–74; see also Wright, *Old South, New South*, 103–6; Manning Marable, "The Politics of Black Land Tenure, 1877–1917," *Agricultural History* 53, no. 1 (January 1979): 142–52.

69. Washington, "Rural Negro and the South," 127. For different perspectives on turn-of-the century yeoman ideology, see Richard Hofstadter, *The Age of Reform from Bryan to F.D.R.* (New York, 1955), 23–59; and Steven Hahn, *The Roots of Southern Populism: Yeoman Farmers and the Transformation of the Georgia Upcountry, 1850–1890* (New York, 1983).

70. Emmett J. Scott, "The Negro and the South After the War" (Address to the Tuskegee Negro Conference, Tuskegee, Ala., January 23, 1919), Box 1, Scott Papers, Department of War, RG 407; "Colored Labor Moves to North," *LaFollette's Magazine* 15, no. 5 (May 1923): 78; Speech by Moton quoted in Atlanta *Constitution*, April 24, 1917, Monroe Work Clipping File, Tuskegee; R[obert] R. Moton to E. T. M. Meredith, August 6, 1920; Meredith to Moton, August 21, 1920; both in "Negroes, Labor," file, U.S. Department of Agriculture, Files of the Secretary of Agriculture, RG 16, NA (I am indebted to John Vernon for providing copies of these letters); Charles Banks to Jackson *News*, June 12, 1917, reprint in Box 86, Series 6, NULR. For a similar view, see George E. Haynes to R. H. Leavell, January 13, 1921, Box 184, DNE-USDL, RG 174. On Charles Banks, see Crockett, *Black Towns*, 124–27.

71. Miller, "Farm the Negro's Best Chance," 96–97; *Method: The Magazine of Negro Business* (Richmond, Va.) 1, no. 1 (December 1920), Box 184, DNE-USDL, RG 174; *Negro Farmer and Messenger*, August 12, 1916; Sutton E. Griggs, *The Negro's Next Step* (Memphis, 1923), 29–30.

72. Birmingham *Weekly Voice*, December 2, 1916, reprint in Box 10, Woodson Collection, LC. See clipping from Montgomery *Advertiser*, n.d., Box C-373, Group 1, NAACP, for indication that "most" southern black newspapers supported the migration. William Cohen, after a more careful survey, concluded that they were "divided." See William Cohen, "The Great Migration: The Lure of the North," 404 (unpublished ms., n.d., copy in possession of author).

73. "Voice of the Press on Migration of Negroes to the North," 131; Joseph C. Manning to New York *Sun*, January 15, 1917, reprint in Box 86, Series 6, NULR; *Christian Recorder*, August 17, 31, 1916, reprints in Box 10, Woodson Collection; "The Exodus," 149–51; Editorial, *Crisis* 12, no. 6 (October 1916): 270. On the *Defender*, see chapter 3.

74. W. E. B. Du Bois, "Brothers, Come North," *Crisis* 19, no. 3 (January 1920): 105–6; *Southwestern Christian Advocate*, December 7, 1916, reprint in Box 86, Series 6, NULR.

75. William Cohen's survey of black southern newspapers convinced him that "virtually all" of them used the exodus as a bargaining point. Cohen, "Lure," 404–9.

76. NAACP Press Release, June 1, 1923, Box C-373, Group 1, NAACP; Wright quoted in Reverdy Ransom, "The Voice of the Press on the Negro Exodus From the South," *AME Church Review* 34, no. 1 (July 1917): 21–22. For a similar sentiment, see Editorial *Crisis* 12, no. 6 (October 1916), 270.

77. Linda McMurry, *Recorder of the Black Experience: A Biography of Monroe Nathan Work* (Baton Rouge, 1985), 81–82.

78. T. W. Coffee to Birmingham *Ledger*, [c.1917], and editorial in Atlanta *Independent*, May 19, 1917; both reprints in Box 86, Series 6, NULR; Atlanta *Independent*, May 26, 1917, reprint in Box 10, Woodson Collection; editorial in Atlanta *Independent*, December 2, 1916, reprint in Box 86, Series 6, NULR; Testimony of George H. Murray, General Counsel for the Colored American Council (Washington, D.C.), *Return of the Railroads to Private Ownership*, Hearings on H.R. 4378, Part 12, 66th Cong., 1st sess., U.S. House of Representa-

tives, Committee on Interstate and Foreign Commerce, 1919, p. 2018. On
T. W. Coffee, see Allen W. Jones, "Alabama," in Henry L. Suggs, ed., *The
Black Press in the South, 1865–1979* (Westport, Conn., 1983), 33–34, 42–43.

79. Draft of letter from Arthur Mitchell (Principal of Armstrong Agricultural and Industrial Institute in West Butler, Ala.) to Birmingham *Ledger*, September 5, 1916, Folder 1, Box 1, Mitchell Papers; excerpt of letter from
R[obert] R. Moton to President Woodrow Wilson, June 15, 1918, Folder 3, Box
53, Rosenwald Papers; Speech by Robert R. Moton, quoted in New York *Age*,
June 7, 1917, Monroe Work Clipping File, Tuskegee; "Professor Moton of
Tuskegee on Negro Question," *Manufacturers Record* 73, no. 22 (May 31, 1923):
53; William Jones to Montgomery *Advertiser*, September 19, 1916, reprint in
Box 86, Series 6, NULR. See also *Minutes of the University Commission on
Southern Race Questions*, Eighth Meeting, August 30, 1917 [Charlottesville,
Va.], 42.

80. See, for example, Monroe N. Work, "The South's Labor Problem,"
South Atlantic Quarterly 19 (January 1920): 4–8.

81. McMurry, *Recorder of the Black Experience*, 64.

82. For an exception, see anonymous black minister to Montgomery *Advertiser*, n.d., quoted in an early draft of the report of the Chicago Commission on Race Relations, "Housing" section [1921], 4, in Victor Lawson Papers,
Newberry Library, Chicago. Although this letter is quoted in the published
edition of CCRR, *Negro in Chicago*, 80–81, the section which deals with "land
monopoly" in the South was excised.

83. Editorial from the Atlanta *Independent*, December 2, 1916, reprint in
Box 86, Series 6, NULR; Atlanta *Independent*, December 16, 1917, reprint in
Box 87, Series 6, NULR. For a good survey of newspaper opinion on the
migration, see the excerpts compiled by Emmett Scott in these two boxes.

84. Speech by Robert R. Moton, quoted in New York *Age*, June 7, 1917, in
Work Clipping File; John Hope, "The Migration From the Standpoint of the
Negro," *Eleventh Annual Meeting of the Home Missions Council* (New York, Janu-
ary 1918): 26–29; John Hope to W. T. B. Williams, November 1, 1919, "1917"
Folder, Box 6, W. T. B. Williams Mss., Tuskegee (I am indebted to John
Vernon for providing a copy of this letter and the quotation from the Moton
speech.). For these leaders' access to white publications, see for example,
"Resolutions, etc. of Negro Bodies," 3, reprinted from the Atlanta *Constitution*, January 2, 1917; Wellborn V. Jenkins to Atlanta *Constitution*, [c. 1916],
both reprints in Box 87, Series 6, NULR; T. W. Coffee to Birmingham *Ledger*,
[c. 1917], reprint in Box 86, Series 6, NULR; "Professor Moton of Tuskegee
on Negro Question," *Manufacturers Record* 73, no. 22 (May 31, 1923): 53; Report of "Negro Baptist Ministers and vicinity" meeting in Memphis *Commercial Appeal*, December 29, 1917, reprint in Box 86, Series 6, NULR. For an
example of a degree of success in using this leverage, see Carl V. Harris,
"Stability and Change in Discrimination Against Black Public Schools: Birmingham, Alabama, 1871–1931," *Journal of Southern History* 51, no. 3 (August
1985): 375–416.

85. T. W. Coffee to Birmingham *Ledger*, [c. 1917], reprint in Box 86, Series
6, NULR; Wellborn V. Jenkins to Atlanta *Constitution* [c. 1916], reprint in Box
87, Series 6, NULR.

86. Sweeney quoted in "Exodus Train," 7, 9, IWP, "Negro in Illinois"; Isaac Fisher, "Do Not Rock the Boat," *Fisk University News* 8, no. 1 (October 1917): 5. See also, 3306 S. Liberty St., New Orleans to *Christian Recorder*, September 20, 1917, reprint in Box 86, Series 6, NULR. In Tampa, Florida, a minister preached against the movement; he was stabbed the next day. Although I am reluctant to assume the causative relationship offered in USDL, *Negro Migration*, 95, it is possible that the attack constituted a particularly angry response to opposition to the popular movement.

87. Fisher, "Do Not Rock the Boat," 4–5; USDL, *Negro Migration*, 36; W. J. Edwards to Montgomery *Advertiser*, January 27, 1917, Migration Letters, NULR; Isaac West to William McAdoo, September 10, 1918, File E-31-11, Vol. 1, Box E 51, Records of the Division of Labor, U.S. Railroad Administration, RG 14, NA. See also Painter, *Exodusters*, for a similar analysis of leadership during the Exodus to Kansas in 1879.

88. W. E. B. Du Bois, "The Migration of Negroes," *Crisis* 14, no. 2 (June 1917): 66; John Hope to W. T. B. Williams, November 1, 1919, "1921" Folder, Box 6, W. T. B. Williams Mss., Tuskegee (I am indebted to John Vernon for this quotation.); USDL, *Negro Migration*, 95.

89. *Southwestern Christian Advocate*, March 9, 1918, reprint in Box 86, Series 6, NULR; clipping from Birmingham *Age-Herald*, March 21, 1917, in Folder 1, Box 1, Mitchell Papers; Folder marked "Migration Study, Newspaper Extracts, 1916–1917," Box 87, Series 6, NULR; *Minutes of the University Commission on Race Questions* (1917), 42. For the consensus that the migration was "leaderless," see Tuttle, *Race Riot*, 93.

Chapter 3

1. Johnson, "Interviews," 2–3, NULR; CCRR, *Negro in Chicago*, 176.

2. Johnson, "Interviews," 15, NULR.

3. Ibid., 3; *Defender*, March 10, 1917; Scott, *Negro Migration*, 40.

4. See for example, Scott, "Additional Letters," 458; Johnson, "Interviews," NULR; Johnson, "The Mississippi Colony in Chicago," 2, "Draft," NULR.

5. Historians have generally accepted the contemporary image of a leaderless movement, probably because the established, nationally and regionally recognized movement was so opposed. Although accepting Charles Johnson's "leaderless" emphasis, William Tuttle has suggested the contours of the network which provided the movement's organizational framework. Allan Spear argued that the movement developed "a certain coherence," which he did not explain before accepting a contemporary description of migrants stealing away "without taking their recognized leaders into their confidence." Florette Henri refers to "new leaders" encouraging migration, but fails to discuss that new leadership. See Tuttle, *Race Riot*, 93–94; Spear, *Black Chicago*, 137–38; Henri, *Black Migration*, 79–80. The concept of a migration "network" was first suggested to me by Tuttle; for a similar analysis of migration networks leading black southerners to Pittsburgh, see Gottlieb, *Making Their Own Way*, 39–59.

6. Bethel, *Promiseland*, 185; Scott, "Additional Letters," 439; Johnson, "In-

terviews," 7; Scott, "Letters," 297, 295. On returnees from Kansas, see Henri, *Black Migration*, 2–3.

7. Scott, "Letters," 296.

8. Johnson, "Beginning of the Exodus of 1916–1917," 1, 3–4, 6, "Draft," NULR; Scott, *Negro Migration*, 38–39, 53–55; Johnson, *Negro in American Civilization*, 27; Cohen, "Lure," 334.

9. Johnson, "Labor Agents," 1–2, "Draft"; "Interviews," 1; "Jackson, Mississippi," 1, "Mississippi Summary," NULR. See also clipping from Birmingham *Age-Herald*, March 21, 1917, Folder 1, Box 1, Mitchell Papers. For evidence of northern agents recruiting in Jacksonville, Florida, see Shofner, "Florida and the Black Migration," 270–71. On recruitment of workers in industries in East Tennessee, but otherwise "spontaneous and unorganized" migration from that state, see Lamon, *Black Tennesseans*, 126.

10. Johnson, "Natchez," 1, "Mississippi Summary," NULR. See also Scroggs, "Interstate Migration of Negro Population," 1037; Donald, "Negro Migration of 1916–1918," 395; William C. Fitts to War Labor Policies Board, May 18, 1918, Box 31, WLPB, RG 1.

11. Gottlieb, *Making Their Own Way*, 43–45, 55–59; Bodnar, et al., *Lives of Their Own*, 190; Trotter, *Black Milwaukee*, 46. Congressional hearings investigating the 1917 riot in East St. Louis turned up little actual evidence of black migrants carried north by labor agents; see Rudwick, *Race Riot at East St. Louis*, 20, 167–70. The extent to which a city was known to black southerners was probably a crucial variable in the extent to which that city's industrial employers sent recruiters south. On the activities of labor agents from Philadelphia, see Allen B. Ballard, *One More Day's Journey: The Story of a Family and a People* (New York, 1984), 185.

12. *Defender*, August 5, September 9, November 11, 1916; Forrest McDonald, *Insull* (Chicago, 1962), 192. See also Wood, *Negro in Chicago*, 10, for evidence of recruitment in the South by Chicago's packinghouse firms.

13. Johnson, "Labor Agents," 1, "Draft," NULR; CCRR, *Negro in Chicago*, 103, 363–64.

14. Scott, "Letters," 321, 323; see also pp. 319–28. On men who returned home and after "several" days, "disappeared with a string of . . . friends," see Johnson, "Stimulation of the Movement," 21, "Draft," NULR.

15. Scott, "Additional Letters," 417; Johnson, "Interviews," 4, NULR; Scott, "Letters," 329. For evidence of agents in *Defender*, see, for example, November 18, 1916, March 24, 1917.

16. Johnson, "Stimulation of the Movement," 5, "Draft," NULR.

17. Scott, "Additional Letters," 415; Johnson, "Interviews," 23, NULR; *Defender*, September 7, 1918, May 12, 1917. Cassani was in fact arrested, but for enticing labor out of the state rather than for fraud. I have presumed that his pitch was a swindle because of the outrageous wages he was promising. Starting daily wages in most Chicago area steel mills were three to four dollars at this time, and it is unlikely that completely inexperienced recruits could have earned significantly more than this.

18. Johnson, "Gulfport," 2, "Mississippi Summary," NULR; Johnson, "Stimulation of the Movement," 5, "Draft," NULR; CCRR, *Negro in Chicago*,

576; George E. Haynes to Felix Frankfurter, August 21, 1918, Box 27, WLPB, RG 1. Although Haynes characterized these stories as "wild rumors," there was some truth to them in some southern states. Albon Holsey and Monroe Work found "definite information which showed that there is a movement on foot to use this Government order [the "Work or Fight" order] referred to in the attached clipping as a means to force Negroes to work in the fields at prices at which the farmers will, themselves, decide upon." Albon Holsey to Robert R. Moton, June 19,1918, Box 1, Scott Papers, Department of War, RG 407.

19. Johnson, "Stimulation of the Movement," 4–5, "Draft," NULR.

20. Haynes, "Effect of War Conditions on Negro Labor," 304. Haynes uses the phrase "guiding hand of the labor agent" in describing the agents as crucial to the onset of migration. He implies that agents, not the migrants, were the actual decision makers in the migratory process. For an argument similar to mine about the migrants making their own decisions while using the resources provided by agents, see Gottlieb, *Making Their Own Way*, 57–59.

21. USDL, *Negro Migration*, 100; Johnson, "Jackson, Mississippi," 1, "Mississippi Summary," NULR; *Defender*, August 12, 1916; Lamon, *Black Tennesseans*, 126.

22. Fanny D. Davidson, Interview with Charles Liggett, May 17, 1937, Box 77, IWP, "Negro in Illinois"; Garnett L. Askew, Interview with Charley Banks, Chicago, April 14, 1939, Drawer 48–3, "Beliefs and Customs" folder, Works Progress Administration, Federal Writers Project, Project O.P. 165-2-26-7. Archive of Folk Song, LC; Johnson, "Interviews," 18–19, NULR.

23. Greene and Woodson, *Negro Wage Earner*, 100; Johnson, "Vicksburg," 4–5, "Mississippi Summary," NULR. On the hiring of black strikebreakers by the Illinois Central, see Sterling D. Spero and Abram L. Harris, *The Black Worker: The Negro and the Labor Movement* (New York, 1931; reprint, 1968), 308. For a discussion of the railroad network to Pittsburgh, see Gottlieb, *Making Their Own Way*, 42.

24. Oscar Hunter, "Negro Music in Chicago," 1940, p. 6, typescript in Box 84, IWP, "Negro in Illinois"; Johnson, "Stimulation of the Movement," 2, "Draft," NULR.

25. Ottley, *Lonely Warrior*, 6, 7, 87–88; Detweiler, *Negro Press in the United States*, 6; *Defender*, May 22, 1915, July 28, 1917. The impact on migrants to other cities is corroborated by the letters to the Detroit Urban League in Box 12, Woodson Collection; most give the *Defender* as their source of information. For Abbott's support of Booker T. Washington, see *Defender*, January 2, 1915. The *Defender*'s policy of using "Race" rather than "Negro" is indicated in *Defender*, January 30, 1915. Portions of the following discussion have been published as "Blowing the Trumpet: The Chicago *Defender* and Black Migration during World War I," *Illinois Historical Journal* 78, no. 2 (Summer 1985): 82–96.

26. *Defender*, May 20, 1916; July 1905 issue quoted in John W. Crawford, "A Brief History of Some Negro Newspapers in the United States With Special Reference to the *Chicago Defender*" (student paper, 1924), 10, Folder 11,

Box 1, Park Papers. See also *Defender*, February 12, March 18, April 8, 15, 29, 1916, September 22, 1917, June 8, 1918.

27. *Defender*, December 8, 1917. For *Defender* coverage of lynchings, see for instance, January 30, May 8, July 10, August 7, September 11, 1915; February 12, April 1, 8, 1916, May 12, 26, 1917.

28. *Defender*, April 29, May 6, 13, 20, 1916. The most sophisticated quantitative analysis of the relationship between lynching and migration is in Fligstein, *Going North*. See also Charles Johnson, "How the Negro Fits in Northern Industry," *Industrial Psychology* 1 (June 1926): 402–3; Johnson, "How Much of the Migration Was a Flight From Persecution," 273–75.

29. *Defender*, January 8, February 19, April 1, August 5, 1916; Charles Johnson, "Stimulation of the Movement," 13, "Draft," NULR. Sweeney's militance was probably more rhetorical than principled. A decade earlier he had been willing to fight Booker T. Washington's opponents on any issue . . . as long as money came from Tuskegee to subsidize his failing Chicago *Leader*, which collapsed in 1905 after less than two years. Sweeney to Emmett J. Scott, December 15, 1905, December 16, 1905; Scott to Sweeney, December 18, 1905; all in Booker T. Washington Papers, LC.

30. *Defender*, February 13, 1915. See also May 21, 1910, January 30, April 10, May 8, 1915; January 1, 1916; Crawford, "Brief History of Some Negro Newspapers," 12. See also *Defender*, January 30, 1915. The *Defender's* support of Pullman porters would prove less than steadfast. It opposed the fledgling Brotherhood of Sleeping Car Porters in 1925, subsequently reversing its position two years later, either because of pressure from its clientele or changing relations with the Pullman company. See William H. Harris, *Keeping the Faith: A. Philip Randolph, Milton P. Webster, and the Brotherhood of Sleeping Car Porters, 1925–1937* (Urbana, 1977), 46–48, 129–33.

31. *Defender*, February 13, September 25, 1915, October 28, November 25, · 1916, February 10, 1917; Ottley, *Lonely Warrior*, 133–39; Chicago *Defender* Shipping List, as of May 29, 1919, including "Standing Dealers List" and "New Names," File no. 10,218–133, MID File, RG 165. This list—the *Defender* shipping manifest—was obtained by Military Intelligence "in strictest confidence" from the *Defender's* distributor.

32. Ottley, *Lonely Warrior*, 133–39, 188, 190, 298; USDL, *Negro Migration*, 30; Scott, *Negro Migration*, 30; Charles Furthmann, "Report on Robert S. Abbott," June 3, 1919, File no. 10,218–133, MID File, RG 165; CCRR, *Negro in Chicago*, 524; James N. Simms, *Simms' Blue Book and National Negro Business and Professional Directory* (Chicago, 1923); Crawford, "Brief History of Some Negro Newspapers," 11 (Crawford's sources are L. C. Anderson of the *Defender* and a booklet published by the *Defender*); John Taitt, *The Souvenir of Negro Progress: Chicago, 1779–1925* (Chicago, 1925), 24. The *Defender* circulation can only be estimated, as its inflated claims must be balanced by guesses of observers. The figures I have presented show the range of estimates, with the upper limit invariably the *Defender's* claim. By comparison, the Baltimore *Afro-American* had a circulation of 18,916 in 1920. See *N. W. Ayer and Son's American Newspaper Annual and Directory* (Philadelphia, 1921), 205, for *Defender* circulation and 392 for *Afro-American* circulation. None of

the other black newspapers listed their circulation in this standard guide, and the *Defender* did begin only in the 1920 edition. The increase in *Defender* circulation during this period cannot be attributed completely to southern readership; the Great Migration expanded its clientele in Chicago and other northern cities.

33. Chicago Defender Shipping List, MID File, RG 165; Johnson, "Stimulation of the Movement," 6, "Draft," NULR, and "Laurel, Mississippi," 2, "Mississippi Summary," NULR.

34. Scott, *Negro Migration*, 30; Ottley, *Lonely Warrior*, 133–39; Walter F. White to Edmund Leigh, March 10, 1920, "Jan.-July, 1920" folder, Box C-319, NAACP; Detweiler, *Negro Press in the United States*, 7; *Defender*, November 4, 1916; CCRR, *Negro in Chicago*, 176. For subscription rates, see *Defender*, October 21, 1916.

35. Johnson, "Stimulation of the Movement," 7, "Draft," NULR; Scott, "Letters," 333; USDL, *Negro Migration*, 103.

36. Scott, "Letters," 327; W. A. McCloud to Editor of the Chicago Defender, December 28, 1916, Box 10, Woodson Collection; Scott, "Additional Letters," 449.

37. Moore, "Migration of the Negro from the Standpoint of the South," 23–24; USDL, *Negro Migration*, 30; Detweiler, *Negro Press in the United States*, 9; Scott, "Letters," 296. On the influence of southern whites on some black southern newspapers, see Frank A. Ross, "Internal Migration and Local Migration," (1925), 8, typescript in LSRM. For an analysis of the Savannah *Tribune* and Atlanta *Independent*, with an emphasis on the political ambitions of their editors, see John M. Mathews, "Black Newspapermen and the Black Community in Georgia, 1890–1930," *Georgia Historical Quarterly* 68, no. 3 (Fall 1984), 356–81.

38. *Defender*, January 2, 1915, January 29, September-November, 1916. For *Defender* stories on Jack Johnson, see e.g. February 20, March 27, April 3, July 17, August 14, 1915, January 1, March 11, 1916, July 6, November 9, 1918. On the "Famous Eighth," see June 24, July 1, 1916; the all-black regiment had a white commanding officer, a fact ignored in these articles. The photograph of Lindblom is in the April 7, 1917, edition.

39. *Defender*, January 16, February 13, July 3, 1915.

40. *Defender*, January 23, 1915.

41. *Defender*, January 23, March 27, October 30, 1915, January 8, 1916. See also *Defender*, February 27, April 17, 1915, January 1, February 12, March 4, 1916.

42. *Defender*, July 31, October 2, 1915, January 5, 1918; Wood, *Negro in Chicago*, 9; Thomas Philpott, *The Slum and the Ghetto: Neighborhood Deterioration and Middle-Class Reform, Chicago, 1880–1930* (New York, 1978), 148.

43. *Defender*, February 5, July 22, August 12, September 2, 1916; see also September 16, 1916. The *Defender's* policy shift is difficult to locate precisely, because of the poor condition of some of the Summer 1916 issues. The July 22 edition probably had a short editorial favoring migration—the editorial is only partly legible but seems to encourage the movement—and the next appearance of favorable editorial comment came on August 12, 1916. William

Cohen also sees this as probably the first encouragement of migration in the *Defender*, but notes that such an item might have been in an issue that is now unavailable or incomplete; see Cohen, "Lure," 369–70, 441.

44. *Defender*, August 12, September 16, 1916.

45. *Defender*, August 26, October 7, 1916, September 22, 1917. Highlighting southern racism to boost migration to a newspaper's community was hardly new to the black press; it was common among black journals that were essentially promotional devices for black towns in Kansas and Oklahoma between 1879 and 1915; see Crockett, *Black Towns*, 43.

46. *Defender*, October 7, 1916, February 10, 1917, May 4, 1918. See also *Defender*, November 1, 1919.

47. *Defender*, September 2, 1916, April 28, November 24, December 1, 1917, April 13, 1918.

48. Scott, "Additional Letters," 420, 437; Scott, "Letters," 293; *Defender*, August 9, 1919.

49. Scott, "Letters," 302, 320–28; Scott, "Additional Letters," 445, 449; Richard Wright, "The Chicago Urban League," (1936), 3–5, typescript in "Negro Studies" drawer, Folder 674, Works Progress Administration, Federal Writers Project O.P. 165-2-26-7, Archive of Folk Song, LC. See also Scott, "Letters," 291–92, 294–95; Scott, "Additional Letters," 416, 420–28, 435.

50. *Defender*, May 8, 1915, October 7, 1916, January 26, February 23, March 30, July 6, 1918; Johnson, "Interviews," 16, NULR.

51. *Defender*, June 23, August 4, 1917, November 2, 1918. This assessment of the American Giants is corroborated by the team's success on the field, where it won the Negro National League pennant from 1920 to 1922, the league's first three years in existence. See Peterson, *Only the Ball Was White*, 257–58.

52. Ottley, *Lonely Warrior*, 141–46; see, for example, Scott, "Additional Letters," 412–13; letters to Abbott in Box 10, Woodson Collection. Scott probably obtained letters from the Chicago Urban League, Woodson from Olivet Baptist Church.

53. Johnson, "Stimulation of the Movement," 6, 14, "Draft," NULR; Scott, "Additional Letters," 422, 426, 448.

54. *Defender*, November 18, 1916, March 10, March 31, April 7, 1917.

55. *Defender*, February 10, 1917; Scott, *Negro Migration*, 33; Scott, "Letters," 331–34; Johnson, "Stimulation of the Movement," 14a, "Draft," NULR; S. Adams to Bethlehem Baptist Association of Chicago, March 31, 1917, Box 10, Woodson Collection.

56. Henri, *Black Migration*, 79; Ottley, *Lonely Warrior*, 160.

57. Scott, "Additional Letters," 419–20; Johnson, "Interviews," 19–20, NULR; Johnson, "Stimulation of the Movement," 1, 3, "Draft," NULR; reprint of letter from a minister (name withheld) in Mississippi to William Pickens, printed in Baltimore *Afro-American*, January 26, 1919, Box 86, Series 6, NULR.

58. On chain migration, see June Granatir Alexander, "Staying Together: Chain Migration and Patterns of Slovak Settlement in Pittsburgh Prior to World War I," *Journal of Ethnic History* 1, no. 1 (Fall 1981): 56–83; Dino Cinel,

From Italy to San Francisco: The Immigrant Experience (Stanford, 1982), 26–27; Joseph Barton, *Peasants and Strangers: Italians, Rumanians and Slovaks in an American City, 1880–1950* (Cambridge, Mass., 1975); Gottlieb, *Making Their Own Way*, 47–52. For a more general presentation of the phenomenon, see J. S. Brown, H. K. Schwarzweller, and J. Mangalam, "Kentucky Mountain Migration and the Stem-family: An American Variation on a Theme by LePlay," in Clifford J. Jansen, ed., *Readings in the Sociology of Migration* (New York, 1970), esp. 111–20. Cinel presents chain migration and "organized" migration as opposing modes of migration, but his use of "organized" to refer to migration promoted from the outside differs from my use of the term to portray coherence and structure.

59. Johnson, "Interviews," 8, NULR; Scott, *Negro Migration*, 34; *Defender*, September 8, 1917; Johnson, "Early Manifestations of the Movement," 2, "Mississippi Summary," NULR; USDL, *Negro Migration*, 20, 27–28, 66; Johnson, "Jackson, Mississippi," 7, "Mississippi Summary," NULR.

60. Johnson, "Interviews," 4, NULR; Scott, "Additional Letters," 457–58; see also Scott, 454–55.

61. Scott, "Additional Letters," 459.

62. Johnson, "Interviews," 8, NULR.

63. *Defender*, February 3, 1917; USDL, *Negro Migration*, 29; Hurtsboro, Georgia, *Tribune*, [1916 or 1917], reprint in Box 87, Series 6, NULR; Johnson, "Stimulation of the Movement," 18, "Draft," NULR; Max Thelen to Walker Hines, June 21, 1919, File P 19–3, Box 114, File of the Director General, U.S. Railroad Administration, RG 14; "Exodus Costing State $27,000,000," 51.

64. Scott, "Additional Letters," 454–57; Johnson, "Interviews," 1, NULR. On similar letters from Poles preparing to leave for the United States and curious about wages, weather, and conditions, see for example, William I. Thomas and Florian Znaniecki, *The Polish Peasant in Europe and America*, 2d ed. (New York, 1927), 1: 319–20, 377. Unfortunately, I have not found enough letters *to* the South for proper comparison with this remarkable collection.

65. See, for example, Marcus Lee Hansen, *The Atlantic Migration* (Cambridge, Mass., 1944), 153–54; Kathleen N. Conzen, *Immigrant Milwaukee: Accommodation and Community in a Frontier City* (Cambridge, Mass., 1976), 37–38.

66. Johnson, "Interviews," 1, 21, NULR; Scott, *Negro Migration*, 34; Johnson, "Stimulation of the Movement," 18, "Draft," NULR. Of those interviewed by Johnson in Chicago in 1917, twenty-nine indicated their source of information about the North. Nine of them said letters were their primary source of information; and two more mentioned letters as a corroborative source; Johnson, "Interviews," NULR.

67. *Defender*, September 22, 1917; October 2, 1920; CCRR, *Negro in Chicago*, 268; G. W. Mitchell to James Weldon Johnson, June 30, 1923, Box C-373, Group 1, NAACP; Johnson, "Jackson, Mississippi," 1, "Mississippi Summary," NULR. The estimate of attendance at the exhibition, probably inflated, is from R. R. Jackson, a member of the commission that operated the exhibition, in *Defender*, September 18, 1915.

68. Chicago *Daily News*, September 7, 8, 1915, clippings in Box 39, IWP,

"Negro in Illinois"; *Defender*, May 4, 11, 18, 1918, August 19, 1916; Richard E. Moore, "The Great Masonic Conclave in Chicago," *Champion Magazine* 1, no. 2 (October 1916): 14–16; Taitt, *Souvenir of Negro Progress*, 45; "ANP [Associated Negro Press] News Releases," Box 1, Barnett Papers.

69. *Defender*, August 19, 1916.

70. USDL, *Negro Migration*, 24–25; Minutes of the Board of Directors [Report of the executive secretary], May 18, 1926, Young Men's Christian Association, Wabash Avenue Branch, Box 3, Papers of the Young Men's Christian Association, Wabash Avenue Branch, UIC; G. R. Wilson, "Mr. B and Miss X" [1921], Folder 14, Box 1, Park Papers; Tuskegee Institute Extension Department, *The Negro Rural School and Its Relation to the Community* (Tuskegee, 1915). For a good discussion of the status of teachers in a southern black community, see Bethel, *Promiseland*, 131–33. For a sampling of *Defender* notices of southerners visiting relatives in Chicago, see local columns in August 11, September 1, and November 24, 1917.

71. *Defender*, March 24, 1917; Robert McMurdy to W. F. Graves, December 30, 1912, Folder 7, Box 31, Rosenwald Papers. See also *Defender*, January 31, 1920.

72. *Defender*, February 20, 1915; January 27, 1917.

73. Johnson, "Gulfport," 2, "Mississippi Summary," NULR; *Defender*, March 10, 1917; Johnson, "Jackson, Mississippi," 7, "Mississippi Summary," and "Stimulation of the Movement," 20, "Draft," NULR. See also Beverly Robinson, Interview with Edith Wilson, May 19, 1977, Tape No. CH77-T097-C, in Interviews conducted for the Chicago Ethnic Arts Project, tapes deposited in American Folklife Center, LC. A week seldom passed without the *Defender's* southern correspondents acknowledging a Chicagoan returned home on family business; see, for example, *Defender*, February 24, 1917, March 3, 10, 17, 24, 1917, April 12, 1919. Bethel, *Promiseland*, 191–92, examines these visits from the perspective of a southern community.

74. Johnson, "Early Manifestations of the Movement," 5, "Mississippi Summary," NULR; Mahalia Jackson and Evan M. Wylie, *Movin' On Up* (New York, 1966), 41; Johnson, "Interviews," 4–5, NULR.

75. CCRR, *Negro in Chicago*, 103; Chicago Board of Education, *Sixty-Fifth Annual Report of the Superintendent of Schools for the Year Ending June 1919* (Chicago, 1919), 73. See also *Defender*, October 2, 1920.

76. CCRR, *Negro in Chicago*, 158, 162–65. On the importance of this flexibility and its role in internal migration within the South, see Jones, *Labor of Love, Labor of Sorrow*, 84.

77. Johnson, "The Spread of the Movement," 4–5, "Draft," NULR; Johnson, "Early Manifestations of the Movement," 6, "Mississippi Summary," NULR; Johnson, "Stimulation of the Movement," 5, "Draft," NULR.

78. *Defender*, June 9, 1917, March 24, 1917; Miles Mark Fisher, *The Master's Slave: Elijah John Fisher, a Biography* (Philadelphia, 1922), 179.

79. W. M. Agnew to Bethlehem Baptist Association, April 1, 1917, Box 10, Woodson Collection. See also Fred D. White to Bethlehem Baptist Association, March 26, 1917, and Cleveland Gailliard to Bethlehem Baptist Association, April 1, 1917, Box 10, Woodson Collection.

80. William H. Holloway, Response to Questionnaire on "Migration of Negroes to the North," [1917], Folder 17, Box 4, Haynes Papers.

81. Johnson, "Vicksburg," 1, "Mississippi Summary," NULR. For a description of this process by an investigator for the Chicago Commission on Race Relations, see Vattel Daniel, "Ritual in Chicago's South Side Churches for Negroes" (Ph.D. dissertation, University of Chicago, 1940), 12–13. A similar process among black migrants to Cleveland is documented in Kusmer, *A Ghetto Takes Shape*, 207–8. See also Scott, *Negro Migration*, 40.

82. Johnson, "Early Manifestations of the Movement," 1–3, "Mississippi Summary," NULR; Scott, *Negro Migration*, 26; Johnson, "Stimulation of the Movement," 1–2, "Draft," NULR.

83. Scott, "Additional Letters," 414, 417, 422, 424, 440–41, 444, 446–47, 451–52; Scott, "Letters," 305, 319–31; U.S. Bureau of the Census, *Negroes in the United States, 1920–1932*, 243.

84. Omah Spencer, "Jasper Taylor—Drummer," typescript in Box 95; "Music History," Boxes 84–85; O. Hunter, "Piano Boogie Woogie and Blues" (1940), 1, typescript in Box 87; all in IWP, "Negro in Illinois"; Gottlieb, *Making Their Own Way*, 25–26; Johnson, "Interviews," 11–12, NULR; Scott, *Negro Migration*, 45; Johnson, "Early Manifestations of the Movement," 4, "Mississippi Summary," NULR; Johnson, "Jackson, Mississippi," 1, NULR; B. B. Thomas to Olivet Baptist Church, April 1, 1917, Box 10, Woodson Collection.

85. Johnson, "Interviews," 1, NULR; *Defender*, March 24, 1917; Johnson, "Labor Agents," 3, 6, "Draft," NULR; Johnson, "Early Manifestations of the Movement," 1, "Mississippi Summary," NULR. See Levine, *Black Culture and Black Consciousness*, on the meaning and importance of oral communication in Afro-American tradition.

86. Allison Davis, Burleigh B. Gardner, and Mary R. Gardner, in their examination of black social life and social structure in the South during the 1930s, argue that the basic unit of social intercourse was the "clique." Within each clique there were people with links to people of higher status, and these people usually exercised leadership roles within the cliques. It is likely that many of the clubs were based in cliques, and that the organizers were people who exercised leadership roles within those cliques. See Allison Davis, Burleigh B. Gardner, and Mary R. Gardner, *Deep South: A Social Anthropological Study of Caste and Class* (Chicago, 1941), 208–27.

87. Johnson, "The Spread of the Movement," 5, "Draft," NULR; Johnson, "Jackson, Mississippi," 2, and "Early Manifestations of the Movement," 5, "Mississippi Summary," NULR. The popularity of the migration clubs is corroborated by a white railroad employee in MIssissippi, who reported that migrants generally "leave in parties." See "Memorandum on Exodus of Negroes from the South" [1917], typescript in File 13/65, Files-USDL, RG 174.

88. Johnson, "The Spread of the Movement," 5, "Draft," NULR; Scott, "Letters," 319–31; Johnson, "Jackson, Mississippi," 2, "Mississippi Summary," NULR; Johnson, "Interviews," 1–2, 6, 9, NULR.

89. Johnson, "Interviews," 1–2, 9, 20–21, NULR.

90. Ibid., 2.

Chapter 4

1. Johnson, "Interviews," 9–10, NULR.
2. Johnson, "Early Manifestations of the Movement," 1, "Mississippi Summary," NULR.
3. Scott, "Letters," 327; Scott, "Additional Letters," 442; Sisk, "Negro Migration in the Alabama Black Belt," 33; Fred Landon [City Librarian of London, Ontario] to George E. Haynes, September 6, 1919, Box 184, USDL-DNE, RG 174.
4. National Urban League, "Special Sleeping Car Party of Business Men" (New York, 1924), advertising leaflet in Folder 18, Box 27, Rosenwald Papers; Johnson, "Interviews," 13, NULR. See also Bethel, *Promiseland*, 183. On the presence of mail-order catalogues in southern black homes, see Lamon, *Black Tennesseans*, 112.
5. Chicago *Defender*, October 21, 28, November 4, 1916; Scott, "Additional Letters," 421.
6. *Defender*, July 7, 1917; Hattie L. Smith to Bethlehem Baptist Association, April 2, 1917, Box 10, Woodson Collection. For the Bethlehem Baptist Association advertisement, see *Defender*, March 24, 1917. For information regarding letters to the association, see S. Mattie Fisher, "Olivet as a Christian Center," *Missions* 10, no. 3 (March 1919): 199; and Miles Fisher, *The Master's Slave*, 179.
7. Johnson, "Letters," 2–3, "Mississippi Summary," NULR; James Pool to T. Arnold Hill, April 29, 1917, Box 86, Series 6, NULR; Scott, "Letters"; Scott, "Additional Letters."
8. Johnson, "Stimulation of the Movement," 2, "Draft"; "Interviews," 22; and "Early Manifestations of the Movement," 2, "Mississippi Summary," NULR.
9. Scott, *Negro Migration*, 38; Johnson, "Early Manifestations of the Movement," 3, "Mississippi Summary," NULR.
10. Johnson, "Early Manifestations of the Movement," 2, "Mississippi Summary," NULR; Johnson, "New Frontage on American Life," 281; *Defender*, March 24, 1917. See also Johnson, "Greenwood," 1, "Mississippi Summary," NULR.
11. *Defender*, August 12, 1916.
12. Scott, *Negro Migration*, 42–43. On fares, see Henri, *Black Migration*, 66.
13. [Alfreda Duster], "Unpublished biography of Ida B. Wells," ch. 9, p. 13, typescript in Folder 1, Box 3, Ida B. Wells Papers, JRL-UC; Scott, "Additional Letters," 429.
14. Scott, "Additional Letters," 453–54; Fisher, "Olivet as a Christian Center," 199.
15. Scott, "Additional Letters," 412, 428; see also Scott, 419–20, 426, 441–42, and passim.
16. Johnson, "Early Manifestations of the Movement," 6, "Mississippi Summary," NULR.
17. Johnson, "Greenwood," 2: 4–5, and "Jackson, Mississippi," 6, "Mississippi Summary," NULR.
18. Johnson, "Jackson, Mississippi," 5, 7; Johnson, "Gulfport," 2, "Mississippi Summary," NULR; Johnson, "Interviews," NULR. See also Wil-

liam H. Holloway, Response to Questionnaire on "Migration of Negroes to the North," [1917], Folder 17, Box 4, Haynes Papers; and Johnson, "Greenwood," 1, "Mississippi Summary," NULR.

19. Johnson, "Early Manifestations of the Movement," 5, "Jackson, Mississippi," 8, "Mississippi Summary," NULR. The quotation is from Sandburg, *Chicago Race Riots*, 11.

20. Bethel, *Promiseland*, 122; Scott, "Additional Letters," 447, 415. See also Scott, "Letters," 296.

21. *Daily News*, March 21, 1917; *Defender*, March 10, 1917, June 9, 1917. See also *Defender*, May 26, 1917, August 11, 1917, September 1, 1917; Elizabeth A. Hughes, *Living Conditions of Small-Wage Earners in Chicago* (Chicago, 1925), 11. Of the thirty Chicago families who provided interviewer Charles Johnson with the relevant information, only eleven had migrated as a unit. The other nineteen families had followed the husband who went North first. Johnson, "Interviews," NULR.

22. *Defender*, July 14, 1917; Johnson, "Interviews," and "Mississippi Summary," NULR; Bethel, *Promiseland*, 122–23; Scott, "Additional Letters," 434. Peter Gottlieb found similar kinship functions in his study of Pittsburgh; see Gottlieb, *Making Their Own Way*, 49–50.

23. USDL, *Negro Migration*, 75. On European immigrants, see for example, Virginia Yans-McLaughlin, *Family and Community: Italian Immigrants in Buffalo, 1880–1930* (Ithaca, 1977). For *Defender* notices mentioning departures of women going North to join husbands, see for example, March 10, May 26, June 9, August 11, September 1, 1917; see also Gottlieb, *Making Their Own Way*, 47–49. For the role of migration in providing a release valve for white and black families, see Joanne J. Meyerowitz, "Holding Their Own: Working Women Apart from Family in Chicago, 1880–1930" (Ph.D. dissertation, Stanford University,1983), 38–39; see also Bethel, *Promiseland*, 124.

24. Scott, "Additional Letters," 416; Scott, "Letters," 314. See also "Letters," 316–18.

25. Woofter, *Negro Migration*, 102–4; Johnson, "Early Manifestations of the Movement," 1, "Mississippi Summary," NULR.

26. Emmett J. Scott, "The Negro and the South After the War" (Address to the Tuskegee Negro Conference, Tuskegee, Alabama, January 23, 1919), Box 1, Scott Papers, Department of War, RG 407; Johnson, "Early Manifestations of the Movement," 1–2, "Mississippi Summary," NULR.

27. Scott, "Additional Letters," 454–55; Johnson, "Jackson, Mississippi," 5, "Greenwood," 1–2, and "General," 2, all in "Mississippi Summary," NULR.

28. Johnson, "The Spread of the Movement," 5, "Draft," NULR.

29. Johnson, "Interviews," 6, 14. For a description of "hill people" replacing migrants in towns see Johnson, "Clarksdale, Mississippi," 1, "Mississippi Summary," NULR.

30. B. B. Thomas to Olivet Baptist Church, April 1, 1917; Charles H. White to Forrester B. Washington, April 30, 1917, both in Box 10, Woodson Collection; Johnson, "Early Manifestations of the Movement," 4; "Jackson," 1, both in "Mississippi Summary," NULR.

31. Johnson, "Efforts to Check the Movement," 2, "Draft," NULR; John-

son, "Gulfport," 2, "Mississippi Summary," NULR; "Horizon," *Crisis*, 13, no. 2 (December 1916): 89. The sidetracking of a club of fifty migrants is described in Johnson, "Early Manifestations of the Movement," 5–6, "Mississippi Summary," NULR.

32. Johnson, "Peonage," 2, "Mississippi Summary," NULR; Ardis Harris, "Bronzeville, A City within a City" (1939), in IWP, "Negro in Illinois." I overlooked this particular document and am indebted to William M. Tuttle for providing me a photocopy of it. See also Levine, *Black Culture and Black Consciousness*, 265. The obligations of tenants did not necessarily—and in fact did not normally—imply a form of peonage, which involved impediments to even local movement that most black southerners did not face. See Daniel, *Shadow of Slavery*, 19–42.

33. Johnson, "Laurel, Mississippi," 2, "Mississippi Summary," NULR; Scott, "Additional Letters," 417; Scott, "Letters," 334–35; Johnson, "Jackson, Mississippi," 1, "Mississippi Summary," NULR; Johnson, "Interviews," 13, NULR. See also Wright, *Black Boy*, 221, 223–25; Charles Johnson to Robert E. Park, November 19, 1917, Folder G, Box 1, Park Papers. On secrecy among Liberia emigrationists, see Redkey, *Black Exodus*, 112–13.

34. *Defender*, November 18, 1916; Johnson, "Greenville," 1, "Mississippi Summary," NULR; Johnson, "Interviews," 9, NULR.

35. *Defender*, March 24, 1917; "Why Stand Ye Idle," clipping from unidentified southern newspaper identified only as "The Herald" [c. 1917], Migration Letters, NULR.

36. Levine, *Black Culture and Black Consciousness*, 262.

37. Langston Hughes, *The Big Sea: An Autobiography* (New York, 1945), 23.

38. Wright, *Black Boy*, 228; *Defender*, April 20, 1918.

39. Wright, *Black Boy*, 181; Chicago *Whip*, February 12, 1921; Gordon Parks, *A Choice of Weapons* (New York, 1966), 6–7.

40. Johnson, "Jackson, Mississippi," 9, "Mississippi Summary," NULR; USDL, *Negro Migration*, 53, 55; [John F. Merry], *About the South on Lines of the Illinois Central and Yazoo and Mississippi Valley* (Chicago, 1905), 40; see also *Defender*, December 30, 1922. Peter Gottlieb has argued that step migration was most likely among young, single males. See Gottlieb, *Making Their Own Way*, 43–47.

41. *Defender*, December 30, 1922; Charles Johnson to Robert Park, November 19, 1917, Folder 6, Box 1, Park Papers; Johnson, "Greenwood," 2, "Jackson, Mississippi," 5, "Greenville," 2, "Mound Bayou and Boliver Co.," 1, "Clarksdale, Mississippi," 1, all in "Mississippi Summary," NULR.

42. Johnson, "Gulfport," 2, "Mississippi Summary," NULR; Johnson, "Interviews," 1, NULR; Johnson, "The Course of the Movement," 1, "Draft," NULR. Most of the letters in the collection published by Emmett Scott (Scott, "Letters" and "Additional Letters") have datelines from southern cities or large towns, possibly because migrants from more rural areas went to the larger places to send the letters safely. See also Sisk, "Negro Migration in the Alabama Black Belt," 33.

43. Johnson, "Hattiesburg," 1, "Mississippi Summary," NULR; Paul F. Mowbray to George E. Haynes, August 31, 1917, Folder 25, Box 2; Mowbray

to L. Hollingsworth Wood, June 13, 1918, Folder 18, Box 3; both in Haynes Papers. Mowbray was the field secretary of the Nashville Public Welfare League.

44. Monroe N. Work, "Research With Respect to Cooperation between Urban and Rural Communities," *Opportunity* 1, no. 2 (February 1923): 8; George E. Haynes, "Negro Migration," *Opportunity* 2, no. 21 (September 1924): 273; ? Curran, "Negro Quarter, Pass Christian, Mississippi," April 1, 1919, field report for a study of labor in Gulf Coast canneries, File 20-21-7, Box 980, Central Files of the U.S. Children's Bureau, U.S. Department of Labor, RG 102, NA. The presence of livestock is documented in Cost of Living Schedules for Memphis, Atlanta, Birmingham, Mobile, and New Orleans, [1919], Boxes 625, 666, 671, 677, 687, Records of the U.S. Bureau of Labor Statistics, RG 257, NA. See also Johnson, "Vicksburg," 3–4, Johnson, "Hattiesburg," 1, both in "Mississippi Summary," NULR; Dittmer, *Black Georgia*, 10–12; Lamon, *Black Tennesseeans*, 137; Woofter, *Negro Migration*, 139–40.

45. U.S. Department of Labor, Press Release, July 9, 1923, Box C-373, Group 1, NAACP; Johnson, "Leland," 1, "Mississippi Summary," NULR; Scott, *Negro Migration*, 60; James H. Robinson, "Migration of Negroes from the South" [1917?], Folder 17, Box 4, Haynes Papers.

46. "Memorandum on Exodus From the South" [1917], File No. 13/65, Files-USDL, RG 174.

47. St. Luke *Herald* (Richmond, Va.), September 29, 1917, quoted in U.S. House of Representatives, Committee on Interstate and Foreign Commerce, *Return of the Railroads to Private Ownership*, Hearings on H.R. 4378, Part 12, 66th Cong., 1st sess., 1919, p. 2027; see also p. 2014.

48. Louis Armstrong, *Satchmo: My Life in New Orleans*, (New York, 1954), 229–30; Myra Young Armstead, Interview with Mary Fluornoy, Chicago, May 1, 1985 (tape in possession of author); Arna Bontemps and Jack Conroy, *They Seek a City* (Garden City, 1945), 136.

49. Matthew Ward, *Indignant Heart* (Detroit, 1957), 27; *Defender*, September 23, 1916, June 16, 1917; Scott, *Negro Migration*, 45–46; Frazier, *Negro Family in Chicago*, 80.

50. Mary F. Adams, "Present Housing Conditions in South Chicago, South Deering, and Pullman" (Master's thesis, University of Chicago, 1926), 20; Wright, *American Hunger*, 1.

51. Johnson, "Stimulation of the Movement," 17, "Draft," NULR; Johnson, "Interviews," 2, NULR. See also Chicago *Daily News*, March 14, 1917.

52. William M. Tuttle Jr., Interview with Chester Wilkins, Chicago, June 25, 1969 (transcript in possession of Tuttle), 1; CCRR, *Negro in Chicago*, 99; Richard Meryman and Louis Armstrong, *Louis Armstrong—A Self-Portrait* (New York, 1966), 28.

53. Travelers Aid Society of Chicago, "Report of the General Secretary for October, 1915," Folder 64; Travelers Aid Society of Chicago, "Report for April—1917," Folder 34; Travelers Aid Society of Chicago, "Minutes of the Second Board Meeting for 1917–1918," May 10, 1917, Folder 34; all in Records of Travelers Aid Society of Chicago, CHS. See also Alfreda Duster, ed., *Crusade for Justice: The Autobiography of Ida B. Wells* (Chicago, 1970), 371–72.

54. Travelers Aid Society of Chicago, "Minutes of Executive Committee Meeting," June 21, 1917, Folder 34, Records of Travelers Aid. The complicated dispute between Travelers Aid, the Urban League, and the Negro Fellowship League over presence in the train stations can be pieced together from reports that give each organization's side of the story. Although the historian of the Chicago Urban League notes that the League "stationed" a worker at the station, there is no other evidence that the League went beyond "cooperating" with Travelers Aid, as the report of the Chicago Commission on Race Relations suggests. Chester Wilkins, a redcap at the Illinois Central station, recalls that "Travelers Aids" had someone at the station, but the League did not. And the League's first annual report notes that it worked with Travelers Aid, which had placed a black aide on its staff. For the role of the Negro Fellowship League, see Louise DeKoven Bowen, *The Colored People of Chicago: An Investigation for the Juvenile Protective Association* ([Chicago], 1913), 22; Duster, ed. *Crusade for Justice*, 306, 333, 353, 371–73; and Duster, "Unpublished biography of Ida B. Wells," ch. 9, p. 10, typescript in Folder 1, Box 6, Wells Papers. On the Urban League's role, see CCRR, *Negro in Chicago,* 94; Chicago Urban League, *First Annual Report of the Chicago Urban League,* (Chicago, 1917), 11; Arvarh Strickland, *History of the Chicago Urban League* (Urbana, 1966), 44; and Tuttle, "Interview with Wilkins," 1.

55. Tuttle, Interview with Wilkins, 1; ? Barker, "Information Regarding Illinois Central Station Set Up, Night Shift 3–11 p.m.," Folder 8, Box 23, Supplement 2, Records of Travelers Aid; Chicago Council of Social Agencies, "Report of a Study of the Travelers Aid Society of Chicago," 27, Box 406, WCMC. By 1928, if not earlier, all porters at the Illinois Central and Dearborn stations were black; see "Memorandum of Conference Between Miss McMaster, Miss Lyons and Mrs. Hennessey," June 16, 1928, Folder 8, Box 23, Records of Travelers Aid.

56. Johnson, "Early Manifestations of the Movement," 6, and "Gulfport," 2, both in "Mississippi Summary," NULR. Most migrants told interviewers for the Chicago Commission on Race Relations that their most difficult adjustment was to the climate; see CCRR, *Negro in Chicago,* 101.

57. Alden Bland, *Behold A Cry* (New York, 1947); Wright, *American Hunger,* 1.

58. Hughes, *Big Sea,* 33.

59. *Whip,* August 15, 1919; Chicago *Broad Ax,* November 22, 1919; Photograph of the corner of 35th and Calumet streets [c.1915–25], in "35th St." file, Graphics Dept., CHS.

60. *Defender,* August 20, 1921, October 20, 1917.

61. *Defender,* May 19, 1917. See also *Whip,* October 9, November 20, 27, December 4, 1920, April 2, 1921.

62. Wright, *American Hunger,* 1–2.

63. CCRR, *Negro in Chicago,* 302; *Defender,* February 16, 1918.

64. CCRR, *Negro in Chicago,* 115; Hughes, *Big Sea,* 33. The imaginary boundary along Wentworth Avenue became increasingly real during the following decade. In 1929, a black man crossed the line and was beaten to death. His wife had retreated to the "black side" of the street and was left alone to

watch the assault. See Associated Negro Press News Release, March 20, 1929, Box 1, Barnett Papers.

65. CCRR, *Negro in Chicago*, 169, 302; Frazier, *Negro Family in Chicago*, 82; Haynes, "Negroes Move North, I," 119; *Defender*, February 10, 1917.

66. CCRR, *Negro in Chicago*, 177, 301.

Chapter 5

1. For the conceptualization and classic description of the "Black Metropolis" on Chicago's South Side, see Drake and Cayton, *Black Metropolis*. The term "Old Settler" specifically identifies members of an extremely exclusive Old Settlers Social Club formed in 1902, closed even to members of "many of our oldest families" (Franklyn A. Henderson to Helen Buckler, September 18, 1947, Folder 79, Box 7, Daniel Hale Williams Papers, Moorland-Spingarn Research Center, Howard University, Washington, D.C.). The club was open only to residents for thirty years or more, and their descendants, but Drake and Cayton (p. 66) indicate that the term customarily designated any blacks resident in Chicago prior to World War I, and I have used the term in that manner. See "History of Chicago Old Settlers Club 1902–1923," 4, pamphlet in Dunmore Collection, DuSable.

2. CCRR, *Negro in Chicago*, 107–8.

3. Spear, *Black Chicago*, 11–27; Philpott, *Slum and the Ghetto*, 119–30. Philpott demonstrates that Spear and others have understated pre-1900 housing segregation. But even his argument does not preclude a decrease in residential proximity between the races after 1900. On the "panic" that "a single Negro householder" could engender, see Philpott, 119, 147–48.

4. Katzman, *Before the Ghetto*, 67–80; Spear, *Black Chicago*, 91–110; Humbert S. Nelli, *Italians in Chicago 1880–1930: A Study in Ethnic Mobility* (New York, 1970), 23–25.

5. Spear, *Black Chicago*, 29–49; CCRR, *Negro in Chicago*, 232–33; Philpott, *Slum and the Ghetto*, 301–8. For school boundary lines, see Michael Homel, "Negroes in the Chicago Public Schools, 1910–1941" (Ph.D. dissertation, University of Chicago, 1972), 36–43, 50–51. A more detailed discussion of race relations follows in chapter 6.

6. U.S. Bureau of the Census, *Thirteenth Census of the United States Taken in the Year 1910*, vol. 4, *Population, Occupations* (Washington, D.C., 1914), 544–47; Spear, *Black Chicago*, 29–36. The often contradictory popular images of "races" and "nationalities" and their aptitudes and charactistics are discussed in Barry Karl, *The Uneasy State: The United States from 1915 to 1945* (Chicago, 1983), 63–64. "City of the Big Shoulders" comes from Carl Sandburg, "Chicago," in *Chicago Poems* (New York, 1916), 3.

7. This discussion of Chicago's black community rests heavily on Spear, *Black Chicago*. For other especially insightful discussions of black social structure in pre-Great Migration northern cities, see Katzman, *Before the Ghetto*, and Kusmer, *A Ghetto Takes Shape*, 91–112. On the status of postal workers, see Henry McGee, "The Negro in the Chicago Post Office" (Master's thesis, University of Chicago, 1961), 70–71, 83; Claude Barnett, "Fly Out of Dark-

ness" (unpublished autobiography), [c. 1965], ch. 1: 1, typescript in Box 4, Section 14 ("Family"), Barnett Papers. For an example of the symbols of respectability, see *Defender*, January 15, 1916.

8. Spear, *Black Chicago*, 51–70.

9. On the evolution of the "new middle class" in black Chicago see Spear, *Black Chicago*, 71–89; since Spear's seminal study, scholars examining other cities have found similar patterns. See for example, Kusmer, *A Ghetto Takes Shape*; Katzman, *Before The Ghetto*; Trotter, *Black Milwaukee*.

10. Ottley, *Lonely Warrior*, 6, 76; *Defender*, July 10, 1915; Harold F. Gosnell, *Negro Politicians: The Rise of Negro Politics in Chicago* (Chicago, 1935), 163–95; Chicago *Record-Herald*[?], 1909, clipping in Archibald J. Carey, Sr., Papers, CHS; Joseph Logsdon, "Reverend Archibald J. Carey and the Negro in Chicago Politics" (Master's thesis, University of Chicago, 1961), 9; Charles R. Branham, "Black Chicago: Accommodationist Politics Before the Great Migration," in Melvin G. Holli and Peter d'A. Jones, eds., *The Ethnic Frontier: Essays in the History of Group Survival in Chicago and the Midwest* (Grand Rapids, Mich., 1977), 218. On the general significance of black politicians who arrived between 1880 and 1915, see Charles R. Branham, "The Transformation of Black Political Leadership in Chicago, 1864–1942" (Ph.D. dissertation, University of Chicago, 1981), 50–94.

11. Spear, *Black Chicago*, 11–126.

12. *Defender*, April 8, 15, 1916; The *Conservator* is discussed in Drake and Cayton, *Black Metropolis*, 47–49.

13. George C. Hall, Speech before the Frederick Douglass Center, reprinted in the Chicago *Broad Ax*, December 31, 1904, quoted in Spear, *Black Chicago*, 73.

14. Estelle Hill Scott, *Occupational Changes among Negroes in Chicago* (Chicago, 1939), 14; Chicago Department of Public Welfare, *Preliminary Report of Bureau of Social Surveys* [Chicago, 1915], 5 (pamphlet); Arthur P. Drucker, et al., *The Colored People of Chicago* (Chicago, 1913), 13–14 (pamphlet); Wright, *87 Years behind the Black Curtain*, 105; *Defender*, May 8, 1915; Gosnell, *Negro Politicians*, 129; Harry Haywood, *Black Bolshevik: Autobiography of an Afro-American Communist* (Chicago, 1978), 38; Drake and Cayton, *Black Metropolis*, 600–57. The quotation is from W. H. A. Moore, "In a Black Belt," *Journal of National Association of Negro Authors* [Chicago] (August 1915): 3–4, copy in Dunmore Collection.

15. CCRR, *Negro in Chicago*, 162–65. For a discussion of women as "kin keepers" among black southerners moving from country to city, with special emphasis on visiting, see Earl Lewis, "Black Migration to Norfolk, Virginia, 1910–1945" (Paper presented at "From Field to Factory" Symposium, Carnegie-Mellon University, January 15, 1988).

16. Scott, "Letters," 317; Hattie L. Smith to Bethlehem Baptist Association, April 2, 1917, Box 10, Woodson Collection; Johnson, "Interviews," 22, NULR. On women coming to the city by themselves see Meyerowitz, "Holding Their Own," 41.

17. Chicago *Whip*, December 11, 1920 for example of migrants arriving penniless. For stranded people referred to YWCA, see datebook of Irene

McCoy Gaines, entry for June 9, 1921, Irene McCoy Gaines Collection, CHS; Chicago Council of Social Agencies, "Report of a Study of the Travelers Aid Society of Chicago," 39, Box 406, WCMC; and *Defender*, May 20, 1922. Judge Trude's policy is noted in CCRR, *Negro in Chicago*, 350.

18. Chicago Urban League, *First Annual Report* (1917), 11; Card distributed by Chicago Urban League, in Folder 6, Arthur Aldis Papers, UIC; Elizabeth Lindsay Davis, *The Story of the Illinois Federation of Colored Women's Clubs* [Chicago, 1922?], 38; *Defender*, March 17, 1917; Chicago Community Trust, *Housing of Non-Family Women in Chicago—A Survey* (Chicago, [1921]), 18–21.

19. *Defender*, July 9, 1921; "Memorandum of Conference on Temporary Shelter, Housing and Care for Colored Women with Young Children," Chicago, July 9, 1926, Box 145, WCMC; Chicago Urban League, *Fifth Annual Report* (1921), 5; Philpott, *Slum and the Ghetto*, 100. For the Urban League's self-image as a clearinghouse, see Chicago Urban League, *Second Annual Report* (1918), 7.

20. *Defender*, May 13, 1916; Ford S. Black, comp., *Black's Blue Book, Business and Professional Directory* (Chicago, 1917), 19–20.

21. *Defender*, March 26, 1921; "General Race News," *Half-Century Magazine* 3, no. 2 (August 1917): 8; Ford S. Black, comp., *Black's Blue Book: Directory of Chicago's Active Colored People and Guide to Their Activities* (Chicago, 1921), 32; CCRR, *Negro in Chicago*, 165.

22. Hughes, *Living Conditions*, 7–9; Scott, *Negro Migration*, 105; *Defender*, July 17, 1920.

23. Charles Johnson, "The Brown Family" [c. 1919–20], 1–2, typescript in Box 86, Series 6, NULR; USDL, *Negro Migration*, 23; CCRR, *Negro in Chicago*, 93.

24. Hughes, *Living Conditions*, 9; Thomas W. Allison, "Population Movements in Chicago," *Journal of Social Forces* 2, no. 4 (May 1924): 533.

25. Hughes, *Living Conditions*, 21–24; Alice Q. Rood, "Social Conditions among the Negroes on Federal Street between Forty-Fifth Street and Fifty-Third Street" (Master's thesis, University of Chicago, 1924), 28–30; Eva Boggs, "Nutrition of Fifty Colored Families in Chicago" (Master's thesis, University of Chicago, 1929), 13–14; [Carrie A. Lyford], *A Study of Home-Economics Education in Teacher Training Institutions for Negroes*, U.S. Office of Education, Federal Board for Vocational Education Bulletin no. 79 (Washington, D.C., 1923), 2–3; Johnson, "Home Life in Mississippi," "Mississippi Summary," NULR; Vance, *Human Factors in Cotton Culture*, 250. Another North Carolina surved cited by Vance (p. 230) found an average of 3.72 rooms per house for black farmers. See also Subcommittee on the Function of Home Activities in the Education of the Child, White House Conference on Child Health and Protection, "Family Relationships and Personality Adjustment" [c. 1920s], 9, typescript in Folder 2, Section 3, "Research," Ernest W. Burgess Papers, JRL-UC. Hughes (p. 23) argued that "contrary to popular current opinion, the overcrowding among Negro households was of relatively infrequent occurrence."

26. Hughes, *Living Conditions*, 29–30; Dickens, *Nutritional Investigation of Negro Tenants*, 11; Scott, "Letters," 292. For a graphic description of blacks'

homes in a Georgia village, see Clifton Johnson, *Highways and Byways of the South* (New York, 1904), 31. Peter Gottlieb found that Pittsburgh's migrants were relegated to housing that was worse than what they had left behind in the South, homes that failed "to meet migrants' customary standards, let alone their hopes for better conditions." Pittsburgh's black migrants lived near the steel mills or in barracks built by employers, facilities vastly different from the old residential neighborhoods on Chicago's South Side. See Gottlieb, *Making Their Own Way*, 66, 69–76.

27. CCRR, *Negro in Chicago*, 93; Memoranda relating to availability of housing in Chicago in 1918–19, in Box 307, Records of the U.S. Housing Corporation, RG 3, NA, especially Charles Bixby to James Ford, July 2, 1919; Bixby to William C. Graves, July 9, 1919; Fred D. McCracken to Ford, July 10, 1919. On the efforts to exclude blacks from white neighborhoods see Philpott, *Slum and the Ghetto*, 146–200; Tuttle, *Race Riot*, 157–83.

28. CCRR, *Negro in Chicago*, 137. In Philadelphia and Homestead, Pa., blacks who had arrived before the Great Migration were able to maintain territorial distance from newcomers, even within the black working class itself. See Ballard, *One More Day's Journey*, 184; Gottlieb, *Making Their Own Way*, 73–74. On the ability of Chicago's white immigrants to move to new neighborhoods, see Nelli, *Italians in Chicago*, 36–54; Edward Mazur, "Jewish Chicago: From Diversity to Community," in Holli and Jones, eds., *The Ethnic Frontier*, 281–82.

29. Philpott, *Slum and the Ghetto*, 197–98; Chicago Urban League, "Block Work," memorandum in Folder 6, Aldis Papers; Frazier, *Negro Family in Chicago*, 99–100; the quotation is on p. 112. Among these landlords who overcharged black newcomers for apartments recently vacated by whites was Oscar DePriest; see Gosnell, *Negro Politicians*, 169.

30. Tuttle, Interview with Chester Wilkins, 1.

31. Fannie Barrier Williams, quoted in Stephen Diner, "Chicago Social Workers and Blacks in the Progressive Era," *Social Service Review* 44, no. 4 (December 1970): 405; *Defender*, January 15, 1916. For information on the Jane Dent Home for Aged and Infirm Colored People, see its *First Annual Report* (Chicago, [1899]), 3, in Papers of the Jane Dent Home for Aged Colored People, UIC. For settlements, see "Frederick Douglass Center," leaflet in Dunmore Collection; E. Jennings, "Institutional AME Church," Box 29 ("Churches"), IWP, "Negro in Illinois"; *Institutional Church and Social Settlement* (Chicago, [1900]), pamphlet in Folder 103, Box 10, Williams Papers; Diner, "Chicago Social Workers," 405; Duster, ed., *Crusade for Justice*, 279–88; B. H. Haynes, "Wendell Phillips Settlement" [Chicago, 1913], handwritten report in Folder 16, Box 30, Rosenwald Papers; Philpott, *Slum and the Ghetto*, 315–16. Philpott found "at least" nine settlements (including the Negro Fellowship League) established in black neighborhoods between 1900 and 1916, but argues that only one still existed by 1919. The Douglass Center was taken over by the Chicago Urban League in 1918.

32. *The Phyllis Wheatley Home for Girls* [Chicago, 1966], pamphlet in Papers of the Phyllis Wheatley Association, UIC; Davis, *Story of the Illinois Federation*, 17, 95.

33. Duster, ed., *Crusade for Justice*, 306, 333, 353, 357–58, 371–73, 414; [Alfreda Duster], "Unpublished biography of Ida B. Wells," ch. 9, p. 10, typescript in Folder 1, Box 3, Wells Papers; Bowen, *Colored People of Chicago*, 22; *Defender*, March 20, 1920.

34. *Defender*, January 7, 1911, October 11, 1911. The Wabash Avenue YMCA was founded in 1911, although its building was not completed until 1913. For *Defender* rhapsodizing about the institution's founding, see January 28, February 4, 11, 18, 25, March 25, 1911.

35. *Whip*, March 13, 1920; Duster, ed., *Crusade for Justice*, 332, 372–73; *YMCA Bulletin* 1, no. 7 (November 13, 1915): 1, copy in Washington Papers. This publication was the newsletter of the Wabash Avenue branch.

36. Kate J. Adams, *Humanizing a Great Industry* (Chicago, [c. 1919]), 21; *Defender*, December 8, 1917, May 10, 1919, October 30, 1920; Bowen, *Colored People of Chicago*, 21; A. L. Jackson to Emmett Scott, November 13, 1915, Folder J, Box 532, Washington Papers; "Statistical and Financial Information Regarding Twelve Young Men's Christian Associations which Operate Buildings for Colored Men" [c.1921?], typescript in Folder 21, Box 10, Rosenwald Papers.

37. *Defender*, January 20, 1917. For lists of arrivals who were staying at the YMCA, see e.g., *Defender*, February 16, April 6, 1918. Activities of the Wabash Avenue YMCA can be traced in the *Defender*, especially after a weekly YMCA column was instituted in 1912. The failure of the institution to serve the "remaining masses" is noted in Maxwell H. Bond, "The Chicago Board of Education Playgrounds and the Colored Child," *Playground* 20, no. 4 (July 1926): 211.

38. Chicago Urban League, *First Annual Report* (1917), 9; Dorothy Crounse, Louise Gilbert, and Agnes Van Driel, "The Chicago Urban League," ([Chicago], 1936), 5, typescript in Chicago Urban League File, Box 286, WCMC. On the establishment of the Chicago Urban League, see Strickland, *History of the Chicago Urban League*, 25–37.

39. Scott, "Letters," 291. For documentation of the "thousands of letters written to the Urban League by Southern Negroes asking for transportation to the North," see Richard Wright, "The Chicago Urban League," (1936), 3–5, typescript in Folder 674, "Negro Studies" drawer, Works Progress Administration, Federal Writers Project, Project O.P. 165-2-26-7, Archive of Folk Song, LC. Statistics on clients can be found in *Defender*, November 24, 1917, November 29, 1919; CCRR, *Negro in Chicago*, 366; Chicago Urban League, *Third Annual Report* (1919), 2, and *Fourth Annual Report* (1920), 5. The opening of the League office is reported in *Defender*, March 10, 1917.

40. W[illiam] C. G[raves] to Julius Rosenwald, November 23, 1917; T. Arnold Hill to Graves, June 23, 1917; both in Folder 13, Box 9, Rosenwald Papers; Chicago Urban League, *Fifth Annual Report* (1921), 10, and *Third Annual Report* (1919), 8; Claude Barnett, "Fly out of Darkness," ch 1: 1, Barnett Papers; CCRR, *Negro in Chicago*, 151; McGee, "Negro in the Chicago Post Office," 83. The "social arbiter" was Julius Avendorph; see *Defender*, January 22, 1921; and Ottley, *The Lonely Warrior*, 109.

41. Davis, *Story of the Illinois Federation*, 38, 96; Chicago Urban League,

Fifth Annual Report (1921), 5; L. Harper, comp., Scrapbook of clippings, Box 106 ("Organizations"), IWP, "Negro in Illinois"; *Defender*, February 7, 1920; CCRR, *Negro in Chicago*, 151. On churches and charity, see Olivet Baptist Church, *Facts and Figures* (Chicago, [1920]), 4, in Folder 6, Papers of the Chicago Commission on Race Relations, Illinois State Archives, Springfield (microfilm); Black, *Black's Blue Book* (1921), 86; Helen C. Harris, "The Negro Church on the South Side in Chicago: How it Meets the Problem of the Need for Charity" (student paper; Chicago, 1929), 4, Folder 5, Box 142, Section 4 ("Others' Work"), Burgess Papers. The increased fundraising by the Wheatley Association is visible in the *Defender*, which during 1916–17 frequently announced and reported its fundraising events; see for example, August 4, September 15, 1917 for the announcement and report of a baseball game that raised $502. On nurseries, see A. Kenyon Maynard to William C. Graves, Folder 16, Box 30, Rosenwald Papers; "Day Nursery Questionnaire," November 12, 1925, Box 419 ("Wendell Phillips Nursery School"), WCMC; Davis, *Story of the Illinois Federation*, 10; *Broad Ax*, April 23, 1921. Home-finding by the YWCA is documented in Young Women's Christian Association of Chicago, Illinois, *Forty-Third Annual Statement*, 1919 (Chicago, [1920]), 14, and the datebook of Irene M. Gaines, Gaines Collection. On the policies of white organizations, see chapter 6.

42. See *Defender*, July 17, 24, 1915, August 3, 1918.

43. *Defender*, January 19, 1918.

44. Ballard, *One More Day's Journey*, 188; *Defender*, March 17, 1917, January 19, 1918. Urban League statement quoted in *Defender*, November 23, 1918. On German and eastern European Jews, see Mazur, "Jewish Chicago," 279–81.

45. Johnson, "New Frontage on American Life," 285; Duster, ed., *Crusade for Justice*, 303. See also Forrester B. Washington, "A Program of Work for the Assimilation of Negro Immigrants in Northern Cities," *Proceedings of the National Conference on Social Work* 44 (1917): 498. Although Washington was an Urban League administrator in Detroit when he wrote this article, it expresses a widespread sentiment; also, Washington had worked in Chicago for a short time, and his observations probably took this experience into consideration.

46. *Defender*, August 17, 1918; USDL, *Negro Migration*, 23; Chicago Urban League, *First Annual Report* (1917), 11; *Daily News*, April 2, 1917. See also the leaflet reproduced in Annual Report of the National Urban League (1919), in *Bulletin of the National Urban League* 9, no. 1 (January 1920): 20–21. *Defender* lectures on proper behavior can be found in almost any issue, 1917–20; this particular one appeared on October 20, 1917. By 1923, the NAACP, which had had very little visibility in Chicago during the war years, was distributing a three-page flyer issued by its Education Committee and carrying a detailed message similar to that previously broadcast by other institutions. The notable differences lie in the NAACP emphasis on voting and citizenship and on its call for "refined and gentle manners," a standard not set by the Urban League, *Defender*, or YMCA. See "Chicago, Great City" (August 1, 1923), typescript in Box G-48, Group 1, NAACP.

47. Charles E. Merriam and Harold F. Gosnell, *Non-Voting: Causes and Methods of Control* (Chicago, 1924), 211; CCRR, *Negro in Chicago*, 478; *Defender*, August 4, 1917, July 13, 1918, July 24, 1920, July 23, 1921, June 17, 1922; Bontemps and Conroy, *They Seek a City*, 142. On community centers, which were open "suitable evenings" in selected public school buildings, see Chicago Board of Education, *Proceedings*, October 22, 1919, p. 872, September 28, 1921, pp. 186–87; and Chicago Board of Education, *64th Annual Report of the Superintendent of Schools for the Year Ending 1918*, 113–16.

48. For statistics on age, see U.S. Bureau of the Census, *Thirteenth Census, 1910*, vol. 2, *Population*, 480; and *Fourteenth Census, 1920*, vol. 3, *Population*, 248. For a comparison of the ages of Illinois-born black Chicagoans and migrants, see Appendix A. The calculation for the proportion of young black Chicagoans in 1920 who were migrants draws on the Forward Census Survival Ratios described in Lee, et al., *Population Redistribution*, 15–25.

49. *Whip*, October 9, 1920; *Defender*, October 20, 1917, May 25, 1918, October 30, 1920, August 13, 1921, September 3, October 22, 1921, June 3, 1922; Leaflet reprinted in *Bulletin of the National Urban League* (1920), 21. For a comparison of the states of birth of Chicago's black population in 1910 and of those who came between 1910 and 1920, see Appendix B.

50. Duster, ed., *Crusade for Justice*, 409; *Defender*, May 19, 1917, July 2, 1921; W. E. B. Du Bois, "A Matter of Manners," *Crisis* 19, no. 4 (February 1920): 170.

51. Kathryn M. Johnson, "Immigration and Segregation," *Half-Century Magazine* 2, no. 2 (February 1917): 8; Frazier, *Negro Family in Chicago*, 82; Gunnar Myrdal, *An American Dilemma: The Negro Problem and Modern Democracy* (New York, 1944), 196; *Defender*, September 24, 1921; *Whip*, July 24, 1920. On "walking the narrow path of liberty and avoiding the precipice of license," see also Haynes, "Effect of War Conditions on Negro Labor," 306. For examples of "golden age" perspectives, see Drake and Cayton, *Black Metropolis*, 73. Not all Old Settlers maintained this nostalgic image; see for example, Wilhelmina Warfield, Interview with William C. King, October 28, 1937, in Box 95, "Music," IWP, "Negro in Illinois." On racial conflict before 1916, see CCRR, *Negro in Chicago*, 291; Charles E. Bentley, Address Delivered before Kenwood Congregational Church, Chicago, 1908, Folder 74, Box 5, Woodson Collection; Philpott, *Slum and the Ghetto*, 146–56. While not suggesting a golden age, Allan Spear, *Black Chicago*, 29–49, argues that race relations in Chicago had seen better days in the nineteenth century and proposes the end of that century as the era of "Jim Crow's triumph," thereby placing the degeneration of race relations before the Great Migration but in an era characterized by a moderate increase in migration from the South. The interest of Chicago settlement-house workers in white immigrant folk culture is discussed in Philpott, *Slum and the Ghetto*, 70.

52. *Defender*, March 24, 1917, May 25, July 6, September 14, 1918; *Searchlight* quoted in CCRR, *Negro in Chicago*, 304. See also *Whip*, March 27, August 7, October 23, December 4, 1920.

53. St. Clair Drake, "Churches and Voluntary Institutions in the Chicago Negro Community," Report of Official Project 465-54-3-386, Work Proj-

ects Administration, (Chicago, 1940), 151; M. P. Webster, "Organized Labor Among Negroes in Chicago," in Frederic Robb, ed., *The Book of Achievement the World Over Featuring the Negro in Chicago* (Chicago, 1929), 196; Oscar Micheaux, *The Conquest: The Story of a Negro Pioneer* (Lincoln, Neb., 1969; reprint, Miami, 1969), 27; Merriam and Gosnell, *Non-Voting*, 211. On the reluctance of Old Settlers to accept business and professional men from the South, see E. Franklin Frazier, "The Negro Community: A Cultural Phenomenon," *Journal of Social Forces* 7 (March 1929): 419. In Philadelphia, according to Allen Ballard, *One More Day's Journey*, 199, "even the Black aristocracy of the South was not good enough for the Old Philadelphians." On immigrants returning to the "old neighborhood" for church and other institutional activities, see Philpott, *Slum and the Ghetto*, 143.

54. E. Franklin Frazier, "Chicago: A Cross-Section of Negro Life," *Opportunity* 7, no. 3 (March 1929): 71.

55. Rood, "Social Conditions among the Negroes on Federal Street," 42–43; Johnson, "Stimulation of the Movement," 3, "Draft," NULR; Helen Wright, *Children of Wage-Earning Mothers: A Study of a Selected Group in Chicago*, U.S. Children's Bureau Publication no. 102 (Washington, D.C., 1922), 16. On housekeeping standards in the rural South, see Jones, *Labor of Love, Labor of Sorrow*, 86–89.

56. CCRR, *Negro in Chicago*, 177, 304.

57. *Whip*, October 23, 1920, March 4, 1922.

58. "Boogie Woogie in Chicago," 1–4, Box 84 ("Music History"); "Native Sons: Rhythm," 8, Box 85 ("Music History"); both in IWP, "Negro in Illinois"; *Defender*, July 22, 1922.

59. Wright, *Black Boy*, 228. On black ambivalence towards the South and the notion of "down home," see Levine, *Black Culture and Black Consciousness*, 364.

60. *Defender*, March 16, 1918, April 12, 1919; *Whip*, June 24, September 20, 1919; T. Arnold Hill to Walter F. White, November 14, 1919, "September-December, 1919" Folder, Box C-319, NAACP; Bontemps and Conroy, *They Seek a City*, 145.

61. Johnson, "The Mississippi Colony," 1, "Draft," NULR; Johnson, "Interviews," 6, 22, NULR; Frazier, *Negro Family in Chicago*, 77.

62. The nine states were Alabama, Arkansas, Kentucky, Louisiana, Mississippi, South Carolina, Tennessee, Texas, and Virginia. Frazier, *Negro Family in Chicago*, 115; Bontemps and Conroy, *They Seek a City*, 145; Lamon, *Black Tennesseans*, 157; *Whip*, March 19, 1921, March 4, 1922; *Defender*, January 23, July 24, October 14, 1915, April 7, 1917, August 24, 1918; *Broad Ax*, November 11, 1922; Drake, "Churches and Voluntary Associations," 153. Emmett Scott, *Negro Migration*, 103–4, mentions a Georgia club and states that these clubs met migrants at train stations, but I have found no other indication of either the existence of a Georgia club or activities of state clubs at Chicago railroad stations.

63. For "invitations," see e.g., *Defender*, February 24, March 3, 17, 24, 31, July 7, September 1, 15, 22, October 20, 27, 1917, March 30, October 19, November 23, 1918, April 5, May 17, 1919. On Olivet and Institutional, see

Black, *Black's Blue Book* (1921), 80; S. Mattie Fisher, "Olivet as a Christian Center," 199; E. Jennings, "Institutional AME Church," Box 29 ("Churches"), IWP, "Negro in Illinois."

64. Myra Young Armstead, Interview with Mary Fluornoy; CCRR, *Negro in Chicago*, 94; George E. Haynes, "Negro Migration," *Opportunity* 2, no. 21 (September 1924): 273; Woofter, *Negro Migration*, 163; Jesse O. Thomas, *My Story in Black and White: The Autobiography of Jesse O. Thomas* (New York, 1967), 21–22.

65. William S. Braddan, *Under Three Banners; An Autobiography* (Nashville, 1940), 249; *Defender*, May 27, 1922; Scott, *Negro Migration*, 110; Drake and Cayton, *Black Metropolis*, 634; Joseph Bougere, Interview with Robert Mays, Chicago, March 9, 1938, Box 77 ("Migration"), IWP, "Negro in Illinois." For ministers at "mainline" churches whipping congregations to a frenzy, see *Whip*, February 12, October 29, 1921, September 30, 1922. On ministers who tried to appeal widely by including both sober and emotional appeals, see Robert Lee Sutherland, "An Analysis of Negro Churches in Chicago" (Ph.D. dissertation, University of Chicago, 1930), 97. This ability to "swing easily" between styles dates back to the antebellum South; see Genovese, *Roll, Jordan, Roll*, 268.

66. Frazier, *Negro Family in Chicago*, 74; Daniel, "Ritual in Chicago's South Side Churches," 12–13; CCRR, *Negro in Chicago*, 144–45; Johnson, "Interviews," 3, 14, 23, NULR; *Defender*, December 13, 1919; A. Williams and E. Jennings, Untitled report on Monumental Baptist Church, Box 24 ("Baptist Church"), IWP, "Negro in Illinois."

67. Johnson, "Interviews," 6 (interviewee discusses St. Luke's M.E. Church, which soon changed its name to South Park M.E.); untitled report in Box 27 ("Religious Cults"), IWP, "Negro in Illinois"; Sutherland, "Analysis of Negro Churches," 84, 118; Drake, "Churches and Voluntary Associations," 195; *Defender*, July 13, 1918, April 12, August 30, 1919, July 8, 1922. For a suggestive discussion of how churches helped migrants to adjust to urban life, see Daniel, "Ritual in South Side Churches," 90–91, 141–43, and passim.

68. Gottlieb, *Making Their Own Way*, 201, offers a similar argument with reference to black migrants in Pittsburgh during this period.

69. CCRR, *Negro in Chicago*, 488. See also Gottlieb, *Making Their Own Way*, 198–203. On the importance of autonomy, control, and status in black religious life, see J. J. Watson, "Churches and Religious Conditions," *Annals of the American Academy of Political and Social Science* 49 (September 1913): 120.

Chapter 6

1. Johnson, "Interviews," 1, NULR; Johnson, "The Brown Family" [c. 1920], 3, typescript in Box 86, Series 6, NULR.

2. U.S. Bureau of the Census, *Thirteenth Census, 1910*, vol. 2, *Population*, 512; *Fourteenth Census, 1920*, vol. 3, *Population*, 274. 1910 statistics show 37 percent of the white population as foreign-born and another 43 percent children of at least one immigrant parent; in 1920, the proportions were 31 percent and 44 percent respectively. In the Second Ward in particular, I have

assumed that Russians and to a lesser extent Germans were likely to be Jewish; see Mazur, "Jewish Chicago," 269.

3. George Harding, an alderman from the Black Belt, falls into two of these categories. Serving his black constitutents as a traditional machine politician, he also bought buildings from whites fleeing the movement of his constituents into their neighborhoods. See Lloyd Wendt and Herman Kogan, *Big Bill of Chicago* (Indianapolis, 1953), 168–69.

4. Chicago *Tribune*, December 10, 1916, January 10, 11, 17, 1917. On the assumption that the migration was a passive process see the quotation from the *Tribune* in CCRR, *Negro in Chicago*, 551, and *Daily News*, January 31, 1917. On the "conceptualization of poverty as a problem in individual cultural adjustment—rather than one of socioeconomic inequality or racism" because of a focus on individual shortcomings rather than structural or other systemic forces, see Kenneth Kusmer, "The Functions of Organized Charity in the Progressive Era: Chicago as a Case Study," *Journal of American History* 60, no. 3 (December 1973): 657–78.

5. *Jewish Daily Courier*, August 5, 1912, May 31, 1917, July 30, 1919, translations of clippings in Box 23, Chicago Foreign Language Press Survey, Chicago Public Library Omnibus Project, Works Progress Administration, 1942, JRL-UC.

6. On nineteenth-century race relations in Chicago, see Drake and Cayton, *Black Metropolis*, 32–39, 41, 50; Gosnell, *Negro Politicians*, 14; CCRR, *Negro in Chicago*, 232–33; Philpott, *Slum and the Ghetto*, 117–18; Spear, *Black Chicago*, 41–42. For a survey of antebellum race relations in the North, see Litwack, *North of Slavery*.

7. Wright, *Life Behind a Veil*; Baker, *Following the Color Line*, 111; Kusmer, *A Ghetto Takes Shape*, 54; Spear, *Black Chicago*, 20–23. Population data from Spear, 12.

8. Thomas Philpott, who has done the most detailed analysis of segregation patterns in Chicago during this period, argues that "there was probably no Southern city in which blacks were so segregated as they were in Chicago." Philpott, *Slum and the Ghetto*, 210.

9. *Defender*, January 29, November 18, 1916, June 30, November 3, 1917, January 26, June 29, September 7, 1918; *Whip*, November 8, 1919. For examples of ethnic tensions, see clippings in the Chicago Foreign Language Press Survey: on Irish and Italians, see e.g., *L'Italia*, May 7, 1916, Box 21; on Poles and Lithuanians, see *Dziennik Zwiazkowy*, August 3, 1918, Box 32, *Lietuva*, February 8, 1901, June 5, 1903, April 23, 1909, October 19, 1917, and *Naujienos*, June 3, 1914, all in Box 28; on Poles and Germans, *Dziennik Zwiazkowy*, February 1, 1908, December 10, 1910, April 26, 1918, Box 32; on Poles and Jews, *Narod Polski*, May 27, 28, June 4, August 6, 1919, *Polonia*, December 12, 1918, *Dziennik Zwiazkowy*, October 20, 1913, all in Box 32, *Daily Jewish Courier*, May 23, June 2, 3, 6, 10, 13, 18, July 7, 10, 25, 1919, *Sunday Jewish Courier*, May 25, June 8, July 6, 13, 27, 1919, *Daily Jewish Forward*, May 28, June 3, 9, 14, 1919, *Lawndale Press*, June 6, 1919, all in Box 23. See also, Edward R. Kantowicz, *Polish-American Politics in Chicago, 1888–1940* (Chicago, 1975), 118–19, 136.

10. Scott, "Additional Letters," 442, 450. On the impact of World War I on ethnic conflict in Chicago, see Melvin G. Holli, "The Great War Sinks Chicago's German *Kultur*," in Holli and Peter d'A. Jones, eds., *Ethnic Chicago* (Grand Rapids, Mich., rev. and exp. ed., 1984), 467–73, 499–508.

11. Bowen, *Colored People of Chicago*, 30. One historian's survey of Chicago's Polish press "failed to locate any material of significance relating to blacks prior to 1917"; see Joseph J. Parot, "Ethnic versus Black Metropolis: The Origins of Polish-Black Housing Tensions in Chicago," *Polish-American Studies*, 29 no. 1–2 (Spring-Autumn 1972): 26n. On southern obsession with racial issues and white supremacy, see Newby, *Jim Crow's Defense*, 3–4. There were northerners who also pointed to the threat of Negro domination, but the point here is that the issue was of little immediacy on any plane other than the theoretical. For a discussion of a northern perception of the imminent Negro threat, see Newby, 57–8.

12. For a good discussion of the importance of a legitimating legal framework for racist race relations, see George Fredrickson, *White Supremacy: A Comparative Study in American and South African History* (New York, 1981).

13. Wright, *American Hunger*, 2–3; *Daily News*, August 24, 1916; Philpott, *Slum and the Ghetto*, 165. Neither the *Defender* nor the Chicago Commission on Race Relations suggests that the streetcar was a locus of conflict. See also the discussion of streetcar segregation in southern cities in Rabinowitz, *Race Relations in the Urban South*, 182–84, 192–94; and Wright, *Life Behind a Veil*, 52–55.

14. CCRR, *Negro in Chicago*, 98–99. See also Johnson, "Interviews," NULR, 30; Scott, "Additional Letters," 459; Drake and Cayton, *Black Metropolis*, 385.

15. Scott, "Additional Letters," 442.

16. Jones, *Labor of Love, Labor of Sorrow*, 149–50; Hastings Hart, "Rising Standards in the Treatment of Negroes" [c. 1920], 1–2, typescript in Folder 4, Box 6, Rosenwald Papers; Myra Young Armstead, Interview with Bert Jones, Chicago, April 19, 1985 (tape in possession of author). One such lynching, in Mississippi in 1916, is described in "The Horizon," *Crisis* 13, no. 4 (February 1917): 195. See also Richard Wright's recollections about the meaning of informal physical contact with white waitresses in Chicago, in *American Hunger*, 11–12.

17. *Daily News*, May 22, 1916.

18. *Tribune*, May 15, 1917; CCRR, *Negro in Chicago*, 524, 529–30, 532; *New World* (Chicago), December 19, 1913; *Defender*, October 5, 1918. See also *Defender*, March 24, 1917 for an attack on the white press for its treatment of blacks.

19. CCRR, *Negro in Chicago*, 438–45; *Defender*, May 17, 1919. On perils to public health, see *Tribune*, March 5, May 15, 1917; *Daily News*, March 14, 1917.

20. *Daily News*, March 16, 1917; *Tribune*, March 5, 1917; E. Jennings, "Report on Interviews on Health Surveys" [c. 1940], typescript in Box 62 ("Health"), IWP, "Negro in Illinois." See also *Tribune*, May 15, 1917; *Daily News*, March 20, 21, 27, 30, April 2, 27, 1917.

21. *Tribune*, March 16, 1917, January 18, 1917, November 20, 1916 for quo-

tations. For headlines about vice investigations involving South Side resorts, DePriest, and blacks, see e.g., *Tribune*, October 14, 16, 17, 19, 1916, January 19, 20, 22, 30, 1917, and *Daily News*, January 18–19, 1917, and the second half of October 1917.

22. "Seventeenth Annual Report of the Committee of Fifteen, 1925," 9, Folder labeled "Committee of Fifteen," Graham Taylor Papers, Newberry Library; *Whip*, April 27, November 20, 1920; *Defender*, July 27, August 3, September 14, 1918, December 31, 1921, May 20, June 10, 1922. On grand jury proceedings, see *Daily News*, October 14, 18, 1916; and *Tribune*, August 11, October 15, 1916. On "mingling" see *Daily News*, January 11, 1917, and similar comments in an untitled Juvenile Protection Association report, December 10, 1922, Folder 92, Juvenile Protection Association Papers, UIC. Taylor and Addams are quoted in Philpott, *Slum and the Ghetto*, 297. For an analogous argument about the reaction of reformers to moral threats posed by young single women in Chicago, see Meyerowitz, "Holding Their Own," 67.

23. Evidence on the exclusion of blacks from social services abounds in the records of various institutions and in comments by both black and white observers. In addition, black institutions frequently stated their mission within the context of black exclusion elsewhere. On homes for dependent children see "Memorandum—Local Community Research Committee Regarding the Proposed Project on the Care of Dependent and Neglected Negro Children in Chicago" [1928], 1, typescript in Box 773, Sophonisba B. Breckinridge Papers, LC; Chicago Council of Social Agencies, "Statement of Committee on Care of Colored Child" (April 17, 1928), typescript in Folder 9, Box 30, Records of the Illinois Children's Home and Aid Society, UIC; "The Amanda Smith Industrial School for Colored Girls" (Harvey, Ill., [1917]), leaflet in Folder 18, Box 75, Records of the Illinois Children's Home and Aid Society; "Report of the Subcommittee of the Advisory Committee of the Cook County Bureau of Public Welfare on the Establishment of a Division of Child Placing in the Cook County Bureau of Public Welfare" [c. 1929], 1, typescript in Box 300 (Cook County Department of Public Aid), WCMC; Minutes of Meeting of the Section on Institutions for Dependent and Neglected Children of the Child Welfare Division of the Chicago Council of Social Agencies, October 23, 1928, Box 35 (Child Welfare), WCMC; Reverend Henry M. Williams to Booker T. Washington, July 8, 1915, Folder W, Box 538, Washington Papers; Philpott, *Slum and the Ghetto*, 304–5. The "lack of facilities for the care of colored dependent women and children and convalescents" is noted in Chicago Urban League, *Eleventh Annual Report* (1927), 9. On the scarcity of day nurseries for blacks, see Wright, *Children of Wage-Earning Mothers*, 19; Ruth Pearson, "Day Nursery Study—Preliminary Report" [1925], 2, typescript in Box 159 (Nursery School), WCMC. On exclusion from or unavailablitity of clinics, dispensaries, infant welfare stations, and public baths, see Harrison L. Harris, "Negro Mortality Rates in Chicago," *Social Service Review* 1 (March 1927): 60; Maude A. Lawrence to Spencer C. Dickerson, January 14, 1928, Folder 1, Box 184, Julius Rosenwald Fund Archives, Fisk. Relief stations and free lodging facilities are discussed in Chicago Urban League, *Fifth Annual Report* (1921), 5; *Defender*, July 9, 1921. On institutions in or near black neigh-

borhoods that refused to serve blacks, see Philpott, 305; Kathleen McCarthy, *Noblesse Oblige: Charity and Cultural Philanthropy in Chicago, 1849–1929* (Chicago, 1982), 140–42.

24. *Defender*, October 12, 1918. Reverend Archibald J. Carey's use of the same phrase is quoted in the *Whip*, November 8, 1919. See also Philpott, *Slum and the Ghetto*, 340–41. For a provocative discussion of Americanization, see Gerd Korman, *Industrialization, Immigrants, and Americanizers: The View From Milwaukee, 1866–1921* (Madison, 1967).

25. Edith Abbott to Wilfred S. Reynolds, January 10, 1913, Folder 6, Box 30, Records of the Illinois Children's Home and Aid Society; Jane Addams, "Has the Emancipation Act Been Nullified by National Indifference?" *Survey* 29 (February 1, 1913): 565–66; Addams, *The Second Twenty Years at Hull House* (New York, 1930), 396–404; Diner, "Chicago Social Workers," 396–400, 402–3; Bowen, *Colored People of Chicago*; Sophonisba P. Breckinridge, "The Color Line in the Housing Problem," *Survey* 29 (February 1, 1913): 575–76; Illinois State Council of Defense, Women's Committee, *Final Report* [Chicago, 1919], 189 (Breckinridge chaired the Committee on Colored Women); Mary McDowell, "The Negro in Industry," *World Tomorrow* 5, no. 3 (March 1922): 72–73; *Defender*, April 5, 1919 (McDowell speaks at Quinn Chapel); Philpott, *Slum and the Ghetto*, 293–301, 312, 323–41. The individuals mentioned in this paragraph are by no means a complete list of reformers who might be considered unusually concerned with racial issues and problems faced by black Chicagoans. Among Chicagoans active in social reform and social service, however, these women were probably in the vanguard of ideas about race relations, racial equality, and the impact of racial discrimination.

26. Louise Wade, *Graham Taylor: Pioneer for Social Justice* (Chicago, 1964), 3; W. E. B. Du Bois, "The Negro and Democracy," *City Club Bulletin* 5, no. 14 (May 28, 1912): 229. See also Fredrickson, *Black Image in the White Mind*, 302; Nancy Weiss, *The National Urban League, 1910–1940* (New York, 1974), 33. On the progressive press and its unconcern and disdain for blacks, see David Southern, *The Malignant Heritage: Yankee Progressives and the Negro Question, 1901–1914* (Chicago, 1968), 43–47, 62–63. Southern notes that the *Independent* constituted a significant exception to this pattern, and one should probably add the *Public*, which was not among the journals he surveyed. For sentiments similar to those expressed by Du Bois, see A. L. Jackson, "Our Negro Neighbor," speech summarized in "Chicago's Negro Problem," *City Club Bulletin* 12, no. 11 (March 17, 1919): 75–76.

27. *Bulletin of the Woman's City Club of Chicago* [c. 1920], quoted in Davis, *Story of the Illinois Federation*, 38; Drake and Cayton, *Black Metropolis*, 69. The United Charities office located at 2959 South Michigan Avenue served the Black Belt as far south as 39th Street. Blacks who lived south of 39th Street had to use the Stockyards district office and would have been less likely to take advantage of the organization's services. See United Charities of Chicago, *Sixty Years of Service* (Chicago, [1922]), 87 (pamphlet).

28. CCRR, *Negro in Chicago*, 144; Wilfred S. Reynolds to Adah M. Waters, January 22, 1919, Folder 18, Box 75, Records of the Illinois Children's Home and Aid Society; Irene Graham, "Six Months of the 'South Side Survey' "

(Chicago, [1930]), 7, typescript in Box 145 (Minorities), WCMC. A careful reading of the material in this box provides a general impression of the frustration felt by social workers unable to convince blacks to accept them and their services. United Charities case statistics can be found in Harriet Cade, "Statistics of Chicago Relief Agencies" (Master's thesis, University of Chicago, 1927), 110. The overrepresentation of black clients reflected in these statistics must be considered within the context of an even greater overrepresentation of blacks among the city's poor. On the reluctance of blacks and Mexicans in South Chicago to request assistance from relief societies, see Adams, "Present Housing Conditions in South Chicago, South Deering, and Pullman," 66. Underutilization of medical facilities and the importance of white staffing as a factor discouraging potential black clients are discussed in Harris, "Negro Mortality Rates," 69–70. Cook County's policy of hiring only white nurses was challenged by the Federation of Civic and Social Agencies in 1922; see *Defender*, July 15, 1922. The reluctance of European immigrants to use certain institutions is discussed in Lizabeth Cohen, "Learning to Live in the Welfare State: Industrial Workers in Chicago Between the Wars, 1919–1939" (Ph.D. dissertation, University of California, Berkeley, 1986), 58–61; Philpott, *Slum and the Ghetto*, 74; and Allen F. Davis, *Spearheads for Reform: The Social Settlements and the Progressive Movement, 1890–1914* (New York, 1967), 88. Olivier Zunz has emphasized religious variables in the attitudes of potential clients towards charities; see Olivier Zunz, *The Changing Face of Inequality: Urbanization, Industrial Development, and Immigrants in Detroit, 1880–1920* (Chicago, 1982), 270–71, 275–77.

29. Graham, "Six Months of the 'South Side Survey,'" 9 Box 145, WCMC; Chicago Urban League, *First Annual Report* (1917), 4; Minutes of meetings of Executive Committee of Chicago Council of Social Agencies, Box 35 (Child Welfare), WCMC. Attention to blacks began to increase in the late 1920s, although the power structure of the charity bureaucracy still included few blacks. The United Charities also lacked black representation on its board of directors at least as late as the early 1920s; see United Charities of Chicago, *Sixty-Six Years of Service*, inside cover. For a debate on the racial attitudes of Chicago's progressive reformers see Diner, "Chicago Social Workers," and Philpott, *Slum and the Ghetto*. To some extent their disagreement can be attributed to Diner's focus on the umbrella organizations, as opposed to Philpott's broader examination of reform activities. The umbrella organizations, whose records document discrimination by specific groups, tended to draw leadership from the ranks of the most broad-minded progressive reformers. On a national level, Nancy Weiss, *History of the National Urban League*, 47, 50–51, 73, draws a careful distinction between deliberate racial discrimination on the part of reformers and the fact that blacks "ranked low among the popular causes of the period."

30. Philpott, *Slum and the Ghetto*, 293–313, 322–23; Minutes of Executive Board Meeting, November 29, 1918 [Secretary's Record], Young Women's Christian Association, 264–65, Box 45, Records of the Young Women's Christian Association of Metropolitan Chicago, UIC; Edith Abbott to Wilfred S. Reynolds, January 10, 1913, Folder 6, Box 30, Records of the Illinois Children's Home and Aid Society.

31. Charles Shanabruch, "The Catholic Church's Role in the Americanization of Chicago's Immigrants: 1833–1928" (Ph.D. dissertation, University of Chicago, 1975), 477–81; *New World*, November 2, 1917; *Defender*, November 17, 1917; Edward R. Kantowicz, *Corporation Sole: Cardinal Mundelein and Chicago Catholicism* (Notre Dame, 1983), 212–13; Chicago Urban League, *Second Annual Report* (1918), 7.

32. CCRR, *Negro in Chicago*, 121; Sandburg, *Chicago Race Riots*, 14; Philpott, *Slum and the Ghetto*, 164. This was not the first time someone had proposed prohibiting the migration of blacks to Chicago; a stockyards businessmen's association had made such a proposal to the mayor during the 1904 labor conflict, apparently because of the threat the black strikebreakers posed to civil order in their neighborhood; see Walter Fogel, *The Negro in the Meat Industry* (Philadelphia, 1970), 22.

33. Mary McDowell, "Hovels or Homes?" *Opportunity* 7, no. 3 (March 1929): 74; Philpott, *Slum and the Ghetto*, 164; *Daily News*, January 31, 1917; *Tribune*, April 5, 1917.

34. Philpott, *Slum and the Ghetto*, 151; On "cultural investment" in ethnic neighborhoods, see Parot, "Ethnic versus Black Metropolis," 20, 22. Parot argues that this "cultural investment" was more important than the financial investment in churches, but see Rudolph Vecoli's convincing response in "'Ethnic versus Black Metropolis': A Comment," *Polish-American Studies* 29, no. 1–2 (Spring-Autumn 1972): 36.

35. Philpott, *Slum and the Ghetto*, 151, 174–75, 326. This discussion relies heavily on Philpott's insightful analysis of housing, race conflict, and reform.

36. Joseph Bougere, Interview with Robert Mays, March 9, 1938, Box 77 ("Migration"), IWP, "Negro in Illinois"; Gosnell, *Negro Politicians*, 19; Merriam and Gosnell, *Non-Voting*, 82–83.

37. *Defender*, March 30, 1918; Gosnell, *Negro Politicians*, 19, 96; Merriam and Gosnell, *Non-Voting*, 199. The migrants' actual propensity to vote, in comparison with other groups in the city, is a matter of dispute. The numbers are sketchy at best. See Gosnell, 16–17, 374; Merriam and Gosnell, 25; and John Allswang, "The Chicago Negro Voter and the Democratic Concensus: A Case Study, 1918–1936" *Journal of the Illinois State Historical Society* 60, no. 2 (Summer 1967): 146.

38. *Denní Hlasatel*, September 6, 1917, Box 1, Chicago Foreign Language Press Survey. Thompson's opposition to prohibition and his attacks on the king of England (whose relevance to Chicago politics and governance remained a mystery to many), coupled with other alliances and his ability to keep his anti-Catholicism out of view when necessary, permitted him to attract significant support from German Catholics. Migrants' equation of "white people" with Democrats is described in Johnson, "Greenwood," 2: 3, "Mississippi Summary," NULR.

39. Gosnell, *Negro Politicians*, 40–44, 49–51, 55–59; *Defender*, September 25, 1915, April 12, 1919; Spear, *Black Chicago*, 187–89; Tuttle, *Race Riot*, 188; Ralph Bunche, "The Thompson-Negro Alliance," *Opportunity* 7 (March, 1929): 78–80. On the significance of patronage and the role of black politicians, despite the lack of significant material benefits, see Ira Katznelson, *Black Men. White Cities: Race, Politics, and Migration in the United States,*

1900–1930, and Britain, 1948–68 (London, 1973), 99–101. For a useful corrective to the notion that blacks followed Thompson blindly, see Branham, "Transformation of Black Political Leadership in Chicago," 160–61. There is no satisfactory biography of Thompson; see Wendt and Kogan, *Big Bill of Chicago.*

40. The best account of the relationship between politics, Thompson, and racial competition is in Tuttle, *Race Riot,* 184–207. Other than among the small minority of whites who lived or worked in close proximity to blacks, it is unlikely that race was as important to voting as the racially interpreted outcome of the election was to racial tensions on the South Side. For ethnocultural interpretations of Chicago mayoral politics during this era see John Allswang, *A House for All Peoples: Ethnic Politics in Chicago, 1890–1936* (Lexington, 1971), 15–59; and Kantowicz, *Polish-American Politics,* 135–36, 141–43. Given the class tensions of the period, the inconsistency of ethnic voting for and against Thompson, and the appeal of the Labor Party in 1919, this approach must be used with caution. Allswang's data are also flawed by neglect of Irish-Americans, who are of paramount importance in this context.

41. Tuttle, *Race Riot,* 112–23; Spear, *Black Chicago,* 36–41. The quotation is from Betty Burke, Interview with Elmer Thomas, May 10, 1939, in folder marked "Occupational Lore," in drawer marked "Folklore-Illinois," Works Progress Administration, Federal Writers Project, Project O.P. 165-2-26-7, Archive of Folk Song, LC. This conflict will be discussed in greater detail in chapter 8.

42. Tuttle, *Race Riot,* 233–40; *Defender,* August 28, 1915, October 20, 1917, July 12, 1919; CCRR, *Negro in Chicago,* 3, 115; Charles S. Johnson, "Digest of Contributing Factors to Racial Outbreak July 29, 1919," 2, typescript in Box 87, Series 6, NULR; Philpott, *Slum and the Ghetto,* 325. On racial conflict in the stockyards, see chapter 8.

43. Tuttle, *Race Riot,* 217–22; "Close Ranks," *Crisis* 16 (July 1918); George E. Haynes, "Report to the Secretary of Labor," August 27, 1919, and "Report to the Secretary," April 12, 1919, both in File 8/102e, Files-USDL, RG 174.

44. Tuttle, *Race Riot,* 236–41.

45. Ibid., 32–64. For detailed descriptions of the riot, see Tuttle, 3–66 and CCRR, *Negro in Chicago,* 1, 4–49. The Illinois National Guard was deployed "late" because Mayor Thompson insisted that the city's police department could handle the situation; he was reluctant to ask for the troops, probably because of political disputes he had with Governor Lowden, who had immediately authorized the guard's detachment to Chicago.

Precipitating incidents seldom sufficiently explain outbreaks of racial violence similar to that which rocked Chicago in 1919, and contemporaries and subsequent historians have attempted to weigh various factors in order to analyze the significance of each source of conflict between black and white Chicago. In addition, historians have disagreed as to whether the riot resulted from racial tensions dating back to the nineteenth century or from antagonisms that grew out of the post-1916 influx of migrants. These two debates are closely related. Emphasis on the importance of competition for space logically highlights the migration as the turning point in Chicago race relations, especially if one magnifies the extent of residential integration in nineteenth-century Chicago. Racial conflicts relating to unionization, on the other hand, apparently had a longer history and had come close to causing riots before the Great Migration. See Spear, *Black Chicago*, and Tuttle, *Race Riot*, for this debate, and Philpott, *Slum and the Ghetto*, 119–42, for an explanation of how integration has been exaggerated.

46. "Exodus of Negroes From Chicago Following Riots," typescript report compiled for the Chicago Commission on Race Relations, Box 87, Series 6, NULR; Walter White, "The Success of Negro Migration," *Crisis* 29, no. 3 (January 1920): 112. Departures from the city after the riot are discussed in CCRR, *Negro in Chicago*, 105. On attempted recruitment by southern agents, see George E. Haynes, "Report to the Secretary of Labor," August 27, 1919, File 8/102e, Files-USDL, RG 174; Chicago *Broad Ax*, August 16, 23, 1919; *Defender*, May 17, 1919; T. Arnold Hill, "Why Southern Negroes Don't Go South," *Survey* 43, no. 6 (November 29, 1919): 183; clipping from *New York Call*, August 14, 1919, Box C-373, Group 1, NAACP; material in folder marked "Employment of Negro Ex-Servicemen," Box 600, Entry 352, Service and Information Branch, RG 165. On the failure of these efforts, see *Whip*, December 25, 1920; [Lieutenant Robert Owen], "Memorandum for Major Kobbe," June 27, 1919, Box 413, Entry 359, Service and Information Branch, RG 165.

47. "The Looking Glass," *Crisis* 13, no. 3 (January 1917): 135. See also P. G. Cooper to George E. Haynes, Folder 22, Box 1, Haynes Papers.

Chapter 7

1. Peter Gottlieb, Interview with Leroy McChester, July 9, 1974, Pittsburgh Oral History Project, Division of History, Pennsylvania Historical Museum Commission, Harrisburg (I am grateful to Dr. Gottlieb for providing me with a copy of this transcript); U.S. Bureau of the Census, *Negro Population, 1790–1915*, 542; Charles B. Spahr, "The Negro as an Industrial Factor," *Outlook* 62, no. 1 (May 6, 1899): 33. See also Gottlieb, *Making Their Own Way*, 118–19, 121.

2. Johnson, "How the Negro Fits in Northern Industry," 408; USDL, *Negro Migration*, 127. Some aspects of southern agricultural labor, such as harvest time on a sugar plantation, required similar speed and coordination, and many migrants therefore had some experience with work practices analogous to factory processes. But, on the whole, the "factories in the field" of the antebellum era had fallen victim to the freedmen's antipathy toward gang labor during Reconstruction. Although there was considerable variation in the work patterns of the rural South, according to the organization of a plantation and the availability of nonfarm labor, few black southerners worked in the types of environments that will be described later in this chapter.

3. Johnson, "Stimulation of the Movement," 2, "Draft," NULR; Scott, "Letters," 301.

4. See Scott, "Letters," for the variety of occupations of prospective migrants. In Pittsburgh, blacks and Poles found it difficult to continue in their trades; Italians, on the other hand, were able to use their skills, especially in

barbering, shoemaking, and the building trades. See Bodnar, et al., *Lives of Their Own*, 66–67.

5. USDL, *Negro Migration*, 24; Greene and Woodson, *Negro Wage Earner*, 316; J. McS to Carter Davis, April 27, 1923, Box 4, Series 4, NULR ("J. McS" was general president of the Wood, Wire and Metal Lathers' International Union). See also "Story of the Attempt of a Negro Plumber to Enter the Chicago Local as Given by the Plumber at the American Negro Congress," October 27, 1925, in Folder 10, Box 1, Park Papers; Report from Morris Lewis to United States Department of Labor, April 1925, Box 1394, Lawrence Oxley File, Records of the U.S. Employment Service, RG 183, NA. The 1915 building construction agreement in Chicago provided for what was essentially a closed shop. See Royal E. Montgomery, *Industrial Relations in the Chicago Building Trades* (Chicago, 1927), 82, 87–88.

6. CCRR, *Negro in Chicago*, 457; U.S. Department of Labor, Division of Negro Economics, *The Negro at Work During the World War and Reconstruction* (Washington, D.C., 1921), 42; Sandburg, *Chicago Race Riots*, 23. Graduates of most of the South's small black industrial schools were likely to find that they had not learned skills useful to modern industry; see Greene and Woodson, *Negro Wage Earner*, 199–203. Along with iron molders, founders, and casters, only coopers and plasterers among skilled workers secured employment in numbers commensurate with the black proportion of Chicago's work force in 1920; see Scott, *Occupational Changes Among Negroes in Chicago*, 203–4. Peter Gottlieb found a similar pattern in Pittsburgh; see Gottlieb, *Making Their Own Way*, 93–95, 97–98.

7. CCRR, *Negro in Chicago*, 94, 166; Chicago Board of Education, *Survey of the Chicago Public Schools* [Chicago, 1914], 17–18.

8. Leo M. Favrot, "Some Problems in the Education of the Negro in the South and How We Are Trying to Meet Them in Louisiana" (Address Before the National Association of Colored People, Cleveland, July 25, 1919; Baton Rouge, 1919), 14–15; Thomas Jesse Jones, "Negro Education," in U.S. Bureau of Education, *Report of the Commissioner of Education*, 1914 (Washington, D.C., 1915), 1: 420; Myra Hill Colson, "Home Work Among Negro Women in Chicago" (Master's thesis, University of Chicago, 1928), 65–66; Wright, *Children of Wage-Earning Mothers*, 53. See also Johnson, "Greenwood," 2, "Mississippi Summary," NULR.

9. Illinois General Assembly Oral History Program, *Corneal A. Davis Memoir* (Springfield, 1984), 1: 29.

10. Colson, "Home Work," 68; U.S. Bureau of the Census, *Negro Population*, 517–23; James W. Johnson to Charles S. Johnson, January 17, 1918, Box 86, Series 6, NULR; "A Plan for the Southern Migrant," *Crisis* 14, no. 5 (September 1917): 217; Dutcher, *Negro in Modern Industrial Society*, 5–6, 22. Jacqueline Jones has argued that even in southern towns and cities, black men and women were unlikely to have jobs that would familiarize them with the industrial work discipline they would encounter in the North. Partly because of the impossibility of advancement, blacks "maintained an aversion to closely supervised, strictly regimented labor." See Jones, *Labor of Love, Labor of Sorrow*, 134.

11. Chicago Urban League, *Seventh Annual Report* (1923), 9; CCRR, *Negro*

in *Chicago*, 94; USDL, *Negro Migration*, 19. The Commission's survey found that 70 percent of 122 migrants had come to Chicago with experience only as unskilled workers, domestics, or farmers; see CCRR, 166.

12. U.S. Bureau of the Census, *Negro Population*, 429; Local Board for Division No. 3, Chicago, "Experience Report—Sections 43 and 95," Box 8, U.S. Selective Service System, Local Board Experience File, RG 163, WNRC; Stanley Lieberson, *A Piece of the Pie: Blacks and White Immigrants since 1880* (Berkeley, 1980), 220. See also Johnson, "School Facilities," in "Mississippi Summary," NULR.

13. "Young Women's Christian Association," *The Champion* (Chicago) 1, no. 7 (March 1917): 34; Tuttle, Interview with Chester Wilkins, 2; Fogel, *Negro in the Meat Industry*, 29; David Brody, *The Butcher Workmen: A Study of Unionization* (Cambridge, Mass., 1964), 85; Edna L. Clarke, "History of the Controversy Between Labor and Capital in the Slaughtering and Meat Packing Industry in Chicago" (Master's thesis, University of Chicago, 1922), 28; William Z. Foster, "How Life Has Been Brought into the Stockyards," *Life and Labor* 8, no. 4 (April 1918): 64. See also *National Provisioner* (May 13, 1922): 18.

14. Fogel, *Negro in the Meat Industry*, 30; Scott, *Negro Migration*, 103; USDL, *Negro Migration*, 22; Johnson, "Interviews," NULR. Although the 1920 census counted only 8,036 black men (17.8 percent of total gainfully employed black males) and 570 black women (2.7 percent of gainfully employed black females) working in the stockyards, it is unlikely that these statistics reflect the full extent of black experience there. The 1920 census was taken after a sharp decline in packinghouse employment but before the 1920–21 depression struck most other industries, so its statistics probably show fewer black meat-packing workers than there had been earlier. The number of black women who had been employed in the industry would be especially underestimated, because many companies had dismissed them by then. These women, hired during the war to replace the white women who had been promoted to jobs formerly performed by white men, were prime candidates for layoffs. Had the census been taken in January 1919, when stockyards employment reached 55,828, at least 11,000 black workers would probably have been counted there, as the black share of positions had probably increased (due to employer fear of unionization) beyond the 20 percent figure cited by one industry executive in 1918. Four months later, when the total had dipped to 42,158, black employment would have dropped commensurately. U.S. Bureau of the Census, *Fourteenth Census* (1920), vol. 4, *Population, Occupations* (Washington, D.C., 1923), 1076–80; U.S. Bureau of the Census, *Fourteenth Census of the United States, State Compendium, Illinois* (Washington, D.C., 1924), 212.

15. Gottlieb, Interview with Leroy McChester; H. M. Robinson, untitled typescript (January 22, 1929), Box 11, Section 7 ("Medicine"), Barnett Papers; Claude A. Barnett, "We Win a Place in Industry," *Opportunity* 7 (March 1929): 82–83; David Brody, *Steelworkers in America: The Nonunion Era* (Cambridge, Mass., 1960), 186; Greene and Woodson, *Negro Wage Earner*, 253; U.S. Bureau of the Census, *Fourteenth Census* (1920), vol. 4, *Population, Occupations*, 1076–77; CCRR, *Negro in Chicago*, 361.

16. U.S. Bureau of the Census, *Fourteenth Census* (1920), vol. 4, *Population*,

Occupations, 1076–79; Scott, *Occupational Changes*, 128, 136–37, 145–49, 190, 192–94, 197–99, 203–4. Scott reassembled the census data into categories slightly different from the reports published by the Bureau of the Census. Her categories are more useful in assessing the character of blacks' jobs, as the census reports focus more on the sector of the economy in which blacks worked. I have accepted Scott's categories wherever I have grouped workers into such classifications as "service," or "unskilled laborers," but have in most cases recalculated her data using the aggregate reports.

17. David M. Katzman, *Seven Days A Week: Women and Domestic Service in Industrializing America* (New York, 1978), 79; U.S. Bureau of the Census, *Fourteenth Census* (1920), vol. 4, *Population, Occupations*, 1079–80; Forrester B. Washington, "Reconstruction and the Colored Woman," *Life and Labor* 9, no. 1 (January 1919): 4. See also Helen Sayre, "Negro Women in Industry," *Opportunity* 2, no. 20 (August 1924): 242.

18. Sandburg, *Chicago Race Riots*, 32; Washington, "Reconstruction," 4; Mary R. Smith, "The Negro Woman as an Industrial Factor," *Life and Labor* 8, no. 1 (January 1918): 8.

19. *Defender*, March 31, 1917, October 5, 12, 1918, December 20, 1919; CCRR, *Negro in Chicago*, 415.

20. *Defender*, September 7, 1918; CCRR, *Negro in Chicago*, 177. For similar findings among black migrants to Pittsburgh during this era, see Gottlieb, *Making Their Own Way*, 78–80.

21. *Defender*, July 7, November 24, 1917, April 27, 1918; Black, *Black's Blue Book* (1917), 8; Theodore T. Cowgill, "The Employment Agencies of Chicago" (Master's thesis, University of Chicago, 1928), 33–34, 36.

22. "Rate of Wages Paid to Workers Placed By Employment Offices in the United States, January, 1918," *Monthly Labor Review* 6, no. 3 (March 1918): 612–17; Illinois Department of Labor, *Third Annual Report* (Springfield, 1921), 16.

23. Chicago Urban League, *Third Annual Report* (1919), 2. For locations of USES branches in Chicago, see *United States Employment Service Bulletin* 1, no. 10 (April 2, 1918): 6, and 1, no. 19 (June 4, 1918): 8; U.S. Employment Service, *Directory of Public Employment Services* (Washington, D.C., 1928), 8, pamphlet in Box 1512, Records of the U.S. Employment Service, RG 183, NA.

24. Chicago Urban League, *Second Annual Report* (1918), 6; *Defender*, March 10, 1917, November 29, 1919; *Whip*, November 22, 1919.

25. Wood, *Negro in Chicago*, 18; *Whip*, July 23, 1921; *Defender*, April 19, 1919, May 10, 1919, September 20, 27, 1919; Young Women's Christian Association of Chicago, *Forty-first Annual Statement*, 1917, 31–32. For descriptions of the YWCA's placement activities, see datebook of Irene McCoy Gaines, in Gaines Collection.

26. Duster, ed., *Crusade for Justice*, 306, 333, 373, 413–14; *Defender*, October 5, 1918, March 20, 1920; E. Jennings, "Institutional AME Church," typescript in Box 29 ("Churches"), IWP, "Negro in Illinois."

27. For a photograph of the employment department of the Chicago Urban League, see Chicago Urban League, *Fourth Annual Report* (1920), 9.

28. U.S. Commission on Industrial Relations, *Final Report and Testimony*

(Washington, D.C., 1916), 4: 3463–64. For evidence that this system was still used in 1917, see R. T. Sims to E. N. Nockels, January 19, 1917, Files-USDL, RG 174.

29. Adams, *Humanizing a Great Industry*, 8. See also Arthur H. Carver, *Personnel and Labor Problems in the Packing Industry* (Chicago, 1928), 43; J. O. Houze, "Negro Labor and the Industries," *Opportunity*, 1, no. 1 (January 1923): 20; "Factory Schedules for McCormick Twine Mill and Deering Twine Mill" (1924), Surveys for Bulletin no. 51, Folder 29, Box 197, Women's Bureau, RG 86.

30. George E. Haynes, "Negroes Move North, II" *Survey* 41 (January 4, 1919): 459; Alma Herbst, *The Negro in the Slaughtering and Meat-Packing Industry in Chicago* (Boston, 1932), 60. None of the factories surveyed by the U.S. Women's Bureau in Alabama in 1922 had an employment manager (see "Factory Schedules for Alabama Industries," Surveys for Bulletin no. 43, Box 189, Women's Bureau, RG 86). For traditional methods of labor relations on even the most rationalized plantations, see Howard A. Turner, "Bledsoe Plantation," (1913), 4–11, typescript in Box 86, OFM-BAE, RG 83.

31. Identification according to check number is apparent in hearings in File No. 33/864, FMCS, RG 280. See also The Pilgrim, "Pilgrim's Progress in a Packing House," *Life and Labor* 10, no. 2 (February 1920): 36. The reference to corporate plantations comes from Turner, "Bledsoe Plantation," 4–11. Men who had worked on the docks in New Orleans, Mobile, or other ports might have had experience with a similar system, in which longshoremen were known to an employer only by a number on a brass check. See David Katzman, "Work in the City: Longshoremen" (Paper presented to Chicago Historical Society Urban History Seminar, May 14, 1987), 12.

32. "Factory Schedule for Armour & Co." (May 1924), and "Factory Schedule for Wilson & Co." (April 1924), both in Surveys for Bulletin no. 51, Folder 5, Box 196, Women's Bureau, RG 86; Emma L. Shields, *Negro Women in Industry*, U.S. Women's Bureau Bulletin no. 20 (Washington, D.C., 1922), 34; Herbst, *Negro in the Slaughtering and Meat-Packing Industry*, 4–5. For more complimentary descriptions of the stockyards, see Robert Shackleton, *The Book of Chicago* (Philadelphia, 1920), 183–84; Adams, *Humanizing a Great Industry*, 5.

33. Herbst, *Negro in the Slaughtering and Meat-Packing Industry*, 63; "Factory Schedule for Wilson & Co." (April 1924), Surveys for Bulletin no. 51, Folder 5, Box 196, Women's Bureau, RG 86. These survey schedules offer the best descriptions of packinghouse environments during the 1910s and 1920s. Fortunately, they sometimes describe men's work areas as well as women's. They seldom state whether workers in a given department were black, but I have used schedules only for those departments that other sources state employed large numbers of blacks. For similar observations about black workers' occupations in Milwaukee's packinghouses see Trotter, *Black Milwaukee*, 53.

34. Herbst, *Negro in the Slaughtering and Meat-Packing Industry*, 170; Paul Aldrich, ed., *The Packers' Encyclopedia; Blue Book of the American Meat Packing and Allied Indusries; A Hand Book of Modern Packing House Practice*. (Chicago, 1922), 24, 26; Testimony of Dennis Lane, "Arbitration between the Packers

and Their Employes on a Demand for Increase of Three Cents per Hour for All Employes in the Industry outside of the Mechanical Trades" (April 7, 1920), 4, in File 170/1064, FMCS, RG 280; Sandburg, *Chicago Race Riots*, 64–65.

35. Shields, *Negro Women in Industry*, 34; Herbst, *Negro in the Slaughtering and Meat-Packing Industry*, 80; Ethel Best and Ruth I. Voris, *Women in Illinois Industries*, U.S. Women's Bureau Bulletin no. 51 (Washington, D.C., 1925), 52; "Factory Schedule for Wilson & Co." (April 1924) and "Factory Schedule for Omaha Packing Co." (February 8, 1924), Surveys for Bulletin no. 51, Folder 5, Box 196, Women's Bureau, RG 86.

36. *Defender*, October 6, 1917, July 7, 1917; Aldrich, ed., *Packers' Encyclopedia*, 27; Lucian W. Chaney, "Trend of Accident Frequency Rates in the Iron and Steel Industry During the World War," *Monthly Labor Review* 5, no. 5 (November 1917): 848.

37. John R. Commons, "Labor Conditions in Slaughtering and Meat Packing," *Quarterly Journal of Economics* 19, no. 3 (November 1904): 6; Brody, *Butcher Workmen*, 2–4. See also Alfred D. Chandler, Jr., *The Visible Hand: The Managerial Revolution in American Business* (Cambridge, Mass., 1977), 391–402.

38. Fogel, *Negro in the Meat Industry*, 17–18; Aldrich, ed., *Packers Encyclopedia*, 8–9; Upton Sinclair, *The Jungle* (New York, 1906), 34. For another invocation of the cliché, see *BW*, February 1916.

39. *BW*, February 1916; Brody, *Butcher Workmen*, 4; Aldrich, ed., *Packers' Encyclopedia*, 13–20. A good description of the various jobs in a packinghouse can be found in U.S. Department of Labor, Bureau of Labor Statistics, *Wages and Hours of Labor in the Slaughtering and Meat-Packing Industry*, Bulletin no. 252 (Washington, D.C., 1919), 1075–1114.

40. Carver, *Personnel and Labor Problems*, 33, 52–53; Herbst, *Negro in the Slaughtering and Meat-Packing Industry*, xvii, 117–18; Aldrich, ed., *Packers' Encyclopedia*, 10, 14.

41. Sinclair, *The Jungle*, 39; Brody, *Butcher Workmen*, 5; Mary McDowell, "A Quarter of a Century in the Stockyards District," *Transactions of the Illinois State Historical Society*, no. 27 (1920), 73–74.

42. Gottlieb, *Making Their Own Way*, 117, 119–20; Dorothy Walton, "Other People's Clothes, or Life in a Laundry," *NM*, March 27, 1920. For a comparison with less rationalized laundries in Mississippi, see "Factory Schedules for Mississippi Laundries, January-February, 1925," Surveys for Bulletin no. 55, Folder 8, Box 199, Women's Bureau, RG 86.

43. Quoted in Vance, *Human Factors in Cotton Culture*, 165.

44. Howard Odum and Guy Johnson, *The Negro and His Songs* (Chapel Hill, 1925), 262–66. On work songs and cadences, see Robert Emmett Kennedy, *Mellows. Negro Work Songs, Street Cries, and Spirituals* (New York, 1925), 26–28; Levine, *Black Culture and Black Consciousness*, 208–16.

45. Levine, *Black Culture and Black Consciousness*, 211.

46. Ibid., 203, 212, 314; Mathilde Bunton, "Negro Work Songs," (1940), 1, typescript in Box 91 ("Music"), IWP, "Negro In Illinois."

47. "A 20 Acre One Horse Cotton Farm in Black Prairie Belt of Alabama and Mississippi," enclosed in M. A. Crosby to W. J. Spellman, January 9, 1912, OFM-BAE, RG 83; Vance, *Human Factors in Cotton Culture*, 77. For a

discussion of the difference between agricultural "task orientation" and industrial "time orientation," see E. P. Thompson, "Time, Work-Discipline, and Industrial Capitalism," *Past and Present* no. 38 (December 1967): 60.

48. T. M. Campbell, *The First Historical Report on Agricultural Extension Work Among Negroes in the States of Alabama, Georgia, Florida, Mississippi, Louisiana, Oklahoma and Texas,* U.S. Department of Agriculture, Social Relations Service Circular no. 1 (Washington, D.C., 1920), 23; A. D. McNair, "Labor Estimates and Records From Arkansas Farms" (Address, November 10, 1913), 10, Box 50, OFM-BAE, RG 83; McNair, "Small Farm Incomes in the Cotton Belt" (1916), 3, typescript in Box 50, OFM-BAE, RG 83; Rosengarten, *All God's Dangers,* 179.

49. Frazier, *Negro Family in Chicago,* 80; McNair, "Small Farm Incomes in the Cotton Belt," 10, Box 50, OFM-BAE, RG 83; Gottlieb, *Making Their Own Way,* 20–21.

50. Wood, *Negro in Chicago,* 7; Helen B. Sayre, "Making Over Poor Workers," *Opportunity* 1, no. 2 (February 1923): 17–18; *Defender,* April 7, 1917; Chicago Urban League, *Fourth Annual Report* (1920), 8; U.S. Department of Labor, *Negro at Work During the World War and Reconstruction,* 50–51; CCRR, *Negro in Chicago,* 372–76. On lateness, see also Haynes, "Negroes Move North, II," 458, and Sayre, "Negro Women in Industry," 243.

51. U.S. Department of Labor, *Negro at Work During the World War and Reconstruction,* 50–51; Herbst, *Negro in the Slaughtering and Meat-Packing Industry,* 127; *Iron Age* 99 (April 12, 1917): 910; CCRR, *Negro in Chicago,* 377; William L. Evans, "An Inquiry Into the Working Conditions of Colored Workmen Employed by the Argo Corn Products & Refining Company, Argo, Illinois, 1920," p. 2, "Jan. 5-April 24, 1922" Folder, Box C-320, NAACP; Howard R. Gold and Byron K. Armstrong, *A Preliminary Study of Inter-Racial Conditions in Chicago* (New York, 1920), 13. These statistics did not distinguish between voluntary and involuntary separations and might have been skewed upward if postwar layoffs had begun. Turnover statistics for different companies must be compared with caution, as there was no single formula used by every compiler of these statistics. To calculate the ratio, employers generally used one of three numerators: total separations; separations less layoffs; or one-half the sum of accessions plus separations. The denominator might be the average number of employees on the payroll or the average number of employees at work. The most commonly used formula was total separations divided by average number of workers on payroll. See Carver, *Personnel and Labor Problems,* 81.

52. Daniel T. Rodgers, *The Work Ethic in Industrial America, 1850–1920* (Chicago, 1978), 163; Paul Douglas quoted in Gordon S. Watkins, *Labor Problems and Labor Administration in the United States During the World War* (Urbana, 1919), 59–60.

53. T. Arnold Hill, "Recent Developments in the Problem of Negro Labor," *Proceedings of the National Conference of Social Work* 48 (1921), 322; Chicago Urban League, *Fourth Annual Report* (1920), 6; Herbst, *Negro in the Slaughtering and Meat-Packing Industry,* 3, 71–73; CCRR, *Negro in Chicago,* 373; Barnett, "We Win a Place," 82.

54. Johnson, "Gulfport," 1, "Mississippi Summary," NULR; USDL, *Negro Migration,* 84–85; Nollie Hickman, *Mississippi Harvest* (Oxford, Miss., 1962), 124; Katzman, *Seven Days A Week,* 213.

55. CCRR, *Negro in Chicago,* 385–87. In her study of working women during World War I, Maurine Greenwald attributed their high turnover rates to "the constant search for better jobs." Entering at the bottom of Chicago's labor market, black migrants employed similar strategies. See Maurine Greenwald, "Women, War, and Work: The Impact of World War I on Women Workers in the United States" (Ph.D. dissertation, Brown University, 1977), 29.

56. Evans, "Inquiry Into the Working Conditions," 3, NAACP; Employment Files of the Pullman Company, Newberry Library, Chicago; Edith Abbott, *The Tenements of Chicago, 1908–1935* (Chicago, 1936), 154; Gold and Armstrong, *Preliminary Study,* 13; Philpott, *Slum and the Ghetto,* 139; Home Registration Service Committee of the [Illinois] State Council of Defense, "Memorandum of Scheduled Running Time and Mileage" (October 1919), in Box 307, Records of the U.S. Housing Corporation, RG 3, NA. The Council of Defense's concern regarding the commute suggests that many of Indiana Harbor's black steelworkers resided in Chicago. Among the migrants interviewed in Chicago by Charles Johnson in 1917 many commuted to Indiana Harbor (see Johnson, "Interviews," NULR).

57. CCRR, *Negro in Chicago,* 365–66, 377, 388–89; Evans, "Inquiry into the Working Conditions," 2–3, 13, NAACP; F. Washington, "Reconstruction," 6.

58. R. Wilson, "Mr. Dorsey" [c. 1921?], Folder 14 ("Life Histories"), Box 1, Park Papers; Hickman, *Mississippi Harvest,* 144; Johnson, "Interviews," 11, NULR.

59. Du Bois, *Souls of Black Folk,* 148–52; *Defender,* May 17, 1919; Howard Odum and Guy Johnson, *Negro Workaday Songs* (Chapel Hill, 1926), 78.

60. "The Superfluous Negro," *New Republic* 7 (June 24, 1916): 187. Railroad spokesman quoted in *Daily News,* February 24, 1916. See also Erie Hardy, "Relation of the Negro to Trade Unionism" (Master's thesis, University of Chicago, 1911), 35–36; Spear, *Black Chicago,* 34–35; Scott, *Occupational Changes,* 128–30, 136–40; Arthur P. Drucker, Sophia Boaz, A. L. Harris, and Miriam Schaffer, *The Colored People of Chicago* (Chicago, 1913), 6; McDonald, *Insull,* 192.

61. *Iron Age* 98 (June 28, 1917): 1563–64; Kennedy, *Negro Peasant Turns Cityward,* 112.

62. "Problem of the Negro Laborer," *Iron Trade Review* 60 (April 12, 1917): 836–37; [George E. Haynes], "Matters of Record" [1917], 10, typescript in Box 184, DNE-USDL, RG 174.

63. Daniel Nelson, *Managers and Workers: Origins of the New Factory in the United States 1880–1920* (Madison, 1975), 81–82; Johnson, *Negro in American Civilization,* 46–47; Houze, "Negro Labor and the Industries," 20.

64. "The Superfluous Negro," 188.

65. *Iron Age* 99 (April 12, 1917): 910; Morris Lewis to Karl D. Phillips, April 9, 1927, File 8/102g, Files-USDL, RG 174.

66. Herbst, *Negro in the Slaughtering and Meat-Packing Industry,* 77.

67. Sayre, "Negro Women in Industry," 244; *Iron Age* 105 (April 1, 1920):

951–54; Korman, *Industrialization, Immigrants, and Americanizers*, 81. On "making men" as an aspect of industrial relations during this era, see Stuart Brandes, *American Welfare Capitalism, 1880–1940* (Chicago, 1976), 33–34.

68. *Defender*, January 19, 1918; Drake and Cayton, *Black Metropolis*, 60. Feminist leaders in the United States approached women's industrial opportunities in a similar vein. They argued that the success of "pioneers" in industry was essential, and often they accorded higher value to individual accomplishment than to protective legislation and collective organization. See Greenwald, "Women, War, and Work," 63–64, 75–76.

69. Sayre, "Making Over Poor Workers," 17. For a discussion of how these institutions dealt with unionism, see chapter 8.

70. George R. Arthur, *Life on the Negro Frontier* (New York, 1934), 186; George Arthur, "The Young Men's Christian Association Movement Among Negroes," *Opportunity* 1, no. 3 (March 1923), 17; *Defender*, October 14, 1922; *Whip*, October 29, 1921.

71. Arthur, "Young Men's Christian Association Movement," 17; Arthur to William J. Parker, April 10, 1920, Folder 6, Box 44, Rosenwald Papers; *Defender*, June 1, 1918; CCRR, *Negro in Chicago*, 148; William M. Tuttle, Jr., Interview with Alexander L. Jackson, Chicago, June 27, 1969 (notes in possession of Tuttle); Tuttle, *Race Riot*, 60–61.

72. Arthur, "Young Men's Christian Association Movement," 17; *Whip*, January 17, 1920; *Defender*, April 27, June 15, 1918, July 12, 1919; Arthur to William J. Parker, April 10, 1920, Folder 6, Box 44, Rosenwald Papers; Minutes of the January Meeting of the Chicago League on Urban Conditions Among Negroes, January 9, [1918], Folder 6, Aldis Papers; Spero and Harris, *Black Worker*, 273.

73. Chicago Urban League, *Third Annual Report* (1919), 3; *Defender*, September 7, 1918; Strickland, *History of the Chicago Urban League*, 48. On screening applicants in Milwaukee by that city's Urban League, which had a close relationship with Chicago's branch, see Trotter, *Black Milwaukee*, 58.

74. Chicago Urban League, *Fourth Annual Report* (1920), 6–8, 10; "The Horizon," *Crisis* 20, no. 5 (August 1920): 192; CCRR, *Negro in Chicago*, 147; "The Horizon," *Crisis* 19, no. 6 (April 1920): 340; A. L. Foster, "Twenty Years of Interracial Goodwill Through Social Service," in Chicago Urban League, *Two Decades of Service* (Chicago, 1936), 13; Sayre, "Making Over Poor Workers," 18.

75. F. Washington, "Program of Work for the Assimilation of Negro Immigrants," 499; Charles Johnson, "Black Workers and the City," *Survey* 63, no. 11 (March 1, 1925): 721; "The Looking Glass," *Crisis* 14, no. 5 (September 1917): 240.

76. Lists of Chicago Urban League contributors in Folders 13–14, Box 9, Rosenwald Papers; W[illiam] C. G[raves] to Julius Rosenwald, November 26, 1919, Folder 15, Box 9, Rosenwald Papers; T. Arnold Hill to Graves, February 8, July 2, September 7, 1921, Folder 16, Box 9, Rosenwald Papers; Strickland, *History of the Chicago Urban League*, 14; Arvarh Strickland, Interview with Irene McCoy Gaines, Chicago, June 26, 1961 (tape in possession of Strickland); Evans, "Inquiry Into the Working Conditions," 14–15, NAACP.

77. Gold and Armstrong, *Preliminary Study*, 11, 13–14; CCRR, *Negro in*

Chicago, 372–78; Houze, "Negro Labor and the Industries," 21; Sayre, "Negro Women in Industry," 243–44; Thomas J. Woofter, "The Negro and Industrial Peace," *Survey* 45, no. 12 (December 18, 1920): 420; Evans, "Inquiry Into the Working Conditions," 2, NAACP. The quotation is from CCRR, *Negro in Chicago*, 373. For company statistics contradicting supervisors' claims that blacks had higher absentee and quit rates than whites, see Cohen, "Learning to Live in the Welfare State," 289. Packinghouse turnover rates during the 1920s were misleading, because in at least one case higher rates among blacks were attributable to discriminatory layoff policies; black quit rates were lower. See Herbst, *Negro in the Slaughtering and Meat-Packing Industry*, 131–40.

78. CCRR, *Negro in Chicago*, 359; *Defender*, February 14, 1920.

79. Thompson, "Time, Work-Discipline," 85–86; Sidney Pollard, *The Genesis of Modern Management: A Study of the Industrial Revolution in England* (London, 1965), 183; Sidney Pollard, "Factory Discipline in the Industrial Revolution," *Economic History Review* 16, no. 2 (December 1963): 257–63; E. J. Hobsbawm, *Industry and Empire: An Economic History of Britain Since 1750* (London, 1968), 67; Herbert Gutman, *Work, Culture, and Society in Industrializing America* (New York, 1977), 3–78.

80. Paul Oliver, *Blues Fell This Morning: The Meaning of the Blues* (New York, 1960), 31.

81. T. Arnold Hill to Walter F. White, November 14, 1919, and enclosed "Memorandum 'A'," "Sept.-Dec., 1919" Folder, Box C-319, NAACP; "Conference on the Negro in Industry," Committee on Industry, Chicago Commission on Race Relations, April 23, 1920, Folder 5, Box 6, Rosenwald Papers.

82. Ralph W. Immel, "The Negro and His Opportunity," *Industrial Management* 58 (July 1919): 76; Charles Johnson, "Negro Migrations" [c. 1926], 16, typescript in Folder 31, Box 167, Johnson Papers; CCRR, *Negro in Chicago*, 439; Cohen, "Learning to Live in the Welfare State," 288.

83. M.V.G. to Chicago Urban League [1918], "Undated, 1920" Folder, Box C-319, NAACP (this letter is reprinted in the *Defender*, August 3, 1918); "Memorandum of Address made June 17 Before the Interracial Committee of the Union League Club," June 17, 1926, pp. 2–3, Folder 2, Box 40, Rosenwald Papers.

Chapter 8

1. *Whip*, July 19, 1919; *NM*, July 5, August 9, 1919.

2. *NM*, July 12, 1919; *BW*, July 1919; Sandburg, *Chicago Race Riots*, 47; *Whip*, July 19, 1919. On the size of the crowd, see note 3 below.

3. Many blacks had expected a riot to erupt on July 4. See Tuttle, Interview with Chester Wilkins, 3. It is always difficult to estimate the size of crowds, and even more problematic to gauge the significance of a given turnout. In this case, union newspapers eschewed their usual practice of estimating the size of the meeting, and Carl Sandburg's estimate of two or three thousand is less than the usual size of Stockyards Labor Council rallies. Given Sandburg's proclivity for exaggeration, his figure should suggest a maximum. See Sandburg, *Chicago Race Riots*, 47.

4. For an exaggerated description of the black community's response to the parade—which nevertheless suggests that there was some significant response, see "Negro Agitation," Military Intelligence Report (July 1919), 3, Box 14, Glasser File, General Records of the U.S. Department of Justice, RG 60, NA.

5. "Strikes and Lockouts, December, 1915 to May, 1916," *Monthly Labor Review* 4, no. 4 (April 1917): 603; Mark L. Crawford to William B. Wilson, April 17, 1916, and Clive Runnels to Crawford, April 14, 1916, both in "Strike of Pullman Car Cleaners," File 33/192, FMCS, RG 280; CCRR, *Negro in Chicago*, 430–31; "International Harvester Workers' Strike," *Life and Labor* 6, no. 7 (July 1916): 111. One Chicago labor leader estimated in May 1916 that 25,000 workers were out on strike in the city; *Daily News*, May 10, 1916.

6. *NM*, December 10, 1921; Joel Seidman, *The Needle Trades* (New York, 1942), 38; Tuttle, *Race Riot*, 129.

7. On blacks and the steel strike of 1919, see Spear, *Black Chicago*, 163–64; Brody, *Steelworkers in America*, 224–25; William Z. Foster, *The Great Steel Strike and its Lessons* (New York, 1920), 205–7; Spero and Harris, *Black Worker*, 260–63; Horace R. Cayton and George S. Mitchell, *Black Workers and the New Unions* (Chapel Hill, 1939), 79; Gottlieb, *Making Their Own Way*, 152, 156–64, 172. Cleveland (along with Wheeling, W. V.) constituted an exception, in that its black steelworkers were "almost completely unionized." There, the steelworkers' union did make a special effort to recruit them. It is also possible that because black Cleveland did not have the institutional framework found in black Chicago, the union did not face some of the competitive obstacles that I discuss below. See Kusmer, *A Ghetto Takes Shape*, 186–87, 197.

8. Spero and Harris, *Black Worker*, 269–70; Herbst, *Negro in the Slaughtering and Meat-Packing Industry*, xviii, 29. For a detailed discussion of packinghouse organizing between 1917 and 1922, see Brody, *Butcher Workmen*, 75–105. See also James R. Barrett, *Work and Community in the Jungle: Chicago's Packinghouse Workers, 1894–1922* (Urbana, 1987), 188–231, 255–63. Most of the discussion that follows was written before the publication of Barrett's book; his interpretation differs from mine at several points.

9. Brody, *Butcher Workmen*, 76; Foster, "How Life Has Been Brought into the Stockyards," 65; Benjamin Stolberg, "The Stock Yards Strike," *Nation* 114 (January 25, 1922): 91. The United States Department of Labor estimated "25–50 percent," probably with reference to Chicago. The Stockyards Labor Council claimed 40,000 members in Chicago—nearly 90 percent—but this seems unlikely at this early date. See U.S. Department of Labor, *Report* (1918), 24; Spero and Harris, *Black Worker*, 270.

10. Brody, *Butcher Workmen*, 77, 81–82; [Frank Walsh], *Over the Top at the Yards* (Chicago, 1918), 117, pamphlet in the Hugh L. Kerwin Files, File 13/110, General Records of the Department of Labor, RG 174, NA. For a concise and evocative description of the Alschuler hearings, see Barrett, *Work and Community in the Jungle*, 198–200.

11. Brody, *Butcher Workmen*, 83–85. Tensions between more radical elements in the Stockyards Labor Council and moderates connected with the craft unions had existed since the beginning of the unionization campaign in

1917. Strategic questions related to the role of arbitration versus the role of strikes were often central to this tension. See Barrett, *Work and Community in the Jungle*, 198, 224–31. Barrett appropriately places greater emphasis than I have on the implications of the decision to channel union energy into the arbitration process at the cost of organization and the freedom to strike.

12. "Arbitration between the Chicago Meat Packers and Their Employees," June 20, 1919, and "Arbitration: Walkout at Wilson & Co., Chicago," July 9, 1919, p. 17, both in File 33/864, FMCS, RG 280; Tuttle, *Race Riot*, 108. The agreement stipulated that "no collecting, soliciting, or advocating for or against unionism shall be permitted on the premises" (See "Agreement," December 25, 1917, in File 33/864B, FMCS, RG 280). Both sides frequently violated this clause.

13. "Arbitration between the Chicago Meat Packers and Their Employees," 103, 131–32, 148, 150–57, 177, File 33/864, FMCS, RG 280.

14. Ibid., 178, 290; Spero and Harris, *Black Worker*, 271.

15. Philip S. Foner, *Organized Labor and the Black Worker, 1619–1973* (New York, 1974), 89 (Ameringer quotation), 113; Spero and Harris, *Black Worker*, 183–86; Johnson, "Meridian," 1, "Mississippi Summary," NULR; Eugene Kinckle Jones to Secretaries of the Affiliated Organizations, April 8, 1918, and T. H. Dwelle to Jones, April 11, 1918, both in Box 87, Series 6, NULR; Paul Worthman, "Black Workers and Labor Unions in Birmingham, Alabama, 1897–1904," *Labor History* 10, no. 3 (Summer 1969): 394–95; Paul Worthman and James Green, "Black Workers in the New South, 1865–1915," in Huggins, et al., *Key Issues in the Afro-American Experience*, 2: 61; *Defender*, October 7, 1916.

16. Walter White, "The Race Conflict in Arkansas," *Survey* 43, no. 7 (December 13, 1919): 233–34.

17. Estimates on black membership in these organizations vary; I have presented a range or a conservative figure. Spero and Harris, *Black Worker*, 331–33; Foner, *Organized Labor*, 49, 56, 115; Vernon H. Jensen, *Lumber and Labor* (New York, 1945), 87–91; Hickman, *Mississippi Harvest*, 236–37; August Meier and Elliott Rudwick, "Attitudes of Negro Leaders toward the American Labor Movement from the Civil War to World War I," in Julius Jacobson, ed., *The Negro and the American Labor Movement* (Garden City, 1968), 33; Lamon, *Black Tennesseans*, 116–17; Martin Dann, "Black Populism: A Study of the Colored Farmers' Alliance Through 1891," *Journal of Ethnic Studies* 2, no. 3 (Fall 1974): 62–69.

18. Dittmer, *Black Georgia*, 30.

19. Spero and Harris, *Black Worker*, 252–53; Lamon, *Black Tennesseans*, 159–60; Greene and Woodson, *Negro Wage Earner*, 186–92; Finney, "Study of Negro Labor during and after World War I," 1–45; Ira DeA. Reid, ed., *Negro Membership in American Labor Unions* (New York, 1930), 43; George S. Mitchell, "The Negro in Southern Unionism," *The Southern Economic Journal* 2, no. 3 (January 1936): 26–33.

20. An Employee of the Illinois Central Railroad Shops, Memphis, Tenn., to Walter Hines, July 7, 1919, File E-38-11, vol. 3, Box E 51, Records of the Division of Labor, U.S. Railroad Administration, RG 14, NA; Spero and Har-

ris, *Black Worker*, 289–92; Worthman and Green, "Black Workers in the New South," 61–62; "The Negro Railway Trainmen and the U.S. Railway Labor Board," Decision No. 307, Docket 138, Chicago, November 4, 1921, Folder 16, Box 43–1, Abram L. Harris Papers, Moorland-Spingarn Research Center, Howard University, Washington, D.C; Lamon, *Black Tennesseans*, 162, 164. See also William H. Harris, *The Harder We Run: Black Workers since the Civil War* (New York, 1982), 46–48.

21. CCRR, *Negro in Chicago*, 424.

22. Meier and Rudwick, "Attitudes of Negro Leaders," 39–41; Kelly Miller, "The Negro as a Workingman," *American Mercury* 6, no. 23 (November 1925): 310–13; Booker T. Washington, "The Negro and the Labor Unions," *Atlantic Monthly* 7 (June 1913): 756–67; [W. E. B. Du Bois], "The Black Man and the Unions," *Crisis* 15, no. 5 (March 1918): 216–17.

23. Spero and Harris, *Black Worker*, 17–22, 92; Reid, ed., *Negro Membership*, 104; Bernard Mandel, "Samuel Gompers and the Negro," *Journal of Negro History* 40, no. 1 (January 1955): 34–60.

24. Marc Karson and Ronald Radosh, "The American Federation of Labor and the Negro Worker, 1894–1945," in Jacobson, ed., *Negro and the American Labor Movement*, 158–60. Gompers did not confine his racial epithets to blacks; he had similar disdain for "Chinamen and Japs." See Mandel, "Samuel Gompers," 46; Arthur Mann, "Gompers and the Irony of Racism," *Antioch Review* 13, no. 2 (June 1953): 208–10.

25. *Defender*, October 2, 1915; Hardy, "Relation of the Negro to Trade Unionism," 35; Van Deusen, *Black Man in White America*, 56; Tuttle, *Race Riot*, 114; Charles S. Johnson, "The Negro and Labor Unions" [c. 1926?], 3, typescript in Box 89, Series 6, NULR; reprint from Chicago *Daily News* [1916 or 1917], Box 86, Series 6, NULR; Montgomery, *Industrial Relations in the Chicago Building Trades*, 87–88; Drucker, et al., *Colored People of Chicago*, 5; Charles S. Johnson to E[ugene] K. Jones, April 17, 1918, Box 87, Series 6, NULR.

26. CCRR, *Negro in Chicago*, 421–22, 426–27; Woofter, "Negro and Industrial Peace," 421; Charles S. Johnson to Eugene K. Jones, April 17, 1918, Box 87, Series 6, NULR; Webster, "Organized Labor Among Negroes in Chicago," 196.

27. Herbst, *Negro in the Slaughtering and Meat-Packing Industry*, 14–19; Spero and Harris, *Black Worker*, 264–68; Scott, *Occupational Changes*, 129–30, 136–40; Tuttle, *Race Riot*, 117–19; U.S. Commission on Industrial Relations, *Final Report and Testimony*, 4: 3518.

28. Chicago *Record Herald*, July 19, 1894, quoted in Spero and Harris, *Black Worker*, 265.

29. Tuttle, *Race Riot*, 113, 120–22; Hardy, "Relation of the Negro to Trade Unionism," 35–36; *Defender*, May 11, 1912. See also Spear, *Black Chicago*, 39–40.

30. Tuttle, *Race Riot*, 116–19; Spero and Harris, *Black Worker*, 132.

31. Tuttle, *Race Riot*, 124–25; Foster, "How Life Has Been Brought into the Stockyards," 64; Fitzpatrick quoted in Spero and Harris, *Black Worker*, 270. Foster, a former Wobbly, was at this time an organizer for the Railway Carmen's Union.

32. *NM*, January 24, 1920; Spero and Harris, *Black Worker*, 112–13, 268–70; Brody, *Butcher Workmen*, 86.

33. CCRR, *Negro in Chicago*, 412–13; Gold and Armstrong, *Preliminary Study*, 14; Brody, *Butcher Workmen*, 42–43, 86; Foster, "How Life Has Been Brought into the Stockyards," 64; Reid, *Negro Membership*, 167; Foster, *Great Steel Strike*, 211; Olive Sullivan, "Chicago League Organizing Stockyards Women Workers," *Life and Labor* 8, no. 4 (April 1918): 84; Sullivan, "The Women's Part in the Stockyards Organization Work," *Life and Labor* 8, no. 5 (May 1918): 104.

34. *BW*, November-December 1917; Charles S. Johnson to Eugene K. Jones, April 17, 1918, Box 87, Series 6, NULR; *BW*, October 1918; Tuttle, *Race Riot*, 127. For dues totals, see *BW* for 1918. I have based my membership estimates on a per capita payment of twenty-five cents from the Local to the International.

35. *NM*, April 26, June 21, 1919; *BW*, May, July, 1919.

36. *NM*, June 21, July 19, 1919; *Whip*, July 19, 1919; dues listings in *BW*, June, July, August, 1919.

37. "Arbitration between the Chicago Meat Packers and Their Employees," 429, 456, 474, 491, File 33/864, FMCS, RG 280. For membership estimates, see Sandburg, *Chicago Race Riots*, 45; CCRR, *Negro in Chicago*, 413; A. Philip Randolph and Chandler Owen, "The Cause of and Remedy For Race Riots," *The Messenger* 2, no. 9 (September 1919): 18; Gold and Armstrong, *Preliminary Study*, 14. Because observers stated that "most" black workers joined Local 651, it is unlikely that other locals included more than 2,000 black members.

38. CCRR, *Negro in Chicago*, 413; "Arbitration between the Chicago Meat Packers and Their Employees," 183–88, File 33/864, FMCS, RG 280.

39. *Defender*, August 30, 1919; CCRR, *Negro in Chicago*, 2–3, 395–96, 399; Tuttle, *Race Riot*, 108–56.

40. *NM*, August 9, 1919; Tuttle, *Race Riot*, 57, 60–61; Brody, *Butcher Workmen*, 87–88.

41. Brody, *Butcher Workmen*, 88; Tuttle, *Race Riot*, 63. Tuttle uses the term "closed shop," but the evidence suggests that Brody's "union shop" reference is probably more accurate. The difference is significant, since the latter does not require an employer to hire only union members; it requires a worker to join after being hired.

42. *NM*, August 9, 1919.

43. CCRR, *Negro in Chicago*, 177, 424. On union aid to blacks during the riot, see *BW*, September 1919; *NM*, August 16, 1919.

44. Tuttle, Interview with Chester Wilkins, 5. The accusation against the packers for their role in the riot's origins is in *NM*, August 9, 1919.

45. *NM*, August 2, 1919; *BW*, July 1919-May 1920.

46. *Whip*, January 24, 1920; *BW*, August 1920.

47. *NM*, March 19, June 11, July 30, September 10, 1921.

48. Brody, *Butcher Workmen*, 97–98; *BW*, November 1921.

49. Herbst, *Negro in the Slaughtering and Meat-Packing Industry*, 63; Stolberg, "Stock Yards Strike," 92; Brody, *Butcher Workmen*, 102–3; *NM*, December 10, 1921.

50. "Negroes in the Packing House Strike in Chicago" [1921], 1, typescript in "Jan. 5-April 24, 1922" Folder, Box C-320, NAACP; *NM*, December 24, 1921; Spero and Harris, *Black Worker*, 281; Clarke, "History of the Controversy between Labor and Capital in the Slaughtering and Meat Packing Industry," 201.

51. Herbst, *Negro in the Slaughtering and Meat-Packing Industry*, xxii, 77; *BW*, February 1922; stockyards executive quoted in Stolberg, "Stock Yards Strike," 92.

52. T. Arnold Hill to J. J. Uhlmann, May 3, 1925, Box 28, Series 4, NULR.

53. Cayton and Mitchell, *Black Workers and the New Unions*, 269; CCRR, *Negro in Chicago*, 428–29; *NM*, July 12, 1919. This willingness to hire black organizers contrasts with the refusal of the leadership of the Amalgamated Association of Iron, Steel, and Tin Workers to heed Foster's advice to use black organizers; Gottlieb, *Making Their Own Way*, 156.

54. *NM*, January 11, August 9, 1919, January 14, 1922; the Foster quotations are from CCRR, *Negro in Chicago*, 429; Foster, *Great Steel Strike*, 211; Spero and Harris, *Black Worker*, 273.

55. Fitzpatrick quoted in Herbst, *Negro in the Slaughtering and Meat-Packing Industry*, 37.

56. Spero and Harris, *Black Worker*, 272, 279; CCRR, *Negro in Chicago*, 429; R. E. Parker to President Warren G. Harding, March 11, 1921, File 170/1365, FMCS, RG 280; George E. Haynes, "Memorandum to the Secretary," March 18, 1921, File 8/102a, Files-USDL, RG 174; *NM*, March 19, 26, 1921; *Defender*, September 23, 1922; *Whip*, September 23, 1922. Parker's organization was also known as the American Unity Packers Union.

57. *The Official Bulletin of the Young Men's Christian Association of Chicago* 17, no. 3 (May-June 1921): 3, copy in "YMCA, 1915–21" folder, Taylor Papers (emphasis in original); Tuttle, *Race Riot*, 151; George R. Arthur to William J. Parker, April 10, 1920, Folder 6, Box 44, Rosenwald Papers.

58. George Arthur to William Parker, April 10, 1920, Folder 6, Box 44, Rosenwald Papers. For a similar event, see *Defender*, October 5, 1918.

59. "Arbitration between the Chicago Meat Packers and Their Employees," 267–69, File 33/864, FMCS, RG 280; Cayton and Mitchell, *Black Workers and the New Unions*, 392–93.

60. George R. Arthur to William J. Parker, April 10, 1920, Folder 6, Box 44, Rosenwald Papers; "Arbitration between the Chicago Meat Packers and Their Employees," 267, 277, File 33/864, FMCS, RG 280; Young Men's Christian Association, Wabash Avenue Branch, Minutes of the Board of Directors, January 22, 1926, Box 3, Papers of the Wabash Avenue YMCA. On Jackson's background, see Tuttle, *Race Riot*, 151.

61. Arthur, "Young Men's Christian Association Movement," 17; *Defender*, October 23, 1920; *Whip*, October 9, 1920, October 29, 1921.

62. Chicago *Broad Ax*, December 21, 1918; Young Women's Christian Association of Chicago, *Forty-fourth Annual Statement*, 1920, p. 30, and *Forty-seventh Annual Statement*, 1923; Datebook of Irene McCoy Gaines, entries for April 1, 9, May 2, June 6, 17, 23, July 4, 19, 1921, Gaines Collection; Davis, *Story of the Illinois Federation*, 52.

63. Young Women's Christian Association of Chicago, *Forty-fifth Annual*

Statement, 1921, pp. 13, 27; "Chicago, Illinois, Colored," entry for February 1923, in Files of the Young Women's Christian Association, microfilm reel 172:3, Historical Records of the National Board, YWCA Archives, New York; YWCA of Chicago, *Forty-fourth Annual Statement*, 1920, p. 30.

64. Herbst, *Negro in the Slaughtering and Meat-Packing Industry*, 64. For employment bureaus at Olivet, Metropolitan, Institutional, and New Trinity churches, see Olivet Baptist Church, *Facts and Figures* (Chicago, [1920]), 4, in Folder 6, Papers of the Chicago Commission on Race Relations, 1919–1920 (microfilm), Illinois State Archives, Springfield; Black, *Black's Blue Book* (1921), 80, 86; E. Jennings, "Institutional AME Church," Box 29 ("Churches"), IWP, "Negro in Illinois"; Logsdon, "Reverend Archibald J. Carey," 17–18; *Whip*, March 11, 1922. A 1916 description of black Chicago observed that "nearly every colored church has an employment agency as one of its most active auxiliaries"; see Wood, *Negro in Chicago*, 9. On the general influence of Chicago's black churches, see Logsdon, "Reverend Archibald J. Carey," 10–33; Carroll Binder, *Chicago and the New Negro* (Chicago, 1927), 17.

65. "Mass Meeting, Tuesday, March 18" [Chicago, 1919], Broadside in Graphics Dept., CHS; *Whip*, November 22, 1919; Sandburg, *Chicago Race Riots*, 51; Myra Young Armstead, Interview with Ida Mae Cress, April 9, 1985 (transcript in possession of author); "Chicago Law and Order League, Hyde Park Protective Association" (December 21, 1925), newsletter in Folder 11, Box 2, Section 12 ("Religion"), Barnett Papers; "[Report of] Meetings Held With Ministers in an Attempt to Secure Their Cooperation in the Interest of Community Welfare," [August 1920?], Box 25, John Fitzpatrick Papers, CHS.

66. Gosnell, *Negro Politicians*, 320; Quinn Chapel AME Church, *102nd Anniversary Record, 1847–1967* (Chicago, 1967), 25; Logsdon, "Reverend Archibald J. Carey," 17, 43, 79–80; Wright, *87 Years Behind the Black Curtain*, 114–15; *Whip*, May 14, 1921; Wood, *Negro in Chicago*, 9; CCRR, *Negro in Chicago*, 415, 421–22; Interviews with black ministers in South Chicago, Folder 5, Box 89, Section 3 ("Research"), Burgess Papers; Cayton and Mitchell, *Black Workers and the New Unions*, 255–56; Paul S. Taylor, *Mexican Labor in the United States*, vol. 2, *Chicago and Calumet Region*, (Berkeley, 1932), 93.

67. *Broad Ax*, November 8, 1919.

68. Because the *Defender* circulated so heavily in the South and circulation data are inconsistent, it is difficult to estimate its Chicago readership. The *Defender's* printer told a federal agent in 1919 that total circulation was 130,000, and the Chicago Commission on Race Relations estimated 185,000 a year later. The Commission estimated that two-thirds of the circulation was outside Chicago, leaving a local circulation of approximately 40,000 in 1919 and 60,000 in 1920, in a city with a black population of 109,458. These figures are obviously inflated, but suggest that the newspaper was widely read in black Chicago. W. E. Rowens, Jr., "Report on Chicago *Defender*," March 5, 1919, File 10,218–133, MID File, RG 165; CCRR, *Negro in Chicago*, 524, 564.

69. *Defender*, March 18, 1911, May 11, November 16, 1912. See also *Defender*, May 27, 1911, August 14, June 19, December 25, 1915, January 8, February 19, September 9, 1916.

70. *Defender*, December 22, 1916.

71. *Defender*, February 16, 1918, April 26, 1919, April 3, October 2, 1920.

72. *Defender*, May 24, 1919. On the nineteenth-century notion of industrial harmony, see Nick Salvatore, *Eugene V. Debs: A Biography* (Urbana, 1982).

73. *Defender*, December 24, 1921, June 17, 1922.

74. For antiunion cartoon, see *Defender*, February 16, 1918. The Alschuler hearings contain many references to discussion and debates "in the street." See "Arbitration between the Chicago Meat Packers and their Employees," 177–78, 215, 270, 286–88, File 33/864, FMCS, RG 280.

75. *Whip*, October 11, 1919, February 7, 1920. Riley's column first appeared July 19, 1919. It and articles by other union leaders continued to run until March 1920. For a comparison of space devoted to "industrial relations" in the *Whip* and *Defender*, see CCRR, *Negro in Chicago*, 558.

76. *Defender*, September 27, 1919.

77. *Defender*, December 17, 1921; Ottley, *Lonely Warrior*, 263; Harris, *Keeping the Faith*, 129–32.

78. Spero and Harris, *Black Worker*, 281–82; *BW*, December 1921; *Defender*, December 17, 1921. See also Jack London, "The Scab," in Philip Foner, ed., *Jack London, American Rebel* (New York, 1947).

79. CCRR, *Negro in Chicago*, 366; *Defender*, November 29, 1919; *Whip*, November 22, 1919.

80. Horace Bridges, "The First Urban League Family," in Chicago Urban League, *Two Decades of Service*, 6; National Urban League, "The Way Out: A Suggested Solution of the Problems of Race Relations Adopted at the National Urban League Annual Conference, Detroit, Michigan, October 15–19, 1919" (1919), typescript in Box 5, Series 4, NULR. The Chicago branch's similar position is indicated in Dorothy Crounse, Louise Gilbert, and Agnes Van Driel, "The Chicago Urban League" (Chicago, 1936), 14–15, typescript in Chicago Urban League File, Box 286, WCMC. See also Eugene K. Jones, "Coming to the Front," *Opportunity* 4, no. 2 (February 1926): 44.

81. *Defender*, February 23, 1918; *NM*, October 11, 25, 1919.

82. Strickland, *History of the Chicago Urban League*, 31; Hill, "Recent Developments in the Problem of Negro Labor," 322–23; A. Philip Randolph et al., to Hugh Frayne, February ?, 1926, Folder 9, Box 2, Victor Olander Papers, CHS; T. Arnold Hill, Address to the Executive Council of the American Federation of Labor, May 4, 1925, Box 87, Series 6, NULR; Hill to Robert S. Abbott, April 5, 1926, Box 1, Series 4, NULR; Hill to George C. Hall, May 18, 1925, Box 28, Series 4, NULR. Hill was characterized by a Rockefeller Foundation official evaluating Urban League branches in 1923 as "the outstanding figure of any person whom I have met in the Urban Leagues." See Kenneth Chorley to Colonel Woods, October 22, 1923, Folder 1006, Box 99, LSRM.

83. Strickland, *History of the Chicago Urban League*, 28; Sandburg, *Chicago Race Riots*, 50; *Defender*, February 23, 1918.

84. [Charles S. Johnson], "Labor and Race Relations," *Opportunity* 4, no. 37 (January 1926): 4–5; William L. Evans to John T. Clark, October 7, 1920, Urban League of Pittsburgh Papers, Archives of Industrial Society, Hilman Library, University of Pittsburgh. I am grateful to Peter Gottlieb for pro-

viding a copy of this letter, which he photocopied from the collection when it was still housed in the offices of the Urban League of Pittsburgh.

85. Bridges, "The First Urban League Family," 6. See also National Urban League, "The Way Out." On Hall, see M. P. Gethner to Helen Buckler, November 17, 1947, Folder 78, Box 7, Williams Papers.

86. For an example of such pressure and the League's continued support of unionization nevertheless, see Bridges, "The First Urban League Family," 6.

87. Evans to John T. Clark, October 7, 1920, Urban League of Pittsburgh Papers. On the East St. Louis rioting, see Rudwick, *Race Riot at East St. Louis.*

88. William C. Graves to Julius Rosenwald, November 26, 1919, Folder 15, Box 9, and T. Arnold Hill to Graves, February 8, 1921, Folder 16, Box 9, both in Rosenwald Papers; Strickland, *History of the Chicago Urban League,* 74. By the mid-1920s the Chicago Urban League had moved even farther from the stated position of the national organization, even to the extent of declaring that national Executive Secretary Eugene K. Jones did not speak for the Chicago branch when he issued a statement in support of the unionization of Pullman porters. A. L. Foster, the executive secretary of the Chicago Urban League, denied any interest in trade unionism or the labor movement. See Spero and Harris, *Black Worker,* 141.

89. *Defender,* May 13, 1922; William L. Evans, "The Negro in Chicago Industries," *Opportunity* 1, no. 2 (February 1923): 15–16.

90. CCRR, *Negro in Chicago,* 432.

91. Card distributed by Chicago Urban League, Folder 6, Aldis Papers; Woofter, "Negro and Industrial Peace," 421; Strickland, *History of the Chicago Urban League,* 69–70; Barnett, "We Win A Place in Industry," 83.

92. Barrett, *Work and Community in the Jungle,* 204; see also 207–8, and Cohen, "Learning to Live in the Welfare State," 24, 35–36. For a more focused analysis of the relationship and the competition between unions and community institutions, see William Kornblum, *Blue Collar Community* (Chicago, 1974).

93. Barrett, *Work and Community in the Jungle,* 258; Robert A. Slayton, *Back of the Yards: The Making of a Local Democracy* (Chicago, 1986), 94–95. Slayton's argument that "the entire community rallied to help those out of work" perhaps overstates the unanimity characterizing a community which also had strikebreakers within its midst, but the larger point stands nevertheless.

94. Spero and Harris, *Black Worker,* 271; "Arbitration between the Chicago Meat Packers and Their Employees," 221–28; *NM,* August 9, 1919.

95. *NM,* April 23, 1921.

96. *NM,* November 1, 1919. See also *NM,* December 20, 1919, November 6, 13, December 16, 1920, April 16, 1921, June 10, 1922; *BW,* July 1920, January 1921. The publications of the National Women's Trade Union League (published in Chicago) and the Illinois State Federation of Labor were even less interested in black workers; see *Life and Labor Bulletin,* 1921–1929; *Illinois State Federation of Labor Weekly News Letter* 6–9 (1920–25).

97. Evans to John T. Clark, October 7, 1920, Urban League of Pittsburgh Papers. The same group of activists was closely tied to the Chicago Labor

Party, whose leadership, according to Robert Bagnall of the NAACP, was "very much advanced in their attitude on the color line"; quoted in Judith Stein, *The World of Marcus Garvey: Race and Class in Modern Society* (Baton Rouge, 1986), 163.

98. Quoted in Herbst, *Negro in the Slaughtering and Meat-Packing Industry*, 36. For evidence of Fitzpatrick's reputation among blacks, see the correspondence in Box 25, Fitzpatrick Papers.

99. Abram L. Harris, "A White and Black World in American Labor and Politics," *Journal of Social Forces* 4 (December 1925): 380.

100. CCRR, *Negro in Chicago*, 420–21; Spero and Harris, *Black Worker*, 128.

101. Walter White, "Chicago and Its Eight Reasons," *Crisis* 18, no. 6 (October 1919), 295. See also Herbst, *Negro in the Slaughtering and Meat-Packing Industry*, xix.

102. CCRR, *Negro in Chicago*, 99. See also Herbst, *Negro in the Slaughtering and Meat-Packing Industry*, 51.

103. Cayton and Mitchell, *Black Workers and the New Unions*, 211.

Chapter 9

1. USDL, *Negro Migration*, 94; William C. Chance to George E. Haynes, January 9, 1917, Folder 14, Box 1, Haynes Papers; Johnson, "Clarksdale, Mississippi," 2–3, "Mississippi Summary," NULR; *Defender*, April 7, June 16, November 10, 1917; Scott, "Additional Letters," 432–33. In 1916, blacks constituted approximately one-fifth of the student body at Phillips; see Wood, *Negro in Chicago*, 21.

2. *Defender*, February 26, March 11, 1916, December 28, 1918; Chicago Board of Education, *Directory of the Public Schools of the City of Chicago*, 1917–1918 (Chicago, 1918), 60, 86, 95–96, 101, 118–19, 129, 152, 169; *Directory*, 1918–1919, pp. 65, 91, 96, 98–99, 120–21, 130, 152, 167; *Directory*, 1920–1921, pp. 60, 84, 90–91, 96–97, 111, 120, 139–40, 154–55; CCRR, *Negro in Chicago*, 242–43. There are minor discrepancies between the School Board's *Directories* and the Commission's surveys regarding physical facilities of schools; I have accepted the school board's inventory.

3. Woofter, *Negro Migration*, 164; *State-Wide Conference Issues Important Address to the Honorable Members of the State Legislature and the White Citizenry of Georgia* [Atlanta?, 1923?], 6–7 (pamphlet); Thomas J. Jones, *Negro Education: A Study of the Private and Higher Schools for Colored People in the United States*, U.S. Bureau of Education Bulletin, 1916, no. 38 (Washington, D.C., 1917), 32–33.

4. Chicago Board of Education, *Directory*, 1916–1917, p. 159; Johnson, "Jackson, Mississippi," 3–4, "Mississippi Summary," NULR; [Thomas Jesse Jones], "Schools for Colored People: Atlanta Private Schools" (Washington, D.C., 1915), 8–9, pamphlet in Folder J, Box 532, Washington Papers; King, *King's Agricultural Digest*, 53; U.S. Bureau of the Census, *Negroes in the United States, 1790–1915*, 383. For a survey of black schooling in the South, see Henry A. Bullock, *A History of Negro Education in the South: From 1619 to the Present* (Cambridge, Mass., 1967).

5. Jones, *Negro Education*, 41; Francis L. Copper, "Physical Education in the High Schools in Chicago" (Master's thesis, University of Chicago, 1918), 43–45, 49, 53, 66; *Defender*, November 12, 1921.

6. CCRR, *Negro in Chicago*, 235, 242; Scott, "Additional Letters," 464.

7. *Defender*, September 30, 1916, October 16, 1920; A. Albertine Wetter, "A Glimpse Into an Unusual Night School," *Chicago Schools Journal* 4 (1921–22): 132–33; Chicago Board of Education, *Proceedings*, October 10, 1923 (Chicago, 1923), 226, April 2, 1924 (Chicago, 1924), 832.

8. Favrot, "Some Problems in the Education of the Negro in the South," 7; Johnson, "Greenwood," 2, "Mississippi Summary," NULR. For the statutory basis for such closings, see Gertrude H. Folks, *Farm Labor vs. School Attendance* (New York, 1922), 5 and passim, pamphlet in File 6-1-0-3, Box 185, Central Files of the U.S. Children's Bureau, U.S. Department of Labor, RG 102, NA. On the relationship between the southern economy and southern education, see Wright, *Old South, New South*.

9. David J. Hogan, *Class and Reform: School and Society in Chicago, 1880–1930* (Philadelphia, 1985), 59–60 (*Tribune* quotation on 59); Edith Abbott and Sophonisba P. Breckinridge, *Truancy and Non-Attendance in Chicago Schools* (Chicago, 1917), 10; Mary J. Herrick, "Negro Employees of the Chicago Board of Education" (Master's thesis, University of Chicago, 1931), 37; Mary K. Plumb, "Truancy," *Educational Bi-Monthly* 9, no. 1 (October 1914): 12; [Chicago Public Schools], "Conditions Which Children Face Today When They Leave School for Employment" [1922], mimeograph; and bookmark enclosed in letter from Anne C. Davis to Grace Abbott, January 25, 1922, both in File 6-1-0, Box 185, Central Files of the U.S. Children's Bureau, RG 102.

10. Bethel, *Promiseland*, 187; *Defender*, August 4, 1917. For school statistics, see Ernest W. Burgess and Charles Newcomb, eds., *Census Data of the City of Chicago, 1920* (Chicago, 1931), 33; and Drake, "Churches and Voluntary Associations," 168. On child labor, see Colson, "Home Work Among Negro Women in Chicago," 110; and Green and Woodson, *Negro Wage Earner*, 225–27. Attitudes towards child labor in the South are suggested in King, *King's Agricultural Digest*, 53. According to one historian of Chicago's Back-of-the-Yards community, eastern European immigrants in that neighborhood exerted "considerably less pressure to finish school than to attend it." Confirmation at age twelve or fourteen or graduation from grammar school usually marked the end of school attendance. See Slayton, *Back of the Yards*, 47. On the tendency of Italian teenagers to leave school and go to work, see Nelli, *Italians in Chicago*, 66–70. Data covering the northeastern and midwestern states as a whole indicate striking gains in the number of years of education attained by black children born in the North between 1915 and 1925. These statistics include children of both migrants and Old Settlers, but given the dramatic rise, they suggest that migrants kept their children in school, especially since higher retardation rates among migrants meant that at any given level of attainment, actual number of years in school would have been higher. See Lieberson, *A Piece of the Pie*, 166, 217–19, 232.

11. CCRR, *Negro in Chicago*, 248, 257–58, 262, 267; Chicago *Broad Ax*, January 29, 1921; Don C. Rogers, "Retardation from the Mental Standpoint," *Chicago Schools Journal* 9 (1926–27): 302; Samuel B. Allison, "Classification of

Exceptional Children in the Elementary School," *Educational Bi-Monthly* 9, no. 5 (June 1915): 388–95; John E. Ransom, *A Study of Mentally Defective Children in Chicago* (Chicago, 1915), 10–11 (pamphlet); Chicago Board of Education, *Directory*, 1916–17, pp. 191, 210–11; Chicago Board of Education, *Proceedings*, December 11, 1918, p. 85, September 3, 1919, pp. 473–743; Chicago Board of Education, *64th Annual Report, 1918*, p. 50, and *71st Annual Report, 1925*, p. 129.

12. CCRR, *Negro in Chicago*, 239, 241, 257–58, 262–65, 439; *Broad Ax*, January 29, 1921; William H. Burton, "The Nature and Amount of Civic Information Possessed by Chicago Children of Sixth Grade Level" (Ph.D. dissertation, University of Chicago, 1924), 170; Rogers, "Retardation from the Mental Standpoint," 302. High levels of retardation were hardly unique to black children; a 1912 report, prepared by a committee chaired by George Herbert Mead of the University of Chicago for the City Club, pointed to "approximately 70,000 retarded children in Chicago elementary schools—or one-third of all the school children"; City Club of Chicago, *A Report on Vocational Training in Chicago and in Other Cities* (Chicago, 1912), v–vi, quoted in Hogan, *Class and Reform*, 160.

13. Interview with Archibald J. Carey, Jr., Chicago, April 27, 1979 (tape in possession of author); Myra Young Armstead, Interview with Ida Mae Cress; CCRR, *Negro in Chicago*, 241. On corrections of southern speech patterns, see Irene McEnroe, "Errors in Speech," *Chicago Schools Journal* 7 (1924–25): 135–37, and Charles H. Thompson, "A Study of the Reading Accomplishments of Colored and White Children" (Master's thesis, University of Chicago, 1920), 56.

14. Homel, "Negroes in the Chicago Public Schools," 10–16; CCRR, *Negro in Chicago*, 246, 249. Michael Homel's dissertation has since been published as *Down From Equality: Black Chicagoans and the Public Schools 1920–41* (Urbana, 1984), but I have retained citations to the dissertation because it presents material on the earlier period in greater depth.

15. CCRR, *Negro in Chicago*, 115, 246–52; Interview with Carey; Alvin L. Hanson, MID Report, January 15, 1919, File 10218–298, Box 3191, MID File, RG 165; *Defender*, October 6, 1917, January 19, 1918.

16. "Memorandum of Eleanor Adams of the Hyde Park High School" [c. 1917?], Box 87, Series 6, NULR; CCRR, *Negro in Chicago*, 253–55; Testimony of Charles Perrine, "Proceedings of Committee on Racial Contacts," March 11, 1920, pp. 7–9, 15–16, Folder 3, CCRR Papers. On the importance of extracurricular activities, see Thomas Gutowski, "The High School as an Adolescent-Raising Institution: An Inner History of Chicago Public Secondary Education, 1856–1940" (Ph.D. dissertation, University of Chicago, 1978), 197–202, 219–20; Elvira D. Cabell, "Social Activities of Chicago High Schools," *Chicago Schools Journal* 5 (May 1923): 361; Chicago Board of Education, *Survey of the Chicago Public Schools*, 51–55. For a discussion of a 1928 boycott at Fenger High School after twenty-five black students transferred there, doubling the school's black enrollment, see Homel, "Negroes in the Chicago Public Schools," 83–84; and "Survey of the Month," *Opportunity* 6, no. 12 (December 1928): 384.

17. *Defender*, October 19, 1918; CCRR, *Negro in Chicago*, 247–48. On the

first black principal, Maudelle Bousfield, see "Along the Color Line," *Crisis* 25, no. 3 (March 1928): 90. The paucity of black teachers, especially before the 1920s, is discussed in "Proceedings of the Committee on Racial Contacts," March 11, 1920, pp. 4–5, Folder 3, CCRR Papers.

18. Testimonies of Charles Perrine and Margaret Madden, "Proceedings of the Committee on Racial Contacts," March 11, 1920, pp. 6, 15, Folder 3, CCRR Papers; Ione M. Mack, "The Factor of Race in the Religious Education of the Negro High School Girl" (Master's thesis, University of Chicago, 1927), 36, 40–41, 52, 55; CCRR, *Negro in Chicago*, 270–71, 439.

19. CCRR, *Negro in Chicago*, 245–47, 249. On the use of the literature of intelligence testing, see, for example, Horace Mann Bond, "Intelligence Tests and Propaganda," *Crisis* 25, no. 2 (June 1924): 62.

20. Thompson, "A Study of the Reading Accomplishments of Colored and White Children," 21, 35–36; Mack, "Factor of Race," 39; Jane P. Cook and John T. McManis, "Fourth Grade Geography," *Educational Bi-Monthly* 11, no. 2 (December 1916): 98–101; CCRR, *Negro in Chicago*, 250–51.

21. Chicago Board of Education, *An Outline of the Course of Study for Elementary Schools* ([Chicago], 1917), 9–13; Chicago Board of Education, *Elementary School Social Science, Geography, History* ([Chicago], 1923), 69–73. On Americanization and the role of the school in the "great American melting pot," see Chicago Board of Education, *65th Annual Report, 1919*, pp. 7–8; Chicago Board of Education, *Proceedings*, December 17, 1919, pp. 1050–51.

22. Homel, "Negroes in the Chicago Public Schools," 26–30; W. E. B. Du Bois, "Dilemma of the Negro," *American Mercury* 3, no. 10 (October 1924): 179–85; CCRR, *Negro in Chicago*, 248.

23. Chicago Board of Education, Education Department, *Subject Failures, Semester I, 1917–18*, Bulletin no. 4 (Chicago, 1918), 7–8; CCRR, *Negro in Chicago*, 271.

24. Wood, *Negro in Chicago*, 22; N. C. Jenkins, "What Chance Has the Trained Student," in Robb, *Book of Achievement*, 89; Katherine M. Johnson, "The Educated Boot-Black," *Half-Century Magazine* 1, no. 3 (October 1916): 9. For dropout rates at Wendell Phillips, see Chicago Board of Education, *Proceedings, 1918–1925*. See also *Defender* complaints about high dropout rates in *Defender*, June 30, 1917, February 9, 16, 1918.

25. Quoted in David B. Tyack, *The One Best System: A History of American Urban Education* (Cambridge, Mass., 1974), 222. The Pittsburgh study is summarized in Lieberson, *A Piece of the Pie*, 238. See Lieberson, 355–57, for an analysis of the "feedback effect" and its discouraging impact on black educational persistence.

26. William J. Parker to William C. Graves, June 16, 1926, Folder 2, Box 40, Rosenwald Papers; Chicago Board of Education, *71st Annual Report, 1925*, p. 130. Kenneth Kusmer has shown that Cleveland's schools reacted similarly. As migration increased the black proportion of a high school's population, emphasis on vocational education increased concomitantly, and fewer electives and academic courses were offered. See Kusmer, *A Ghetto Takes Shape*, 184.

27. On the meaning of "Negro education" as a separate category, see

statement by George C. Hall in "Proceedings of the Inter-Racial Conference" (New Haven, December 19–21, 1927), 106, Folder 1024, Box 102, LSRM.

Conclusion

1. On the participation of blacks in Employee Representation Councils, see Cohen, "Learning to Live in the Welfare State," 287. A survey of employers indicating the receptivity of black workers to "industrial democracy" programs is summarized in "Memorandum of Address made June 17 Before the Interracial Committee of the Union League Club," June 17, 1926, pp. 2–3, Folder 2, Box 40, Rosenwald Papers.

2. Branham, "Transformation of Black Political Leadership," 130–31; Arthur I. Waskow, *From Race Riot to Sit-In, 1919 and the 1960s* (Garden City, 1966), 60–104. For a description of the *Defender's* statistical coverage, which "appeared like box scores," see Ottley, *Lonely Warrior*, 177.

3. The quotation is from CCRR, *Negro in Chicago*, 439, and summarizes views that were "frequently expressed" by Chicago industrial employers in 1920. The limits of black power and the significance of clientage are discussed in Katznelson, *Black Men, White Cities*, 86–104, and Martin Kilson, "Political Change in the Negro Ghetto, 1900–1940s," in Huggins, et al., *Key Issues in the Afro-American Experience*, 2: 167–92. For a somewhat different, although not entirely contradictory perspective, see Branham, "Transformation of Black Political Leadership," 28–49, 147–50, 153–57. School segregation and other aspects of racial policies in the Chicago public schools are detailed in Homel, *Down From Equality*, and Herrick, "Negro Employees of the Chicago Board of Education," 92–97. What Drake and Cayton called the "job ceiling" in Chicago's economy during the two decades following the Great Migration is discussed in *Black Metropolis*, 214–62. The opportunites for limited promotion are discussed in Hughes, *Living Conditions*, 52–53. See also Scott, *Occupational Changes*, 179–82, 230–32, for data on movement into semiskilled occupations between 1920 and 1930.

4. CCRR, *Negro in Chicago*, 386.

5. Jackson and Wylie, *Movin' On Up*, 46. For a similar observation, see Drake and Cayton, *Black Metropolis*, 387.

6. For the comparison with white immigrants see Cohen, "Learning to Live in the Welfare State," 189, 209–10. The Detroit survey is in Charles S. Johnson, "Abstracts of a Report of the Research Committee to the National Interracial Commission" (1928), 29, typescript in Folder 8, Box 61, Johnson Papers. The survey included a sample of one thousand heads of families who had migrated from the South. Detroit's migrants were likely to have come from backgrounds similar to those of Chicago's newcomers; many had probably passed through Chicago before going to Detroit. The ownership of radios by blacks in northern and southern cities is detailed in U.S. Bureau of the Census, *Negroes in the United States, 1920–1932*, p. 259. On the paucity of moving picture theaters, even in the more substantial southern towns and cities, and the reluctance of blacks to attend the Jim Crow theaters, see the surveys in "Theaters" folder, Box 590, Entry 12 HN-A4, Records of the Negro

Press Section, U.S. Food Adminstration, Educational Division, RG 4, WNRC.

7. On barbecue stands and other southern cooking, see *Defender*, March 16, 1918, October 22, 1921, June 3, 1922. On southern music in Chicago during this era, see George Bushnell, "When Jazz Came to Chicago," *Chicago History* 1, no. 3 (Spring 1971): 135–38; Beverly Robinson, "Chicago: An Overview of the African-American History and Folklore," in "A Report on the Chicago Ethnic Arts Project" (1978), 45–46, typescript in American Folklife Center, LC; *Defender*, October 29, 1921, and January 21, 1922.

8. Disfranchisement had an important class dimension that was less obvious to black southerners than it is from a historical perspective. Its partisan dimensions were likely to be interpreted as a racial issue by many black southerners, given the conflation of "white" with "Democratic." For a comprehensive analysis of the process of disfranchisement, see J. Morgan Kousser, *The Shaping of Southern Politics: Suffrage Restriction and the Establishment of the One-Party South, 1880–1910* (New Haven, 1974).

9. Drake and Cayton, *Black Metropolis*, 80. For an observation that migrants were more likely than other black Chicagoans to patronize black professionals, see Frazier, *Negro Family in Chicago*, 108–9.

10. This view of Garvey and the UNIA is indebted to insights in Lawrence W. Levine, "Marcus Garvey and the Politics of Revitalization," in John Hope Franklin and August Meier, eds., *Black Leaders of the Twentieth Century* (Urbana, 1982), 113–18, and Kusmer, *A Ghetto Takes Shape*, 228–34. See also Stein, *World of Marcus Garvey*, 256 and passim. UNIA activity in Chicago was reported most frequently in the *Whip*; see, e.g., October 11, November 1, 1919, October 23, November 13, 27, December 18, 25, 1920, January 1, 15, July 9, October 15, 1921. Robert Abbott led the opposition to Garvey in Chicago, and the *Defender* ignored the movement except to ridicule it. See for example articles appearing on September 9, 16, 23, 30, and October 7, 1922. The *Broad Ax* was at first amicable towards Garvey, perhaps because of editor Julius Taylor's sympathy with Garvey's lawsuits against Robert Abbott, who had driven the UNIA leader out of Illinois by arranging to have him arrested for irregularities in the sale of Black Star Line securities. By 1922, Taylor had turned against Garvey. See *Broad Ax*, October 4, 11, 1919, January 24, 1920, May 13, July 29, August 12, 1922. Although Drake and Cayton, *Black Metropolis*, 752, argue that "Garveyism was never very popular in Chicago," they admit that "the UNIA did recruit several thousand fanatical members from the lower class and lower middle class, who spread its influence far beyond the small circle of its membership." Indications of the movement's strength in Chicago can be found also in Gosnell, *Negro Politicians*, 113; Drake, "Churches and Voluntary Associations," 235, 238–39; and Bontemps and Conroy, *They Seek a City*, 171. Bontemps and Conroy refer to Chicago as "one of his towers of strength," and estimate membership at 7,500 in 1920; Drake argues that "five thousand is a very conservative estimate." The composition of the movement is analyzed in Haywood, *Black Bolshevik*, 103–4. Haywood views the UNIA claim of 9,000 members as "probably exaggerated" (p. 107). These estimates suggest that at a minimum the movement was popular in Chicago and that its membership drew heavily upon migrants, although for

reasons different from those I have suggested here. Stein's evidence that the leadership of the movement was more entrepreneurial is not incompatible with my assumptions about its membership, to whom I have ascribed values similar to those Stein labels "petit bourgeois." We agree more on the content of the movement's ideological appeal than on the meaning of that appeal, which she argues is evidence that the movement was driven by narrow class imperatives and relevant mainly to the world of the petit bourgeoisie.

11. Ralph Ellison, "An American Dilemma: A Review," essay written in 1944, first published in *Shadow and Act* (New York, 1964), 304.

Selected Bibliography

This bibliography includes all cited archival and oral sources, but only those printed sources that have been cited more than once in the Notes.

Manuscript Collections

Aldis, Arthur T., Papers. Special Collections, the University Library, University of Illinois at Chicago, Chicago.

Barnett, Claude A. Papers. Chicago Historical Society, Chicago.

Breckinridge, Sophonisba B. Papers. Library of Congress, Washington, D.C.

Burgess, Ernest W. Papers. Joseph Regenstein Library, University of Chicago, Chicago.

Carey, Archibald J., Sr. Papers. Chicago Historical Society, Chicago.

Chicago Commission on Race Relations. Papers, 1919–20. Illinois State Archives, Springfield. Microfilm.

Chicago Foreign Language Press Survey. Chicago Public Library Omnibus Project, U.S. Works Progress Administration, 1942, Joseph Regenstein Library, University of Chicago, Chicago.

Jane Dent Home for Aged Colored People. Papers. Special Collections, the University Library, University of Illinois at Chicago, Chicago.

Dunmore Collection. DuSable Museum of African-American History, Chicago.

Federal Writers Project. U.S. Works Progress Administration. Official Project 165-2-26-7. Archive of Folk Song, Library of Congress, Washington, D.C.

Fitzpatrick, John. Papers. Chicago Historical Society, Chicago.

Gaines, Irene McCoy. Collection. Chicago Historical Society, Chicago.

Harris, Abram Lincoln. Papers. Moorland-Spingarn Research Center, Howard University, Washington, D.C.

Haynes, George Edmund. Papers. Special Collections Division, Fisk University Library, Nashville.

Illinois Children's Home and Aid Society. Records. Special Collections, the University Library, University of Illinois at Chicago, Chicago.

Illinois Writers Project. "The Negro in Illinois." Vivian Harsh Collection, Carter Woodson Regional Library, Chicago.

Johnson, Charles. Papers. Fisk University Library, Nashville.

Juvenile Protective Association. Papers. Special Collections, the University Library, University of Illinois at Chicago, Chicago.

Lawson, Victor. Papers. Newberry Library, Chicago.

Mitchell, Arthur W. Papers. Chicago Historical Society, Chicago.

National Association for the Advancement of Colored People. Records. Manuscripts Division, Library of Congress, Washington, D.C.

National Urban League. Records. Manuscripts Division, Library of Congress, Washington, D.C.

National Urban League, Southern Regional Office. Records. Manuscripts Division, Library of Congress, Washington, D.C.

Olander, Victor. Papers. Chicago Historical Society, Chicago.

Park, Robert E. Papers. Joseph Regenstein Library, University of Chicago, Chicago.

Pullman Company. Employment Files. Newberry Library, Chicago.

Laura Spelman Rockefeller Memorial. Collection. Rockefeller Archives, Tarrytown, New York.

Rosenwald, Julius. Papers. Joseph Regenstein Library, University of Chicago, Chicago.

Julius Rosenwald Fund. Archives. Fisk University Library, Nashville.

Taylor, Graham. Papers. Newberry Library, Chicago.

Travelers Aid Society of Chicago. Records. Special Collections, the University Library, University of Illinois at Chicago, Chicago.

Washington, Booker T. Papers. Manuscripts Division, Library of Congress, Washington, D.C.

Welfare Council of Metropolitan Chicago. Records. Chicago Historical Society, Chicago.

Wells, Ida B. Papers. Joseph Regenstein Library, University of Chicago, Chicago.

Phyllis Wheatley Association. Papers. Special Collections, the University Library, University of Illinois at Chicago, Chicago.

Williams, Daniel Hale. Papers. Moorland-Spingarn Research Center, Howard University, Washington, D.C.

Woodson, Carter G. Collection. Manuscripts Division, Library of Congress, Washington, D.C.

Young Men's Christian Association, Wabash Avenue Branch. Papers of the Young Men's Christian Association. Special Collections, the University Library, University of Illinois at Chicago, Chicago.

Young Women's Christian Association of Metropolitan Chicago. Records. Special Collections, the University Library, University of Illinois at Chicago, Chicago.

Young Women's Christian Association National Board. Historical Records. National Board of the Young Women's Christian Association, New York.

Government Records

U.S. Council of National Defense. Field Division. Correspondence. Series 15-A4, Record Group 62. WNRC.

U.S. Department of Agriculture. Files of the Secretary of Agriculture. Records of the U.S. Department of Agriculture. Record Group 16. NA.

———. Bureau of Agricultural Economics. Office of Farm Management. Manuscripts. Series 133, Record Group 83. NA.

U.S. Department of Labor. Files of the Chief Clerk. Record Group 174. NA.

———. Children's Bureau. Central Files. Record Group 102. NA.

———. Division of Negro Economics. Records. In General Records of the Department of Labor. Record Group 174. NA.

———. Women's Bureau. Records. Record Group 86. NA.

U.S. Department of Justice. General Records. Record Group 60. NA.

U.S. Department of War. General and Special Staffs. Files of the Military Intelligence Division. Entry 65, Record Group 165. NA.

———. General and Special Staffs. Records of the Service and Information Branch. Record Group 165. NA.

———. Papers of Emmett J. Scott, Special Assistant to the Secretary of War. Records of the Adjutant General's Office. Boxes 1–2, Record Group 407. NA.

U.S. Employment Service. Records. Record Group 183. NA.

U.S. Federal Mediation and Conciliation Service. Records. Record Group 280. WNRC.

U.S. Food Administration. Records of the Negro Press Section. Entry 12HN, Record Group 4. WNRC.

U.S. Housing Corporation. Records. Record Group 3. NA.

U.S. National War Labor Board. Case Files. Record Group 2. WNRC.

U.S. Railroad Administration. File of the Director General. Record Group 14. WNRC.

———. Records of the Division of Labor. Record Group 14. NA.

U.S. Selective Service System. Local Board Experience File. Record Group 163. WNRC.

U.S. War Labor Policies Board. Records. Record Group 1. NA.

Newspapers and Newsletters

Broad Ax (Chicago), 1917–22
Butcher Workman, 1915–22
Chicago City Club *Bulletin*, 1910–22
Chicago *Defender*, 1910–22
Chicago *Daily News*, 1916–19
Chicago *Tribune*, 1916–19
Crisis, 1916–28
Illinois State Federation of Labor Weekly News Letter, 1920–25.
National Provisioner, 1917–22

Negro Farmer and Messenger (Tuskegee), 1916–17
New Majority, 1919–22
New World, 1910–22
Whip (Chicago), 1919–22

Interviews

Armstead, Myra Young. Interview with Ida Mae Cress. Chicago, April 9, 1985. Transcript in possession of author.
———. Interview with Bert Jones. Chicago, April 19, 1985. Tape in possession of author.
———. Interview with Mary Fluornoy. Chicago, May 1, 1985. Tape in possession of author.
Gottlieb, Peter. Interview with Leroy McChester. July 9, 1974. Pittsburgh Oral History Project, Division of History, Pennsylvania Historical Museum Commission, Harrisburg. Transcript provided by Dr. Gottlieb.
Grossman, James R. Interview with Archibald J. Carey, Jr. Chicago, April 27, 1979. Tape in possession of author.
Interview with Milt Hinton. Transcript at Institute of Jazz Studies, Newark, N.J.
Illinois General Assembly Oral History Program. *Corneal A. Davis Memoir.* Springfield: Sangamon State University, 1984.
Robinson, Beverly. Interviews conducted for the Chicago Ethnic Arts Project. Tapes deposited in the American Folklife Center, LC.
Strickland, Arvarh. Interview with Irene McCoy Gaines. Chicago, June 26, 1961. Tape in possession of Strickland.
Tuttle, William M., Jr. Interview with Chester Wilkins. Chicago, June 25, 1969. Transcript in possession of Tuttle.
———. Interview with Alexander L. Jackson. Chicago, June 27, 1969. Notes in possession of Tuttle.

Government Documents

Best, Ethel L., and Ruth I. Voris. *Women in Illinois Industries.* U.S. Women's Bureau Bulletin no. 51. Washington, D.C.: GPO, 1925.
Chicago Board of Education. *Annual Report of the Superintendent of Schools.* 1915–26. Chicago.
———. *Directory of the Public Schools of the City of Chicago.* 1916–26. Chicago.
———. *Survey of the Chicago Public Schools.* [Chicago, 1914].
———. *Proceedings.* 1918–25. Chicago.
Dickins, Dorothy. *A Nutritional Investigation of Negro Tenants in the Yazoo Mississippi Delta.* Mississippi Agricultural Experiment Station Bulletin no. 254, 1928.
Illinois Department of Labor. *Third Annual Report.* Springfield: Illinois State Journal Co., 1921.
Jones, Thomas J. *Negro Education: A Study of the Private and Higher Schools for*

Colored People in the United States. U.S. Bureau of Education Bulletins no. 38 and 39. Washington, D.C.: GPO, 1917.

Shields, Emma L. *Negro Women in Industry.* U.S. Women's Bureau Bulletin no. 20. Washington, D.C.: GPO, 1922.

U.S. Bureau of the Census. *Thirteenth Census of the United States Taken in the Year 1910.* Vol. 2, *Population.* Washington, D.C.: GPO, 1913.

———. *Thirteenth Census of the United States Taken in the Year 1910.* Vol. 3, *Population, Reports by States.* Washington, D.C.: GPO, 1913.

———. *Thirteenth Census of the United States Taken in the Year 1910.* Vol. 4, *Population, Occupations.* Washington, D.C.: GPO, 1914.

———. *Fourteenth Census of the United States Taken in the Year 1920.* Vol. 3, *Population.* Washington, D.C.: GPO, 1922.

———. *Fourteenth Census of the United States Taken in the Year 1920.* Vol. 4, *Population, Occupations.* Washington, D.C.: GPO, 1922.

———. *Fourteenth Census of the United States. State Compendium, Illinois.* Washington, D.C.: GPO, 1924.

———. *Negro Population, 1790–1915.* Washington, D.C.: GPO, 1918.

———. *Negroes in the United States, 1920–1932.* Washington, D.C.: GPO, 1935.

U.S. Bureau of Education. *Report of the Commissioner of Education, 1914–19.* Washington, D.C.: GPO, 1915–20.

U.S. Commission on Industrial Relations. *Final Report and Testimony.* Vol. 4. Washington, D.C.: GPO, 1916.

U.S. Congress. House. Committee on Interstate and Foreign Commerce. *Return of the Railroads to Private Ownership: Hearings on H.R. 4378, Part 12.* 66th Cong., 1st sess. Washington, D.C.: GPO, 1919.

U.S. Department of Agriculture. *Yearbook, 1921–25.* Washington, D.C.: GPO, 1922–26.

U.S. Department of Labor. *Reports of the Department of Labor, 1916–18, 1920.* Washington, D.C.: GPO, 1917–19, 1921.

———. *U.S. Employment Service Bulletin.* January 28, 1918-Feb. 29, 1919 (weekly).

———. Division of Negro Economics. *The Negro at Work During the World War and Reconstruction.* Washington, D.C.: GPO, 1921.

———. Division of Negro Economics. *Negro Migration in 1916–17.* Washington, D.C.: GPO, 1919.

Wright, Helen R. *Children of Wage-Earning Mothers: A Study of a Selected Group in Chicago.* U. S. Children's Bureau Publication no. 102. Washington, D.C.: GPO, 1922.

Books, Pamphlets, and Reports

Adams, Kate J. *Humanizing a Great Industry.* Chicago: Armour, [c. 1919].

Aldrich, Paul, ed. *The Packer's Encyclopedia: Blue Book of the American Meat Packing and Allied Industries. A Hand Book of Modern Packing House Practice.* Chicago: National Provisioner, 1922.

Arthur, George R. *Life on the Negro Frontier*. New York: Association Press, 1934.

Baker, Ray Stannard. *Following the Color Line*. New York: Doubleday, Page and Co., 1908. Reprint. New York: Harper and Row, 1964.

Ballard, Allen B. *One More Day's Journey: The Story of a Family and a People*. New York: McGraw-Hill, 1984.

Barrett, James R. *Work and Community in the Jungle: Chicago's Packinghouse Workers, 1894–1922*. Urbana: University of Illinois Press, 1987.

Berlin, Ira. *Slaves Without Masters: The Free Negro in the Antebellum South*. New York: Pantheon, 1974.

Berlin, Ira, and Ronald Hoffman, eds. *Slavery and Freedom in the Age of the American Revolution*. Charlottesville: University Press of Virginia, 1983.

Bethel, Elizabeth Rauh. *Promiseland: A Century of Life in a Negro Community*. Philadelphia: Temple University Press, 1981.

Black, Ford S. *Black's Blue Book, Business and Professional Directory*. Chicago: [Ford S. Black], 1917.

Black, Ford S., comp. *Black's Blue Book: Directory of Chicago's Active Colored People and Guide to Their Activities*. Chicago: Ford S. Black, 1921.

Bodnar, John, Roger Simon, and Michael P. Weber. *Lives of Their Own: Blacks, Italians, and Poles in Pittsburgh, 1900–1960*. Urbana: University of Illinois Press, 1982.

Bontemps, Arna, and Jack Conroy. *They Seek a City*. Garden City: Doubleday, Doran, and Co., 1945.

Bowen, Louise DeKoven. *The Colored People of Chicago: An Investigation Made for the Juvenile Protective Association*. [Chicago]: Press of Rogers and Hall Co., 1913.

Brandfon, Robert L. *Cotton Kingdom of the New South: A History of the Yazoo Mississippi Delta from Reconstruction to the Twentieth Century*. Cambridge: Harvard University Press, 1967.

Brody, David. *The Butcher Workmen: A Study of Unionization*. Cambridge: Harvard University Press, 1964.

———. *Steelworkers in America: The Nonunion Era*. Cambridge: Harvard University Press, 1960.

Burgess, Ernest W., and Charles Newcomb, eds. *Census Data of the City of Chicago, 1920*. Chicago: University of Chicago Press, 1931.

Carver, Arthur H. *Personnel and Labor Problems in the Packing Industry*. Chicago: University of Chicago Press, 1928.

Cayton, Horace R., and George S. Mitchell. *Black Workers and the New Unions*. Chapel Hill: University of North Carolina Press, 1939.

Chicago Commission on Race Relations. *The Negro in Chicago*. Chicago: University of Chicago Press, 1922.

Chicago Urban League. *Annual Report of the Chicago Urban League*. Chicago, 1917–21, 1923, 1927.

———. *Two Decades of Service*. Chicago: William Mason Press, 1936.

Crockett, Norman L. *The Black Towns*. Lawrence: The Regents Press of Kansas, 1979.

Daniel, Pete. *Breaking the Land: The Transformation of Cotton, Tobacco, and Rice Cultures Since 1880*. Urbana: University of Illinois Press, 1985.

————. *The Shadow of Slavery: Peonage in the South, 1901–1969*. Urbana: University of Illinois Press, 1972.

Davis, Elizabeth Lindsay. *The Story of the Illinois Federation of Colored Women's Clubs*. [Chicago, 1922].

Detweiler, Frederick G. *The Negro Press in the United States*. Chicago: University of Chicago Press, 1922.

Dittmer, John. *Black Georgia in the Progressive Era, 1900–1920*. Urbana: University of Illinois Press, 1977.

[Dorsey, Hugh M.]. *A Statement From Governor Hugh M. Dorsey as to the Negro in Georgia*. Atlanta, 1921.

Drake, St. Clair. "Churches and Voluntary Associations in the Chicago Negro Community." Report of Offical Project 465-54-3-386, Work Projects Administration. Chicago, 1940.

Drake, St. Clair, and Horace R. Cayton. *Black Metropolis: A Study of Negro Life in a Northern City*. New York: Harcourt, Brace, and Co., 1945.

Drucker, Arthur P., Sophia Boaz, A. L. Harris, and Miriam Schaffner. *The Colored People of Chicago*. Chicago: Juvenile Protective Association, 1913.

Du Bois, William Edward Burghardt. *The Souls of Black Folk*. Chicago: A .C. McClurg and Company, 1903.

Duncan, Otis D., and Beverly Duncan. *The Negro Population of Chicago: A Study of Residential Succession*. Chicago: University of Chicago Press, 1957.

Duster, Alfreda, ed. *Crusade for Justice: The Autobiography of Ida B. Wells*. Chicago: University of Chicago Press, 1970.

Dutcher, Dean. *The Negro in Modern Industrial Society: An Analysis of Changes in the Occupations of Negro Workers, 1910–1920*. Lancaster, Pa: Science Press, 1930.

Eldridge, Hope T., and Dorothy Swaine Thomas. *Population Redistribution and Economic Growth, United States, 1870–1950*. Vol. 3, *Demographic Analysis and Interrelations*. Philadelphia: American Philosophical Society, 1964.

Favrot, Leo M. *Some Problems in the Education of the Negro in the South and How We Are Trying to Meet Them in Louisiana*, Address before the National Association of Colored People, Cleveland, July 25, 1919. Baton Rouge: Ramires Jones Printing Co., 1919.

Fisher, Miles Mark. *The Master's Slave: Elijah John Fisher, a Biography*. Philadelphia: Judson Press, 1922.

Fligstein, Neil. *Going North: Migration of Blacks and Whites from the South, 1900–1950*. New York: Academic Press, 1981.

Fogel, Walter A. *The Negro in the Meat Industry*. Philadelphia: University of Pennsylvania, 1970.

Foner, Philip S. *Organized Labor and the Black Worker, 1619–1973*. New York: Praeger Publishers, 1974.

Foster, William Z. *The Great Steel Strike and Its Lessons*. New York: B. W. Huebsch, 1920.

Frazier, E. Franklin. *The Negro Family in Chicago*. Chicago: University of Chicago Press, 1932.

Fredrickson, George M. *The Black Image in the White Mind: The Debate on Afro-American Character and Destiny, 1817–1914*. New York: Harper and Row, 1971.

Genovese, Eugene D. *Roll, Jordan, Roll: The World the Slaves Made*. New York: Pantheon, 1974.

Gold, Howard R., and Byron K. Armstrong. *A Preliminary Study of Inter-Racial Conditions in Chicago*. New York: Home Missions Council, 1920.

Gosnell, Harold F. *Negro Politicians: The Rise of Negro Politics in Chicago*. Chicago: University of Chicago Press, 1935.

Gottlieb, Peter. *Making Their Own Way: Southern Blacks' Migration to Pittsburgh, 1916–1930*. Urbana: University of Illinois Press, 1987.

Greene, Lorenzo J., and Carter G. Woodson. *The Negro Wage Earner*. Washington, D.C.: Association for the Study of Negro Life and History, 1930.

Harris, William H. *Keeping the Faith: A. Philip Randolph, Milton P. Webster, and the Brotherhood of Sleeping Car Porters, 1925–1937*. Urbana: University of Illinois Press, 1977.

Haywood, Harry. *Black Bolshevik: Autobiography of an Afro-American Communist*. Chicago: Liberator Press, 1978.

Henri, Florette. *Black Migration: Movement North, 1900–1920*. Garden City: Anchor Press/Doubleday, 1975.

Herbst, Alma. *The Negro in the Slaughtering and Meat-Packing Industry in Chicago*. Boston: Houghton Mifflin, 1932.

Hickman, Nollie. *Mississippi Harvest*. Oxford: University of Mississippi Press, 1962.

Hogan, David J. *Class and Reform: School and Society in Chicago, 1880–1930*. Philadelphia: University of Pennsylvania Press, 1985.

Holli, Melvin, and Peter d'A. Jones, eds. *The Ethnic Frontier: Essays in the History of Group Survival in Chicago and the Midwest*. Grand Rapids, Mich.: William B. Eerdmans, 1977.

Homel, Michael. *Down From Equality: Black Chicagoans and the Public Schools, 1920–41*. Urbana: University of Illinois Press, 1984.

Hughes, Elizabeth A. *Living Conditions of Small-Wage Earners in Chicago*. Chicago: Chicago Department of Public Welfare, 1925.

Hughes, Langston. *The Big Sea: An Autobiography*. New York: Alfred A. Knopf, 1945.

Jackson, Mahalia, and Evan M. Wylie. *Movin' On Up*. New York: Hawthorn Books, 1966.

Jacobson, Julius, ed. *The Negro and the American Labor Movement*. Garden City: Anchor Books, 1968.

Jaynes, Gerald D. *Branches without Roots: Genesis of the Black Working Class in the American South, 1862–1882*. New York: Oxford University Press, 1986.

Johnson, Charles S. *The Negro in American Civilization: A Study of Negro Life and Race Relations in the Light of Social Research*. New York: Henry Holt and Co., 1930.

Jones, Jacqueline. *Labor of Love, Labor of Sorrow: Black Women, Work, and the Family from Slavery to the Present*. New York: Basic Books, 1985.

Jones, Leroi [Amiri Baraka]. *Blues People: Negro Music in White America.* New York: William Morrow and Co., 1963.

Kantowicz, Edward R. *Polish-American Politics in Chicago, 1888–1940.* Chicago: University of Chicago Press, 1975.

Katzman, David M. *Before the Ghetto: Black Detroit in the Nineteenth Century.* Urbana: University of Illinois Press, 1973.

———. *Seven Days a Week: Women and Domestic Service in Industrializing America.* New York: Oxford University Press, 1978.

Katznelson, Ira. *Black Men, White Cities: Race, Politics, and Migration in the United States, 1900–1930, and Britain, 1948–1968.* London: Published for the Institute of Race Relations by Oxford University Press, 1973.

Kennedy, Louise V. *The Negro Peasant Turns Cityward: Effects of Recent Migrations to Northern Centers.* New York: Columbia University Press, 1930.

King, George F., ed. *King's Agricultural Digest.* Clayton, N. J.: George F. King, 1923.

Kiser, Clyde Vernon. *Sea Island to City: A Study of St. Helena Islanders in Harlem and Other Urban Centers.* New York: Columbia University Press, 1932.

Kolchin, Peter. *First Freedom: The Responses of Alabama's Blacks to Emancipation and Reconstruction.* Westport, Conn.: Greenwood Press, 1972.

Korman, A. Gerd. *Industrialization, Immigrants, and Americanizers: The View from Milwaukee, 1866–1921.* Madison: State Historical Society of Wisconsin, 1967.

Kusmer, Kenneth L. *A Ghetto Takes Shape: Black Cleveland, 1870–1930.* Urbana: University of Illinois Press, 1976.

Lamon, Lester C. *Black Tennesseans, 1900–1930.* Knoxville: University of Tennessee Press, 1977.

Lee, Everett S., Ann R. Miller, Carol Brainerd, and Richard A. Easterlin. *Population Redistribution and Economic Growth, United States, 1870–1950.* Vol. 1, *Methodological Considerations and Reference Tables.* Philadelphia: American Philosophical Society, 1957.

Levine, Lawrence W. *Black Culture and Black Consciousness: Afro-American Folk Thought from Slavery to Freedom.* New York: Oxford University Press, 1977.

Lieberson, Stanley. *A Piece of the Pie: Blacks and White Immigrants since 1880.* Berkeley and Los Angeles: University of California Press, 1980.

Litwack, Leon F. *Been in the Storm So Long: The Aftermath of Slavery.* New York: Alfred A. Knopf, 1979.

———. *North of Slavery: The Negro in the Free States, 1790–1860.* Chicago: University of Chicago Press, 1961.

Locke, Alain, ed. *The New Negro: An Interpretation.* New York: Albert and Charles Boni, 1925.

McDonald, Forrest. *Insull.* Chicago: University of Chicago Press, 1962.

McMurry, Linda. *Recorder of the Black Experience: A Biography of Monroe Nathan Work.* Baton Rouge: Lousiana State University Press, 1985.

Magdol, Edward. *A Right to the Land: Essays on the Freedmen's Community.* Westport, Conn.: Greenwood Press, 1977.

Mandle, Jay R. *The Roots of Black Poverty: The Southern Plantation Economy after the Civil War.* Durham: Duke University Press, 1978.

Meier, August. *Negro Thought in America, 1880–1915: Racial Ideologies in the Age of Booker T. Washington.* Ann Arbor: University of Michigan Press, 1963.

Meier, August, and Elliott Rudwick. *From Plantation to Ghetto.* 3d ed. New York: Hill and Wang, 1976.

Merriam, Charles E., and Harold F. Gosnell. *Non-Voting: Causes and Methods of Control.* Chicago: University of Chicago Press, 1924.

Minutes of the University Commission on Race Questions. Eighth Meeting, August 30, 1917. [Charlottesville, Va., c. 1917].

Montgomery, Royal E. *Industrial Relations in the Chicago Building Trades.* Chicago: University of Chicago Press, 1927.

Myrdal, Gunnar. *An American Dilemma: The Negro Problem and Modern Democracy.* New York: Harper and Bros., 1944.

National Association for the Advancement of Colored People. *Tenth Annual Report for the Year 1919.* New York: National Association for the Advancement of Colored People, 1920.

National Urban League. *Bulletin of the National Urban League* 9 (January 1920).

Nelli, Humbert S. *Italians in Chicago 1880–1930: A Study in Ethnic Mobility.* New York: Oxford University Press, 1970.

Newby, I. A. *Jim Crow's Defense: Anti-Negro Thought in America, 1900–1930.* Batón Rouge: Louisiana State University Press, 1965.

Oliver, Paul. *Blues Fell This Morning: The Meaning of the Blues.* New York: Horizon Press, 1960.

Osofsky, Gilbert. *Harlem: The Making of a Ghetto.* 2d ed. New York: Harper and Row, 1971.

Ottley, Roi. *The Lonely Warrior: The Life and Times of Robert S. Abbott.* Chicago: Henry Regnery Co., 1955.

Painter, Nell Irvin. *Exodusters: Black Migration to Kansas after Reconstruction.* New York: Alfred A. Knopf, 1977.

Peterson, Robert. *Only the Ball Was White.* Englewood Cliffs: Prentice-Hall, 1970.

Philpott, Thomas L. *The Slum and the Ghetto: Neighborhood Deterioration and Middle-Class Reform, Chicago 1880–1930.* New York: Oxford University Press, 1978.

Rabinowitz, Howard N. *Race Relations in the Urban South, 1865–1890.* New York: Oxford University Press, 1978. Reprint. Urbana: University of Illinois Press, 1980.

Ransom, Roger L., and Richard Sutch. *One Kind of Freedom: The Economic Consequences of Emancipation.* Cambridge, Eng.: Cambridge University Press, 1977.

Redkey, Edwin S. *Black Exodus: Black Nationalist and Back-to-Africa Movements, 1890–1910.* New Haven: Yale University Press, 1969.

Reid, Ira De A., ed. *Negro Membership in American Labor Unions.* New York: Alexander Press, 1930.

Robb, Frederic, ed. *The Book of Achievement the World Over Featuring the Negro in Chicago.* Chicago: Washington Intercollegiate Club, 1929.

Rosengarten, Theodore. *All God's Dangers: The Life of Nate Shaw.* New York: Alfred A. Knopf, 1974.

Rudwick, Elliott M. *Race Riot at East St. Louis, July 2, 1917.* Carbondale: Southern Illinois University Press, 1964.

Sandburg, Carl. *The Chicago Race Riots July, 1919.* New York: Harcourt, Brace and Howe, 1919.

Scott, Emmett J. *Negro Migration during the War.* New York: Oxford University Press, 1920.

Scott, Estelle Hill. *Occupational Changes among Negroes in Chicago.* Chicago: U.S. Work Projects Adminstration, 1939.

Simms, James N. *Simms' Blue Book and National Negro Business and Professional Directory.* Chicago: James N. Simms, 1923.

Sinclair, Upton. *The Jungle.* New York: Doubleday, Page and Co., 1906.

Slayton, Robert A. *Back of the Yards: The Making of a Local Democracy.* Chicago: University of Chicago Press, 1986.

Spear, Allan H. *Black Chicago: The Making of a Negro Ghetto.* Chicago: University of Chicago Press, 1967.

Spero, Sterling D., and Abram L. Harris. *The Black Worker: The Negro and the Labor Movement.* New York: Columbia University Press, 1931. Reprint. New York: Atheneum, 1968.

State-Wide Conference Issues Important Address to the Honorable Members of the State Legislature and the White Citizenry of Georgia. [Atlanta?, 1923?].

Stein, Judith. *The World of Marcus Garvey: Race and Class in Modern Society.* Baton Rouge: Louisiana State University Press, 1986.

Strickland, Arvarh. *History of the Chicago Urban League.* Urbana: University of Illinois Press, 1966.

Taitt, John. *The Souvenir of Negro Progress: Chicago, 1779–1925.* Chicago: De-Saible Association, 1925.

Tindall, George B. *The Emergence of the New South, 1913–1945.* Baton Rouge: Louisiana State University Press, 1967.

———. *South Carolina Negroes, 1877–1900.* Columbia: University of South Carolina Press, 1952.

Trotter, Joe W., Jr. *Black Milwaukee: The Making of an Industrial Proletariat, 1915–1945.* Urbana: University of Illinois Press, 1985.

Tuttle, William M., Jr. *Race Riot: Chicago in the Red Summer of 1919.* New York: Atheneum, 1970.

United Charities of Chicago. *Sixty-Six Years of Service.* Chicago: United Charities of Chicago, [1922].

Vance, Rupert B. *Human Factors in Cotton Culture: A Study in the Social Geography of the American South.* Chapel Hill: University of North Carolina Press, 1929.

Van Deusen, John G. *The Black Man in White America.* Washington, D.C.: Associated Publishers, 1938.

[Walsh, Frank]. *Over the Top at the Yards.* Chicago: Chicago Labor News, 1918.

Weiner, Jonathan. *Social Origins of the New South: Alabama, 1860–1885.* Baton Rouge: Louisiana State University Press, 1978.

Weiss, Nancy. *The National Urban League: 1910–1940.* New York: Oxford University Press, 1974.

Wendt, Lloyd and Herman Kogan. *Big Bill of Chicago.* Indianapolis: Bobbs Merrill, 1953.

Wharton, Vernon L. *The Negro in Mississippi, 1865–1890.* Chapel Hill: University of North Carolina Press, 1947. Reprint. New York, 1965.

Wood, Junius B. *The Negro in Chicago.* Chicago: Chicago Daily News, 1916.

Woodson, Carter G. *A Century of Negro Migration.* Washington, D.C.: Association for the Study of Negro Life and History, 1918.

Woofter, Thomas J. *Negro Migration: Changes in Rural Organization and Population of the Cotton Belt.* New York: W. D. Gray, 1920. Reprint. New York, 1969.

Wright, Gavin. *Old South, New South: Revolutions in the Southern Economy since the Civil War.* New York: Basic Books, 1986.

Wright, George C. *Life Behind a Veil: Blacks in Louisville, Kentucky, 1865–1930.* Baton Rouge: Louisiana State University Press, 1985.

Wright, Richard. *American Hunger.* New York: Harper and Row, 1977.

———. *Black Boy.* New York: Harper and Brothers, 1937.

Wright, Richard Robert. *87 Years Behind the Black Curtain: An Autobiography.* Philadelphia: Rare Book Co., 1965.

Young Women's Christian Association of Chicago, Illinois. *Annual Statement.* 1917, 1919–23. Chicago: Young Women's Christian Association, 1918, 1920–24.

Dissertations, Theses, and Unpublished Manuscript

Adams, Mary F. "Present Housing Conditions in South Chicago, South Deering, and Pullman." Master's thesis, University of Chicago, 1926.

Branham, Charles R. "The Transformation of Black Political Leadership in Chicago, 1864–1942," Ph.D. dissertation, University of Chicago, 1981.

Clarke, Edna L. "History of the Controversy Between Labor and Capital in the Slaughtering and Meat Packing Industry in Chicago." Master's thesis, University of Chicago, 1922.

Cohen, Lizabeth. "Learning to Live in the Welfare State: Industrial Workers in Chicago between the Wars, 1919–1939." Ph.D. dissertation, University of California, Berkeley, 1986.

Cohen, William. "The Great Migration: The Lure of the North." Unpublished ms. Copy in possession of author.

Colson, Myra Hill. "Home Work Among Negro Women in Chicago." Master's thesis, University of Chicago, 1928.

Cowgill, Theodore T. "The Employment Agencies of Chicago." Master's thesis, University of Chicago, 1928.

Daniel, Vattel E. "Ritual in Chicago's South Side Churches for Negroes." Ph.D. dissertation, University of Chicago, 1940.

Finney, John D. "A Study of Negro Labor during and after World War I." Ph.D. dissertation, Georgetown University, 1967.

Greenwald, Maurine. "Women, War, and Work: The Impact of World War I on Women Workers in the United States." Ph.D. dissertation, Brown University, 1977.

Hardy, Erie. "Relation of the Negro to Trade Unionism." Master's thesis, University of Chicago, 1911.

Herrick, Mary J. "Negro Employees of the Chicago Board of Education." Master's thesis, University of Chicago, 1931.

Homel, Michael. "Negroes in the Chicago Public Schools, 1910–1941." Ph.D. dissertation, University of Chicago, 1972.

Logsdon, Joseph. "Reverend Archibald J. Carey and the Negro in Chicago Politics." Master's thesis, University of Chicago, 1961.

McGee, Henry. "The Negro in the Chicago Post Office." Master's thesis, University of Chicago, 1961.

Mack, Ione M. "The Factor of Race in the Religious Education of the Negro High School Girl." Master's thesis, University of Chicago, 1927.

Meyerowitz, Joanne J. "Holding Their Own: Working Women Apart from Family in Chicago, 1880–1930." Ph.D. dissertation, Stanford University, 1983.

Rood, Alice Q. "Social Conditions among the Negroes on Federal Street between Forty-fifth Street and Fifty-third Street." Master's thesis, University of Chicago, 1924.

Sutherland, Robert Lee. "An Analysis of Negro Churches in Chicago." Ph.D. dissertation, University of Chicago, 1930.

Thompson, Charles H. "A Study of the Reading Accomplishments of Colored and White Children." Master's thesis, University of Chicago, 1920.

Vickery, William E. "The Economics of Negro Migration, 1900–1960." Ph.D. dissertation, University of Chicago, 1969.

Wilson, Evelyn H. "Chicago Families in Furnished Rooms." Master's thesis, University of Chicago, 1929.

Wright, Richard Robert. "The Industrial Condition of Negroes in Chicago." B.D. thesis, University of Chicago Divinity School, 1901.

Articles

Arthur, George. "The Young Men's Christian Association Movement among Negroes." *Opportunity* 1, no. 3 (March 1923): 16–18.

Barnett, Claude A. "We Win a Place in Industry." *Opportunity* 7, no. 3 (March 1929): 82–86.

Bridges, Horace. "The First Urban League Family." In Chicago Urban League, *Two Decades of Service*, 4–8. Chicago: William Mason Press, 1936.

Clark, Howard L. "Growth of Negro Population in the U.S. and Trend of Migration from the South Since 1860. Economic Conditions the Reason Negroes are Leaving South." *Manufacturers Record* 83, no. 4 (January 25, 1923): 61–63.

Cohen, William. "Black Immobility and Free Labor: The Freedmen's Bureau and the Relocation of Black Labor, 1865–1968." *Civil War History* 30, no. 3 (September 1984): 221–34.

———. "Negro Involuntary Servitude in the South, 1865–1940: A Preliminary Analysis." *Journal of Southern History* 42, no. 1 (February 1976): 31–60.

Davis, P. O. "Negro Exodus and Southern Agriculture." *American Review of Reviews* 63 (October 1923): 401–7.

Diner, Steven J. "Chicago Social Workers and Blacks in the Progressive Era." *Social Service Review* 44, no. 4 (December 1970): 393–410.

Donald, Henderson H. "The Negro Migration of 1916–1918." *Journal of Negro History* 6, no. 4 (October 1921): 388–498.

Du Bois, W. E. B., "The Migration of Negroes." *Crisis* 14, no. 2 (June 1917): 63–66.

Evans, William L. "The Negro in Chicago Industries." *Opportunity* 1, no. 2 (February 1923): 15–17.

"The Exodus." *AME Church Review* 33, no. 3 (January 1917): 149–51.

"Exodus Costing State $27,000,000." *Journal of the American Bankers Association* 16, no. 1 (July 1923): 51–52.

Farley, F. W. "Growth of the Beef Cattle Industry in the South." U.S. Department of Agriculture *Yearbook*, 1917. Washington, D.C.: GPO, 1918.

Fisher, Isaac. "Do Not Rock the Boat," *Fisk University News* 8, no. 1 (October 1917): 4–5.

Fisher, S. Mattie. "Olivet as a Christian Center." *Missions* 10, no. 3 (March 1919): 199–202.

Foster, William Z. "How Life Has Been Brought into the Stockyards." *Life and Labor* 8, no. 4 (April 1918): 63–72.

Frazier, E. Franklin. "Chicago: A Cross-Section of Negro Life." *Opportunity* 7, no. 3 (March 1929): 70–73.

Harris, Harrison L. "Negro Mortality Rates in Chicago." *Social Service Review* 1 (March 1927): 58–77.

Haynes, George E. "Effect of War Conditions on Negro Labor." *Proceedings of the Academy of Political Science* 8, no. 2 (February 1919): 299–312.

———. "Migration of Negroes into Northern Cities." *Proceedings of the National Conference of Social Work* 44 (1917): 494–96.

———. "Negroes Move North, I." *Survey* 40 (May 4, 1918): 115–22.

———. "Negroes Move North, II." *Survey* 41 (January 4, 1919): 455–61.

Higgs, Robert. "The Boll Weevil, the Cotton Economy, and Black Migration: 1910–1930." *Agricultural History* 50, no. 2 (April 1976): 335–50.

Hill, T. Arnold. "Recent Developments in the Problem of Negro Labor." *Proceedings of the National Conference of Social Work* 48 (1921): 321–25.

———. "Why Southern Negroes Don't Go South." *Survey* 43, no. 6 (November 29, 1919): 183–95.

Holmes, William F. "Labor Agents and the Georgia Exodus, 1899–1900." *South Atlantic Quarterly* 79, no. 4 (Autumn 1980): 436–48.

Houze, J. O. "Negro Labor and the Industries." *Opportunity* 1, no. 1 (January 1923): 20–22.

Johnson, Charles S. "How Much of the Migration Was a Flight from Persecution." *Opportunity* 1, no. 9 (September 1923): 273–75.

———. "How the Negro Fits in Northern Industry." *Industrial Psychology* 1 (June 1926): 399–412.

———. "The New Frontage on American Life." In Alain Locke, ed. *The New Negro: An Interpretation*, 278–98. New York: Albert and Charles Boni, 1925.

Kilson, Martin. "Political Change in the Negro Ghetto, 1900–1940s." In Nathan I. Huggins, Martin Kilson, and Daniel Fox, eds., *Key Issues in the Afro-*

American Experience, vol. 2. New York: Harcourt, Brace, Jovanovich, 1971.

Kirby, Jack T. "The Southern Exodus, 1910–1960: A Primer for Historians." *Journal of Southern History* 49, no. 4 (November 1983): 585–600.

Litwack, Leon F. "The Ordeal of Black Freedom." In Walter J. Fraser, Jr., and Winfred B. Moore, Jr., eds., *The Southern Enigma: Essays on Race, Class, and Folk Culture*. Westport , Conn.: Greenwood Press, 1983.

Mandel, Bernard. "Samuel Gompers and the Negro," *Journal of Negro History* 40, no. 1 (January 1955): 34–60.

Mazur, Edward. "Jewish Chicago: From Diversity to Community." In Melvin G. Holli and Peter d'A. Jones, eds., *The Ethnic Frontier: Essays in the History of Group Survival in Chicago and the Midwest*. Grand Rapids, Mich.: William B. Eerdmans,1977.

Meier, August, and Elliott Rudwick. "Attitudes of Negro Leaders toward the American Labor Movement from the Civil War to World War I." In Julius Jacobson, ed., *The Negro and the American Labor Movement*, 27–48. Garden City: Anchor Books, 1968.

Miller, Kelly. "The Farm the Negro's Best Chance." *Manufacturers Record* 90, no. 5 (August 5, 1926): 96–97.

Moore, Rev. John M. "The Migration of the Negro from the Standpoint of the South." *Eleventh Annual Meeting of the Home Missions Council* (January 1918): 21–26.

Parot, Joseph J. "Ethnic versus Black Metropolis: The Origins of Polish-Black Housing Tensions in Chicago." *Polish-American Studies* 29, nos. 1–2 (Spring-Autumn 1972): 5–33.

Rogers, Don C. "Retardation from the Mental Standpoint." *Chicago Schools Journal* 9 (1926–27): 302–3.

Sayre, Helen B. "Making Over Poor Workers." *Opportunity* 1, no. 2 (February 1923): 17–18.

———. "Negro Women in Industry." *Opportunity* 2, no. 20 (August 1924): 242–44.

Scott, Emmett J., comp. "Additional Letters of Negro Migrants of 1916–1918." *Journal of Negro History* 4 (October 1919): 412–75.

———. "Letters of Negro Migrants of 1916–1918." *Journal of Negro History* 4 (July 1919): 290–340.

Scroggs,William O. "Interstate Migration of Negro Population." *Journal of Political Economy* 25, no. 10 (December 1917): 1034–43.

Shofner, Jerrell H. "Florida and the Black Migration." *Florida Historical Quarterly* 57, no. 3 (January 1979): 267–88.

Sisk, Glenn N. "Negro Migration in the Alabama Black Belt—1875–1917." *Negro History Bulletin* 17 (November 1953): 32–34.

Spillman, W. J., and E. A. Goldenweisser. "Farm Tenantry in the United States." U.S. Department of Agriculture *Yearbook*, 1923. Washington, D.C.: GPO, 1924.

Stolberg, Benjamin. "The Stock Yards Strike." *Nation* 114 (January 25, 1922): 91–92.

Strickland, Arvarh. "Toward the Promised Land: The Exodus to Kansas and Afterward." *Missouri Historical Review* 69, no. 4 (July 1975): 376–412.

"The Superfluous Negro." *New Republic* 7 (June 24, 1916): 187–88.

Thompson, E. P. "Time, Work-Discipline, and Industrial Capitalism." *Past and Present* 38 (December 1967): 56–97.

"Voice of the Press on Migration of Negroes to the North." *AME Church Review* 33, no. 3 (January 1917): 130–33.

Washington, Booker T. "The Rural Negro and the South." *Proceedings of the National Conference of Charities and Corrections* 41 (1914): 121–27.

Washington, Forrester B. "A Program of Work for the Assimilation of Negro Immigrants in Northern Cities." *Proceedings of the National Conference of Social Work* 44 (1917): 497–500.

———. "Reconstruction and the Colored Woman." *Life and Labor* 9, no. 1 (January 1919): 3–7.

Webster, M[ilton] P. "Organized Labor Among Negroes in Chicago." In Frederic Robb, ed. *The Book of Achievement the World Over Featuring the Negro in Chicago*, 196–97. Chicago: Washington Intercollegiate Club, 1929.

White, Walter. "Chicago and Its Eight Reasons." *Crisis* 18, no. 6 (October 1919): 294–97.

Woofter, Thomas J. "The Negro and Industrial Peace." *Survey* 45, no. 12 (December 18, 1920): 420–21.

Worthman, Paul, and James Green. "Black Workers in the New South, 1865–1915." In Nathan I. Huggins, Martin Kilson, and Daniel Fox, eds., *Key Issues in the Afro-American Experience*, 2: 47–69. New York: Harcourt, Brace, Jovanovich, 1971.

Index

Abbott, Edith, 171

Abbott, Robert S., 35, 78, 79, 88, 144; on economic opportunity, 82; founding of *Defender*, 74, 130; as hero to black southerners, 80, 85; ideas on political economy, 233; leadership role in Chicagó, 83; on migration from South, 33; migration to Chicago (1897), 130; on prohibition, 75; on race, 75, 82. *See also* Chicago *Defender*

Aberdeen, Mississippi, 87, 94

Abernethy, H. B., 54

Abolitionism, 163

Adams, Henry, 24

Adaptation, 5, 7, 133; defined as "Negro Problem," 163, 169; of families, 106; of industrialists to black workers, 198; to industrial work, 7, 181–207, 262; to northern race relations, 1–2, 112, 117–19, 150–53, 166, 253; pressures on migrants, 144–53; role of churches, 158–59; to schools, 249–57; to urban life, 112, 117, 145, 150, 153–54, 156, 260–62. *See also* Race relations; Work

Addams, Jane, 170–71

African Methodist Episcopal Church, 3, 58, 61, 94, 129. *See also* Quinn Chapel

Agnew, W. M., 94

Alabama: boll weevil, 29; domestic slave trade, 20; migration from, 6, 112; reactions to Great Migration, 52; schools, 247; trade unions, 213

Alabama Federation of Labor, 213

Albany (Georgia) *Herald*, 51

Alexander, Will W., 51

Algiers, Louisiana, 106

Alpharetta, Georgia, 34

Alschuler, Samuel B., 211–12, 221, 242, 244

Amalgamated Assocation of Iron and Steel Workers, 214

Amalgamated Meat Cutter and Butcher Workmen (AMC&BW), 218, 223; assistance to blacks during 1919 riot, 223; Local 213 (Chicago), 220–21, 224, 226; Local 651 (Chicago), 208, 219–21, 223, 224–26, 235, 237; membership, 211; opposition to postriot strike, 223; organizing strategies, 224; racial policies, 219–21, 224–26, 237, 241; rallies, 208; relations with Stockyards Labor Council, 211, 212, 223, 226

AME Church Review: on Great Migration, 17, 52, 60; on opportunities in South, 34

American Colonization Society, 25

American Federationist, 216

American Federation of Labor, 214, 215–16, 220, 231, 237

American Giants, 4, 86, 93

Americanization, 169, 171, 256

American Railway Union, 217

American Revolution, 20

American Unity Welfare Labor Union, 227

Americus, Georgia, 48

Ameringer, Oscar, 213

Andalusia, Alabama, 110

Anderson, Louis B., 35, 130, 177

Anniston, Alabama, 36, 68, 113, 213

Anti-enticement legislation, 20, 27, 46
Argo, Illinois, 196
Argo Corn Products Company, 184, 200, 204, 206
Arkansas: black restlessness before Great Migration, 30; domestic slave trade, 20; migration from, 6; migration to, 21, 26, 68
Arkansas Club, 156
Armour, Philip, 230
Armour & Company, 71, 142, 190; Armour Glee Club, 228; Armour Star Lambs (baseball team), 201; discrimination against black employees, 206; hiring practices, 187; philanthropy in black community, 223; satisfaction with black work force, 206
Armstrong, Louis, 113, 114–15
Arthur, George, 228
Associated Charities of Atlanta, 43
Association of Colored Railway Trainmen, 214
Athletic clubs, 178
Atlanta, Georgia: race riot (1906), 32; schools, 247
Atlanta *Constitution*, 50, 51, 63
Atlanta *Independent*, 61, 62
Augusta, Georgia, 1, 72, 103
Austell, Georgia, 3

Back-of-the-Yards, 240–41
Baker, Ray Stannard, 164
Baltimore *Afro-American*, 88
Banks, Charles, 59
Banks, Charley, 74
Baptist Church, 92, 94, 129
Baraka, Amiri, 7
Barber, Jesse Max, 32
Baseball, 4, 81, 86, 89, 93, 99, 130, 142, 201, 228
Bedford, Robert, 212–13, 215
Berean Baptist Church, 157
Bethlehem Baptist Association, 94, 102, 104, 132
Bilbo, Theodore, 50, 78
Binga, Jesse, 174
Birmingham, Alabama: anti-enticement legislation, 46; availability of jobs, 112; reaction to Great Migration, 41; steel mills, 181; unions, 213, 214
Birmingham *Reporter*, 61
Birmingham *Weekly Voice*, 60

Black Metropolis (Drake and Cayton), 15
Black press: Chicago newspapers and migrants, 145, 152–54; role in Great Migration, 3–4, 7, 60, 68–69, 76–77 (map), 79, 81–88, 99, 102; in South, compared with *Defender*, 80; and trade unions, 223, 227, 231–36. *See also individual newspapers*
Black towns, 24–25
Blackwell, Rev. W. A., 157
Bland, Alden, 116
Blockbusting, 162
Bolivar County, Mississippi, 55
Boll weevil, 14, 28–30, 41, 42, 70
Boston, Massachusetts, 32
Bowen, Louise DeKoven, 171
Braddan, Rev. William, 157
Breckinridge, Sophonisba, 171
Bridges, Horace, 236, 238
Brinley, Arkansas, 181
Broad Ax (Chicago), 231
Brookhaven, Mississippi, 103, 104, 108
Broonzy, Bill, 192
Brotherhood of Sleeping Car Porters, 230, 235
Brotherhood of Timber Workers, 213
Brown, Edwin, 133
Building trades, 182, 213, 214, 216–17, 232, 243
Bullock City, Alabama, 99
Burnette, Texas, 117
Butcher Workman, 220, 224, 226, 235

Canada, 99
Carey, Rev. Archibald J., Jr., 252
Carey, Rev. Archibald J., Sr., 130, 176, 230
Carolina Sea Island Candy Store, 155
Carrier, Mississippi, 14
Carroll, Jack, 190
Carroll County, Mississippi, 17
Cassani, C. (labor agent), 73
Catholic Church, 173
Cayton, Horace, 15, 131, 200
Central Training School (Charity, Alabama), 57
"Chain Gang Blues," 197
Chain migration, 89–94, 99
Chamber of Commerce: Houston, 46; Mississippi, 51; New Orleans, 56
Chattanooga, Tennessee, 71
Chicago: antebellum black community,

20; arrival of migrants in 2, 3, 106, 113–16, 123; black community's links with South, 67–68, 91–94, 132, 155, 158; as destination for migrants, 4, 7, 13, 16, 33, 48, 74, 94, 98, 99–102, 108, 109, 110, 130, 214; education, 246–58; employment, 2, 7, 13, 35, 128, 131, 153, 154, 177, 182–85, 197, 206, 239, 252, 257; image in black South, 4, 9, 18, 36, 74, 79, 81, 86, 93, 98, 99, 132, 161, 165; leisure opportunities, 86, 117; letters from, 89–91; politics, 130, 162, 175–77, 178, population, 123, 127, 162–64; race riot (1919), 138, 165, 172, 179–80, 222–23, 239, 245, 259–60; racial segregation, 126–28, 134, 152, 163–64, 166, recruitment of labor to, 70–71; residential patterns, 126–27, 154, 163, 174–75, 241; return migration from, 43, 179–81; white reactions to Great Migration, 162–63, 168–75. *See also* Education; Old Settlers; Packinghouses; Race relations, in Chicago

Chicago Black Belt, 126 (map); autonomy, 261, 263; boundaries, 118, 123, 124–25 (maps), 126–27, 137, 139; difficulty of organizing workers in, 240–41; housing shortage, 135–38; population, 123; public health, 168; schools, 247–49, 253; social service institutions, 172; social structure, 123, 127, 128–30, 143; ubiquity and influence of southern culture, 262; vice, 169–70

Chicago Board of Education, 128, 258, 260

Chicago Chamber of Commerce, 179

Chicago City Council, 130

Chicago Commission on Race Relations, 185; analysis of 1919 riot, 222; blacks in industry, 205, 206; causes of Great Migration, 15; characteristics of migrants, 183; education and schools, 252, 253; housing, 134; interviews with migrants, 168, 180, 259

Chicago Committee of Fifteen, 170

Chicago *Conservator*, 130

Chicago Council of Social Agencies, 173

Chicago *Daily News:* on black involvement in vice, 169; praised by *Defender*, 168; reaction to Great Migration, 168–69

Chicago *Defender*, 54, 69, 71, 74–88, 113, 130, 135, 260; advice to black southerners before Great Migration, 33, 81–82; analysis of 1919 riot, 222, 259; on attractions of North, 55; on black opposition to Great Migration, 56, 58, 63; on causes of Great Migration, 16; on Chicago daily press, 168; circulation, 69, 74, 76–77 (map), 78–80; on community institutions, 140–41; correspondence columns, 93, 105, criticism of migrants, 130, 146, 150, 152; early view of Great Migration, 82; on education and schools, 81, 247, 251; and entertainers, 78; on European immigrants, 164; Help Wanted columns, 185; on impact of Great Migration in South, 40; influence in Chicago, 144, 153; influence in South, 66, 69, 75, 78–81; instructing migrants, 118, 144, 145–46, 197, 200; and labor agents, 72; letters from prospective migrants, 49, 104, 109, 132; links to industrial employers, 185; local sales agents in South, 95, 97; on opportunities in North, 35, 81, 144, 251; on opportunities in South, 81–82, 251; promotion of Great Migration, 60, 82–88, 139; and Pullman porters, 78; race consciousness, 75, 82, 233, 236, 240; on racial violence in South, 75, 78, 81, 82; role in Great Migration, 4, 7, 68, 69, 81–88, 94, 99, 102; on segregation in Chicago, 174; and southern images of Chicago, 14, 36, 66, 74, 81, 94, 132, 156, 246; on success of migrants, 205; suppression of, in South, 44, 86; on unions and strikes, 209, 217, 231–36, 242; on white reformers, 171; on William Hale Thompson, 176; on work ethic, 35. *See also* Abbott, Robert S.

Chicago Federation of Labor: racial policies, 216, 219, 226, 241–42; relationship to Stockyards Labor Council, 211, 219; on YMCA, 201

Chicago *Herald Examiner*, 168

Chicago Loop, 123

Chicago Real Estate Board, 174

Chicago Shipbuilding Company, 185

Chicago *Tribune:* on black involvement in vice, 169; campaign to induce blacks to return to South, 179; criticized by

Chicago *Tribune* (*continued*)
New Majority, 224; on proposal to restrict black migration, 174; reaction to
Great Migration, 163, 168–70
Chicago Urban League: assistance to
migrants, 116, 134, 141–43, 186, 236,
240; attractiveness to white reformers,
174; employment bureau, 186, 187,
188–89 (photos), 236; on Great Migration, 16, 183; industrial program, 196,
202, 204, 206; influence among migrants, 142, 236; instructing migrants,
144, 146, 147, 150, 151, 152, 154,
203–4; leadership, 131; letters from
prospective migrants, 68, 71, 102,
104, 105, 132, 142; position on unionization, 208–9, 236–40; recruitment of
black workers, 85; role in Great Migration, 85, 86, 139; ties to Chicago
industrialists, 203–4, 238–40
Chicago *Whip*, 155, 234; criticism of migrants, 150, 154; on State Street, 117;
on unions and strikes, 234–36; on
YMCA, 141
Child labor, 249–51
Christian Industrial League, 134
Christian Recorder, 60
Christ Temple Mission, 158
Churches. *See* Religion
Church of the New Jerusalem, 158
Cincinnati, Ohio, 112
Citizenship: denial of rights of, 163; and
education, 258; and Great Migration,
8–9, 19, 36–37, 53, 57, 60, 180, 263;
and Kansas Fever Exodus, 24; and
land ownership, 13, 24; migrants'
definition of, 265; in schools, 250, 254;
and voting, 259
City Club of Chicago, 172
Civil War, 13, 19, 20, 256
Class consciousness, 6, 210, 263
Class formation, 5, 6, 7, 8, 250
Clemons, Jefferson, 17
Cleveland, Ohio, 112
Club Home for Colored Girls, 134
Cobb, Ned, 34, 194
Coffee, Rev. T. W., 61, 63
Colored Farmers Alliance, 214
Colored Methodist Episcopal Church, 58,
92
Columbia (South Carolina) *State*, 40
Columbian Exposition (1893), 4, 130

Columbus, Georgia, 112
Come and See Baptist Church, 159
Commonwealth Edison, 71, 198
Communist Party, 264
Congress of Industrial Organizations
(CIO), 228
Connecticut, recruitment of black work-
ers, 69
Cook County Hospital, 172
Corinth, Mississippi, 93
Cotton cultivation: annual cycle, 30; con-
trasted with industrial work, 192–94;
and diversification, 30, 41, 51; expan-
sion in early nineteenth century, 20;
mechanization, 19, 41; westward ex-
pansion, 28. *See also* Boll weevil
Cottonseed-oil mills, 31, 181
Cottrell, Bishop Elias, 58
Councils of Defense, 49, 56
Crawford, I. W., 55
Cress, Ida Mae, 252
Crisis: on Great Migration, 60; suppres-
sion of, 44
Crop lien system, 19
Crystal Springs, Mississippi, 55
Custer, Frank, 213, 215

Dallas (vicinity), labor shortage, 40
Davis, Corneal, 182
Davis, P. O., 42
Dawes Hotel, 134
Dearborn Station (Chicago), 116
Decatur, Alabama, 105
Democratic Party, 176, 263
DePriest, Oscar, 130, 169
DeRidder, Louisiana, 17
Detroit: formation of ghetto, 127; migra-
tion to, 4, 99, 112; premigration lei-
sure activities of black southerners,
262
Detroit Urban League, 203
Dewey, John, 254
Dillard, James H., 15
Dismond, Binga, 81
Dixon, Charles, 226
Domestic service work, 15, 31, 131, 164,
244, 257
Doolittle School, 253, 254
Douglas, Paul, 195
Downing, G. W., 220
Drake, St. Clair, 15, 131, 200
Drew, Howard, 81

Du Bois, W. E. B., 4; on Great Migration, 16, 60, 64; on plantation system, 197; on problems of school integration, 256; on racial etiquette, 151; on Reconstruction and black achievement, 34; on South, 32; on trade unions, 215; on "twoness," 25; on white reformers, 172; on World War I, 179
Dukis, Gertrude Jones, 106
Dyersburg, Tennessee, 75

East St. Louis, riot (1917), 55, 178, 238
Ebenezer Baptist Church, 230
Education, 6, 241, 246–58, 263; curriculum, 256; and disillusionment, 251, 257–58; influence of Booker T. Washington, 58; intelligence testing, 255; as means of upward mobility, 8, 246; before migration, 183; motivation for migration, 8, 17, 18, 36, 81, 90, 91, 93, 246; at night for adults, 248–49; school attendance, 249–51, 252, 257; school buildings, 247–48; segregation and integration, 127–28, 164, 246, 248, 254, 256–57, 260; in South, 36, 52, 54, 62, 182, 247, 248 (photo), 249–50, 263; theories of, in Chicago, 251, 254, 255. *See also* Teachers
Eighth Illinois Regiment, 81, 130, 178
Elks Lodge, 92
Ellis, Hugh, 53
Ellison, Ralph, 265
Ellisville, Mississippi, 96, 98
Emancipation, 6, 19, 21–22, 259
Emancipation Proclamation, 141
Emigrationism: Africa, 25; Oklahoma, 24. *See also* Kansas Fever Exodus
Empire Mattress Company, 207
Employment. *See individual industries*
Employment agencies, 102, 185–87
Englewood, 123
Evans, William, 202, 238, 239, 242
Exodusters, 24. *See* Kansas Fever Exodus
Expectations of migrants, 3, 15, 18, 36, 86, 89–90, 99, 132, 137, 161, 165, 181, 183, 246, 264. *See also* Chicago, image in black South

Family: impact of migration on, 20, 106–7; role in migration and adaptation, 6, 21, 133; strategies during migration process, 105–7. *See also* Migration networks, family and kin
First Baptist Church (Hattiesburg), 67
Fisher, Isaac, 63, 64
Fisk University *News*, 64
Fitzpatrick, John, 219, 227, 242
Florida: domestic slave trade, 20; migration from, 16, 69; migration to, 26, 68
Florida East Coast Shine Parlor, 155
Fluornoy, Mary, 113, 156
Foote, A. K., 221
Ford, Charles, 208
Foster, Rube, 93
Foster, William Z., 219, 220, 226–27
Franklin, Mississippi, 44
Frederick Douglass Center, 140
Freedmen's Bureau, 22, 23
Freetown, Louisiana, 81

Gaines, Irene, 229
Galveston, Texas, 213
Garment industry, 185, 210, 230, 240
Garvey, Marcus, 4, 264
Georgia: attitudes of labor leaders, 214; blacks' images of North, 18; domestic slave trade, 20; labor market, 41; labor shortage, 40; migration from, 1, 3, 6, 17, 26, 106, 112; schools, 247; white-capping, 17
Ghettoization, 5, 6, 7, 9, 123–28
Goins, Irene, 220
Gompers, Samuel, 216
Grady, Henry, 39
Great Migration: attempts to stop by force, 44–50, 104, 105, 108, 110; attempts to stop by incentives, 50–52, 54; benefits to Chicago's black community, 83, 130, 144; blamed for 1919 Chicago race riot, 179; causes and motivations, 14–37, 44, 50, 52, 53, 57, 62, 68, 78, 162, 180, 241, 246, 265; challenge to southern white values, 38–39; characteristics of participants, 147, 148–49 (map), 150, 183, 195, 214; continuities with Kansas Fever Exodus, 24, 44, 56; geographic patterns, 4, 99, 100–101 (map); historical meaning of, 4–6, 7, 8–9, 13, 19, 37, 57, 68, 97, 200, 246; hope and disillusion, 259; ideology, 243–44, 264; impact on Chicago, 138, 143, 152, 156, 162–63, 165, 248, 260; impact on family life, 106–7; impact on South, 38, 40–41,

Great Migration (*continued*)
  52; impact on southern black communities, 58, 107–8; and labor shortage
  in South, 40; and labor turnover in
  North, 195; magnitude and direction,
  3–4; migrants' perceptions of, 7, 87,
  98, 103, 205; origins, 69; and patterns
  of black leadership, 55–65, 88–89, 95,
  96–97, 133, poetry and music, 96; as
  political lever for southern black leadership, 60–63, 246; role of federal
  government in, 48–49; southern black
  opposition, 38, 56–60, 64, 67, southern black support, 60, 88; southern
  white approval, 38, 41–43; southern
  white opposition, 6, 38, 57, 98; and
  unionization, 210, 243
Great Northern Drive, 87
Greek Americans, 253
Greenville, Mississippi: migration from,
  3, 107, 108, 109; wages, 52
Greenwood, Mississippi, 107
Griggs, Sutton, 60
Gulfport, Mississippi, 73, 80, 105, 113
Guy, Ira, 155

Half-Century (magazine), 152
Half-Century of Negro Progress (1915), 91
Hall, George C., 131, 146, 237, 238
Hammond, Louisiana, 106
Hampton Institute, 57, 58, 74, 130, 215,
  233
Handsboro, Mississippi, 113
Harper, L. C., 78
Harris, Abram, 243
Harris, Nathan W., 141
Hattiesburg, Mississippi: community in
  Chicago, 66–67; *Defender* circulation,
  79; labor agent activity, 71; letters to,
  89; migration clubs, 96, 97; migration
  from, 4, 66–67, 109, 111, 113; wages,
  52
Hattiesburg Shaving Parlor, 66, 155
Hawkinsville, Georgia, 14
Hayes, Cornelius J., 225
Haynes, George E., 15
Helena, Arkansas, 213
Henderson, Rev. James, 230
Hill, James, 117
Hill, T. Arnold, 205–6, 208, 237–38, 239
Holiness churches, 158
Hope, John, 63, 64

Hope Well Baptist Church, 159
Horton, Robert, 66–67, 95, 97, 155
Housing, 127, 132–39, 145, 166; relation
  between residence patterns and
  unionization, 241. *See also* Chicago,
  residential patterns
Houston, Texas, Chamber of Commerce
  reaction to Great Migration, 46
Houston *Observer*, 17
Houston *Post*, 53
Howard, Perry, 55
Howard University, 59, 215
Hughes, Langston, 110, 117, 118
Hull House, 171
Hyde Park, 174

Idlewild Hotel, 134
Illinois, prohibition against black immi-
  gration (1848), 23
Illinois Central Railroad, 4, 69, 71, 74, 99,
  100–101 (map), 111; Chicago Terminal, 114–16, 123, 141; labor relations
  and race, 214, 215; relationship with
  YMCA, 228
Illinois Federation of Labor, 237
Illinois State Employment Service, 186
Illinois Steel, 184
Immigrants (from Europe), 162, 207; access to social services compared with
  Afro-Americans', 170–71; attitudes
  of Afro-Americans toward, 164; attitudes of reformers toward, 151; and
  Chicago politics, 176–77; conflicts
  among, 164, 217; experience compared with Afro-Americans', 127,
  128, 139, 144, 169, 185, 250–51, 262;
  interactions with Afro-Americans,
  118, 162, 175, 177–78, 208–9, 217–19,
  253; and labor supply in northern cities, 3, 13; in packinghouses, 217; reaction to Great Migration, 175; and
  southern labor supply, 40, 41
Immigrants (from Mexico), 40, 198
Industrial employment: in Chicago, 36,
  128, 181–207, 260–61; and education,
  258; meaning of to black southerners,
  36; in North (pre–1916), 33, 128; in
  South, 31. *See also individual industries*
Industrial Workers of the World, 213, 230
Information and migration, 6, 44, 67–69,
  89, 97, 98, 161; rumors, 73, 98
Inland Steel, 196

Institutional AME Church, 140, 156, 230
Interchurch World Movement, 204
International Harvester, 200, 202, 203, 206, 210
International Ladies Garment Workers Union, 230
Irish Americans, 118, 162, 164, 178, 217, 220
Iron Age, 199
Iron Trade Review, 198
Italian Americans, 253

Jackson, A. L., 201, 228
Jackson, Giles, 56
Jackson, Mahalia, 93, 261
Jackson, Mississippi: images of Chicago, 18; impact of Great Migration, 107, 108; labor agent activity, 70; migration clubs, 96; migration from, 2, 105; schools, 247; white response to Great Migration, 54, 55
Jacksonville, Florida, 56, 107; anti-enticement legislation, 46; black opposition to Great Migration, 58
Jane Dent Home, 140
Jenkins, Wellborn, 18, 63
Jewish Daily Courier, 163
Jews, 144, 162, 164, 253
Jim Crow, 1, 15, 81, 99, 112, 166, 214, 248
Johnson, Charles S.: on acculturation of migrants, 203; on causes of Great Migration, 15, 16, 30; on *Defender*, 80, 87; on labor agents, 70, 72, 73; on limits to black achievement, 206; on migration networks, 90, 93, 95, 97; on migration process, 102, 107; on migration's impact on families, 106; in Mississippi (1917), 30, 43, 54; on role of leaders in Great Migration, 64, 88; on southern housing, 136; on Stockyards Labor Council, 220; on unionization of black workers, 238
Johnson, Jack, 81
Johnson, James Weldon, 4, 16, 53, 237
Johnson, Kathryn, 152
Johnstone, Jack, 208, 219, 224
Jones, Bert, 167
Jones, William, 62
Julia Johnson Home for Working Girls, 134

Kansas Fever Exodus (1879–80), 23–24, 44, 56, 68

Kentucky: domestic slave trade, 20; labor shortage, 40; migration to Kansas, 23
Kenwood, 174
Kikulski, John, 208, 226
Knights of Labor, 213–14
Knights Templar, 92
Kohlsaat, H. H., 230
Kohlsaat Restaurants, 217
Ku Klux Klan, 17, 214

Labor agents: as alleged cause of black migration, 20, 27, 44–46, 47, 53, 58; and federal government, 49; and fraud, 26, 72–73; and migration within South, 26; in post–Civil War South, 22; reputation among black southerners, 26, 27, 47, 70, 71–73, 96; returnees as agents, 71, 93; role in Great Migration, 3, 47, 66, 68, 69, 73, 96, 103–4; suppression of, 20, 27, 46, 104
Labor market: in Chicago, 13, 14, 82, 196; and education, 258; national, 15, 49; in North, 69; and racial discrimination, 258; in South, 14, 15, 26, 39–41, 44, 250
Labor shortage: in Chicago, 162, 185, 198; in North, 3, 14; in post–Civil War South, 22; in South after Great Migration, 39, 40–41, 60
Land ownership: abandonment of as ideal, 36; barriers to, 22–23, 29, 34–35, 62; and black opposition to Great Migration, 58–59; and black progress, 59; and black towns, 24; and independence, 6, 13, 19, 21–26, 31, 33; and Kansas Fever Exodus, 24; white vs. black chances, 35
Lane, Dennis, 218
Laundries, 181, 184; unionization, 210; work process, 192
Laurel, Mississippi, 52, 79, 80, 99, 104, 109
Leisure, 131–32, 142, 146, 150; and adaptation to urban life, 262; and class structure of black community, 131, 264; concerns of reformers about temptations and vice, 131, 173; motivation for migration, 18, 86, 90; in South, 262; and work, 194. *See also* Baseball; Movies; State Street
Leland, Mississippi, 112

Liberia, 25, 109
Liggett, Charles, 74
Lincoln, Abraham, 176
Lithonia, Georgia, 40
Locke, Alain, 7, 36–37
Lodging, 66, 133, 135
Louisiana: boll weevil, 28; domestic slave trade, 20; labor shortage, 40, 41; migration from, 4, 6, 16, 17, 21; racial violence, 16; schools, 247
Louisville, Kentucky, 164
Lumber industry, 70, 95, 106, 181, 197, 213
Lutcher, Louisiana, 71, 109
Lynch, Rev. James, 13

McChester, Leroy, 181, 184
McCloud, W. A., 80
McCormick, Cyrus, 230
MacDowell, Mary, 171
McLeod, Thomas, 54
Macon, Georgia, 17, 48, 102, 109
Macon (Georgia) *Telegraph*, 40, 50, 51
Marcel, Mississippi, 85
Marshall, Texas, 213
Mason, R. L., 155
Masons: and class structure, 129; and migration networks, 92
Mays, Robert, 175
Meat packing. *See* Packinghouses
Memphis, Tennessee: Ida B. Wells forced to leave, 32; migration from, 2; as stopping or transfer point for migrants, 2, 102, 111; railway unions, 214
Memphis *Commercial Appeal*, 54
Meridian, Mississippi: black opposition to Great Migration, 58; confiscation of *Defender*, 44; impact of Great Migration, 108; migration from, 16, 93
Merritt, George, 200
Mexico, 40
Miami, Florida, 81
Michora, Louis, 212
Migration (pre–WWI): after Civil War, 19, 21–23; during Civil War, 20–21; impediments to, 19, 23, 27; motivations for, 6, 8, 14–19, 35–37; to North, 1–3, 23, 32–33, 66, 130, 132, 148–49 (map), 150; opposition to among black leadership, 22; repressive response to, 22; of slaves, 19,

20–21; within South after Reconstruction, 26–32. *See also* Kansas Fever Exodus
Migration clubs: Great Migration, 64, 66, 96–97, 98, 104, 114; Liberia, 25; migration within South in late nineteenth century, 26; Oklahoma Land Rush, 24
Migration networks, 8, 66–97, 102; and activism of migrants, 68, 90–91, 98; and adaptation, 113, 132–33; barber shops, 66, 79, 80, 95; black newspapers, 3, 68; businesses, 95, 155; churches, 67, 80, 92, 94–95, 158; establishment of before Great Migration, 33; family and kin, 66, 69, 90, 92–94, 106, 133; and finding employment, 185; formation of, 68, 69, 89; fraternal organizations, 92; letters, 3, 66, 68, 69, 89–91, 95, 132; musicians, 95; nurses, 92; railroad workers, 68, 69, 74, 78; rumors and gossip, 3, 73; seasonal work, 95; teachers, 92; and unionization, 215; visiting, 47, 68, 69, 71, 91–93, 102, 155. *See also* Chicago *Defender*; Labor agents
Migration process, 6, 8, 66–67, 98–119; arrival, 113–16, 123, 133; assembling resources, 48, 103–5; choosing destination, 4, 99–102; departure, 48, 96, 107–10; family dynamics, 105–7; first impressions, 117; journey northward, 112–13; obtaining information, 49, 68–96, 102–3; stopping in southern city, 111–12
Miller, Kelly, 59, 215
Milwaukee, migration to, 70
Mississippi: anti-enticement legislation, 46; black restlessness before Great Migration, 30; blacks' images of North, 18, 86; boll weevil, 28; cost of living, 135; dissatisfaction among blacks, 14; domestic slave trade, 20; labor agents, 72; labor shortage, 40; migration from, 2, 3, 4, 6, 21, 74, 93, 102, 155; migration to, 26; reactions to Great Migration, 43, 51; remittances from migrants in Chicago, 90; schools, 247; whitecapping, 17
Mississippi Coal and Wood Company, 155
Mississippi River, floods (1912–13), 30

Mississippi Rural Association, 56
Missouri, domestic slave trade, 20
Mitchell, Arthur, 112
Mitchell, G. W., 91
Mobile, Alabama, 213
Mobile Young Men's Progressive Club, 142
Montgomery, Alabama: anti-enticement legislation, 46; trade unions, 213
Montgomery *Advertiser*: on Chicago's climate and black migration, 43; on Great Migration, 40, 52; on keeping blacks in South, 50, 51; on labor agents, 46
Montgomery Ward, 203
Monumental Baptist Church, 158
Morgan Park, 139
Morris & Company, 70, 190, 201, 206, 225, 228
Moseley Elementary School, 247, 249 (photo)
Moses, Kingsley, 43
Moton, Robert R.: on blacks' affinity for agriculture, 59; on causes of black migration, 61; relations with southern white establishment, 53, 57; on trade unions, 237; on why blacks should remain in South, 56
Mound Bayou, Mississippi, 59
Movies, 86, 262
Mundelein, Archbishop George, 173–74
Municipal Lodging House, 134
Murphy, Edgar Gardner, 38
Music, and Great Migration, 28, 95, 96, 154–55. *See also* Work songs

NAACP, 79, 88, 131, 199, 243; defends prepaid railroad tickets, 48; on Great Migration, 60; praised by *New Majority*, 242. See also *Crisis*
Nachman Spring-Filled Mattress Company, 194, 203
Nashville, Tennessee: reaction to Great Migration, 41; as stopping or transfer point for migrants, 111–12
Nashville *Banner*, 46
Natchez, Mississippi, 70
National Civic Improvement Association, 56
National Committee for Organizing Iron and Steel Workers, 211
National Malleable Castings Company, 198, 200, 228

National Negro Business League, 92, 131
National Urban League, 16, 69, 203, 237; position on unionization, 236
Negro Advocate, 227, 231
Negro Farmer and Messenger, 57, 60
Negro Fellowship League, 140, 141, 186
Newborn, Alabama, 88
New Deal, 42
New Galilee Baptist Church, 159
New Majority, 220, 223 224, 226, 228, 237, 241–42
New Orleans, 21, 66, 98; Chamber of Commerce attempts to stem migration, 56; influence of Chicago *Defender*, 79, 80; labor agent activity, 70, 72; migration from, 36, 68, 99, 107, 113; as stopping or transfer point for migrants, 102, 103, 111; unionization, 213
New Orleans *States*, 53
New Orleans *Times-Picayune*, 42, 44, 46
New Republic, 198
New World (Chicago), 168
New York City, 33, 99, 123; migration to, 4
Nockels, Ed, 226
North Carolina: housing, 136; migration from in late nineteenth century, 26
Nova Scotia, 20

Oglethorpe University, 41
Ohio River, 1, 90, 113
Oklahoma, migration to, 24–25, 68
Old Settlers: assistance to migrants, 140–43; attitudes toward migrants, 82, 131, 132, 138–40, 141, 144, 150–53, 166, 252, 264; avoidance of migrants, 139, 153, 174, 264; differences with migrants on unionization, 212–13; economic ideology, 215; instructing migrants, 140, 144–53, 200, 261; mythology of pre–Great Migration Chicago, 152, 164; occupational patterns, 184; reaction of migrants to, 153–54, 253; shared interests with Chicago industrialists, 199, 215
Oliver, Joe, 115
Olivet Baptist Church, 94, 156, 157, 159, 230, 256
O'neal, A. R., 105
O'neal, Viola, 105
Overton Hygienic Manufacturing Company, 4
Owen, Robert, 41

Packinghouses, 3, 112, 132, 153, 183–93;
    black employment in, 7, 183–84, 185,
    197, 225, 239; hiring practices, 187;
    image in South, 4; labor recruitment,
    71; labor turnover, 195, 197; physical
    environments, 188–90; race relations
    in, 178; racial discrimination, 206; ru-
    mors about in South, 73; strikes, 178,
    212, 217–19, 221, 225, 233–34, 239,
    241; ties to YMCA, 200, 228; unioniza-
    tion, 7, 208–13, 217–28, 233–44;
    wages, 15; work process, 188, 190–92,
    193, 195
Palatine, Texas, 167
Parker, James, 117
Parker, Richard E., 227–28, 231
Pass Christian, Mississippi, 106, 112
Pass riders. *See* Labor agents
Paternalism, 39, 42, 103, 164
Peacock, Ethel, 92
Pecan Point, Arkansas, 183
Pensacola, Florida, 104, 105, 108
Perrine, Charles, 256
Perry County, Mississippi, 107
Peters, James S., 47
Petersburg, Virginia, 130
Philadelphia, Pennsylvania, 33
Phyllis Wheatley Home, 134, 140–41, 143
Pickens, William, 88
Pilgrim Baptist Church, 157
Pittsburgh, Pennsylvania: employment
    opportunities, 257; migration to, 5, 70
Pittsburgh, Texas, 34
Plantation Café, 117
Plantation system, 19, 22, 26, 39–42, 51,
    52, 62, 197
Planters, 22–23, 27, 41; dependence on
    black labor, 39–40; opposition to
    black migration, 19, 26, 47
Playgrounds, 86
Pluralism, 8, 264–65
Police, 115, 117, 208, 209; assistance to
    employers, 222; attitudes toward, 2;
    and racial violence in Chicago, 178,
    179, 260; treatment of blacks in South,
    16, 98, 108
Polish Americans, 162, 164, 208, 217
Politics, 6, 8; athletic clubs, 178; Chicago
    leadership, 130, 209; and Kansas
    Fever Exodus, 24; limits to black par-
    ticipation and power, 260; meaning
    of, to migrants, 263; and post–Civil

War migration, 22; and racial conflict,
    175–77; role of ministers, 176; state
    clubs, 156. *See also* Democratic Party;
    Republican Party; Voting
Prattville, Alabama, 52
President's Mediation Commission, 211.
    See also Alschuler, Samuel B.
Promiseland, South Carolina, 105, 106, 250
Provident Hospital, 92, 140, 238
Public health, 168, 169, 172
Pullman, George, 230
Pullman Company, 184, 200, 210
Pullman Hotel, 134
Pullman porters: and class structure in
    Chicago, 129, 139; and *Defender,* 78;
    and Great Migration, 74; and mys-
    tique of railroad, 110; and unions,
    216, 224, 235

Quinn Chapel AME Church, 130, 230

Race consciousness, 5, 6, 7–8, 75, 127,
    130, 159–60, 210, 236, 240, 245, 263,
    264, 265
Race relations: adaptation to new pat-
    terns of, 1–2, 112, 150–53, 166; in
    Chicago, 2, 117–19, 123, 127, 129,
    138, 150–53, 161–80, 253–54, 259–61;
    in Chicago vs. South, 164–67; and
    employment relations, 197; in North
    vs. South as cause of Great Migration,
    14, 90, 161; and northern ghettos, 5;
    and politics, 175–77; and residential
    patterns, 174–75; in South, 7, 8, 9,
    52, 63, 109; and unionization, 208–9,
    212, 214–20, 221–28; at workplaces,
    177–78, 187, 202, 212, 222. *See also*
    Jim Crow; Racial discrimination
Racial discrimination, 2; as cause of
    Great Migration, 14, 16–18; in Chi-
    cago before Great Migration, 128–29,
    163, 164; in Chicago schools, 247,
    254–57; employers, 128, 182, 185, 196,
    198, 206, 218, 233, 236, 238, 240, 243,
    257, 260; housing, 126–27, 174–75,
    196; influence on black conscious-
    ness, 227; migrants' perceptions of,
    260–63; public employment services,
    186; reformers, 143; social services,
    134, 170–74; unions, 182, 214, 215,
    216–17, 219–20, 231–33, 236,
    239–40, 243

Racial ideology, 6, 162–66; as barrier to
  unionization, 212; legitimacy of racial
  dominance, 166; race as category,
  7–8, 162, 219, 227, 240, 242, 255, 258,
  263; stereotypes, 55, 128, 152, 162,
  198–99, 206, 218, 227, 238; and teachers, 254–56. *See also* Race
  consciousness
Racial violence: bombings, 174, 178; and
  decision to migrate, 16–18, 32; and labor issues, 218–19; lynching, 15–16,
  50–51, 54, 61, 75, 78, 82, 167; in
  North vs. South, 259; riots, 5, 32, 55,
  138, 165, 172, 178–80, 213, 222–23,
  238, 239, 245, 259–60; threat of, 208,
  224; turf battles, 175, 178
Ragen's Colts, 178, 179
Railroads: impact of rates on migration
  process, 103–4; journey north, 109–
  14; mystique of, 28, 110; prepaid tickets, 47, 90; role in Great Migration, 3,
  4, 28, 48, 68, 69, 74, 96, 99
Railroad workers, 68, 69, 192; unions and
  strikes, 213, 214–15, 216. *See also*
  Pullman porters
Railway Labor Board, 215
Rakestraw, W. M., 57
Randolph, A. Philip, 235, 237
Raymond School, 254, 257
Reconstruction, 22–23, 34, 39
Reed, Henry, 34
Reed, Mrs. G. W., 221
Reese, James, 13
Reformers (Chicago), 146, 151, 261; and
  education, 250; on housing, 135; on
  interracial vice, 170; racial discrimination, 143; relations with blacks,
  171–74; on "social disorganization,"
  170
Reformers (South): reaction to Great
  Migration, 50–52, 54; on whitecap-
  ping, 17
Religion, 156–59, 262; in Chicago vs.
  South, 94; and class structure, 129;
  churches and strikebreaking, 230–31;
  links between churches and employers, 187, 229–31; and migrants, 90;
  prounion ministers, 230; role of ministers in politics, 176. *See also individual denominations;* Storefront
  churches
Republican Party, 162, 176–77, 260, 263

Restrictive covenants, 175
Return migration (to South), 3; after 1919
  race riot, 179–80; argument against
  migration, 55; expected, 43; federal
  policies, 49
Riley, John, 220, 221, 234
Robert Lindblom High School, 81
Roberts, Adelbert H., 176
Robertson, John Dill, 169
Rome, Georgia, 79, 106
Rosenwald, Julius, 141, 203
Rule, John Wesley, 93
Russell Sage Foundation, 52

St. James School, 173
St. John AME Church, 158
St. Monica's Church, 173
Salvation Army, 134
Savannah, Georgia, 79, 102, 109, 130
Sawmills. *See* Lumber industry
Sayre, Helen, 203
Scales, Helen, 93
Scott, Emmett J., 15, 59, 64, 237
Scott, Lation, 75
Searchlight (Chicago), 152
Sears, Roebuck & Company, 203, 229
Selma, Alabama, 108, 213
Settlement houses. *See* Frederick Doug-
  lass Center; Reformers (Chicago);
  Wendell Phillips Settlement
Sharecropping, 26, 27, 30, 42, 103, 197
Shreveport, Louisiana, 46
Sinclair, Upton, 191
Singleton, Benjamin ("Pap"), 23
Slave trade: domestic, 20; foreign, 20
Slidell, Louisiana, 175
Smith, Hattie L., 102, 133
Snavely, T. A., 53
Snow Hill Normal and Industrial Insti-
  tute, 64
Social gospel, 171–72
Social services, 133–34, 140–43, 170–74
Social workers, 170, 172–73
South Carolina: circulation of Chicago
  Defender, 79; domestic slave trade, 20;
  migration from, 26, 67
Southern Christian Recorder, 60
Southern Home Cooking (restaurant),
  155
Southern Lunch Room, 155
South Park Methodist Episcopal Church,
  158

Southwestern Christian Advocate, 60, 64
State Street, 9, 123, 135, 141, 145; employment agencies, 185; headquarters for Local 651 (AMC&BW), 208; images in South, 9, 86, 90, 92; leisure and "temptation," 86, 90, 92, 117, 131, 142, 145, 265; storefront churches, 131
Steel mills, 3, 112, 181; and assumptions about aptitudes of blacks, 198; employment of blacks, 153, 184, 197, 198, 239; labor turnover rates, 195; neighborhoods, 240; occupational hazards in, 190; strike (1919), 211; unionization, 210, 211, 214; work process, 7, 192, 193, 195
Stephenson, Gilbert, 42
Stockyards. *See* Packinghouses
Stockyards Labor Council: black membership, 221, 224; organizing strategies, 211–12, 219–22; position of *Defender* on, 232; racial policies, 209, 219–20, 225–26, 237, 239, 242; rallies, 208–9, 211, 220, 221, 224; relations with AMC&BW, 211, 212, 226
Storefront churches, 95, 131, 158, 187, 229–30
Street Pavers' Union, 220
Streetcars, 17, 99, 119, 128, 150, 151, 152, 154, 166–67, 169
Strikebreaking, 128, 177, 184–85, 210–19, 221, 224–25, 230, 235, 239–43
Strikes, 128, 178, 210–14, 217–18, 221, 224, 225, 234, 235
Sugar plantations, organization of labor, 193
Summit, Mississippi, 48, 87
Sunflower County, Mississippi, 56
Sweeney, W. Allison, 63, 78
Swift, Gustavus, 230
Swift & Company: discrimination against black employees, 206; industrial relations policies, 199; philanthropy in black community, 223, 229, 230; position in industry, 190; Swifts' Premiums (baseball team), 201, 228; ties to YWCA, 229; work processes, 190–92

Tampa Red, 74
Taylor, Graham, 170
Teachers: black, in Chicago schools, 254; difficulty of finding employment as,

182; and migration networks, 92; theories and attitudes on race, 254–56; treatment of migrants, 252–55
Tennessee: domestic slave trade, 20; migration from, 4, 6, 23; racial violence in, 16
Tennessee Coal and Iron Company, 46
Tennessee Home League, 156
Texas: domestic slave trade, 20; migration from, 6; migration to, 21, 26, 68; recruitment of Mexican laborers, 40
Thirteenth Amendment, 13
Thomas, George, 104
Thomas, Rev. John F., 230
Thompson, William Hale, 130, 176–77, 178, 260
Travelers Aid Society, 116, 133, 134, 141, 186
Trinity AME Church, 140, 230
Trude, Daniel P., 134
Turner, Henry McNeal, 25
Turner, James, 105
Tuskegee Institute, 53, 56, 57, 62, 64, 154, 215, 246, 258

Unionization, 7, 132; and employers' expectations about Great Migration, 162; incentive to hire blacks, 207, 212, 214, 217, 225. *See also* Unions
Unions, 6, 197, 208–45; and black churches, 230; black membership, 212–14, 220–21, 223–25, 227, 235; brewery workers, 213; building trades, 182, 213–14, 216–17, 232, 243; dockworkers and longshoremen, 213; exclusion of black workers, 182, 214–17, 219, 231–32, 236; garment industry, 230; lumberjacks, 213; meat packing, 208–13, 217–28, 233–44, 265; miners, 213, 218; and neighborhoods, 240–41; newsboys, 218; railroad workers, 213, 214–15, 216–17, 232, 243; relations with black leadership, 208–10, 217, 225, 226–41; relations with black workers, 208–11, 212–27, 241, 243, 245; restaurant workers, 217, 232; in South, 213–15; steel, 210–11, 214; teamsters, 218, 219
United Charities of Chicago, 172
United Mine Workers, 213, 216
United States Bureau of Agricultural Economics, 30

United States Department of Agriculture, 29, 41
United States Department of Labor, 15, 39, 49, 106; Division of Negro Economics, 35, 49
United States Department of War, 41, 49
United States Employment Service (USES), 48–49, 186
United States Office of Education, 258
Universal Negro Improvement Association, 264
University of Chicago Settlement, 171
U.S. Steel, 184

Vagrancy laws, 23, 27
Veterans, 182
Vice, 168, 169–70
Vicksburg, Mississippi, 79, 94
Vicksburg (Mississippi) *Herald*, 41, 42
Voting: disfranchisement, 17, 32, 163, 176, 263; meaning of, to migrants, 175–76, 259; as motivation for migration, 8, 90, 161

Wadley, Georgia, 80
Wages: in Chicago, 14–15, 90, 93, 211, 214; in South, 41, 52, 54; as symbol of racial patterns, 263
Walters AME Zion Church, 134, 156, 157
Ward, George, 99
Ward, Matthew, 113
War Labor Policies Board, 49
Washington, Booker T., 15, 56, 74, 81, 131; Atlanta Compromise, 32; influence of, 63–65, 80, 130, 215; on migration from South, 33, 56, 59; on self help, 56; on southern economy, 39; and trade unions, 215
Waters, Muddy, 193
Webster, Milton, 217
Webster School, 253
Welfare capitalism, 199, 201–2, 224, 228–29, 259, 261
Wells, Ida B., 32, 141, 145, 150
Wendell Phillips High School, 36, 81, 91, 92, 246, 247, 248, 251, 254, 256
Wendell Phillips Night School, 249
Wendell Phillips Settlement, 140, 143
Wentworth Avenue, 118, 175
West, Isaac, 64
West Side ghetto, 123, 127, 140, 253
White, Walter, 79, 243

Whitecapping, 17, 34
Williams, Austin ("Heavy"), 212–13
Williams, Rev. Lacey K., 230, 256
Williams, W. T. B., 64, 73
Wilmington, North Carolina, race riot (1898), 32
Wilson, George, 250
Wilson, William B., 49
Wilson, Woodrow, 15, 152
Wilson & Company, 212, 213, 228, 241
Women's City Club of Chicago, 172
Women's Trade Union League, 220, 229
Wood, Wire, and Metal Lathers' International Union, 182
Woodlawn, 174
Woods, Clem, 103
Woodson, Carter G., 14
Work, Monroe, 64, 112
Work, 6, 181–207; and cash nexus, 261–62; physical environment, 188; and time, 181, 191–95
Work discipline, 112, 146, 262; inculcation by black institutions, 199–204; industrial vs. agricultural, 181, 191–97; performance of migrants in Chicago, 204–6; and racial stereotypes, 198–99; and schools, 250, 258
Work songs, 1, 192–93
World War I, 3, 19, 165, 178, 209; impact on labor market, 15, 36, 185; impact on northern economy, 13, 14
Wright, Rev. Daniel, 79
Wright, Richard: on anonymity of urban life, 166; first impressions of Chicago, 116, 117; on meaning of migration, 38; migration to Chicago, 2–3; on South, 155; on southern black images of North, 18
Wright, Richard Robert, 1–3, 140, 164; on Great Migration, 60

Yazoo and Mississippi Valley Railroad, 74, 215
Yazoo-Mississippi Delta: migration patterns, 26, 30, 68, 70, 111; music, 154
Yellow Cab, 206
Yeoman ideology. See Land ownership
Young Men's Christian Association (YMCA): antiunion activities, 228–29; assistance to migrants, 116, 134, 143; and class structure, 129; Efficiency Clubs, 200–202, 228; employment ser-

Young Men's Christian Association
(YMCA) (*continued*)
vice, 186; establishment and growth,
130, 140–42; influence among black
workers, 201, 228; praised by *Defender*, 150, 235; recreational programs, 81, 150, 201, 228; segregation
at, 81, 128, 134; ties to Chicago industrialists, 186, 200–202, 228–29, 240;
and welfare capitalism, 201, 202, 228,
261
Young Women's Christian Association
(YWCA), 150; assistance to migrants,
116, 133–34, 143; employment service, 186; and unions, 229; and welfare capitalism, 229, 261